PSYCHOLOGICAL WARFARE

PSYCHOLOGICAL WARFARE

EXPANDED EDITION

Paul M. A. Linebarger

Coachwhip Publications

Landisville, Pennsylvania

Psychological Warfare, by Paul M. A. Linebarger
Copyright © 2012 Coachwhip Publications
Introduction © 2012 Joseph A. Dixon
First edition published 1948.
Second edition published 1954.
No claims made on public domain material.

ISBN 1-61646-127-6
ISBN-13 978-1-61646-127-0

CoachwhipBooks.com

CONTENTS

INTRODUCTION
JOSEPH A. DIXON

I am not going to pretend that I can add anything significant to this work as it represents some of the most in-depth and serious writings on the subject. Though it may be dated it still holds significance in current and future military conflicts. While the circumstances have changed the essential reasoning and theory remains as they are still controlled by politics, culture, and the psychology of man. This introduction is merely to let the reader know the importance and relevance of Linebarger's work, which has been studied by military leaders and students since its publication. Finally after long last we have both first edition and second edition together, all the author's chapters and forewords, so as to allow a complete view of his work. Also a brief history of the author and publishing history is also touched upon as to give a clear perspective of both the man and his work.

Paul Myron Anthony Linebarger was born 1913 in Milwaukee, Wisconsin. Throughout his early life he lived in such diverse places as Chicago, Mississippi, China, Japan, and Germany. During this time, he suffered an accident and lost one eye in the process. By the time he was an adult he knew six languages and had a vast and collective knowledge of these and other cultures. Though this was gained from both personal experience and general education, it helps to give notice of his credentials to understand an essential part of his work on psychological warfare. That "essential part" is knowledge of an opponent's culture and mode of thought, as well as the importance of speaking and understanding their language.

By the relatively young age of 19, he graduated from George Washington University in 1933 with an A.B degree. In 1935 he earned an M.D., and in 1936 graduated from John Hopkins University at the age of 23 with a doctorate in political science. During the same year he also married his first wife, Margaret Snow. On September 7, 1937, he published his first book entitled *The Political Doctrines of Sun Yat-sen*. In 1938, he published his second book, *Government in Republican China*. In 1941, while professing in political science and economics he published *The China of Chiang Kai-shek*. In 1942, Linebarger then joined the U.S. military. He was placed in the Far East section, becoming a second lieutenant. During this period, he formed the Office of War Information, the Operation Planning and Intelligence Board, and the Section of Psychological Warfare—and incidentally this was the same year his first daughter Rosana was born. Later in 1943, Linebarger was assigned to China to coordinate psychological operations as well as the American and Chinese war relation effort. By 1945 he had managed to secure the rank of Major. After the war in 1947, he became a professor of Asiatic politics at Johns Hopkins University's School of Advanced International Studies. During that same year he published his first novel *Ria* under the pen name Felix C. Forest, and his second child, Marcia, was born. It was not until 1948 that he published his landmark book *Psychological Warfare*. In 1949 Linebarger divorced his first wife; he remarried in 1950 to Genevieve Collins, while continuing to publish various works. These included two more novels and several other publications such as the science fiction story "Scanners Live in Vain" (published in *Fantasy Magazine* in 1950) and the story "You Will Never Be the Same" in 1963. He also became an adviser, as a Colonel, to both the British in Malaya as well as the U. S. in Korea, though he passed on Vietnam, holding the belief that the U.S. should never have gone in. Linebarger also became an adviser to President Kennedy and was a member of the Foreign Policy Association. He died in 1966 and was buried in Arlington National Cemetery, leaving behind two daughters and a widow.

As can be inferred by this history of the man's life, he had a vast amount of experience in politics, foreign culture, and military affairs. Since psychological warfare deals heavily with these three key issues there should be no question as to why he and his work are still held in such high regard both in political and military circles. But of course the question remains as to what makes it so influential and how it can remain relevant from war to war in an ever-changing climate of world affairs, military tactics, and technology.

The answer is that though these things do in fact change, the human mind does not, and no matter what new technology may come to bear it still will not change the base behavior of man or his reactions to the world around him. Even when we look to the definition of psychological operations we find that the definition indeed does not change. At the time of his writing there did not yet exist a working definition of "psychological operations" or (PSYOPS), yet he still managed to craft a precise and relevant one. By his understanding he defined it as "the use of propaganda against an enemy, together with such other operational measures of a military, economic, or political nature as may be required to supplement propaganda." Reading this definition also raises the question as to the meaning of propaganda. That definition is critical in understanding psychological operations as it plays the main role of changing or otherwise affecting the opponent's mind. In understanding the earlier definition we can relate to the term propaganda which he defines as "the planned use of any form of communication designed to affect the minds and emotions of a given enemy, neutral or friendly foreign group for a specific strategic or tactical purpose." In explaining the meaning of propaganda Linebarger also outlined five distinct elements: source, time, audience, subject, and mission.

In terms of the specific duties and skills needed by those who sought to effectively employ PSYOP techniques we find that even this was understood and outlined by Linebarger. He specifically noted the qualifications necessary in choosing those for such a delicate and potentially important task. He believed that while all such qualities may not be present in each individual, that it would still be possible to identify a specific important quality in each person, thus bringing together multiple people from various backgrounds yet all together forming a useful and coercive group most suited to the job at hand. In outlining the specific qualities he noted, "1. An effective working knowledge of U.S. government administration and policy, so that the purposes and plans of the government may be correctly interpreted, 2. An effective knowledge of correct military and naval procedure and of staff operations, together with enough understanding of the arts of warfare, weather naval or military, to adjust propaganda utterance to military situations and to practical propaganda operations in forms which will dovetail, 3. Professional knowledge of the media of information, or of at least one of them (book publishing, magazines, newspapers, radio, advertising in various branches), or some closely related field (practical political canvassing, visual or adult education, etc.), 4. Intimate, professional-level understanding of a given area (Italy, Japan, New Guinea, Kwangtung, Algeria), based on first hand acquaintance, knowledge of the language, traditions, history, practical politics, and customs, 5. Professional scientific understanding of psychology, anthropology, sociology, history, political science, or a comparable field." Interestingly enough, Linebarger stated that "the man who steps up and says that he meets all five of these qualifications is a liar, a genius, or both." This restates the previous sentiment that finding a single person capable of providing all the necessary qualifications would be quite rare, that instead it would be most useful to employ multiple individuals who all have their own specific relevance to the topic at hand. However, still in relation to this, it can be found that Linebarger's belief that while no man may be a master of all, it still is possible for those working together to learn from each other, thus gaining rudimentary skill at all the qualifications—the man versed in advertising can learn from the one versed in politics, and vice versa. As a team works together in this fashion one has both a useful and skilled group of "components," but at the same time each one has working knowledge at all important levels.

This is why psychological warfare is such a potent weapon when utilized by either military or civilian groups, though with varying tactics and delivery systems. The effect remains the same; that is changing or manipulating an opponent's mentality to a desired degree. However Linebarger was clear in his statement that PSYOPS was not an unbeatable weapon that can be used without any violent or military action, for it was just the opposite. Rather, psychological warfare is a useful tactic when employed in addition to other military operations—a tool used to augment and weaken an opponent's position in order defeat militarily or diplomatically but not one to be used independently. From reading his position on the subject it becomes clear that the myth that it can be used behind the shadows to a high and effective degree without any other support was a prominent mistaken idea at the time that he was trying to dispel. He was also aware that it could at times be very difficult to gauge effectiveness as his techniques left no physical trace. It is invisible warfare and therefore more difficult to discern in effects on minds than physical bodies show with conventional weapons. Still he was confident in the ability of this misunderstood weapon to soften up opponents in order to bring a finishing and painful blow through physical military force.

In attempting to explain the realistic use of psychological warfare and its effectiveness he couldn't help but relate the topic to the archives of history. As the saying goes, "those who do not understand history are doomed to repeat it," giving great credence to his understanding of said historical events in the context of PSYOPS. Linebarger gave many references in his first chapter on the subject, so much in fact that trying to explain each and every one as he wrote it would defeat the purpose of this brief introduction. However in excerpt he used historical anecdotes such as "The Use of Panic by Gideon," where Gideon used torches and trumpets to incite panic and eventual retreat by the Midianites. He gave praise in his example, "Field Propaganda of the Athenians and the Han," the tale of Themistocles who engraved messages on stones. These stones were set close to drinkable water, acting as a sort of leaflet, ensuring the presence of an audience. The message itself was crafted in a way to both demoralize and elicit sympathy, sapping readers of their desire to fight. This type of propaganda remains incredibly similar to the propaganda used during Linebarger's time, and which continues to be used in modern wars though utilizing more advanced delivery systems.

In today's world of light speed video, as well as the great social online networks, psychological warfare has taken center stage as an effective and reasonably afforded tactic. Technology has developed well beyond the boundaries of general imagination from Linebarger's time. The technology of communication has evolved beyond recognition in the span of just a few decades, connecting everyone from all nations, rich or poor. As noted by Linebarger this is, of course, a key portion of psychological warfare on any stage, as it plays the part of a delivery system without which there can be no attack. Today and in the future, the ability to change and manipulate an opponent, whoever they may be, becomes more and more important. During Linebarger's lifetime a fairly large infrastructure or system was needed to properly disseminate subversive or manipulative ideas and communications, but now this ability is given to individuals and groups with very little financial or other structural support; in fact, all that's needed for mass dissemination of ideas is a "lone computer." This makes the business of psychological warfare far more dangerous and difficult to discern. In fact Limburger's work has become more relevant now than it has ever been in the past and will most likely continue in importance as communication and social technology improves. The truth of the matter is that war has undergone many changes from the so-called first generation warfare of our ancestors all the way up to fourth-generation warfare, which has been used to describe guerrilla or asymmetrical warfare today. This is the type of warfare that the world seems to find itself in today and has proven to be difficult to handle—but we are now at the edge of a new generation of battle. This has been called information warfare and is fast becoming the weapon of choice for those who favored asymmetrical or guerrilla warfare in the past, as it has made the changing or controlling both people and public opinion infinitely easier. Today the Internet and mass communication supplements or even in some instances entirely replaces the more upfront and violent strategies of the past. What we have today is a much more dubious way of attack where an opponent can appear on the Internet, disseminate subversive information, and then disappear as fast as he appeared. Too, with today's mass media the coverage of wars is greatly enhanced at an even greater level, which can influence the public and its leaders.

Even with all these advances and the growing power of the war on the mind, Linebarger's opinions still remain relevant. Though psychological warfare can be employed efficiently, physical military conflict is still necessary to take full advantage of its effect. From his statements it can be inferred that he wholeheartedly believed that military action without psychological operations was a terrible blunder; he also affirmed that psychological operations without military action was also a mistake, for each feeds off the other and it is with both techniques operating in unison that the full and terrible effect comes to bear.

Using as an example the riots that have multiplied greatly among dictatorships in the Middle East as well as more industrialized nations like Great Britain, the need for violent action working in tandem with psychological warfare remains. That is, while the use of social media employed among disenfranchised and restless youth has allowed subversive and ideological messages to become viral among them, it has only been through the use of violent resistance and even military support that their overall goals have been met. While it is true that in times past certain ideas proliferated without violence even insofar as to bring about major alterations in policy, in the environment of a dictatorship this seems very unlikely to occur. By disseminating ideas to bring about passionate indignation and by spreading constant pleas and news of abuse that has come out of these countries, the rest of the world has taken charge and helped them to fight, prying them from the grip of past leadership, for better or for worse. Live feeds of abuses by various dictatorships have not only rallied support of the populace in such places as Tunisia and Egypt, but from the rest of the world as well. The use of modern communication has replaced the leaflets of old used; even radio has become displaced with the growing use of the Internet and cell phones even in some of the more poverty-stricken nations. However as was stressed earlier, technology itself does not change minds. Today's media technology only represents an evolution in the delivery system, not the ammunition. The goal is still to effectively blunt or control a given target population. Whether messages that spark and fan the flames of revolution are used by the indigenous population to bring change or if governments wage wars on others, it is in this seminal writing of Linebarger that the positives and pitfalls of this technique of war are outlined.

It should also be noted that while both first and second editions of this book shared almost all the text, different circumstances did force some changes. The first edition was published in 1947, directly after WWII, and it was thought the great wars of the world were finally over. The author mostly spoke of the coming disarmament and its difficulties but then removed this chapter from his second edition, published in 1953. That was the time of the communist threat and here he devoted a new chapter to the true war of ideas. That chapter becomes most relevant as it speaks of the disaster and danger of the fanaticism that came about through the spread of communism.

Linebarger went into great detail in his second edition about the destructiveness of subversive culture but also raised an interesting point. He believed that no matter what, fanaticism would eventually fail within a secure and safe environment. By this was meant that fanaticism only grows and spreads if the emotional "high" and fervor remains. There must be a goal to be attained, one to be attained at all costs, which must be constantly reinforced and drilled into the masses. The goal must always remain; there must always be something to fight for. This is how such culture sustains itself. Whether indeed it comes from cultures of revolution, religious fanaticism, or anything in between, the enemy must always loom and the goal must always be clear. If we were to look back on the history of such nations or cultures that have relied on this approach, we find that they all fall in the end. The saying goes that "the candle that burns twice as bright burns for half as long."

This aptly describes how cultures and ideas have spread as if by a virus but die out from lack of a viable host. In the end Linebarger apparently believed that democracy would always win out against communism. Today the world waits to see how current trends in fanaticism fare in their efforts to break apart stability in favor of their own ideals. Nearly all political systems, whether radical, democratic, or dictatorship, have a finite lifespan and thus live and die, only to be reborn once more. However when we look upon Linebarger's final chapter we see that he held onto the notion that in the battle of culture, the safe and secure life of a democracy would check the spread of the scourge of fanaticism, not by a lack of comparable passion, but through the longevity that it holds over its contenders.

QUICK LOOK REFERENCE TERMS

IDEOLOGY A system of deep-rooted beliefs about fundamental questions in human life and affairs.

EDUCATION The process, usually institutional, by which the people of a given area transmit to their successors, their own children, practical information needed in modern life, together with a lot of other teachings designed to make good men and women, good citizens, good Christians or other believers of them.

PROPAGANDA The planned use of any form of communication designed to affect the minds and emotions of an enemy, neutral, or friendly foreign group for a specific strategic or tactical purpose.

PSYCHOLOGICAL WARFARE The use of propaganda against an enemy, together with other operational measures of a military, economic, or political nature as may be required to supplement propaganda.

FIVE ELEMENTS OF PROPAGANDA Source, Time, Audience, Subject, Mission.

WHITE PROPAGANDA Issued from an acknowledged source, usually a government or an agency of a government, including military commands at various levels. This type of propaganda is associated with overt psychological warfare.

GREY PROPAGANDA Does not clearly identify any source.

BLACK PROPAGANDA Purports to emanate from a source other than the true one. This type of propaganda is associated with covert psychological warfare operations.

16

STRATEGIC PROPAGANDA   Directed at enemy forces, enemy peoples, and enemy-occupied areas in their entirety, and in coordination with strategic planning is designed to effectuate results planned and sought over a period of weeks, months, or years.

TACTICAL PROPAGANDA   Directed at specific audiences, usually named, and prepared and executed in support of localized combat operations.

DEFENSIVE PROPAGANDA   Designed to maintain an accepted operating form of social or other public action.

CONVERSIONARY PROPAGANDA   Designed to change the emotional or practical allegiance from one group to another.

DIVISIVE PROPAGANDA   Designed to split apart the component subgroups of the enemy and therefore reduce the effectiveness of the enemy group as a single unit.

CONSOLIDATION PROPAGANDA   Directed toward civil populations in areas occupied by military force and designed to insure compliance with the commands or policies promulgated by the commander of the occupying force.

COUNTERPROPAGANDA   Designed to refute a specific point or theme of enemy propaganda.

POLITICAL WARFARE   Consists of the framing of national policy in such a way as to assist propaganda or military operations, whether with respect to the direct political relations of governments with one another or in relation to groups of people possessing a political character.

ENEMY IN RELATION TO PSYCHOLOGICAL WARFARE   A ruler, or ruling group, or unspecified manipulators, or any definite minority.

MEDIA OUTLETS   Radio, loudspeakers, leaflets, pamphlets, books, novelties (and more recently television, cell phones, and Internet, including social networks).

GENERAL ELEMENTS OF PSYOP GOAL   Specific kinds of demoralization and discord desired, the particular enemy audiences to address, the types of argument proposed to use, and the media through which to project propaganda.

ESTIMATE OF SITUATION DURING PSYCHOLOGICAL OPERATIONS   Definition of audience, psychological goals sought, limitations of policy,

media available, the propaganda developed, competitive factors, and relation to general military estimate of the situation.
ELEMENTS OF OVERT PROPAGANDA   Communications from the legitimate authority, novelty materials appealing to children, gifts,
and appeals to women.

THE 1ST EDITION

ACKNOWLEDGMENTS

This book is the product of experience rather than research, of consultation rather than reading. It is based on my five years of work, both as civilian expert and as Army officer, in American psychological warfare facilities at every level from the Joint and Combined Chiefs of Staff planning phase down to the preparing of spot leaflets for the American forces in China. Consequently, I have tried to avoid making this an original book, and have sought to incorporate those concepts and doctrines which found readiest acceptance among the men actually doing the job. The responsibility is therefore mine, but not the credit.

Psychological warfare involves exciting wit-sharpening work. It tends to attract quick-minded people—men full of ideas. I have talked about psychological warfare with all sorts of people, all the way from Mr. Mao Tse-tung in Yenan and Ambassador Joseph Davies in Washington to an engineer corporal in New Zealand and the latrine-coolie, second class, at our Chungking headquarters. I have seen one New York lawyer get mentally befuddled and another New York lawyer provide the solution, and have seen Pulitzer Prize winners run out of ideas only to have the stenographers supply them. From all these people I have tried to learn, and have tried to make this book a patchwork of enthusiastic recollection. Fortunately, the material is non-copyright; unfortunately, I cannot attribute most of these comments or inventions to their original proponents. Perhaps this is just as well: some authors might object to being remembered.

21

A few indebtednesses stand out with such clarity as to make acknowledgment a duty. These I wish to list, with the caution that this list is not inclusive.

First of all, I am indebted to my father, Judge Paul M. W. Linebarger (1871-1939), who during his lifetime initiated me into almost every phase of international political warfare, whether covert or overt, in connection with his life-long activities on behalf of Sun Yat-sen and the Chinese Nationalists. On a limited budget (for years, out of his own pocket) he ran campaigns against imperialism and communism, and for Sino-American friendship and Chinese democracy, in four or five languages at a time. For five and a half years I was his secretary, and believe that this experience has kept me from making this a book of exclusively American doctrine. There is no better way to learn the propaganda job than to be whipped thoroughly by someone else's propaganda.

Second only to my debt to my father, my obligation to the War Department General Staff officers detailed to Psychological Warfare stands forth. By sheer good fortune, the United States had an unbroken succession of intelligent, conscientious, able men assigned to this vital post, and it was my own good luck to serve under each of them in turn between 1942 and 1947. They are, in order of assignment: Colonel Percy W. Black, Brigadier General Oscar N. Solbert, Colonel Charles Blakeney, Lieutenant Colonel Charles Alexander Holmes Thomson, Colonel John Stanley, Lieutenant Colonel Richard Hirsch, Lieutenant Colonel Bruce Buttles, Colonel Dana Johnston, Lieutenant Colonel Daniel Tatum, and Lieutenant Colonel Wesley Edwards. Their talents and backgrounds were diverse but their ability was uniformly high. I do not attribute this to the peculiar magic of Psychological Warfare, nor to unwonted prescience on the part of The Adjutant General, but to plain good luck.

Especial thanks are due to the following friends, who have read this manuscript in whole or in part. I have dealt independently with the comments and criticism, so that none of them can be blamed for the final form of the book. These are Dr. Edward K. Merat, the Columbia-trained MIS propaganda analyst; Mr. C. A.

H. Thomson, State Department international information consultant and Brookings Institution staff member; Professor E. P. Lilly of Catholic University and concurrently Psychological Warfare historian to the Joint Chiefs of Staff; Lieutenant Colonel Innes Randolph; Lieutenant Colonel Heber Blankenhorn, the only American to have served as a Psychological Warfare officer in both World Wars; Dr. Alexander M. Leighton, M.D., the psychiatrist and anthropologist who as a Navy lieutenant commander headed the OWI-MIS Foreign Morale Analysis Division in wartime; Mr. Richard Hirsch; Colonel Donald Hall, without whose encouragement I would never have finished this book; Professor George S. Pettee, whose experience in strategic intelligence lent special weight to his comment; Colonel Dana Johnston; Mr. Martin Herz, who may some day give the world the full account of Yakzif operations; and my wife, Margaret Linebarger.

Further, I must thank several of my associates in the propaganda agencies whose thinking proved most stimulating to mine. Mr. Geoffrey Gorer was equally brilliant as colleague and as ally. Dean Edwin Guthrie brought insights to Psychological Warfare which were as much the reflection of a judicious, humane personality as of preeminent psychological scholarship. Professor W. A. Aiken, himself a historian, provided data on the early history of U. S. facilities in World War II. Mr. F. M. Fisher and Mr. Richard Watts, Jr., of the OWI China Outpost, together with their colleagues, taught me a great deal by letting me share some of their tasks and my immediate chief in China, Colonel Joseph K. Dickey, was kind to allow a member of his small, overworked staff to give time to Psychological Warfare. Messrs. Herbert Little, John Creedy and C. A. Pearce have told me wonderful stories about their interesting end of propaganda. Mr. Joseph C. Grew, formerly Under Secretary of State and Ambassador to Japan, showed me that the processes of traditional responsible diplomacy include many skills which Psychological Warfare rediscovers crudely and in different form.

Finally, I wish to thank Colonel Joseph I. Greene in his triple role of editor, publisher and friend, to whom this volume owes its actual being.

While this material has been found unobjectionable on the score of security by the Department of the Army, it certainly does not represent Department of the Army policy, views, or opinion, nor is the Department responsible for matters of factual accuracy. I assume sole and complete responsibility for this book and would be glad to hear the comment or complaint of any reader. My address is indicated below.

Paul M. A. Linebarger

2831 29th Street N.W.
Washington 8, D. C.
20 June 1947

PART ONE
DEFINITION AND HISTORY

CHAPTER 1
HISTORIC EXAMPLES OF PSYCHOLOGICAL WARFARE

Psychological warfare is waged before, during, and after war; it is not waged against the opposing psychological warfare operators; it is not controlled by the laws, usages, and customs of war; and it cannot be defined in terms of terrain, order of battle, or named engagements. It is a continuous process. Success or failure is often known only months or years after the execution of the operation. Yet success, though incalculable, can be overwhelming; and failure, though undetectable, can be mortal.

Psychological warfare does not fit readily into familiar concepts of war. Military science owes much of its precision and definiteness to its dealing with a well defined subject, the application of organized lawful violence. The officer or soldier can usually undertake his task of applying mass violence without having to determine upon the enemy. The opening of war, recognition of neutrals, the listing of enemies, proclamation of peace—such problems are considered political, and outside the responsibility of the soldier. Even in the application of force short of war, the soldier proceeds only when the character of the military operation is prescribed by higher (that is, political) authorities, and after the enemies are defined by lawful and authoritative command. In one field only, psychological warfare, is there endless uncertainty as to the very nature of the operation.

Psychological warfare, by the nature of its instruments and its mission, begins long before the declaration of war. Psychological warfare continues after overt hostilities have stopped. The enemy

Figure 1: A Basic Form of Propaganda. This American leaflet, issued during the Philippine landings, was dropped on inhabited Philippine areas in order to obtain local civilian cooperation with the landing forces. It can be called the ''civilian-action'' type.

often avoids identifying himself in psychological warfare; much of the time, he is disguised as the voice of home, of God, of the church, of the friendly press. Offensively, the psychological warfare operator must fight antagonists who never answer back—the enemy audience. He cannot fight the one enemy who is in plain sight, the hostile psychological warfare operator, because the hostile operator is greedily receptive to attack. Neither success nor defeat are measurable factors. Psychological strategy is planned along the edge of nightmare.

The Understanding of Psychological Warfare. In a formal approach to this mysterious part of the clean-cut process of war, it might be desirable to start with Euclidian demonstrations, proceeding from definition to definition until the subject-matter had been delimited by logic. Alternatively it might be interesting to try a historical approach, describing the development of psychological warfare through the ages.

The best approach is perhaps afforded by a simplification of both a logical and historical approach. For concrete examples it is most worthwhile to look at instances of psychological warfare taken out of history down to World War II. Then the definitions and working relationships can be traced and—with these in mind—a somewhat more detailed and critical appraisal of World Wars I and II organizations and operations can be undertaken. If a historian or philosopher picks up this book, he will find much with which to quarrel, but for the survey of so hard-to-define a subject, this may be a forgivable fault.

Psychological warfare and propaganda are each as old as mankind; but it has taken modern specialization to bring them into focus as separate subjects. The materials for their history lie scattered through thousands of books and it is therefore impossible to brief them. Any reader contemplating retirement from the army to a sedentary life is urged to take up this subject.[1] A history of propaganda would provide not only a new light on many otherwise odd or trivial historical events; it would throw genuine illumination on the process of history itself. There are however numerous instances which can be cited to show applications of psychological warfare.

The Use of Panic by Gideon. One of the earliest (by traditional reckoning, 1245 B.C.) applications was Gideon's use of the lamps and pitchers in the great battle against the Midianites.

The story is told in the seventh chapter of the Book of Judges. Gideon was in a tactically poor position. The Midianites outnumbered him and were on the verge of smiting him very thoroughly. Ordinary combat methods could not solve the situation, so Gideon—acting upon more exalted inspiration than is usually vouchsafed modern commanders—took the technology and military formality of his time into account.

Retaining three hundred selected men, he sought for some device which would cause real confusion in the enemy host. He knew well that the tactics of his time called for every century of men to have one light-carrier and one torch-bearer for the group. By equipping three hundred men with a torch and a trumpet each, he could create the effect of thirty thousand. Since the lights could not be turned on and off with switches, like ours, the pitchers concealed them, thus achieving the effect of suddenness.

He had his three hundred men equipped with lamps and pitchers. The lamps were concealed in the pitchers, each man carrying one, along with a trumpet. He lined his forces in appropriate disposition around the enemy camp at night and had them—himself setting the example—break the pitchers all at the same time, while blowing like mad on the trumpets.

The Midianites were startled out of their sleep and their wits. They fought one another throughout their own camp. The Hebrew chronicler modestly gives credit for this to the Lord. Then the Midianites gave up altogether and fled. And the men of Israel pursued after the Midianites.[2] That settled the Midianite problem for a while; later Gideon finished Midian altogether.

This type of psychological warfare device—the use of unfamiliar instruments to excite panic—is common in the history of all ancient countries. In China, the Emperor-usurper Wang Mang on

Figure 2: Nazi Troop Morale Leaflet. In this leaflet, used on the Italian front in 1944, the Nazis did not call for any specific action from their American GI readers. Their aim was merely depression of American morale for future exploitation by action propaganda. Note the extreme simplicity of the message. Throughout World War II, the Nazis were misled by their own tendentious political intelligence reports and consequently overestimated the kind and degree of American opposition to Franklin D. Roosevelt. They mistook normal complaint for treasonable sedition; hence, leaflets such as this seemed practical to the Germans.

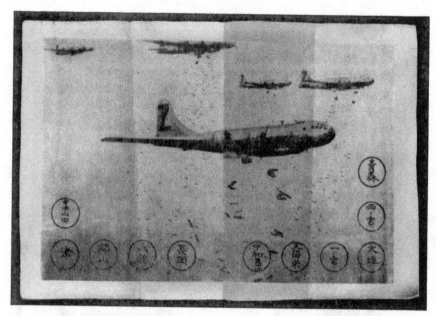

Figure 3: One of the Outstanding Leaflets of the War. Prepared in 1945 for distribution by B-29s operating over Japan, this leaflet lists eleven Japanese cities which were marked for destruction. The leaflet is apparently of the civilian-action type, calling on Japanese civilians to save their own lives. At the same time, it had the effect of shutting down eleven strategically important cities, thus hurting the Japanese war effort while giving the Americans a reputation for humanity and also refuting enemy charges that we undertook indiscriminate bombing.

one occasion tried to destroy the Hunnish tribes with an army that included heavy detachments of military sorcerers, even though the Han Military Emperor had found orthodox methods the most reliable; Wang Mang got whipped at this. But he was an incurable innovator and in 23 A.D., while trying to put down some highly successful rebels, he collected all the animals out of the Imperial menagerie and sent them along to scare the enemy: tigers, rhinoceri, and elephants were included. The rebels hit first, killing the Imperial General Wang Sun, and in the excitement the animals got loose in the Imperial army where they panicked the men. A hurricane which happened to be raging at the same time enhanced the excitement. Not only were the Imperial troops defeated, but the military propaganda of the rebels was so jubilant in tone and so successful in effect that the standard propaganda theme, "Depress and unnerve the enemy commander," was fulfilled almost to excess on Wang Mang. Here is what happened to him after he noted the progress of the enemy: "A profound melancholy fell upon the Emperor. It undermined his health. He drank to excess, ate nothing but oysters, and let everything happen by chance. Unable to stretch out, he slept sitting up on a bench."[3] Wang Mang was killed in the same year, and China remained without another economic new deal until the time of Wang An-shih (A.D. 1021-1086), a thousand years later. Better psychological warfare would have changed history.

Field Propaganda of the Athenians and the Han. A more successful application of psychological warfare is recorded in the writings of Herodotus, the Greek historian:

> Themistocles, having selected the best sailing ships of the Athenians, went to the place where there was water fit for drinking, and engraved upon the stones inscriptions, which the Ionians, upon arriving the next day at Artemisium, read. The inscriptions were to this effect, 'Men of Ionia, you do wrong in fighting against your fathers and helping to enslave Greece. Rather, therefore, come over to us or if you cannot do that, withdraw your forces from the contest and entreat the Carians to do the same. But if neither of these things is possible, and you are bound by too strong a necessity, yet in action, when we are engaged, behave ill on purpose, remembering that you are descended from us and that the enmity of the barbarians against us originally sprang from you.'[4]

This text is very much like leaflets dropped during World War II on reluctant enemies, such as the Italians, the Chinese puppet troops, and others. (Compare this Greek text with Figure 5.) Note that the propagandist tries to see things from the viewpoint of his audience. His air of reasonable concern for their welfare creates a bond of sympathy. And by suggesting that the Ionians should behave badly in combat, he lays the beginning of another line—the

Paſſierſchein

(GÜLTIG FÜR EINEN ODER MEHRERE ÜBERBRINGER)

Der deutſche Soldat, der dieſen Paſſierſchein vorzeigt,
benutzt ihn als Zeichen ſeines ehrlichen Willens, ſich zu
ergeben. Er iſt zu entwaffnen. Er muß gut behandelt
werden. Er hat Anſpruch auf Verpflegung und, wenn
nötig, ärztliche Behandlung. Er wird ſo bald wie möglich
aus der Gefahrenzone entfernt.

Dwight D Eisenhower

DWIGHT D. EISENHOWER
Oberbefehlshaber
der Alliierten Streitkräfte

*Übersetzung nachstehend. Sie dient als
Anweisung an die alliierten Vorposten.*

SAUF CONDUIT | SAFE CONDUCT

Le soldat porteur de ce
laissez-passer a sincèrement
l'intention de cesser le combat. Il doit être désarmé
et correctement traité. Il
doit être nourri et recevoir
les soins médicaux néces-
saires. Il sera éloigné dès
que possible de la zone
dangereuse.

The German soldier who
carries this safe conduct is
using it as a sign of his
genuine wish to give himself
up. He is to be disarmed,
to be well looked after, to
receive food and medical
attention as required and to
be removed from the danger
zone as soon as possible.

Dwight D Eisenhower

DWIGHT D. EISENHOWER
Commandant Suprême,
des Forces Interalliées

Dwight D Eisenhower

DWIGHT D. EISENHOWER
Supreme Commander,
Allied Expeditionary Force

propaganda to the Persians, "black" propaganda making the Persians think that any Ionian who was less than perfect was a secret Athenian sympathizer. The appeal is sound by all modern standards of the combat-leaflet.

Another type of early military propaganda was the political denunciation which, issued at the beginning of war, could be cited from then on as legal and ethical justification for one side or the other. In the Chinese *San Kuo* novel, which has probably been read by more human beings than any other work of fiction, there is preserved the alleged text of the proclamation of a group of loyalist pro-Han rebels on the eve of military operations (about A.D. 200). The text is interesting because it combines the following techniques, all of them sound: 1) naming the specific enemy; 2) appeal to the "better people"; 3) sympathy for the common people; 4) claim of support for the legitimate government; 5) affirmation of one's own strength and high morale; 6) invocation of unity; 7) appeal to religion. The issuance of the proclamation was connected with rather elaborate formal ceremony:

> The House of Han has fallen upon evil days, the bonds of Imperial authority are loosened. The rebel minister, Tung Cho, takes advantage of the discord to work evil, and calamity falls upon honorable families. Cruelty overwhelms simple folk. We, Shao and his confederates, fearing for the safety of the imperial prerogatives, have assembled military forces to rescue the State. We now pledge ourselves to exert our whole strength, and to act in concord to the utmost limit of our powers. There must be no disconcerted or selfish action. Should any depart from this pledge may he lose his life and leave no posterity. Almighty

Figure 4: The Pass Which Brought them in. Germans liked things done in an official and formal manner, even in the midst of chaos, catastrophe and defeat. The Allies obliged, and gave the Germans various forms of very official-looking "surrender passes," of which this is one. The original is printed in red and has banknote-type engraving which makes it resemble a soap-premium coupon. (Western Front, 1944-45, issued by SHAEF.)

←

Heaven and Universal Mother Earth and the enlightened spirits of our forefathers, be ye our witnesses.[5]

Any history of any country will yield further examples of this
kind of material. Whenever it was consciously used as an adjunct
to military operations, it may appropriately be termed military
propaganda.

Emphasis on Ideology. In a sense, the experience of the past
may, unfortunately, provide a clue to the future. The last two great
wars have shown an increasing emphasis on ideology or political
faith (see definition, endnote 1 of chapter 2) as driving forces behind warfare, rather than the considerations of coldly calculated
diplomacy. Wars become more serious, and less gentlemanly; the
enemy must be taken into account not merely as a man, but as a
fanatic. To the normal group-loyalty of any good soldier to his
army, right or wrong, there is added the loyalty to the Ism or the
Leader. Warfare thus goes back to the Wars of Faith. It is possible
that techniques from the Christian-Mohammedan or from the
Protestant-Catholic wars of the past could be reexamined with a
view to establishing those parts of their tested experience which
may seem to be psychologically and militarily sound in our own
time. How fast can converts be made from the other side? In what
circumstances should an enemy word of honor be treated as valid?
How can heretics (today, read "subversive elements") be uprooted?
Does the enemy faith have weak points which permit enemy beliefs to be turned against personnel at the appropriate times? What
unobjectionable forms should leaflets and broadcasts follow in
mentioning subjects which are reverenced by the enemy but not
by ourselves?

Figure 5: *Revolutionary Propaganda.* When revolution favors one side or the other in war, revolutionary propaganda becomes an instrument which is used by one constituted government against
another. This leaflet was issued by the Azad Hind Fauj (Free India Army) of the Japanese puppet
Subhas Chandra Bose. (Singapore, then called Shonan, 1943 and 1944.) The leaflet avoids direct
reference to the Japanese, and is therefore "black" propaganda. Its theme is simple: the British
are alleged to eat while the Hindus starve. At the time, this argument had some plausibility. There
was famine in Bengal, but no white men were found among the thousands of emaciated dead.

$\longrightarrow$

जरा देखो खाने पीने के सामानों का अंग्रेज कैसी नेपरवा के साथ इस्तेमाल कर रहे है. पर हिंदुस्तानि खाने पीने के सामानों के नहोनेसे भुखसे मरे जा रहे ।

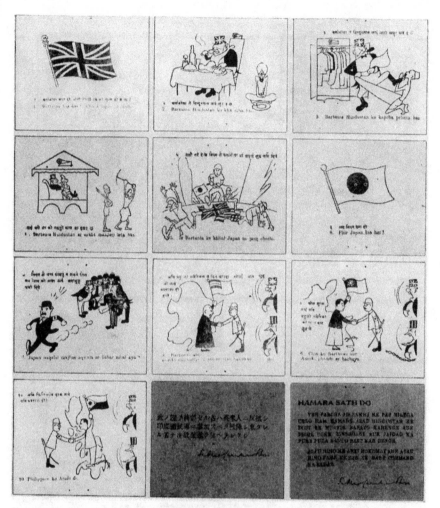

Figure 6: Propaganda for Illiterates. Propaganda reached out for the mass audience in World War II. Some of the most interesting developments in this line were undertaken by CBI Theater facilities and their Japanese competitors. The leaflet shown above is designed to tell its story in Hindu-

The expansion of the Islamic Faith-and-Empire provides a great deal of procedural information which cannot be neglected in our time. It has been said that men's faith should not be destroyed by violence, and that force alone is insufficient to change the minds of men. If this were true, it would mean that Germany can never be de-Nazified, and that there is no hope that the democratic peoples captured by totalitarian powers can adjust themselves to their new overlords or, if adjusted, can be converted back to free

stani (Devanagari script) or in Romanized Hindustani to Indians who could read either form, and in pictures to the illiterates. It starts with the Union Jack and ends with the Congress flag used by the puppet pro-Japanese Indian leader, Subhas Chandra Bose.

principles. In reality warfare by Mohammed's captains and successors demonstrated two principles of long-range psychological warfare which are still valid today:

A people can be converted from one faith to the other if given the choice between conversion and extermination, stubborn individuals being rooted out. To effect the initial conversion, participation in the public ceremonies and formal language of the new faith must be required. Sustained counterintelligence must remain

l'Empereur Roi p... Lui (Koubilai - Khan) dans une Tour portée par quatre Eléphants ... jour de Parade.

Figure 8: One of the Mongol Secret Weapons. The Mongol conquerors used rumor and terror in order to increase their military effectiveness. Once they came to power, they used spectacular military displays as a means of intimidating conquered peoples. This old French engraving shows a warhowdah mounted on four elephants allegedly used by Kublai Khan, grandnephew to Genghis Khan and friend of Marco Polo the Venetian. Obviously impractical for field use, the vehicle is well suited for ceremonial display and mere mention of it is a factor for "warfare psychologically waged."

on the alert against backsliders, but formal acceptance will become genuine acceptance if all public media of expression are denied the vanquished faith.

If immediate wholesale conversion would require military operations that were too extensive or severe, the same result can be effected by toleration of the objectionable faith, combined with the issuance of genuine privileges to the new, preferred faith. The conquered people are left in the private, humble enjoyment of their old beliefs and folkways; but all participation in public life, whether

Figure 7: Propaganda Through News. News is one of the best carriers of psychological warfare to the enemy. One of these newspapers is directed by the Allies to the German troops in the Ægean Islands; the other by the Germans to the Americans in France. Of the two, the Allied paper (in German) is the more professional job. Note the separation of appeals from the news, the greater newsiness of the news columns, and the explanation provided for third-party civilians in their own Greek language (top right).

←

political, cultural or economic, is conditioned on acceptance of the new faith. In this manner, all up-rising members of the society will move in a few generations over to the new faith in the process of becoming rich, powerful, or learned; what is left of the old faith will be a gutter superstition, possessing neither power nor majesty.

These two rules worked once in the rise of Islam. They were applied again by Nazi overlords during World War II, the former in Poland, the Ukraine and Byelorussia, the latter in Holland, Belgium, Norway and other Western countries. The rules will probably be seen in action again. The former process is difficult and bloody, but quick; the latter is as sure as a steam-roller. If Christians, or democrats, or progressives—whatever free men may be called—are put in a position of underprivilege and shame for their beliefs, and if the door is left open to voluntary conversion, so that anyone who wants to can come over to the winning side, the winning side will sooner or later convert almost everyone who is capable of making trouble. (In the language of Vilfredo Pareto, this would probably be termed "capture of the rising elite"; in the language of present-day Marxists, this would be described as "utilization of potential leadership cadres from historically superseded classes"; in the language of practical politics, it means "cut in the smart boys from the opposition, so that they can't set up a racket of their own.")

The Black Propaganda of Genghis Khan. Another demonstration of psychological warfare in the past was so effective that its results linger to this day. It is commonly thought that the greatest conqueror the world has seen—Temujin, the Genghis Khan—effected his Mongol conquests with "limitless hordes" of wild Tatar horsemen, who flooded the world by weight of sheer numbers. Recent research shows that the sparsely settled countryside of Inner Asia could not have produced populations heavy enough to overwhelm the densely settled areas of the great Mongol periphery by weight alone. The empire of the Khan was built on bold military inventiveness—the use of highly mobile forces, the full use of intelligence, the coordination of half-global strategy, the application of propaganda in all its forms.[6] The Mongols were fighting the Sung Dynasty in China and the Holy Roman Empire in Prussia four thousand miles apart when neither of their adversaries knew (in more than rumor) that the other existed. The Mongols used espionage to plan their campaigns and deliberately used rumor and other means to exaggerate accounts of their own huge numbers, stupidity, and ferocity. They did not care what their enemies thought as long as the enemies became frightened. Europeans described light, hard-hitting numerically inferior cavalry as a "numberless horde" because Mongol agents whispered such a story in the streets. To this day most Europeans do not appreciate the lightness of the forces nor the cold intelligence of command with which the Mongols hit them seven centuries ago.

Genghis even used the spies of the enemy as a means of frightening the enemy. When spies were at hand he indoctrinated them with rumors concerning his own forces. Let the first European biographer of Genghis tell, in his own now-quaint words, how Genghis put the bee on Khorezm (Carizme):

> And a Historian, to describe their Strength and Number, makes the Spies whom the King of *Carizme* had sent to view them, speak thus: They are, say they to the Sultan, all compleat Men, vigorous, and look like Wrestlers; they breathe nothing but War and Blood, and show so great an Impatience to fight, that the Generals can scarce moderate it; yet though they appear thus fiery, they keep themselves within the bounds of a strict Obedience to Command, and are intirely devoted to their Prince; they are contented with any sort of Food, and are not curious in the choice of Beasts to eat, like Mussulmen [Mohammedans], so that they are subsisted without much trouble; and they not only eat Swines-Flesh, but feed upon Wolves, Bears, and Dogs, when they have no other Meat, making no distinction between what was

> lawful to eat, and what was forbidden; and the Ne-
> cessity for supporting Life takes from them all the
> Dislike which the *Mahometans* have for many sorts
> of Animals; As to their Number, (they concluded)
> *Genghizcan's* Troops seem'd like the Grasshoppers,
> impossible to be number'd.
>
> In reality, this Prince making a Review of his
> Army, found it to consist of seven hundred thousand
> men. . .[7]

Enemy espionage can now—as formerly—prove useful if the net effect of it is to lower enemy morale. The ruler and people of Khorezm put up a terrific fight, nevertheless, despite their expectation of being attacked by wolf-eating wrestlers without number; but they left the initiative in Genghis' hands and were doomed.

However good the Mongols were in strategic and tactical propaganda, they never solved the problem of consolidation propaganda (see chapter 3). They did not win the real loyalty of the peoples whom they conquered; unlike the Chinese, who replaced conquered populations with their own people, or the Mohammedans, who converted conquered peoples, the Mongols simply maintained law and order, collected taxes, and sat on top of the world for a few generations. Then their world stirred beneath them, and they were gone.

The Blindness of John Milton. Moving across the centuries for an example, it is interesting to note that John Milton, author of *Paradise Lost* and of other priceless books of the English-speaking world, went blind because he was so busy conducting Oliver Cromwell's psychological warfare that he disregarded the doctors' warning and abused his ailing sight. And the sad thing about it was that it was not very good psychological warfare.

Milton fell into the common booby-trap of refuting his opponents item by item, thus leaving them the strong affirmative position, instead of providing a positive and teachable statement of his own faith. He was Latin Secretary to the Council, in that

Commonwealth of England which was—to its contemporaries in Europe—such a novel, dreadful, and seditious form of government. The English had killed their king, by somewhat offhanded legal procedures, and had gone under the Cromwellian dictatorship. It was possible for their opponents to attack them from two sides at once. Believers in monarchy could call the English murderous king-killers (a charge as serious in those times as the charge of anarchism or free love in this); believers in order and liberty could call the British slaves of a tyrant. A Frenchman called Claude de Saumaise (in Latin form, Salmasius) wrote a highly critical book about the English, and Milton seems to have lost his temper and his judgment.

In his two books against Salmasius, Milton then committed almost every mistake in the whole schedule of psychological warfare. He moved from his own ground of argument over to the enemy's. He wrote at excessive length. He indulged in some of the nastiest name-calling to be found in literature, and went into considerable detail to describe Salmasius in unattractive terms. He slung mud whenever he could. The books are read today, under compulsion, by Ph.D. candidates, but no one else is known to find them attractive. It is not possible to find that these books had any lasting influence in their own time. (In these texts written by Milton in Latin but now available in English, Army men wearying of the monotonous phraseology of basic military invective can find extensive additions to their vocabulary.) Milton turned to disappointment and poetry; the world is the gainer.

The vocabulary of seventeenth-century propaganda had a strident tone which is, perhaps unfortunately, getting to be characteristic of the twentieth century. The following epithets sound like an American Legion description of Communists, or a Communist description of the Polish democrats, yet they were applied in a book by a Lutheran to Quakers. The title of the tirade reads, in part:

> . . . a description of the . . . new Quakers, making
> known the sum of their manifold blasphemous opin-
> ions, dangerous practices, Godless crimes, attempts

THE

Sad Estate

OF THE

KINGDOM,

Being an account of the first years charge of our Reformation.

It is an old Custom in England among Tradesmen, to Cast up their Books at Christmas: After their example I have thought fit to draw up the last years Account of the Kingdom, by way of Debtor and Creditor, so plainly, that he that runs may read it. They that love England I am sure cannot like it, but for that reason they should help to mend it. When they know the Disease, it will not be hard to find out the Cure. If our miserys do not mend our Hearts, I wish, at least, they may our Understandings.

Kingdom Debtor,

I. TO the loss of three, of the ten Commandments, Honour thy Father: Thou shalt not Steal: Nor covet any thing that is thy Neighbours: And those of the Gospel, Do as you would be done by: Don't do evil that good may come of it, nor reward evil with evil, but love one another.

II. To the loss of the Doctrine of Passive-Obedience, and Non-resistance, which first recommended the Primitive Christians to the mercy and Protection of Kings and Emperours, and has ever since the Reformation been the Characteristick of the Church of England.

III. To the loss of an English King in the right Line, by the new art of Abdication, who with all his faults, was Affable, Sober, Just and diligent; and Innocent of the main matters suggested against him.

IV. To the loss of Ireland, by that means, worth thirty Millions of pounds sterling, and the Conveniencies of its Neighbourhood, Trade and Ports for our safety and benefit, unattainable.

V. To five Millions expended this year to beat the French and recover Ireland.

VI. To thirteen Thousand Souldiers dead in Schombourgs Army, without Sword or Gun, in an unusual and lamentable manner.

To three Thousand Men killed, taken and deserted to King James.

To the loss of Dundalk, Carlingford, James-Town and Siege, with four Counties in Ulster, which is the only Province of Ireland, where the English Forces have any footing.

To eleven Thousand Souls that perished in London-derry besides many English and Scotch Inhabitants that dyed of the same defeats in the North.

VII. To six Thousand Men that died in Flanders, out of the nine Thousand, forced into the Dutch and Spanish service last year against the French for helping King James.

VIII. To seven Thousand Sea-men that died upon the Fleet, of strange distempers.

IX. To five Thousand Sea-men taken by the French, both upon men of War and Marchant men, notwithstanding our Fleet.

X. To twenty Men of War taken and lost: the value, at least two hundred thousand pound, which is more then has been lost in three Dutch Wars.

Kingdom Creditor,

I. TO the pretence of preserving us from Popery and Arbitrary Government, by reforming abuses in Elections of Parliament, setting Corporations, leaving the Prerogative, and Securing our Laws and Liberties against a standing Army, specially of Foreigners and Papists.

II. To the Doctrines of Might is Right, and the Jus Divinum of the MOBB.

III. To a Dutch King, such an one as he is, with abundance of new Lords and Officers of both houses of Parliament, that are yet to deserve their honour, and learn their businels.

IV. To a standing Army of Foreigners, brought in and upheld without advice of Parliament, that will Certainly do as King William pleases.

V. To Schomberg's success against the Irish and Herbert's against the French, such as it was.

VI. To fifteen Hundred men killed and taken, and a Thousand Shams and Stories to keep up the Spirits of the People, especially of mighty Victories, Slaughters and REVOLTS, that time has detected with a Vengeance.

VII. To the Dutch-friendship, especially in Trade, and that of the Spaniard and confederates, though good for little else but to pick our pockets.

VIII. To poysoned Victuals, or any thing else but the hand of God Almighty.

IX. To five Hundred twenty nine French Prisoners taken by us.

X. To one small man of War, and two Privateers taken by us; the first of which was retaken, and other two lately destroyed by the storm at Plymouth.

XI. To

Figure 9: Black Propaganda from the British Underground, 1690. When William of Orange took the crown of England away from the timid rascal, James II, he met opposition from the Loyalists de-

XI. To four Hundred Sail of *Merchant-men* taken by the French, & twenty five loſt by ſtorms, of which nine were driven off of our own Coaſt to *France*, whoſe Hulls and Cargo are valued at two Millions five Hundred Thouſand pounds, many of the Ships being as big as our large fourth rate Frigats.

XII. To thirty Thouſand pounds for pulling down and building up one ſide of *Hampton-Court*, and altering the Gardings, and rebuilding what *fell down*.

XIII. To twenty Thouſand pounds for my Lord *Nottingham* and his houſe, and twenty thouſand more to re-build it, with that which *fell down* of the new building ; for it ſeems they have built with *untempered Mortar*.

XIV. To the *Navy*, *Army* and *Houſhold* for the moſt part three quarters Sallery *unpayd*.

XV. To the loſs of a great part of *Scotland*, and the *hazard* of the Reſt.

XVI. To the loſs of fifteen Hundred Engliſh, *Horſe and Foot*, in that Kingdom ; beſides more Scotch.

XVII. To a whole year loſt in *Trade* and *War*, not to be computed.

XVIII. To two Millions that we are yet in Debt.

The total of loſs in Money	l. Money
Ireland	30000000
Taxes	05000000
Merchants Ships	02500000
Men of War	00200000
Hampton-Court	00030000
Nottingham-houſe	00040000
	37770000

The total of men loſt	Men
By death, in *Shomburgs* Army	13000
Killed, taken and deſerted	03000
Periſhed in *Londondery*	11000
Dead, deſerted & killed in *Flanders*	06000
Dead in the Fleet	07000
Dead, taken and deſerted in *Scotland*	03000
Men taken by the French	05000
	48000

XI. To twenty five French prizes taken by us, of ſmall burden and mean loading.

XII. To a more modiſh apartment with convenient back Stairs, though the old one had ſerved well enough *eight crowned Heads* in better times, beſides *Cromwel*, that loved it of all places.

XIII. To a Good *Receipt* for the *Piſſick*.

XIIII. To ſix Hundred Thouſand pounds ſent to *Holland* for fear of the worſt, and as much more to fetch over *foreign Ships and Troops*, for the better perſerving our Rights and Privileges, Engliſh men not being to be *truſted* in a buſineſs that ſo nearly concerns them.

XV. To the Maintaining of the *Prerogative* of the Crown againſt Scotch *Republicans*, in that Our Antient Kingdom.

XVI. To the exploits of *Mackay*.

XVII. To our own *folly and Gods Judgments*.

XVIII. To three ſhillings in the pound, and a new Parliament with more *foreign Forces* and *home Levies*, and forty Thouſand *Bayonets* (inſtead of Dr *Oates* forty Thouſand *black Bils*) now beſpoken, and making ; and *ſaddles*, *bridles*, and other furniture coming from *Germany*, by the *Jews* means ; for all Nations muſt have a ſhare of us.

To ballance this, we may perhaps have taken and deſtroyed, in all, three Thouſand of our Enemies, got twenty five Sale of ſmall Craft, worth twenty Thouſand pound at the moſt, but remain a moſt ſick Army in *Ireland* ; the *aſtoniſhment* of all beholders and *a mutinous*, tattered and *diſeaſed Fleet ſtill*.

Hear you ſee the firſt years account of our deliverance. *Vaſt Taxes*, *mighty Loſſes*, *great Mortality*, ſo that we have been delivered of more *Men*, *Money* and *Ships*, then our *Civil* and *Dutch* Wars formerly coſt us, inſomuch as they that ſee not the *heavy hand* of God upon us, are blind to providence ; our ſufferings in *Intereſt* as well as *Reputation*, having ſurpaſſed all remedy as well as example, unleſs we ſpeedily repent of our impiety to God, our Injuſtice to our King and our malice againſt one another.

FINIS.

voted to the Stuarts. This broadsheet demonstrates an early form of black propaganda. It also provides a good instance of propaganda material borrowing a familiar form of expression in order to get its message across, in this case, the tradesman's enumeration of debit and credit.

to subvert civil government in the churches and in
the community life of the world; together with their
idiotic games, their laughable action and behavior,
which is enough to make sober Christian persons
breathless, and which is like death, and which can
display the lazy stinking cadaver of their fanatical
doctrines. . .

In its first few pages, the book accuses the Quakers of obscenity, adultery, civil commotion, conspiracy, blasphemy, subversion
and lunacy.[8] Milton was not out of fashion in applying bad manners to propaganda. It is merely regrettable that he did not transcend the frailties of his time.

Other Instances from History. Innumerable other instances of
propaganda in warfare and diplomacy could be culled out of history; these would not mean much if they were presented as mere
story-telling. The cultural factors would have to be figured out;
the military situation would need to be appraised in realistic terms;
the media available for psychological warfare would have to be
charted pretty carefully, before the instances would become usable
examples. Here are some of the most promising topics:

Naval psychological warfare techniques used by the Caribbean pirates to unnerve prospective victims.

Cortez's use of horses as psychological disseminators of terror among the Aztecs, along with his exploitation of
Mexican legends concerning the Fair God.

The failure of Turkish psychological warfare in the great
campaigns of 1683 which left the issue one of purely
physical means and cost Turkey the possible hegemony
of central Europe.

The propaganda methods of the British East India Company
in the conquest of India against overwhelming Indian
numerical superiority. (Edmond Taylor mentions these
in his *Richer by Asia.*)

Addrefs to the Soldiers.

GENTLEMEN,

YOU are about to embark for America, to compel your Fellow Subjects there to fubmit to POPERY and SLAVERY.

It is the Glory of the Britifh Soldier, that he is the *Defender*, not the *Deftroyer*, of the Civil and Religious Rights of the People. The *Englifh* Soldiery are immortalized in Hiftory, for their Attachment to the Religion and Liberties of their Country.

When King JAMES the Second endeavoured to introduce the Roman-catholic Religion and arbitrary Power into Great Britain, he had an Army encamped on Hounfow-Heath, to terrify the People. Seven Bifhops were feized upon, and fent to the Tower. But they appealed to the Laws of their Country, and were fet at Liberty. When this News reached the Camp, the Shouts of Joy were fo great, that they re-echoed in the Royal Palace. This, however, did not quite convince the King, of the Averfion of the Soldiers to be the Inftruments of Oppreffion againft their Fellow Subjects. He therefore made another Trial. He ordered the Guards to be drawn up, and the Word was given, that thofe who did not chufe to fupport the King's Meafures, fhould ground their Arms. When, behold, to his utter Confufion, and their eternal Honour—the whole Body grounded their Arms.

You, Gentlemen, will foon have an Opportunity of fhewing equal Virtue. You will be called upon to imbrue your Hands in the Blood of your Fellow Subjects in *America*, becaufe they will not admit to be Slaves, and are alarmed at the Eftablifhment of Popery and Arbitrary Power in one Half of their Country.

Whether you will draw thofe Swords which have defended them againft their Enemies, to butcher them into a Refignation of their Rights, which they hold as the Sons of *Englifhmen*, is in your Breafts. That you will not ftain the Laurels you have gained from *France*, by dipping them in Civil Blood, is every good Man's Hope.

Arts will no doubt be ufed to perfuade you, that it is your Duty to obey Orders; and that you are fent upon the juft and righteous Errand of crufhing Rebellion. But your own Hearts will tell you, that the People may be fo ill treated, as to make Refiftance neceffary. You know, that Violence and Injury offered from one Man to another, has always fome Pretence of Right or Reafon to juftify it. So it is between the People and their Rulers.

But, whatever hard Names and heavy Accufations may be beftowed upon your Fellow Subjects in America, be affured they have not deferved them; but that, by the moft cruel Treatment, into Defpair. In this Defpair they are compelled to defend their Liberties, after having tried, in Vain, every peaceable Means of obtaining Redrefs of their manifold Grievances.

Before God and Man they are right.

Your Honour then, Gentlemen, as Soldiers, and your Humanity as Men, forbid you to be the Inftruments of forcing Chains upon your injured and oppreffed Fellow Subjects. Remember that your firft Obedience is due to God, and that whoever bids you fhed innocent Blood, bids you act cuntrary to his Commandments.

I am, GENTLEMEN,

your fincere Well-wifher,

AN OLD SOLDIER.

Figure 10: Secret American Propaganda Subverting the Redcoats. Readers of Charles Dickens' great novel, *Barnaby Rudge*, will remember that anti-Catholicism was a lively propaganda issue in England at the time of the American Revolution. This American propaganda avoids discussion of the theme of American independence—a topic on which Englishmen were liable to hold united opinions—and instead attempts to subvert British troops by means of the anti-Catholic appeal. (Original source unknown; from War Department files. Probable date, 1775.)

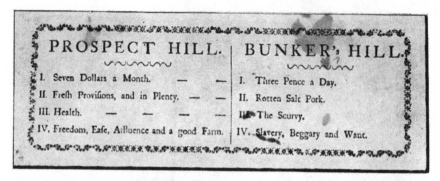

Figure 11: Desertion Leaflet from Bunker Hill. This leaflet is as valid today as the day it was written. No source is indicated, but neither is any attempt made to suggest a false source different from the true one; it is in modern parlance "grey" propaganda. Wealth, food, health and economic status are played up simultaneously; difficult political issues are not argued—they are side-stepped.

The preventive psychological warfare system set up by the Tokugawa shoguns after 1636, which bottled up the brains of the Japanese through more rigorous control than has ever been established elsewhere over civilized people.

The field psychological warfare of the Manchus, who conquered China against odds running as much as 400 to one against them, and who used terror as a means of nullifying Chinese superiority.

The propaganda of the European feudal classes against the peasant revolts, which identified the peasants with filth, anarchy, murder, and cruelty.

The Inquisition considered as a psychological warfare facility of the Spanish Empire.

The agitational practices of the French Revolutionaries.

Early uses of rockets and balloons for psychological effect.

The beginnings of leaflet-printing as an adjunct to field operations.

Such a list just begins to touch on subjects which can and should be investigated, either as staff studies or by civilian historians. Collection of the materials and framing of sound doctrines for psychological warfare are no minor task.

The American Revolution. In the American Revolution, psychological warfare played a very important role. The Whig campaign of propaganda which led up to colonial defiance of Britain was energetic and expert in character, and the very opening of hostilities was marked by passionate appeals to the civilian population in the form of handbills. The American forces at the Battle of Bunker Hill used one of the earliest versions of front-line combat propaganda (see Figure 11). The appeal was as direct as could be wished. Artful use was made of the sharp class distinctions then existing between British officers and enlisted men; fear was exploited as an aid to persuasion; the language was pointed. Even in our own time, the Bunker Hill propaganda leaflet stands as a classic example of how to do good field propaganda.

The Americans made extensive use of the press.[9] When the newspaper proprietors veered too far to the Loyalist side, they were warned to keep to a more Patriotic line. If, in the face of counter-threats from the Loyalists, the newspaper threatened going out of business altogether, it was warned that suspension of publication would be taken as treason to America. The Whigs, before hostilities, and their successors, the Patriots of the war period, showed a keen interest in keeping the press going and in making sure that their side of the story got out and got circulated rapidly. In intimidation and control of the press, they far outdistanced the British, whose papers circulated chiefly within the big cities held as British citadels throughout the war. Political reasoning, economic arguments, allegations concerning the course of the war, and atrocity stories all played a role.

George Washington himself, as commander of the Continental forces, showed a keen interest in war propaganda and in his just, moderate political and military measures provided a policy base from which Patriot propagandists could operate.

Some wars are profoundly affected by a book written on one side or the other; the American revolutionary war was one of these. Thomas Paine's *Common Sense* (issued as a widely sold series of pamphlets) swept American opinion like wildfire; it stated some of the fundamentals of American thinking, and put its bold but

JINGHPAW NI!

JAPAN NI GAW NANHTE HPE JAI LANG SHANGUN AI, NDAI ZAWN MANU N DAN AI MAISAU GUMHPRAW HPE ALOISHA GALAW LU MA AI.

SHAHPA, COOLIE AMU HTE RA AI ARAI NI GAW SHANHTE GUMHPRAW LU LOI AI DARAM, NANHTE LU YAK NGA MA NIT DAI.

MAWP SHA HKUM HKAM MU! JAPAN GUMHPRAW KOI GAM MU!

Ginjang Japan ni Myen mung de nga ai shanhte a hpyen ma ni hpe ip da let, amying jaw tawn ai gaw "Majan aten e, shahpa, coolie hte ra ai arai ni lu na matu sha Nippon hpyen hpung ni gaw maisau gumhpraw hpe dip shapraw nga ai. Mung masha ni hte ndai gumhpraw a lam hpe nkum bawng mu. Ra ai hte maren lang mu."

← ↑

Figure 12: Money as a Carrier of Propaganda. The note on the left above is French revolutionary currency; observe the use of revolutionary slogans. Next to it is the famous Russian 10,000-ruble bill which calls for the world revolution in seven languages. The Japanese peso note (at top of page *38*) carries American propaganda on the reverse; captured notes were overprinted by Psychological Warfare Branch during the Philippine campaign and dropped back on the enemy. The two five-rupee notes date from the Japanese occupation of Burma. The lower of the two was issued by Americans as a means of deriding the Japanese.

reasonable revolutionary case in such simple terms that even conservatives in the Patriot group could not resist using it for propaganda purposes.[10] *Common Sense* has become a classic of American literature, but it has its place in history too, as "the book that won the war." Other pamphleteers, with the redoubtable Sam Adams in the lead, also did well.

American experience in the Mexican war was less glorious. The Mexicans waged psychological warfare against us with considerable effect, ending up with traitor American artillerymen dealing out heavy murder to the American troops outside Mexico city. Historians in both countries gloss over the treason and subversion which occurred on each side.

In the Civil War, psychological warfare was practised by both Lincoln and the Confederacy in establishing propaganda instrumentalities in England and on the continent of Europe. The Northern use of Negro troops, which was followed, at the end of the war by the Confederate plans for raising Negro troops, did not become the major propaganda issue it might have because of the community of feeling on the two sides, indecision on each side as to the purpose of the war (apart from the basic issue of union or disunion), and the persistence of politics-as-usual both North and South of the battle line.

Boers and Burmese. In the latter part of the nineteenth century, two sets of British wars indicate the effect psychological warfare can play. The British conquered both Burma and the Boers. The Burmese were more numerous, had the larger country, and (if they had had leadership comparable to the Japanese leadership of the time) could have developed the larger military potential. But Burma was conquered by the British in a final war which went on quietly and ingloriously. No nation came to their aid. They did not even get a chance to surrender. The British simply ended the war in the middle by announcing the end of the Burmese government, and by making a one-sided declaration that Burma was annexed to the Empire of India. The political death of Burma occurred on 1 January 1886, but the event has been forgotten.

The Boers, on the other hand, made a stir throughout the world. They got in touch with the Germans, Irish, Americans, French, Dutch, and everybody else who might criticize Britain. They stated their case loudly and often. They waged commando warfare, adding the word *commando* to international military parlance, and sent small units deep into the British rear, setting off a mad uproar and making the world press go crazy with excitement. When they finally gave in, it was on reasonable terms for themselves; they left the British with an internationally blacked eye.

Nobody remembered the Burmese; everybody remembered the Boers. The Boers used every means they could think of; they did everything they could. They even captured Winston Churchill.

These examples may show that the military role of propaganda and related operations is not as obscure or intangible as it may have seemed. They cannot be considered history but must be regarded as a plea for the writing of history. More recent experience is another question, and involves tracing the doctrines pertaining to psychological warfare which have now become established military procedure in the modern armies.

NOTES:

[1] Histories of warfare, of politics (though there are no good recent ones, Edward Jenks' little book being half a century out of date), of political theory (especially the excellent though dissimilar volumes by G. H. Sabine and by G. E. C. Catlin), of particular countries, of diplomacy, of religion and even of literature all cast a certain amount of light on the subject. No writer known to the author specializes in the topic of historical propaganda; none takes up the long-established historical role of non-violent persuasion in warfare. Some of the sociologists and anthropologists such as Karl Mannheim, Max Weber, Talcott Parsons, Geoffrey Gorer, Ruth Benedict (to mention a few at random) have presented approaches which would justify re-evaluations of history in a way useful to propaganda students; but they have not yet persuaded the historians to do the work.

[2] 7 Judges 22-23.

[3] Leon Wieger, S. J., *Textes Historiques*, Hsien-hsien, 1929, vol. 1, pp. 628-633.

[4] The author's attention to this reference was drawn by an unpublished undated typescript article in the War Department files by Lt. Col. Samuel T. Mackall, Inf.

[5] Lo Kuan-chung, *San Kuo chih Yen-i*, translated by C. H. Brewitt-Taylor as *San Kuo or Romance of the Three Kingdoms*, Shanghai, 1929, vol. 1, p. 46.

[6] Recent writers on Genghis, such as Lamb, Vladimirtsov, Fox and Lattimore all credit the Mongols with a higher technological level of warfare than has been the custom among most Western historians. H. G. Wells' simple but compelling description of the Mongols in his *Outline of History* is worth re-reading in this connection.

[7] Petis de la Croix, *The History of Genghizcan the Great, First Emperor of the Antient Moguls and Tartars* . . ., London, 1722, p. 154.

[8] Benedict Figken, *Historia Fanaticorum*, Danzig, 1664.

[9] Philip Davidson's *Propaganda and the American Revolution*, Chapel Hill, 1941, is a careful scholarly study of this period. Comparable studies have not yet been written concerning other American wars. Military and civilian historians have a fascinating piece of research awaiting them in the material concerning Confederate and Federal psychological warfare. Each participant in the Civil War was vulnerable to the propaganda of the other. Subversive and clandestine pro- Confederate propaganda in the North is outlined in George Fort Milton's engrossing *Abraham Lincoln and the Fifth Column*, New York and Washington, D. C., 1942, but no comparable study covering all forms of propaganda on either side is yet available.

[10] Various new editions of Paine's chief works are available in popular and inexpensive form. They are worth study as good propaganda.

CHAPTER 2
THE FUNCTION OF PSYCHOLOGICAL WARFARE

Psychological warfare, in the broad sense, consists of the application of parts of the science called psychology to the conduct of war; in the narrow sense, psychological warfare comprises the use of propaganda against an enemy, together with such military operational measures as may supplement the propaganda. Propaganda may be described, in turn, as organized persuasion by non-violent means. War itself may be considered to be, among other things, a violent form of persuasion. Thus if an American fire-raid burns up a Japanese city, the burning is calculated to dissuade the Japanese from further warfare by denying the Japanese further physical means of war and by simultaneously hurting them enough to cause surrender. If, after the fire-raid, we drop leaflets telling them to surrender, the propaganda can be considered an extension of persuasion—less violent this time, and usually less effective, but nevertheless an integral part of the single process of making the enemy stop fighting.

Neither warfare nor psychology is a new subject. Each is as old as man. Warfare, being the more practical and plain subject, has a far older written history. This is especially the case since much of what is now called psychology was formerly studied under the heading of religion, ethics, literature, politics, or medicine. Modern psychological warfare has become self-conscious in using modern scientific psychology as a tool.

In World War II the enemies of the United States were more fanatical than the people and leaders of the United States. The consequence was that the Americans could use and apply any expedient psychological weapon which either science or our version of common sense provided. We did not have to square it with Emperor myths, the Führer principle, or some other rigid, fanatical philosophy. The enemy enjoyed the positive advantage of having an indoctrinated army and people; we enjoyed the countervailing advantage of having skeptical people, with no inward theology that hampered our propaganda operations. It is no negligible matter to be able to use the latest findings of psychological science in a swift, bold manner. The scientific character of our psychology puts us ahead of opponents wrapped up in dogmatism who must check their propaganda against such articles of faith as Aryan racialism or the Hegelian philosophy of history.

Psychological Warfare as a Branch of Psychology. Good propaganda can be conducted by persons with no knowledge of formal psychology. The human touch, the inventive mind, the forceful appeal—things such as these appear in the writings of gifted persons. Thomas Paine never read a word of Freud or Pavlov, yet Paine's arguments during the Revolutionary War played subtly on every appeal which a modern psychologist could catalogue. But war cannot, in modern times, assume a statistical expectation of talent. Psychology makes it possible for the able but ordinary statesman or officer to calculate his persuasion systematically and to obtain by planning those results which greater men might hit upon by genius.

What can psychology do for warfare?

In the first place, the psychologist can bring to the attention of the soldier those elements of the human mind which are usually kept out of sight. He can show how to convert lust into resentment, individual resourcefulness into mass cowardice, friction into distrust, prejudice into fury. He does so by going down to the *unconscious* mind for his source materials. (During World War II, the fact that Chinese babies remain unimpeded while they commit a nuisance, while Japanese babies are either intercepted or punished if they make a mess in the wrong place, was found to be of significant importance in planning psychological warfare. See chapter 9.)

In the second place the psychologist can set up techniques for finding out how the enemy really does feel. Some of the worst blunders of history have arisen from miscalculation of the enemy state of mind. By using the familiar statistical and questionnaire procedures, the psychologist can quiz a small cross section of enemy prisoners and from the results estimate the mentality of an entire enemy theater of war at a given period. If he does not have the prisoners handy, he can accomplish much the same end by an analysis of the news and propaganda which the enemy authorities transmit to their own troops and people. By establishing enemy opinion and morale factors he can hazard a reasoned forecast as to how the enemy troops will behave under specific conditions.

In the third place, the psychologist can help the military psychological warfare operator by helping him maintain his sense of mission and of proportion. The deadliest danger of propaganda consists of its being issued by the propagandist for his own edification. This sterile and ineffectual amusement can disguise the complete failure of the propaganda as propaganda. There is a genuine pleasure in talking-back, particularly to an enemy. The propagandist, especially in wartime, is apt to tell the enemy what he thinks of him, or to deride enemy weaknesses. But to have told the Nazis, for example, "You Germans are a pack of murderous baboons and your Hitler is a demented oaf. Your women are slobs, your children are halfwits, your literature is gibberish and your cooking is garbage," and so on, would have stiffened the German will to fight. The propagandist must tell the enemy those things which the enemy will heed; he must keep his private emotionalism out of the operation. The psychologist can teach the propaganda operator how to be objective, systematic, cold. For combat operations, it does not matter how much a division commander may dislike the enemy; for psychological warfare purposes, he must consider how to persuade them, even though he may privately thirst for their destruction. The indulgence of hatred is not a working part of the soldier's mission; to some it may be helpful; to others, not. The useful mission consists solely of making the enemy stop fighting, by combat or other means. But when the soldier turns to propaganda, he may need the advice of a psychologist in keeping his own feelings out of it.

Finally, the psychologist can prescribe media—radio, leaflets, loudspeakers, whispering agents, returned enemy soldiers, and so forth. He can indicate when and when not to use any given medium. He can, in conjunction with operations and intelligence officers, plan the full use of all available psychological resources. He can coordinate the timing of propaganda with military, economic or political situations.

The psychologist does not have to be present in person to give this advice. He does not have to be a man with an M.D. or Ph. D. and years of postgraduate training. He can be present in the manuals he writes, in the indoctrination courses for psychological warfare officers he sets up, in the current propaganda line he dictates by radio. It is useful to have him in the field, particularly at the higher command headquarters, but he is not indispensable. The psychologist in person can be dispensed with; the methods of scientific psychology cannot. (Further on, throughout this book, reference will be made to current psychological literature. The general history of psychology is described in readable terms in Gregory Zilboorg and George W. Henry, *A History of Medical Psychology*, New York, 1941, and in Lowell S. Selling, *Men Against Madness*, New York, 1940, cheap edition, 1942.)

Propaganda can be conducted by rule of thumb. But only a genius can make it work well by playing his hunches. It can become true psychological warfare, scientific in spirit and developed as a teachable skill, only by having its premises clearly stated, its mission defined, its instruments put in systematic readiness, and its operations subject to at least partial check, only by the use of techniques borrowed from science. Of all the sciences, psychology is the nearest, though anthropology, sociology, political science, economics, area studies and other specialties all have something to contribute; but it is psychology which indicates the need of the others.

Psychological Warfare as a Part of War. An infantry officer does not need to study the whole nature of war, in order to find his own job. Tradition, military skill, discipline, sound doctrine—these have done the job for him. Sun Tzu, Vegetius, Frederick, Clausewitz and a host of lesser writers on war have established the place of combat in war, and have appraised its general character.

How much the traditional doctrines may be altered in the terrible light of atomic explosion, no one knows; but though the weapons are novel, the wielders of the weapons will still be men. The motives and weaknesses within war remain ancient and human, however novel and dreadful the mechanical expedients adopted to express them.

Warfare as a whole is traditionally well defined, and psychological warfare can be understood only in relation to the whole process. It is no mere tool, to be used on special occasion. It has become a pervasive element in the military and security situation of every power on earth.

Psychological warfare is a part of war. The simplest, plainest thing which can be said of war—any sort of war, anywhere, anytime—is that it is *an official fight between men.* Combat, killing, and even large-scale group struggle are known elsewhere in the animal kingdom, but war is not. All sorts of creatures fight; but only men declare, wage, and terminate war; and they do so only against other men.

Formally, war may be defined as the "reciprocal application of violence by public, armed bodies."

If it is not *reciprocal*, it is not war, the killing of persons who do not defend themselves is not war, but slaughter, massacre, or punishment.

If the bodies involved are not *public*, their violence is not war. Even our enemies in World War II were relatively careful about this distinction, because they did not know how soon or easily a violation of the rules might be scored against them. To be public, the combatants need not be legal—that is, constitutionally set up; it suffices, according to international usage, for the fighters to have a reasonable minimum of numbers, some kind of identification, and a purpose which is political. If you shoot your neighbor, you will be committing mere murder; but if you gather twenty or thirty friends, together, tie a red handkerchief around the left arm of each man, announce that you are out to overthrow the government of the United States, and *then* shoot your neighbor as a counterrevolutionary impediment to the new order of things, you can have the satisfaction of having waged war. (In practical terms, this means that you will be put to death for treason and rebellion, not merely for murder.)

Finally, war must be *violent*. According to the law of modern states, all the way from Iceland to the Yemen, economic, political, or moral pressure is not war; war is the legalization, in behalf of the state, of things which no individual may lawfully do in time of peace. As a matter of fact, even in time of war you cannot kill the enemy unless you do so on behalf of the state; if you had shot a Japanese creditor of yours privately, or even shot a Japanese soldier when you yourself were out of uniform, you might properly and lawfully have been put to death for murder—either by our courts or by the enemies'. (This is among the charges which recur in the war trials. The Germans and Japanese killed persons whom even war did not entitle them to kill.)

The governments of the modern world are jealous of their own monopoly of violence. War is the highest exercise of that violence, and modern war is no simple reversion to savagery. The General Staffs would not be needed if war were only an uncomplicated orgy of homicide—a mere getting-mad and throat-cutting season in the life of man. Quite to the contrary, modern war—as a function of modern society—reflects the institutional, political complexity from which it comes. A modern battle is a formal, ceremonialized and technically intricate operation. You must kill just the right people, in just the right way, with the right timing, in the proper place, for avowed purposes. Otherwise you make a mess of the whole show, and—what is worse—you lose.

Why must you fight just so and so, there and not here, now and not then? The answer is simple: you are fighting against *men*. Your purpose in fighting is to make them change their minds. It is figuratively true to say that the war we have just won was a peculiar kind of advertising campaign, designed to make the Germans and Japanese like us and our way of doing things. They did not like us much, but we gave them alternatives far worse than liking us, so that they became peaceful.

Sometimes individuals will be unpersuadable. Then they must be killed or neutralized by other purely physical means—such as isolation or imprisonment. (Some Nazis, perhaps including the Führer himself, found our world repellent or incomprehensible and died because they could not make themselves surrender. In the Pacific many Japanese had to be killed before they became acceptable to us.) But such is man, that most individuals will stop fighting at some point short of extinction; that point is reached when one of two things happens:

Either, the defeated people may lose their sense of organization, fail to decide on leaders and methods, and give up because they can no longer fight as a group. This happened to the American Southerners in April, 1865. The President and Cabinet of the Confederate States of America got on the train at Richmond; the men who got off farther down the line were "refugees." Something happened to them and to the people about them, so that Mr. Davis no longer thought of himself as President Davis, and other people no longer accepted his commands. This almost happened in Germany in 1945 except for Admiral Doenitz.

Or, the defeated people can retain their sense of organization, and can use their political organization for the purpose of getting in touch with the enemy, arranging the end of the war, and preparing, through organized means, to comply with the wishes of the conquerors. That happened when Britain acknowledged American independence; when the Boers recognized British sovereignty; when Finland signed what Russia had dictated; and when Japan gave up.

Sometimes these things are mixed. The people might wish to make peace, but may find that their government is not recognized by the enemy. Or the victors may think that they have smashed the enemy government, when the new organization is simply the old one under a slightly different name, but with the old leaders and the old ideas still prevailing.

It is plain that whatever happens wars are fought to effect a psychological change in the antagonist. They are then fought for a psychological end unless they are wars of extermination. These are rare. The United States could not find a people on the face of the earth whose ideas and language were unknown to all Americans. Where there is a chance of communication, there is always the probability that one of the antagonistic organizations (governments)—which have already cooperated to the extent of meeting one another's wishes to fight—will subsequently cooperate on terms of primary advantage to the victors. Since the organizations comprise human beings with human ways of doing things, the change must take place in the minds of those specific individuals who operate the existing government, or in the minds of enough other people for that government to be overthrown.

The fact that war is waged against the minds, not the bodies, of the enemy is attested by the comments of military writers of all periods. The dictum of Carl von Clausewitz that "war is politics continued by other means" is simply the modern expression of a truth recognized since antiquity. War is a kind of persuasion—uneconomical, dangerous, and unpleasant, but effective when all else fails.

Ideology. An ideology is a system of deep-rooted beliefs about fundamental questions in human life and affairs.[1] Ideology also plays a part in psychological warfare. A difference in beliefs which does not touch fundamentals is commonly termed a difference of *opinion*. You may believe in high tariffs; and I, in no tariff. You may believe in One World; I may not. You may support Republicans; I, Democrats. Despite these differences both of us can still believe in dollars as a method of paying income, in marriage as a system of setting up the family, in private property for most goods industrial or personal, in the Government of the United States, in majority rule, in democratic elections, in free speech, and so on.

If our difference of opinion is so inclusive that we can agree on nothing political, our differences have gone from mere opinion into the depths of *ideology*. Here the institutional framework is affected. You and I would not want to live in the same city; we could not feel safe in one another's presence; each would be afraid of the effect which the other might have on the morals of the community. If I were a Nazi, and you a democrat, you would not like the idea of my children living next door to yours. If I believed that you were a good enough creature—poor deluded devil—but that you were not fit to vote, scarcely to be trusted with property, not to be trusted as an army officer, and generally subversive and dangerous, you would find it hard to get along with me.

It was not metaphysical theories that made Protestants and Catholics burn one another's adherents as heretics in early wars. In the seventeenth century, the Protestants knew perfectly well what would happen if the Catholics got the upper hand, and the Catholics knew what would happen if the Protestants came to power. In each case the new rulers, fearful that they might be overthrown, would have suppressed the former rulers, and would have used the rack, the stake, and the dungeon as preventives of counterrevolution. Freedom cannot be accorded to persons outside the ideological pale. If an antagonist is not going to respect your freedom of speech, your property, and your personal safety, then you are not obliged to respect his. The absolute minimum of any ideology is the assumption that each person living in an ideologically uniform area (what the Nazi General Haushofer, following Rudolf Kjellen, would call a *geo-psychic* zone) will respect the personal safety, etc., of other individuals in the same area.

In our own time, we have seen Spaniards get more and more mistrustful of one another, until years of ferocious civil war were necessary before one of the two factions could feel safe. Spain went from republican unity to dictatorial unity in four years; in neither case was the unity perfect, but it was enough to give one government and one educational system control of most of the country. The other countries of the world vary in the degree of their ideological cohesion. Scandinavia seemed serene until the German invasion brought to the surface cleavages, latent and unseen, which made Quisling a quisling. Russia, Italy, Germany and various other states have made a fetish of their ideologies and have tried to define orthodoxy and heresy in such a way as to be sure of the mentality of all their people. But most of the countries of the world suffer from a considerable degree of ideological confusion—of instability of basic beliefs—without having any immediate remedy at hand, or even seeking one.

Education. Education is a process usually institutional by which the people of a given area transmit to their successors, their own children, the purely practical information needed in modern life, together with a lot of other teachings designed to make good men and women, good citizens, good Christians or other believers, of them. In the democratic states this process is ideological only in some parts of the curriculum; elsewhere in the field of opinions, the government seeks to control ideology only negatively—through laws concerning obscenity, blasphemy, subversion, and so on.

In the states which are ideologically self-conscious and anxious to promote a fixed mentality, the process of education is combined with agitation and regulation, so that the entire population lives under conditions approximating the psychological side of war. Heretics are put to death or are otherwise silenced. Historical materialism and the Marxian "objectivity," or the *Volk,* or *Fascismo,* or *Yamato-damashii,* or "new democracy" is set up as the touchstone of all good and evil, even in unrelated fields of activity. Education and propaganda merge into everlasting indoctrination. And when such states go to war against states which do not have propaganda machinery, the more liberal states are at a disadvantage for sheer lack of practice in the administrative and mechanical aspects of propaganda. Education is to psychological warfare what a glacier is to an avalanche. The mind is to be in both cases captured, but the speed and techniques differ.

Salesmanship. Salesmanship is related to psychological warfare. Propaganda is often compared to another art of our time—

industrialized salesmanship through mass printing and telecommunications. This bad parallel was responsible for much of the inept American propaganda overseas in the early part of the war; some of our propagandists had a fundamental misconception of the nature of wartime propaganda.

Allegiance in war is a matter of ideology, not of opinion. A man cannot want his own side to lose while remaining a good citizen in all other respects. The desire for defeat—even the acceptance of defeat—is of tragic importance to any responsible, sane person. A German who wanted the Reich to be overthrown was a traitor to Germany, just as any American who wished us to pull out of the war and exterminate American Jews would have been a traitor to his own country. These decisions cannot be compared with the choice of a toothpaste, a deodorant, or a cigarette.

Advertising succeeds in peacetime precisely because it does not matter; the choice which the consumer makes is of slight importance to himself, even though it is of importance to the seller of the product. A Dromedary cigarette and an Old Coin cigarette are both cigarettes; the man is going to smoke one anyhow. It does not matter so much to him. If Dromedaries are associated in his mind with mere tobacco, while Old Coins call up unaccountable but persistent memories of actresses' legs, he may buy Old Coins. The physical implements of propaganda were at hand in 1941-1942, but we Americans had become so accustomed to their use for trivial purposes that much of our wartime propaganda was conducted in terms of salesmanship.

In a sense, however, salesmanship does serve the military purpose of accustoming the audience to appeals both visual and auditory. The consequence is that competing, outside propaganda can reach the domestic American audience only in competition with the local advertising. It is difficult for foreign competition to hold attention amid an almost limitless number of professionally competent commercial appeals. A Communist or Fascist party cannot get public attention in the United States by the simple expedient of a "mass meeting" of three hundred persons, or by the use of a few dozen posters in a metropolitan area. Before the political propagandist can get the public attention, he must edge his media past the soap operas, the soft drink advertisements, the bathing beauties advertising Pennsylvania crude or bright-leaf tobacco. The consequence is that outside propaganda either fails to get much public attention, or else camouflages itself to resemble and to exploit existing media. Clamorous salesmanship deadens the American citizen to his own government's propaganda, and may to a certain extent lower his civic alertness; but at the same time, salesmanship has built up a psychological Great Wall which excludes foreign or queer appeals and which renders the United States almost impervious to sudden ideological penetration from overseas.

Psychological Warfare and Public Relations. Psychological warfare and public relations are different in the direction in which they apply. Psychological warfare is designed to reach the enemy. Public relations is designed primarily to reach the home audience. Both reach neutrals, sometimes confusingly much. In some nations, the two functions were combined in a single instrumentality, as in the Japanese *Joho Kyoku* (see chapter 10). The American army and navy traditions of public relations are based on the ideas that the news should be as complete as military security may permit, that it should be delivered speedily and interestingly, that it should enhance the confidence of the people in their armed services, and that its tenor (no less than its contents) should not aid the enemy morale. These ideas are justified in terms of sound newspaper practice, but they can lead to a weak psychological warfare position when we must deal with an inventive and enterprising enemy.

It is not possible to separate public relations from psychological warfare when they use the same media. During World War II, the Office of War Information prepared elaborate water-tight plans for processing war news to different audiences; at their most unfortunate, such plans seemed to assume that the enemy would listen only to the OWI stations, and that the American public releases issued from Army and Navy would go forth to the world without being noted by the enemy. If a radio in New York or San Francisco presented a psychological warfare presentation of a stated battle or engagement, while the theater or fleet public relations officer presented a very different view, the enemy press and radio were free to choose the weaker of the two, or to quote the two American sources against each other.

Psychological Warfare and Morale Services. All modern armies, in addition to public relations, also employ morale services facilities—officers or employees whose function it is to supply troops with entertainment, educational materials, political indoctrination, and other attention-getting materials. Morale services are the prime overt defense against enemy psychological warfare, and by a program of keeping the attention of the troops, can prevent the enemy from establishing effective communication. During World War II, the Armed Forces Radio Service of the United States established global radio service for Americans, and incidentally turned out material of top importance to United States propaganda. Naturally, enemy and allied peoples would pay more serious heed to communications from Americans to Americans than they would to materials which they knew had been concocted for themselves. The American morale services in the last war indignantly rejected the notion that they were a major propaganda facility, rightfully insisting that their audience counted on getting plain information, plain news, and plain education without ulterior propaganda content. The fact that in a theater of war all communication has propaganda effect was not always taken into account, and only on one or two critical occasions was there coordination of stress and timing.

It must be said, however, that propaganda by any other name is just as sweet, and that the conviction of the propagandist that he is not a propagandist can be a real asset. Morale services provided the American forces with news, entertainment, and educational facilities. Most of the time these morale facilities had huge parasitical audiences—the global kibitzers who listened to our broadcasts, read our magazines, bought our paper-bound books on the black markets. (It was a happy day for Lienta University at

Kunming, Yünnan, when the American Information and Education set-up began shipping in current literature. The long-isolated Chinese college students found themselves deluged with good American books.)

The morale services lost the opportunity to ram home to their G.I.-plus-foreign audience some of the more effective points of American psychological warfare, but they gained *as propagandists* by not admitting, even to themselves, that they *were* propagandists. Since the United States has no serious inward psychological cleavages, the general morale services function coordinated automatically with the psychological warfare function simply because both were produced by disciplined, patriotic Americans.

In the experience of the German and Soviet armies, morale services were parts of a coordinated propaganda machine which included psychological warfare, public relations, general news, and public education. In the Japanese armies, morale services were directed most particularly to physical and sentimental comforts (edible treats, picture postcards, good luck items) which bore little immediate relation to news, and less to formal propaganda.

Related Civilian Activities. In a free nation, the big media of communication will remain uncoordinated even in time of war. The press, the stage, motion-pictures, part of the radio, book publishing and so on will continue. Psychological warfare has in such private facilities a constantly refreshed source of new material for news or for features. By a sparing but well considered liaison with censorship, psychological warfare can effect negative control of non-governmental materials, and can prevent the most overt forms of enemy propaganda from circulating on the home front.

News becomes propaganda when the person issuing it has some purpose in doing so. Even if the reporters, editors, writers involved do not have propaganda aims, the original source of the news (the person giving the interview; the friends of the correspondents, etc.) may give the news to the press with definite purposes in mind. It is not unknown for government officials to shift their rivalries from the conference room to the press, and to provide on-the-record or off-the-record materials which are in effect *ad hoc* propaganda campaigns. A psychological warfare campaign must be planned on the assumption that these civilian facilities will remain in being, and that they will be uncoordinated; the plan must allow in advance for interference, sometimes of a very damaging kind, which comes from private operations in the same field. The combat officers can get civilian cars off the road when moving armored forces into battle but the psychological warfare officer has the difficult task of threading his way through civilian radio and other communication traffic over which he has no control.

Psychological warfare is also closely related to diplomacy. It is an indispensable ingredient of strategic deception. In the medical field, psychological warfare can profit by the experiences of the medical corps. Whenever a given condition arises among troops on one side, comparable troops on the other are apt to be facing the same condition; if the Americans are bitten by insects, the same insects will bite the enemy, and enemy soldiers can be told how much better the American facilities are for insect repulsion. Finally, psychological warfare is intimately connected with the processing of prisoners of war and with the protection of one's own captured personnel.

Psychological warfare is a field to itself, although it touches on many sciences and overlaps with all the other functions of war. It is generally divisible into three topics: the general scheme of psychological warfare, the detection and analysis of foreign psychological warfare operations, and the tactical or immediate conduct of psychological warfare. Sections of this book deal with each of these in turn. In each case it must be remembered, however, that psychological warfare is not a closed operation which can be conducted in private, but that—to be effective—psychological warfare output must be a part of the everyday living and fighting of the audiences to which it is directed.

NOTES

[1] In his *The Political Doctrines of Sun Yat-sen*, Baltimore, 1937, page 17 and following, this author attempted to present some of the relationships of ideology to other methods of social control and, in connection with that enterprise, was furnished by the philosopher, A.O. Lovejoy, with a definition of "ideology" more systematic and more elaborate than the one used here.

CHAPTER 3
DEFINITION OF PSYCHOLOGICAL WARFARE

Psychological warfare seeks to win military gains without military force. In some periods of history the use of psychological warfare has been considered unsportsmanlike.[1] It is natural for the skilled soldier to rely on weapons rather than on words, and after World War I there was a considerable reluctance to look further into that weapon—propaganda—which Ludendorff himself considered to be the most formidable achievement of the Allies. Nevertheless, World War II brought a large number of American officers, both Army and Navy, into the psychological warfare field: some of the best work was done without civilian aid or sponsorship. (Capt. J. A. Burden on Guadalcanal wrote his own leaflets, prepared his own public-address scripts, and did his own distributing from a borrowed Marine plane, skimming the tree tops until the Japanese shot him down into the surf. He may have heard of OWI at the time, but the civilians at OWI had not heard of him.)

Psychological warfare has become familiar. The problems of psychological warfare for the future are problems of *how better* to apply it, not of whether to apply it. Accordingly, it is to be defined more for the purpose of making it convenient and operable than for the purpose of finding out what it is. The whole world found out by demonstration, during World Wars I and II.

Psychological warfare is not defined as such in the dictionary.[2] Definition is open game. There are three ways in which "psychological warfare" and "military propaganda" can be defined:

73

first, by deciding what we are talking about in a given situation, book, conversation, or study course;

second, by determining the responsibilities and authority involved in a given task;

or *third*, by stating the results which are believed to be accomplishable by the designated means.

Plainly, the staff officer needs a different definition from the one used by the combat officer; the political leader would use a broader definition than the one required by soldiers; the fanatic would have his own definition or—more probably—two of them; one (such as "promoting democracy" or "awakening the masses") for his own propaganda and another (such as "spreading lies," "corrupting the press," or "giving opiates to the people") for antagonistic propaganda.[3] Definition is not something which can be done once and forever for any military term, since military operations change and since military definitions are critically important for establishing a chain of command.

The first method of definition is satisfactory for research purposes; it may help break a politico-military situation down into understandable components. The second method—the organizational—is usable when there exists organization with which to demonstrate the definition, such as, "Propaganda is what OWI and OSS perform." The third method, the operational or historical, is useful in evaluating situations after the time for action has passed; thus, one may say, "This is what the Germans did when they thought they were conducting propaganda."

Since the first lesson of all propaganda is *reasoned disbelief*, it would be sad and absurd for anyone to believe propaganda about propaganda. The "propaganda boys" in every army and government are experts at building up favorable cases, and they would be unusual men indeed if they failed to work up a fine account of their own performance. Propaganda cannot be given fair measurement by the claims made for it. It requires judicious proportioning to the military operations of which it is (in wartime) normally a part.

Broad and Narrow Definitions. The term *propaganda* springs from the name of that department of the Vatican which had the duty of propagating the faith. A multitude of definitions is available. Among Americans, Walter Lippmann, Harold Lasswell and Leonard W. Doob have done some of the most valuable critical, analytical, and historical writing, but a host of other scholars have also made contributions, some of them works of very real importance.[4] For the purposes of explaining what this book is about, propaganda may be defined as follows: *Propaganda consists of the planned use of any form of communication designed to affect the minds, emotions, and action of a given group for a specific purpose.*

This may be called the broad definition, since it would include an appeal to buy Antident toothpaste, to believe in the theological principle of complete immersion,[5] to buy flowers for Uncles on Uncles' Day, to slap the Japs, to fight fascism at home, or to smell nice under the arms. All of this is propaganda, by the broad definition. Since War and Navy Department usage never put the Corps of Chaplains, the PX system, the safety campaigns, or the anti-VD announcements under the rubric of propaganda, it might be desirable to narrow down the definition to exclude those forms of propaganda designed to effect private or nonpolitical purposes, and make the definition read:

> Propaganda consists of the planned use of any form of public or mass-produced communication designed to affect the minds and emotions of a given group for a specific public purpose, whether military, economic, or political.

This may be termed the everyday definition of propaganda, as it is used in most of the civilian college textbooks.[6] For military purposes, however, it is necessary to trim down the definition in one more direction, applying it strictly against the enemy and making it read:

> Military propaganda consists of the planned use
> of any form of communication designed to affect the
> minds and emotions of a given enemy, neutral or
> friendly foreign group for a specific strategic or tac-
> tical purpose.

Note that if the communication is not planned it cannot be called propaganda. If a lieutenant stuck his head out of a tank turret and yelled at some Japs in a cave, "Come on out of there, you qwertyuiop asdfgs, or we'll zxcvb you all to hjkl, you etc.'s!," the communication may or may not work, but—in the technical sense— it is not propaganda because the lieutenant did not employ that form of communication planned and designed to affect the minds or emotions of the Japanese in the cave. Had the lieutenant given the matter thought and had he said, in the Japanese language, "Enemy persons forthwith commanded to cease resistance, otherwise American Army regrets inescapable consequences attendant upon operation of flamethrower," the remark would have been closer to propaganda.

Furthermore, propaganda must have a known purpose. This element must be included in the definition; a great deal of communication, both in wartime and in peacetime, arises because of the pleasure which it gives to the utterer, and not because of the result it is supposed to effect in the hearers. Sending the Japanese cartoons of themselves, mocking the German language, calling Italians by familiar but inelegant names—such communications cropped up during the war. The senders got a lot of fun out of the message but the purpose was unintelligently considered. The actual effect of the messages was to annoy the enemy, stiffening his will-to-resist. (Screams of rage had a place in primitive war; in modern military propaganda they are too expensive a luxury to be tolerated. Planned annoyance of the enemy does, of course, have its role—a minor, rare and special one.)

"Psychological warfare" is simple enough to understand if it is simply regarded as application of propaganda to the purposes of war, as in the following definition:

> Psychological warfare comprises the use of pro-
> paganda against an enemy, together with such other
> operational measures of a military, economic, or
> political nature as may be required to supplement
> propaganda.

In this sense, "psychological warfare" is a known operation which was carried on very successfully during World War II under the authority of the Combined and Joint Chiefs of Staff. It is in this sense that some kind of a "Psychological Warfare Unit" was developed in every major theater of war, and that the American military assimilated the doctrines of "psychological warfare."

However, this is only one of several ways of using the term, "psychological warfare." There is, in particular, one other sense, in which the term became unpleasantly familiar during the German conquest of Europe, the sense of *warfare psychologically waged*. In the American use of the term, psychological warfare was the supplementing of normal military operations by the use of mass communications; in the Nazi sense of the term, it was the calculation and execution of both political and military strategy on studied psychological grounds. For the American uses, it was modification of traditional warfare by the effective, generous use of a new weapon; for the Germans it involved a transformation of the process of war itself. This is an important enough distinction to warrant separate consideration.

Warfare Psychologically Waged. Various labels were devised to name Hitler's queer, terrifying strategy for the period 1936-1941. One writer, Edmond Taylor, called it the *"strategy of terror"* in a book by that name (Boston, 1940), and also *"the war of nerves."* Another, Ladislas Farago, a political journalist who started out as an authority on the Axis fifth column in the Near East and ended up in American naval psychological warfare planning, put forth a book called *German Psychological Warfare: A Critical, Annotated and Comprehensive Survey and Bibliography* (New York, 1941), which digested hundreds of German works on topics pertaining to psychology and war, much of this material concerned personnel practices, psychosomatic medicine, and other non-propaganda aspects of psychology, but the book as a whole was an impressive demonstration of how much the Germans had done to make their war scientific. Other articles and books on the Nazi "inventions" followed in rapid succession.

After the excitement had died down, it was found that the novelty of the German war effort lay in two special fields:

first, the perfect or perfect-seeming synchronizing of po-
    litical, propaganda, subversive, and military efforts;
second, the use of the findings of modern psychology for
    the attainment of military goals.

The Germans set the pace, in the prewar and early war period and United Nations psychological warfare tried to keep up, even though the two efforts were different in scope and character.

In conquering Europe, the German staff apparently used opinion analysis. Much of this analysis has turned out to have been superb guesswork; at the time, it looked as though the Nazis might have found some scientific formula for determining just when a nation would cave in. In the conduct of war, the Germans waged a rapid war—which was industrially, psychologically and militarily sound, as long as it worked. Their "diplomacy of dramatic intimidation" used the war threat to its full value, with the result that the Czechoslovaks surrendered the Sudetenland without a shot and then submitted themselves to tyranny half a year later; the Germans wrung every pfennig's worth of advantage out of threatening to start war, and when they did start war, they deliberately tried to make it look as horrible as it was. The psychologists had apparently taught the German political and military intelligence people how to get workable opinion forecasts; German analysis of anti-Nazi counterpropaganda was excellent. Add all this to strategy and field operations which were incontestably brilliant: the effect was not that of mere war, but of a new kind of war—the psychological war.

The formula for the psychological war is not to be found in the books of the psychologists but in the writings of the constitutional lawyers. The totality of war is a result of dictatorship within government; total coordination results from total authority. The "secret weapon" of the Germans lay in the power which the Germans had openly given Hitler, and in his use of that power in a shrewd, ruthless, effective way. The Führer led the experts, not the experts the Führer. If the Germans surprised the world by the cold calculation of their timing, it was not because they had psychological braintrusters inventing a new warfare, but because they had a grim political freak commanding the total resources of the Reich. Even in wartime, no American President has ever exercised the authority which Hitler used in time of peace; American Cabinet members, military and naval figures, press commentators and all sorts of people are free to kibitz, to offer their own opinions, to bring policy into the light of day. That is as it should be. The same factors which made "psychological warfare" possible in the beginning of the war were the ones which led to Germany's futile and consummate ruin in 1944-45: excessive authority, an uninformed public, centralized propaganda, and secret political planning.

That kind of "psychological warfare"—war tuned to the needs of fanatically sought lusts for power, war coordinated down to the nth degree, waged in the light of enemy opinion and aiming at the political and moral weaknesses of the enemy—is not possible within the framework of a democracy. Even from within Imperial Japan, Pearl Harbor had to be waged secretly as a *purely* naval operation; those Japanese who would have told the Board of Field Marshals and Fleet Admirals that an unannounced attack was the best way to unify all American factions *against* Japan were obviously not brought into the planning of the Pearl Harbor raid. The Japanese still had too much of their old parliamentary spirit left over, as Ambassador Grew's reports show; the military had to outsmart the home public, along with the foreigners. In the Western dictatorships, the home public is watched by elite troops, secret police, party cells, and is made the subject of psychological warfare along with the victim nations. Hitler could turn the war spirit on and off; the Japanese did not dare do so to any effective extent. "Psychological warfare" was too dictatorial a measure even for prewar Japan; it is therefore permanently out of reach of the authorities of the United States. After war starts, we are capable of surprising the enemy with such things as incendiary raids, long-range bombers, and nuclear fission; but we cannot startle with the start of war. The United States is not now capable and—under the spirit of the Constitution, can never be capable—of surprising an enemy by *the timing of aggression.* If the same were true of all other nations, peace would seem much nearer than it does.

German psychological warfare, in the broad sense of warfare psychologically waged, depended more on political background than on psychological techniques. Disunity among the prospective victims, the complaisance of powers not immediately affected, demonstration of new weapons through frightful applications, use of a dread-of-war to harness pacifism to appeasement, the lucky geographic position of Germany at the hub of European communications—such factors made the German war of nerves seem new. Such psychological warfare is not apt to be successful elsewhere except for aggressions by dictatorships against democracies; where the democracies are irritable, tough, and alert, it will not work at all.

The psychological warfare which remains as a practical factor in war is therefore not the Hitlerian war of nerves, but the Anglo-American application of propaganda means to pre-decided strategy. Let him who will advocate American use of the war of nerves! He will not get far with commentators publishing his TOP SECRET schedule of timing, with legislators very properly catechizing him on international morality, with members of his own organization publishing their memoirs or airing their squabbles right in the middle of the operation. He would end up by amusing the enemy whom he started out to scare. Psychological warfare has its place in our military and political system, but its place is a modest one and its methods are limited by our usages, morality, and law.

Propaganda: Definitions. Propaganda has been defined. It remains to distinguish some of the other technical and professional terms which apply in this field. In operational terms, propaganda can be distinguished by the consideration of five elements:[7]

1. Source (including Media)
2. Time
3. Audience
4. Subject
5. Mission

These factors are given in approximate order of importance to the analyst, and provide a good working breakdown for propaganda analysis when expert staffs are not available. The five factors can be remembered by memorizing the initial letters in order: S-T-A-S-M. The last factor, "Mission," covers the presumed effect which the enemy seeks by dissemination of the item.

Without going into the technique of field propaganda analysis (described in chapter 7), it is useful to apply these analysis factors to the definition of some surbordinate types of military propaganda.

Source is the most important. If the source is open and acknowledged, the government issuing it is putting the propaganda on the record before the world, and must therefore issue the propaganda with a certain amount of dignity and with an eye to the future. If the source is faked, then it is important for the government or army to make sure that the faking is a good job, and that the propaganda cannot readily be traced back. Two very different techniques are employed. Open sources require responsible public officials, preferably men with international reputations, who will get the best effect from use of the name and facilities of the government. Use of an open source usually (but not always) implies belief of the disseminator in the veracity of his materials. Fabricated sources require persons adept at illicit imaginativeness, impromptu forgery, and general devilment, combined with a strong sense of discipline and security. The United States was so chary of mixing the two kinds of propaganda during World War II that it operated them in different categories, giving rise to the two following types:

Overt propaganda (also called white propaganda) is issued from an acknowledged source, usually a government or an agency of a government, including military commands at various levels.

Covert propaganda (also called black propaganda) has an ostensible source other than the real source and normally involves utterances or acts which are unlawful under the domestic law of the attacked area.

The two forms are shown in figure 4. Figure 4 does everything possible to make the message the official message of the British and American governments. The border is done up in handsome banknote fashion; the great seals of the nations are handsomely displayed; the signatures of the commanding generals are shown as further attestation of the openness and good faith of the issuer of the propaganda.

Figure 38 was also prepared by British-American authority; it too had the job of making Germans surrender. But in this case, nothing was done to make the British-American source evident; indeed, every effort was made to hide the source, so that the German who read it would think that it came from within his own territory. The two different kinds of propaganda were both of them needed; each supplemented the other but they had to be kept apart as far as possible.

In the field of radio, the difference between Covert and Overt was even more plain. During World War II, the ether over Europe was filled with appeals from radio stations both public and covert in character. The British spoke to the Germans over B.B.C., making no effort to conceal the fact that they were British. But they also spoke to the Germans over clandestine stations, which pretended to be free-lancing Nazis, German army stations, or freedom group operations. The Germans, comparably, beamed official German news to the United States in English; but they also pretended to be

Americans broadcasting from an isolationist radio in the American mid-west. In some cases, the belligerent powers used the identical radio transmission facilities for overt and covert propaganda. Radio Saipan, under the Americans, was most of the time the relay for the acknowledged San Francisco programs; intermittently OSS borrowed it, and it then became a "Japanese" station. (Under such conditions, black radio cannot remain black very long.)

In terms of the timing, propaganda can be subdivided into two further categories, strategic and tactical. Strategic propaganda is conducted with no immediate effect in view. Its purpose is to wear down the enemy by psychological changes that may extend over months. Figure 19, warning the Germans of the remote future, is an example of this in leaflet form. Tactical propaganda is operated to accomplish an immediate short-range purpose, and normally does not cover a long time-span. Only in a few cases, such as leaflets for a besieged enemy unit, is tactical propaganda run for a purpose that encompasses a long delay between the operation and the expected result. These two forms may be defined as follows:

Strategic propaganda is directed at enemy forces, enemy peoples, and enemy-occupied areas in their entirety, and—in coordination with strategic planning—is designed to effectuate results planned and sought over a period of weeks, months, or years.

Tactical propaganda is directed at specific audiences, usually named, and is prepared and executed in support of localized combat operations.

Another set of distinctions can be set up, depending on the relationship of the propaganda operation to the simultaneous hostile propaganda operations, namely offensive or defensive propaganda. Before the advent of World War II, this distinction appeared to be significant but experience on almost all fronts indicated that it meant little when applied to day-in day-out necessities of actual practice. Propaganda is so intimately keyed to the news and opinion situation that it does not usually bear elaborate pre-operational analysis. Elaborate planning very often ends up in the locked files; the distinction of offensive and defensive means little in routine work. However, for the sake of the record, the distinction can be listed:

> *Defensive propaganda* is designed to maintain an accepted and operating form of social or other public action. (Soviet propaganda for the Five Year Plans is a conspicuous instance.)
>
> *Offensive propaganda* is designed to interrupt social action not desired by the propagandist, or to predispose to social action which he desires, either through revolutionary means (within the same society) or international, either diplomatic or belligerent (between different societies).

Another set of distinctions arises from the purpose which the propaganda officer or group may have in mind for the people whom he addresses. These distinctions, like offensive-defensive, are theoretical rather than practical, and did not often appear in the actual operations, although all the more hush-hush plans made elaborate references to them:

> *Conversionary propaganda* is designed to change the emotional or practical allegiance of individuals from one group to another.
>
> *Divisive propaganda* is designed to split apart the component subgroups of the enemy and thereby reduce the effectiveness of the enemy group considered as a single unit. (An instance is provided by the Allied effort to make German Catholics think first as Catholics, then as Germans.)
>
> *Consolidation propaganda* is directed toward civil populations in areas occupied by a military force and is designed to insure compliance with the commands or policies promulgated by the commander of the occupying force.

Counterpropaganda is designed to refute a specific point
or theme of enemy propaganda. (Japanese charges of
American atrocities usually followed American charges
of Japanese atrocities.)

All six of the distinctions last mentioned can be forgotten, except for the fact that in exercises or research the terms will be found
to crop up; the basic working distinctions are those determined by
the task involved.

World War II brought up a very sore issue between military
and civilians with respect to propaganda in areas with unsettled
governments—such as Darlanist North Africa, Communist China,
all of Siam. (See, also, discussion of World War II, chapter 6.) In
these areas every military act involved the definition of the political relations of the United States Government to the governments
locally enjoying authority. Were we at war with them, or not? And
so on. In these cases, politics itself became a vital foundation to
propaganda, especially when the local authorities were themselves
active in the propaganda field. The American theater and unit commanders had to decide what kinds of political promises they could
or could not make. In this job, they had a more difficult task than
did the British, who possessed in the Political Warfare Executive a
pooling facility which coordinated foreign policy with propaganda.[8]
Could we promise freedom from France to the Algerians? Or im-
munity to the Siamese who re-doublecrossed in the matter of allegiance and got ready to subvert the Japanese? Or the Yenan people
who wanted us to highjack the Generalissimo as a price of their
support? Or the Indonesians who might oppose the Japanese and
already opposed the Dutch? Such questions transcended propaganda. Their decision made propaganda, or unmade it; but the
deciding power was outside the authority of the propaganda people.

Political warfare is therefore, in administrative terms, a higher-
level activity than propaganda, and may be defined as follows:

Political warfare consists of the framing of national policy in such a way as to assist propaganda

or military operations, whether with respect to the
direct political relations of governments with one
another or in relation to groups of people possessing a political character.

Such policy-framing does not normally fall within the authority of the Army or Navy, though these may be consulted and called
upon to effect appropriate military action. An outstanding instance
of the use of political warfare was President Roosevelt's impromptu
enunciation of the theme "Unconditional Surrender" at Casablanca.
The theme affected not only our propaganda, but the types of surrenders which American generals could accept from Germans.

Notes:

[1] For example, in the 1920's the Soviet press expressed
resentment and amusement over a ruse adopted by the
British during the course of operations along the North-
west Frontier. Plane- mounted loudspeakers had told the
tribesmen, in Pushtu, that God was mad at them for having broken the pledged peace, with the result that they
scattered and gave up. This maneuver exasperated the
Russians, who themselves were making equally sweeping
propaganda inroads on the other side of the Pamirs. The
Russians were attacking religion, and having heavy going; it struck them as improper warfare to make use of
local superstition.

[2] Webster's *New International Dictionary*, Second
Edition, Springfield, 1944.

[3] The late Huey Long is reported to have created a
new word in the language of rustic Louisiana, the word
"damlyingnewspapers." By instilling in his followers
contempt for the "capitalist" press, he got them to the
point where they *disbelieved* anything which they saw in
print, and *believed* everything which "Ol' Huey, the King-
fish" himself told them. This operation was technically

competent, since one of the most effective means of putting propaganda across is to draw alarmed attention to unfriendly propaganda and then just "happening to mention" the "truth" (that is, the promoted side). Long attributed to the newspapers a large number of lies which they did not print, along with the "lies" (which were in historical fact true) that they *did* actually print. Since most of his followers either boycotted the press or read it in a hostile frame of mind, they never found out whether the newspapers said what Huey said they said, or not. You can try this out on your neighbors or friends by making up some idiotic "quotation" (such as, "The Jewish *Vorwaerts* says that pickled onions are a cause of immorality" or "*Le Temps* of Paris says that Alaska is preparing to secede") and the listener will be so busy scoffing at *what* the paper allegedly said that he will take no time to find out whether the paper did say it or not. Such attributions occur in everyday life; the smart propagandist attributes plenty of rich, ripe, silly quotations to his opponent. How many people actually *know* what the Communists have said on any given topic? Or bother to check on the actual claims of the Zionist organization? Or the statements of the Arabs in Palestine?

⁴ The literature in this field is carefully described in two volumes by a three-man team consisting of Harold D. Lasswell, Ralph B. Casey and Bruce Lannes Smith, the first being *Propaganda and Promotional Activities, An Annotated Bibliography*, Minneapolis, 1935, and the sequel being *Propaganda, Communication and Public Opinion, A Comprehensive Reference Guide*, Princeton, 1946. The booklists provide material in plenty for any academic-minded inquirer. The essays in the two volumes are well worth reading, although the authors have undergone the professorial delight of inventing a private language of their own. Parts of the latter book, especially, read like proceedings out of an unfamiliar lodge meeting; but there is sound sense and acute observation behind the vocabulary. It must, however, be parenthetically noted that during World War II the key propaganda jobs

were held by a radio commentator, a dramatist, a newspaperman, a New York banker, and an absolutely astonishing number of men from commercial radio—along, of
course, with a sprinkling of Army and Navy officers in
Washington, and a heavy majority of non-specialist officers in the field. The propaganda experts were not, in
most instances, called in to do the actual chore of propaganda. Among the exceptions were Leonard W. Doob, author of *Propaganda, Its Psychology and Technique*, New
York, 1935, who served in the War Department's Psychological Warfare Branch and in the Washington propaganda center at OWI; C. A. H. Thomson, who served as a
propaganda staff officer both in Washington and overseas
after being a collaborator with the Lasswell group; and
Drs. Edwin Guthrie and A. L. Edwards, whose chapter
"Psychological Warfare" in [E. G. Boring, editor] *Psychology for the Fighting Man*, Washington, 1943, pp. 430-
447, is a lucid epitome of the topic.

[5] This means that if you want to get baptised, you've
got to get *all* the way under the water or it doesn't count.

[6] See Doob's book, mentioned above, especially pages
71 through 89 and 413 through 417.

[7] See the bibliographies by Harold Lasswell and others,
mentioned above, for a wealth of literature giving more
technical and scientific breakdowns than this. The formula STASM represents what was actually used in preparation of up-to-the-minute propaganda spot analysis for
the War Department General Staff by Propaganda Branch
during World War II. Some further aspects of this formula are presented in my article, "Stasm: Psychological
Warfare and Literary Criticism" in *The South Atlantic
Quarterly*, Vol. 46, No. 3, July 1947, pp. 344-348,

[8] See Harold Lasswell's *Propaganda Technique in the
World War*, New York, reissue 1938, Chapter II, "Propaganda Organization," for a description of the attempts to
coordinate policy and propaganda in World War I.

CHAPTER 4
THE LIMITATIONS OF PSYCHOLOGICAL WARFARE

Psychological warfare cannot be known simply in terms of what it is; it must also be understood in relation to the limits which are imposed on it. The limitations can be described under four headings:

political limitations;
security limitations;
limitations arising from media;
limitations of personnel.

Like all limitations, these are handicaps only to the person who lacks the courage and resourcefulness to turn them into assets. Propaganda is dependent on politics, even for such front-line requirements as "definition of the enemy," yet intelligent exploitation of political goals yields valuable results. Security is an asset to any army; its price is rarely too high a price to pay for protection, but a selective and flexible censorship can lead to positive advantages. Media—that is, the actual instrumentalities by which propaganda is conveyed—are the ordnance of psychological warfare. They limit the performable job but they also make it possible in the first place. And as in any military operation, success depends most of all on proper use of personnel.

Each of these merits discussion. The experience drawn upon has, in almost all instances, been that of World War IL As in most other fields, common sense runs a close second to experience as a guide in new methods of struggle.

Political Limitations of Psychological Warfare. Politics has great influence on the content of psychological warfare. The relationship between two warring states is not one of complete severance; on the contrary, in wartime the relationship becomes abnormal, acute, sensitive. Each belligerent takes a strong interest in the other, in its affairs and weaknesses. During World War II the American armed services, government, and people learned more about the Japanese than they would have in twenty years of peacetime education. Japanese names made news. The purposes and weaknesses of the Japanese became the objects of hatred and—along with the hatred—intense scrutiny.

Each warring nation tries to turn the known enemy interest in itself into favorable channels. The propagandists of each country try to give the enemy the news which the enemy wants, while so arranging that news as to create a drop in enemy morale, to develop uncertainty in enemy policies, to set enemy cliques into action against each other. The propagandist sometimes becomes very agitated because he recognizes as a technician propaganda opportunities which national policy prohibits his using. The propagandist who is so intent on his target that he forgets his broader responsibilities can often spoil the entire operation.

German broadcasters who emphasized the anti-capitalist character of National Socialism in the programs beamed to Eastern Europe found that B.B.C. picked up the most tactless statements and repeated them to Western Europe, where the Germans posed as anti-Bolshevik champions of private property. American attacks on the Germans for associating with Japanese monkey-men were passed along by the Japanese to the Chinese, who did not like the slur either. The most notorious example of backfiring propaganda was of course the famous "Rum, Romanism, and Rebellion" phrase, which may have made James G. Blaine lose to Grover Cleveland in the national election of 1884; the phrase was used by a Republican clergyman in New York, referring to the Democrats, and implied that the Wets (anti-prohibitionists), Catholics, and Southerners were important components in the Democratic Party. (This may have been true, but it pleased none of them to have the matter pointed out with such epithets; the phrase succeeded in its short-range purpose, that of rousing Republicans, but failed by rousing the enemy even more and offending neutral-minded persons as well.)

The balance between home-front politics and field psychological warfare is difficult to maintain. The closer the psychological warfare officer is to the enemy, the more apt he is to think of the mission in terms of getting the enemy to come on over. Why quibble about a few phrases if the words will save lives, materiel, and time? Unfortunately the phrase that is successful against the enemy on the battle front may prove to be an irritant to the home public, with the sure consequence that the enemy will pick it up and send it back to do harm. Similarly, home-front propaganda can get out to do the theaters of operation harm: "Do your utmost—save lard!" sounds silly to men in combat areas.

This can be illustrated by the propaganda problem of the Japanese Emperor. It would have helped domestic American politics to call the Japanese Emperor a monkey, a swine, a lunatic, a witch-doctor or comparable names; some people did so. But if the American government had done so at home for the purpose of rousing its own public, the Japanese home public would have been roused even more with the net result that the Americans would have lost by such attacks. If the Russians promised—as in another instance they are reported to have done—good food and warm clothes to the Germans on the winter fronts, the Nazis passed that promise along to the Russian civilians, who would not think well of Stalin's letting Fascist invaders be plump and snug while they themselves nearly starved. For the enemy audience, it is good to portray excellent care of enemy personnel; for the home audience, it is poor. For the home audience it is sometimes good to present the enemy as ruthless lunatics, beasts in human form, cruel degenerates, and so on; but the same claims, falling into enemy hands, can be used to the disadvantage of the originator by being relayed to the enemy home audience.

Furthermore, sound psychological warfare must take account of the fact that its ultimate aim is the successful ending of the war.

For the end to be successful it must occur—the fighting must stop and the nations must enter into altered but renewedly peaceful relations. Propaganda that promises the enemy too much will alienate both allies and home public. But propaganda that promises bloody vengeance hurts possible peace movements in the enemy camp. None of the great powers in World War II went so far as to promise specific frontiers for the postwar period. They kept their promises vague, knowing that a definite promise would please somebody but alienate everyone else; furthermore, by not promising, the expectations of the hopeful parties can be kept at a higher pitch. If the French do not *know* that they will get the Saar they will fight so much the harder; but if they are promised the Saar they come in a very short while to regard the promise as a settled matter, and proceed to ask for something else. Meanwhile, other possible claimants to the Saar either have a sense of grievance or lose interest in the matter. For this reason, postwar political uncertainty can be a propaganda asset.

President Roosevelt, in his conduct of the political world role of the United States, promised Manchuria to the Chinese, Korea "in due course" to the Koreans, and the integrity of the French Colonial Empire to the French; outside of that he avoided specific promises. In another instance (to put a complicated matter baldly), the British promised Palestine to both the Arabs and to the Jews in World War I, and consequently got themselves into a political mess which, thirty years later, was still a mess.

Definition of the Enemy. Another significant connection between politics and propaganda is found in definition of *the nature of the enemy.* For combat operations, it is easy (most of the time) to tell who the enemy is; he is the man with the other uniform, the foreign language, the funny color or physique. For psychological operations, it is not that easy. The sound psychological warfare operator will try to get enemy troops to believing that the enemy is not themselves but somebody else—the King, the Führer, the elite troops, the capitalists. He creates a situation in which he can say, "We're not fighting *you*." (This should not be said too soon after extensive use of bombs or mortars.) "We are fighting the So-and-so's who are misleading you." Some of the handsomest propaganda of World War II was produced by the Soviet experts along this line. Before the War was over, Soviet propaganda created a whole gallery of heel-clicking reactionary German generals *on the Russian side*, and made out that the unprofessional guttersnipe Hitler was ruining the wonderful German Army in amateurish campaigns. Joseph Stalin's ringing words, "The German State and the German *Volk* remain!" gave the Russians a propaganda loophole by which they implied that Germany was not the enemy—no, not Germany! just the Nazis. This was superb psychological warfare, since the Russians had already built up the propaganda thesis that the common people (workers and peasants) were automatically—by virtue of their class loyalty—on the side of the workers' country, Russia. That left very few Germans on the other side.

For psychological warfare purposes, it is useful to define the enemy as:

(1) the ruler;
(2) or the ruling group;
(3) or unspecified manipulators;
(4) or any definite minority.

It is thoroughly unsound to define the enemy too widely. On the other hand, too narrow a definition will leave the enemy the opening for a peace offensive if the ruler dies, or if the ruling group changes part of its composition. It was fear of a peace move by the German generals, plus the desire to maintain the precarious anti-German unity of the occupied countries, which led the United States and Britain to adopt the policy of defining the German Reich rather than Naziism as the enemy. In the instance of Japan, we defined the enemy as the militarists and "Fascists," with the capitalists a poor second, and left the Emperor and people with whom to make peace.

If the psychological warfare campaign is operated for a definite political purpose, it is possible for politics to be an aid rather than a limitation. The operator can describe his own political system in its most radiant light. He can say complimentary things about the enemy leaders or groups who might come over (though he should avoid giving them the kiss of death which the Nazis gave certain prominent American isolationists, by praising them too much). He can promise his own brand of Utopia.

If the politics are defensive, vague, well-meaning but essentially non-committed, psychological warfare has to avoid making blunders. In World War II we could not say that we were against one-party states, because our largest ally (Russia) was a one-party state. We could not attack the ruin of free enterprise by the Japanese and German governments since socialism existed on the Allied side too. We could not bring up the racial issue, because our own national composition rendered us vulnerable to racial politics at home. There was a huge catalog of *Don'ts* (usually not written down but left to individual judgment) in every propaganda office. Whenever we violated them, we paid the price in adverse opinion.

Promises. Finally, psychological warfare must avoid promises that may not be kept. The Americans during World War II never promised much as a government, but individual American agents promised all sorts of things which could not be delivered. We promised the Dutch their homeland and empire by implication; we promised the Indonesians self-government, also by implication; and we promised everybody, including the Japanese, access to Indonesian raw materials. It is highly probable that individual Americans, off-the-record, stated that they "expected," "hoped," or "thought" that their government would fulfill each of these promises. The three are not compatible, especially the first and second. The New York banker, James Warburg, has written a book, *Unwritten Treaty*, pointing out that the United States promised just about everything to everybody during the war (he was in OWI and he ought to know), and that it is going to take a generous, wise, and intelligent foreign policy to fulfill—even in part—the promises which we made. The promises of the loser are forgotten; he can write them off and start international policies with a clean slate. But the promises of the victor remain, and have to be carried out or else repudiated.

The psychological warfare officer should not make promises to persons in occupied territory, to friendly guerrillas, to underground movements, or to enemy troops when those promises are not backed up by word-for-word quotations from the head of his government or someone of Cabinet rank. The promises may not conform with promises which other psychological warfare officers are making to other groups. (In China, some American officers told the Chinese Communists that the Chinese Communists were wonderful people, and would be sure to get American material aid and political sympathy against Chiang Kai-shek. At the same time, other American officers told the Chinese government people that the United States did not propose to short-circuit recognition of the Chinese government, or to interfere in internal Chinese affairs. The two sets of Chinese heard about the American promises and, for a while, could not decide whether Americans were fools or liars. Much the same sort of thing happened in our dealings with French, Serbs, and Poles.) It is a poor piece of work for a combat officer to promise elections, liberties, labor rights, or even food to people in his path, unless the rear echelon people will be able to deliver the goods when they come up. And it is an irresponsible radio or leaflet man who makes promises without finding out whether his government is in a position, in relation to the political situation, to back up the promises one way or other. His nation itself will be called a liar if he slips up.

Security Limitations. Another serious set of limitations arises from security problems.

The very conduct of psychological warfare encroaches upon perfectionist plans for security. Security is designed to keep useful information from reaching the enemy; propaganda operations are designed to get information to him. Security is designed to keep the enemy from knowing true figures; but propaganda must have a lot of good, current, true information if it is to be believed. Security demands that military and naval news be withheld until the extent of the enemy's knowledge is known; propaganda is designed to tell the enemy the news faster than his own sources tell him, thus discrediting enemy news. Security demands that dubious persons, intimately associated with the enemy, be kept away from communications facilities; propaganda officers have to keep an eye open for people who speak the enemy language well, who can address the enemy sympathetically and get his attention, who have a keen appreciation of the enemy culture.

Often, it is plain, psychological warfare and security officers get in each other's way. This conflict was lessened by American censorship organization during World War II. The United States Office of Censorship under Byron Price achieved a distinguished record of smooth, reasonable, and modest operation. It took an adult view of the intelligence of the American public, and permitted bad news to reach the public except when the Services or the White House intervened. Much of the story of this office is told in Theodore Koop's exciting book, *Weapon of Silence*,[1] which makes it plain that censorship sought to avoid developing negative psychological warfare campaigns on its own initiative.

The usual wartime security procedures apply with special force to psychological warfare operations. Civilian employees who are qualified as political experts, as writers, or as propaganda analysts are often well-educated and artistic. They are apt to value classified information highly for the pleasure which they can derive by violating security—that is, by showing "people they can trust" how much they are "in on" certain operations. The temptation to show off is almost irresistible. (The vice is not unknown even in military echelons.) An atmosphere of excessive security easily degenerates into melodrama, bringing out in many individuals a silly zest for displaying to others how much TOP SECRET information they possess. Where military and civilian personnel work together, this human weakness is stimulated by rivalry. Even among the Germans in World War II, propaganda groups were easily infected by an atmosphere of gossip and intrigue.

Security Procedures. Security procedures for psychological warfare involve the usual common-sense precautions which apply to all operations, and which may be summarized in the following rules:

(1) Classification should be kept at an absolute minimum. No information should be classified unless there are genuinely strong reasons for supposing that it would benefit the enemy. Classification and declassification should be the responsibility of designated officers trained for the task. (In World War II, many American civilians classified information recklessly, with the result that all classification became a subject of disrespect. The author once found a highly classified inter-Allied plan in the hands of an elderly woman stenographer in Washington, who safeguarded the information by leaving the papers in a desk drawer which had no pull. The drawer had to be opened with a nail file and that fact comprised the "security.")

(2) Security should apply, generally speaking, to units as a whole, taking working units up to the limit of face-to-face working acquaintance as a base. It is unsound procedure to give certain individuals a higher level of information than others, since the privileged individuals will be tempted to display their inside knowledge, and the underprivileged individuals will be goaded by unwholesome, resentful, and acute curiosity. Either the entire unit should be given the information, or denied it.

(3) Security should not be applied for editorial purposes. Censorship is a separate function. Improper security procedures, vesting arbitrary powers in stated officers, may tempt the security officer to express his personal literary, artistic, or political preferences under the guise of maintaining security. The inevitable consequence is the breakdown of both security and of procedure. Censorship should be applied in conformity with national or theater censorship policies. Review and estimate of radio or leaflet output is another function.

(4) Security for printed materials is easy enough to maintain. The leaflets can be sent to the G-2 to check, or wherever else security functions may be vested. Radio security is another problem.

Experience in World War II indicates that spot news cannot wait
for routine security, but must be processed through. Two types of
control, supplementing one another, are desirable:

> *Security liaison* on a 24-hour basis should be available to
> the radio operatives for the rapid processing of military
> news. The security duty officer should be indoctrinated
> with an attitude of cooperativeness, based on an under-
> standing of the value of propaganda, and should con-
> ceive it as his mission to explain the needs of radio pro-
> paganda to his superiors, rather than taking the atti-
> tude of being superior to the radio operatives. There is
> a sound psychological reason for this. The presence of a
> sympathetic security officer will increase cooperative-
> ness on the part of the propaganda broadcaster. An un-
> sympathetic one will merely maintain the official dig-
> nity of his office and position. High morale on the part
> of script writers is more important than high morale of
> security officers.
>
> *Security supervision* can be exercised by monitoring facili-
> ties: that is, the security officers can equip themselves
> with a good radio receiver and listen to the broadcasts
> without ever meeting the broadcasters. A critical frame
> of mind on the part of such security personnel is desir-
> able. Unlike liaison officers, they need not be coopera-
> tive. Since their criticism applies after the operation,
> they can afford to apply rigorous standards. (During
> most of 1942 and 1943, no one in Washington had any
> idea of what actually *went out* from San Francisco. The
> civilians who broadcast to Japan received elaborate or-
> ders to do this and to do that, but the Washington policy-
> makers did not know what was going on the air. On one
> occasion, the civilian propaganda broadcasters told the
> Army in Washington that the information was too highly
> classified to be released or circulated. The result was
> that Army and Navy found out what OWI was doing by
> receiving reports from listeners in the Pacific.)

Security liaison can check propaganda output in the process of transmission; security supervision can check the output after it goes on the air, and can transmit through channels recommendations for punitive or corrective action. The final military connection should exist (for an all-military psychological warfare group) in the person of a responsible commanding or executive officer. For a civilian group functioning under Military control the military connection should lie in the hands of an officer capable of watching a great deal and of saying little. Attempts by security to act as propagandists have been found to be as disastrous as the efforts of operators to get along without security.

Media Limitations. Psychological warfare should not broadcast into areas in which radio sets are unknown. Psychological warfare should not drop books to illiterates. These rules seem obvious but they have often been violated. Psychological warfare should not assume that an extensive news or morale campaign is going to achieve the desired results unless there is trustworthy intelligence to the effect that propaganda is getting through.

It is ridiculous to broadcast to the masses of a country when the masses are known not to have radio facilities. This was done in the anti-Japanese broadcasts of OWI, at least in the early part of the war, in which mass-audience soap operas and popular music were sent to Japan on the short-wave—this despite reports that short-wave sets were almost unknown outside governmental or plutocratic circles. What was known was that the Japanese government itself had listening facilities, and that the content of American broadcasts was relayed through Japanese military and governmental groups. The propaganda (to fit the medium, radio) should have been designed *to affect the persons actually reached*, and not an audience known to be out of reach. The mere fact that enemy counterpropaganda mentions one's own material is nothing more than a professional exchange of compliments. Goading the enemy radio into a reply may be fun, but unless non-propagandists are known to be listening, the fun is expensive and unprofitable.

(It is really fun, though. The author suggested in the spring of 1942 that the San Francisco radio carry an item to the effect that "American art lovers" hoped the Japanese would move their price-less books and paintings away from the great cities. This was prepa-ration for eventual nagging on the topic, "the air raids will get you if you don't watch out!" The radio civilians in San Francisco put the item on the air. Nothing was heard from the Japanese on the subject. Four days later, Radio Luxembourg [then under Nazi con-trol, of course] broadcast in German to Europe that a spokesman for the "beastly American Air Ministry" had told the Japanese that the Americans planned to destroy cultural monuments. The Nazi commentator added that this was characteristic of the actions of uncivilized Americans, New York picked up the German broadcast. The author enjoyed seeing his item go all the way around the world, but in retrospect he wonders whether he did any good other than to please himself. He did do the actual harm of giving the Nazis another point to distort.)

Media consist simply of the facilities possessed. These are, most commonly:

(1) Standard-wave radio;
(2) Short-wave radio;
(3) Loudspeakers;
(4) Leaflets;
(5) Pamphlets;
(6) Books;
(7) Novelties.

The limitations consist simply of applying the right medium at the right time. Radio broadcasts need be made only when receiv-ing sets are known to exist. Written material should be dropped only to areas in which at least some people can read. (The OWI in China, at the request of CBI Forward Echelon Headquarters, made up the leaflet showing pictures only. This was designed for the aboriginal hillmen between China and Tibet—to tell them to rescue downed American pilots. Broadcasting to these people would have been as profitable as spitting in the ocean. None of them could read, much less understand radio.) The probable number of listeners or readers should be calculated conservatively, taking enemy policing, amount of enemy interest, customs of the people, tension among enemy troops or civilians and other appropriate factors into account.

Occasionally propaganda media exceed the expected limitations. The Americans and British dropped leaflets on Berlin. The leaflets had little key numbers in the corners, showing to which series they belonged, and could thus be arranged in series. The Germans prohibited civilians from picking up the leaflets. The Nazi authorities followed up the prohibition by sending the *Hitlerjugend* and *Hitlermädel* out to pick up the leaflets and turn them in for destruction. The boys and girls did their job with gusto. Vast quantities were turned in for destruction. What the Nazis discovered—too late, too late—was that the schoolchildren had begun collecting the leaflets, using the key numbers to make up perfect sets. Some numbers were rarer than others, so that the Hitlerite children swapped Allied leaflets all over Berlin, trying to make up attractive albums. Mother and Father—who did not dare pick the leaflets up off the street for fear the Gestapo might be watching—found a convenient file, reasonably complete, in the room of little Fritzl or Ermintrude! The most hopeful British or American planner could not have counted on such a happy result.

Maximum Performance of Personnel. Another limitation, to be found in any psychological warfare operation, is that imposed by the types of personnel available. It would be a rash commander who assumed that he had air support because he saw airplanes—without knowing whether air crews were available. A microphone does not make a propagandist. Personnel using the speaking voice have to be good speakers; merely knowing the language is not enough. Writing personnel must be up to the level of professional writers. On the other hand, the available personnel must not be driven above its limits of performance: often an attempt to do a too-professional job will defeat the propaganda. (When the Japanese pretended to be perfectly American, and used the corny obsolete slang of the 1920's, they aroused more contempt than they would have done had they confined themselves to rather bookish, plain English.)

The psychological warfare operation must be gauged to the personnel facilities no less than to the material facilities, (In China, the author sat in with an expert on medieval and modern Japanese art, who was writing leaflets which were to be dropped on the Japanese garrisons of the Yangtze cities. The expert wrote pure, dignified Japanese, but the Chinese-Japanese language experts brought up the point, "Would the Japanese common soldier understand this kind of talk?" For a while, we had no plain-spoken Japanese at hand, and we had to send our Japanese leaflets from Chungking up to Yenan, where the Japanese Communists read the leaflets and wrote back long detailed criticisms.)

Whenever the politico-military situation permits, it is sound procedure to check output with live enemies, either interned civilians or captured military personnel. A shrewd interrogator can soon find out whether the comments from the enemy jury are honest or not.

Intelligent psychological warfare procedures have often turned liabilities into assets. Absence of a good orchestra has compelled propagandists to make up current music schedules by recording enemy musical programs, re-broadcasting them with new spoken commentary. Failure to obtain native speakers (such as genuine home-grown Japanese, or Chinese with the properly slurred Wu dialect) has led to the use of substitutes that proved better than the original. There is no point in trying to establish *rapport* with the enemy unless you talk his language with effortless perfection on the one end of the scale—or else admit that you really are a foreigner, on the other end of the scale. It is easier to build up the image of a trustworthy enemy than it is to create trust in a traitor. Frequently the attempt to talk the enemy's own language is less successful than a frank acceptance of handicaps.

In actual practice this means that either—

(a) the speaker should be authentically perfect in use of the enemy language, whether spoken or written as script; *or*

(b) the speaker should make no effort to conceal his foreign accent.

In British broadcasts to Germany, for example, it was found to be desirable for the radio announcers to have British accents in their German, rather than the Viennese or Jewish lilt which many of them did have. A Nazified audience was so infected with anti-Semitism that no Jewish speaker could carry much weight, no matter how cogent his arguments nor how eloquent his appeals. The British tone in the voices of other speakers actually helped carry conviction. The Germans were prepared to listen to a genuine Britisher, and might have been disappointed if he had spoken letter-perfect *German*.[2]

Furthermore, with the perfect speaker of the enemy language there is always the question, "What is that guy doing over there?" A traitor is less appealing than an open enemy spokesman; a traitor has to be sensationally good in order to get across at all. Lord Haw Haw was one of a kind, but he seems to have had genuine theatrical talent along with a crazy zeal which persuaded his hearers that though he was on the wrong side, he did believe his own line. The perfect speaker, whether enemy renegade or friendly linguist, has an inglorious role at the beginning of war, when enemy morale is high and the enemy population has not had time to think over the problem of changing sides. Only toward the end of the war, or in any morale downgrade, the man who says, "Come on over! See? I'm here. It's fine," has a chance of being believed.

The propaganda administrator must use his personnel thoughtfully. It is a waste of talent and—in advance field units, of life as well—to impose tasks which operatives cannot handle. An American *nisei* from California should not be asked to talk slangy *Edokko* Japanese; a soldier detailed to psychological warfare, because of some special linguistic qualification, should not be considered a great journalist, radio commentator, or actor just because he speaks the right language. If he is given a microphone, and the feeling of having an audience (one that cannot write adverse fan mail), it will be easy for the average man to overestimate the effect of his own talk. The intelligent officer tries to see his staff as the enemy would see them; he keeps their limitations in mind. If they speak the enemy language perfectly, they fall under suspicion as traitors; if they speak it poorly, they may sound like bunglers or jackasses. Nevertheless, propaganda must come from men and through words written by men, and the flavor must be fitted to the situation. Advance planning should therefore consider the available personnel as an actual factor in estimating the situation.

Counterpropaganda. Counterpropaganda could be listed as a limitation, as the enemy combat strength is sized up in physical warfare. This, however, is one of the points at which psychological warfare differs from other forms. If the propaganda message is worth putting across, it need not be geared to what the enemy is saying. Enemy propaganda should, in well conducted operations, be taken into account only when it becomes an asset. That is, the enemy need only be heeded when he tells a whopping lie, or comes forth with a piece of hypocrisy so offensive to his own people that it needs little improvement to be adapted for counterpropaganda. Most enemy themes are beyond reach, especially those of inter-ideological warfare. The Nazis and Russians made the best propaganda against each other when they got down to the basic necessities of life, not when they were trying to weave finespun theories about each other's way of thinking or of life. Refutation is a joy; it is delightful to talk back. But the best propaganda is only incidentally counterpropaganda. It uses enemy blunders and counteracts enemy success by building up unrelated successes of its own.

This does not mean that propaganda analysis is not needed. Somewhere in every psychological warfare unit there must be an intelligence group servicing the operation. If, for example, the enemy has announced that the candy your aviators are dropping is poisoned (and has proved it by dropping some of "your" candy, made by his black-operations boys and actually poisoned), there is no point in calling him a liar; you may not know for some time whether poisoned candy has been dropped or not. If the enemy commander has shown his troops photographs of prisoners whom your side has taken and "murdered" (according to his well staged photos), it is not a good idea to ask people to surrender without sending along equally convincing pictures of well cared for prisoners. If the enemy alleges that you and your allies are rioting in the streets or stealing each other's womenfolk, or that one of you is doing all the fighting while the other sits around in safe staging areas, it may be a good idea to send along some leaflets showing inter-allied cooperation on your side, or to run a few radio shows on the subject.

This consists merely of reckoning the enemy propaganda as part of the psychological warfare situation, and of using the enemy as part of the background to your own advantage. The moment you start letting him take the initiative, your propaganda wags along behind his. Tell *his* people something *he* can't deny. Let him sit up nights worrying about how he will counteract *you*. Make him drive his security officers crazy trying to release figures that will please your G-2 in order to reassure his home audience. Really good propaganda does not worry about counterpropaganda. It never assumes that the enemy propagandist is a gentleman: he is by definition a liar. Your listeners and you are the only gentlemen left on earth.

NOTES:

[1] Chicago 1946. The discussion of what censorship authorities regarded as propaganda material possessing value for the enemy, of the wartime OC-OWI relationship, and of censorship of short-wave broadcasts are of particular interest to the student of psychological warfare.

[2] In a somewhat different context, it is interesting to note that Chinese Protestant churches, made up of Chinese church members, like to hire ministers who mouth their Chinese with a strong American accent. The

American missionaries established the American accent
as part of the liturgical paraphernalia of Protestantism,
and the Chinese preachers trained under them accepted
the American mispronouncing of Chinese as a part of the
religion. It is odd to see a church full of Chinese using
absolutely unbelievable tones while singing hymns or
making appropriate individual responses. At that, they are
no funnier than the Chinese Buddhists, who memorize
long Indian sutras without understanding a single syl-
lable.

CHAPTER 5
PSYCHOLOGICAL WARFARE IN WORLD WAR I

World War I saw psychological warfare transformed from an incidental to a major military instrument, and later it was even called the weapon which won the war. The story spread, since the Germans liked to imagine that they had been talked out of winning, and since ex-propagandists among the Allies enjoyed thinking that their own cleverness had been decisive when even the tremendous violence of trench warfare had produced nothing more than a stalemate. If psychological warfare is considered in the broad sense, it seems plain that it was among the decisive weapons of 1914-1918. The political decency of the Allies, the appeal of President Wilson's Fourteen Points, the patent obsolescence of the Kaiser and what he stood for, the resurgence of Polish, Baltic, Finnish, Czechoslovak and South Slav nationalisms—all these played a real part in making Germany surrender in 1918. More real than the role of guns, men, ships, planes, tanks? This cannot be answered: it is like asking of a long-distance runner whether his heart, lungs, legs, or head contributed most to his success. Since war is waged by and against all parts of the human personality—physical condition, skills, intelligence, emotions, and so on—it is impossible to distinguish between the performance of one kind of weapon and the other in the attainment of a goal itself complex—governmental surrender. Only a weapon which left no enemy survivors could claim for itself undisputed primacy in victory.

Propaganda came to prominence in war because the nations involved had made mass-communications part of their civilian lives. The appearance of huge newspapers, systematic advertising, calculated political publicity, and opinion manipulation in other forms made it inevitable that skills which developed in civilian life should be transferred to the military. In general, *the psychological warfare efforts of each belligerent were the direct equivalents of his peacetime nonpolitical propaganda facilities.* (By way of exception, the peculiar genius of the Bolshevik leaders stimulated a propaganda effort disproportionate to the facilities, either of personnel or materiel, to be found in pre-1914 Russia.)

Nations rarely change their basic character in time of war. When war starts it is usually too late to re-educate generations already grown up, teach them wholly new skills, or develop administrative or operational procedures unknown in peacetime life. Sometimes, by great effort, a nation can transform a small available cadre into large, new and effective units on the political, military, economic or social fronts. Even then, the character of the war effort will be colored and influenced by the experience of the men undertaking it. The British had, in 1914, one of the world's finest news systems, a highly sophisticated press, and extensive experience in international communication for technical and commercial purposes, notably the undersea cable system, and they turned these to war use with considerable smoothness. The Germans had a far more regimented press and a more limited network of commercial and technical connections. The British, furthermore, had a diplomatic and consular service of superb quality; comparable German services included a much higher proportion of bunglers and enthusiasts.

From the very beginning the British had the lead. They nailed German propaganda as propaganda, while circulating their own as news, cultural relations, or literature. The Germans who boasted that they were a "cultured" people had their naïveté rewarded when the British let the German word *Kultur* become a synonym for boorish pedantic arrogance. The Germans had the awful habit of putting many of their own unattractive emotions into words, and the even more ruinous habit of then printing the words. In many instances, the British simply let the Germans think up braggadocio or vengeful phrases, then circulated the German phrases to the world. The English language was permanently enriched by some of these: *strafe* comes from the German plea that God "strafe" (punish) England. The actual "Hymn of Hate" was originally a song made up by Germans for Germans. The word "Hun" was applied to the German Army by Kaiser Wilhelm himself, and so on. Furthermore, the Germans created in their press and information services a condition of bureaucratic snafu which has rarely been excelled in any war. National character certainly worked out its automatic vengeances in World War I.

The American psychological warfare effort of 1917-1919 also drew heavily on familiar skills: the American press, second only to that of the British at the time; the church, Y.M.C.A., and Chautauqua groups; and the wealth of private clubs which flourish under our liberal system of laws and usages. Other nationalities made efforts similarly in keeping with their peacetime facilities. The Japanese were adroit, but even at that time confused by the mixup of trying to be a "civilized" power but simultaneously expansionist. The French showed high professional skill in adapting their military and diplomatic personnel to propaganda tasks. France's position as battleground ensured her of the rage of her own people and the sympathy of neutrals, giving propaganda from Paris a hearing. The Chinese, though undergoing the downfall of the Yüan Shihk'ai dictatorship and lapsing into chaos, maintained an impeccable diplomatic front and played a weak hand for everything it was worth; they had their private quasi-war with the Japanese in 1915. That they did so while putting the blame for Allied disunity squarely on the Japanese where it belonged is to their credit.

The weight of the propaganda war, as of the material war, fell on its prime contestants, Britain, Germany, and the United States. The private and revolutionary groups which emerged as the revolutionary governments played a vigorous part because they had few other functions to distract their attention. The Republic of Czechoslovakia got its start in Pittsburgh, Pennsylvania, in 1918, and fought psychological warfare from the instant it took form; not till later did it assume the weightier and more expensive responsibilities of ruling and warring.

The British Effort. In World War I, the British made most of
the mistakes and learned most of the lessons which the Americans
were to make and to learn in World War II. The British Foreign
Office formed a War Propaganda Bureau in 1914, but a great deal
of the effort was done by private facilities (patriotic associations)
or by lower political and military echelons of the government and
armed forces—and without coordination. Things became so confused that at the mid-point of the war, the British organized a Department of Information with Colonel John Buchan at its head.
(Buchan will be remembered by all adventure-lovers as author of
The Thirty-nine Steps, The Courts of the Morning, and other first-
class thrillers; he was also made a peer under the style, Lord
Tweedsmuir, and became a popular Governor-General of Canada.)
Buchan did not always get along with the committee which floated
above him, telling him how to run his business.

The British, like the Germans, had immense organizational difficulties. The British ended up by inventing a distinction of roles.
Thus they finished World War I with two separate propaganda
agencies. The Ministry of Information, under Lord Beaverbrook,
with Colonel Buchan as Director of Intelligence, carried on civilian psychological warfare outside Britain; the National War Aims
Committee carried on civilian psychological warfare within Britain. Military psychological warfare was carried on by military and
civilian agencies, both. The British required five years of honest
effort, bitter wrangling, and positive political invention in order
to devise a psychological warfare system sufficient to meet the
needs of a great power at war. They did not let their administrative difficulties prevent their conduct of correct, poised and highly
moral propaganda, nor impede their use of plentiful funds and high
ingenuity in getting their propaganda across.[1]

The British set the pace in coordinating political warfare with
news-propaganda, and in effecting workable liaison between national policy-makers and operational and public-relations chiefs
of the armed services. It is not likely that, even in World War II,
the Americans—within the looser, younger, bigger framework of
our more compendious government—achieved as good results in

terms of timing. State-War-Navy-OWI-OSS-Treasury timing of related events or news items was obtained through most of World War II in the following manner: the federal agency affected did whatever it was going to do anyhow, and other federal agencies took notice after the event, initiating their related actions, if any were feasible, then and only then. The British sought to get around this in World War I by correlating their policy toward various countries with their policy involving different departments. They were not totally successful but they learned a lot; the net product of their propaganda was, for most of its purposes, superb.

The German Failure in Propaganda. German writers, after World War I, sometimes attributed the superiority of the British in propaganda to the innate fiendishness of Britishers as contrasted with the gullible purity of Germans. The psychoneurotic non-com who made himself famous to the world's cost did not make this mistake. In *Mein Kampf* Hitler stated categorically that the British had understood the professional touch in propaganda while the Germans had not. Hitler's contempt for the masses was shown in his explicit statement of their inattentiveness, their poor response to formal logic, their affirmative reaction to simple one-sided reiteration. He said: "[In England] . . . propaganda was a weapon of the first class, while with us it was a sop to unemployed politicians . . ." German nationalists of whatever stripe found themselves in accord when they blamed their military defeat on the enemy's use of propaganda. They thus succeeded in maintaining the myth, already sedulously inculcated for two centuries, that the German army could not be beaten in the field. The extremists and crackpots among them went on to develop the "stab-in-the-back" theory that an unbeaten Germany was betrayed from within by Jews, socialists, and democratic people. (The mutually exclusive alternatives— namely, that either Allied propaganda was fiendishly good, and the Germans merely innocent victims, or else that Allied propaganda was ineffectual and the anti-war sentiment a purely German development—did not keep the Hitlerites from exploiting both alibis simultaneously.)

The postwar period of the 1920's saw, therefore, the curious spectacle of the Germans lauding American psychological warfare, and counting it as a major factor of defeat, while the Americans naturally emphasized the fighting record of American troops.

As for Kaiserist propaganda, it started out with the twin curses of amateurishness and bureaucracy, each of them crippling but deadly when paired. German writers and scholars ran wild in 1914 and 1915 in trying to put the blame on the Allies; amateurish in public relations, they succeeded in arousing a tremendous amount of antagonism. They were handicapped by the ponderosity of the German Imperial Government, by the intervention of persons unfamiliar with news or advertising (at that time the most obvious sources of civilian propaganda personnel), and by a military stodginess which made German press communiqués infuriating even to anti-British readers. Overseas propaganda developed through poorly secured clandestine channels, and was mixed up with espionage and sabotage personnel. Inescapable "breaks" gave all German agents a bad name. George Sylvester Viereck, who has enjoyed the odd distinction of being our most vocal pro-German sympathizer in both wars with Germany, later wrote a naïve but revealing account of his operations under the title *Spreading Germs of Hate* (Boston, 1930). (No British information officer was guilty, even after the war, of a comparable breach of taste.) Viereck praises the British for their sang-froid and skill; coming from him, the praise is more than deserved.

More seriously, German propaganda lacked both organization and moral drive. Lieutenant Colonel Nicolai, the Imperial German General Staff officer responsible, puts part of the blame on the German press and on the press officers of the Army and the Reich: "In fact, the enemy remained virtually untouched by any kind of German propaganda. This reproach falls against the press, it would seem, as well as on the responsible officials. . . . Internationally minded papers themselves failed to cooperate. Yet it was precisely these which were circulated and esteemed abroad. Newspapers with other (pro-militarist) editorial policies, failing to get leadership from the Government, could not aim at any unified effect. . . .

Instead, the goal of the governmental press leadership remained a thoroughly negative one: to prevent the press from doing harm to national policy."[2]

Without developing his theme into systematic doctrine for psychological warfare, the German colonel stated the basic defect of World War I from the German point of view. Writing in 1920, he went on to say: "The enemy alleges simply to have copied our frontline propaganda when he initiated his. In so doing, he is guilty of a deliberate untruth, made for the sake of removing the moral blot which is attached to his victory. . . ." Nicolai could not overcome the supposition that propaganda was a dirty and unsoldierly device and that it was much more honorable for armies to exchange loss of life than to save men on both sides by talking the enemy into surrendering; but he went on to the real point at issue. "Furthermore, it was not moralistic misgivings which kept us from applying to the enemy front lines a propaganda campaign as successful as theirs, but very sober practical obstacles. There were available to us none of the (psychological) points of attack at which propaganda would have been effective against the enemy forces, points such as the enemy found in our own domestic conditions. What was lacking was political propaganda as precursor of military."

What the Germans failed to learn in World War I. they later learned and applied in World War II. The German Imperial Government started in 1914 with a defiant assurance of its own power. Power was not sought among the masses so far as Kaiser Wilhelm was concerned; one inherited it from one's ancestors, along with an army, and the masses had better keep their noses out of it. The Hitlerite German government of 1939 began its world war only after two decades of shrewd, conscienceless, bitter domestic propaganda. Hitlerism had come to power by first wooing and then bullying the common man, and the Nazi chiefs, in their strategy of terror or "warfare psychologically waged," subsequently applied the same tactics to the international community. Hitler conquered Europe with these tactics; he started with flattery, made scenes, and ended with cold brutality. These were the skills of the urban slum.

The Creel Committee. The fabulous American propaganda, of which the Germans expressed such dread, was the work of two agencies. The civilian agency was the Committee on Public Information, universally known as the "Creel Committee" after its chairman, Mr. George Creel. The military agency was the Propaganda Section (or Psychologic Section), G-2D), General Headquarters, American Expeditionary Forces, under Captain Heber Blankenhorn.

The Creel Committee had the superlative advantage of possessing a chief who enjoyed the confidence of the President and whose participation in national policy was on a high enough level to give propaganda coordination to other governmental policies on a basis of equality. Creel himself considered the task to be one of advertising, and he organized his Committee with extreme looseness, expanding it rapidly. Although his total gross budget for the war was only a fraction of OWI's budgets in World War II, he systematized most of the publicity activities then available.

News services were maintained by means of a news bureau in Washington that fed material to the commercial press and processed other material to publicity missions abroad. Heavy emphasis was placed on the home audience for Creel's mission covered all phases of propaganda work. Sections were set up for posters, advertising, "Four Minute Men" (volunteer local speakers in all American communities), films, American minority groups and the foreign-language press, women's organizations, information bureaus, syndicated features, and cartoons. The young but already large American motion picture industry was made a channel whereby American propaganda movies went to both the United States and overseas audiences. In one instance Creel got the American producers to threaten Swiss exhibitors with a boycott unless they showed American propaganda film along with the features.

Missions were sent to France, England, Italy, Switzerland, Holland, Spain, Scandinavia, Mexico and other Latin American countries, China, and Russia. It was not considered necessary to send American propagandists to Japan in World War I. The Japanese were given the American propaganda file and were asked to use it; they said they would.

The Creel Committee was run in simple, almost chaotic fashion. Agencies proliferated whenever a new idea turned up. The basic concept was that of domestic American agitation, as practiced commercially through advertising and socially through the civic clubs. The war propaganda left a rather bad taste in the mouth of many Americans, and the boisterous joviality of the arousers probably produced negative attitudes which encouraged pacifism and isolationism in the postwar years. The purely technical side of the work was done well, but at the terrible cost of overshooting national commitments.

America emerged from the war disappointed at home and discredited abroad—so far as the heated propaganda of "making the world safe for democracy" was concerned. A more modest, more calculated national propaganda effort would have helped forestall those attitudes which, in turn, made World War II possible. Creel and his fellow-workers did not remember that beyond every war there lies a peace, in its own way as grim and difficult as war. They did not understand that no war is the last war, that leeway must be left for propaganda to be effective *again*. They said that World War I would be the last of all wars; perhaps they believed it themselves.

General Pershing's Headquarters. The civilians of the Creel committee patronizingly claimed to have helped the G-2 men at A.E.F. Headquarters run psychological warfare. In the official history of Captain Blankenhorn's group, which centered from the very beginning on leaflet production, there is little reference to outside aid. Radio did not exist as a means of mass communication, and loudspeakers then surpassed an ordinary megaphone very little, if at all; hence communication with the enemy had to be through print. Leaflets were basic.

The Americans at A.E.F. concentrated on morale and surrender leaflets. They did work that was superb from the point of view of commonsense psychology. They used British and French experience in applying techniques of leaflet distribution, making inventions and improvements of their own. Balloons and airplanes were the chief methods for air distribution; the plane-borne leaflet bomb was a development of World War II. Extensive improvements were made in the procedures of leaflet distribution by means of mortars.

The morale leaflets used the anti-militarist, pro-democratic sentiments of the world at that time. The autocracy and inefficiency of the German government provided an excellent target. Since propaganda against the upper classes was not yet regarded as a Communist monopoly, considerable appeal was introduced for the common German soldier against his generals, nobles, officials, and capitalists. German nationalism was attacked by means of sectional appeals to Lorrainers and Bavarians. The news that America was in fact producing vast weapons, that the American army was truly in Europe, that the German retreats were really serious—these were used in morale form (see below) rather than as spot-news leaflets.

It was in the primary mission of combat propaganda—the inducement to surrender—that the Americans excelled themselves. They produced limitless appeals (see Figure 13) promising the Germans first-class American food when they surrendered. Emphasis was indeed on all surrender themes—good food, human care, privileges under international law, patriotic value of remaining alive, opportunity to return to loved ones, and so forth. But the Americans went over these variously, and came back to the topic of food. For an army of hungry men who knew that their homeland starved behind them, the enumeration of things to eat had obsessive value.

Haughty and incompetent, the German high command tried to counteract Allied leaflets—particularly the American leaflets—by the use of appeals to "disregard propaganda." While the German armies plainly backed down toward defeat, such German statements preached about the situation. They did not put the common soldier's plight in concrete terms. They did not say, "You will be unemployed, poor, sick, dishonored, lonely, if you surrender. Your wife will be beaten by Frenchmen, your daughters raped by savages, your father and mother starved to death by the food prices." Such tactics had to wait for a later war. In 1918, the German command, senile and fussy, pointed out that enemy leaflets

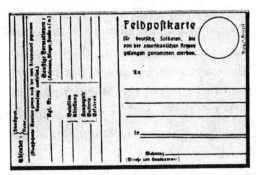

Figure 13: Surrender Leaflet from the AEF. Though this American combat leaflet from World War I copies the original form of the German *Feldpostkarte* (field postcard, an early precursor of the V-mail form), it is not black propaganda since neither source nor intent is concealed. "When you are taken prisoner, by the Americans, give this to the first officer who checks your identities." The prisoner is commanded to fill in his own battle-order history. By marking out appropriate items, he indicates whether he is hurt or not and can explain that he is well cared for and fed "beef, white bread, potatoes, beans, plums, genuine bean coffee, milk, butter, tobacco, etc."

were propaganda (nasty! nasty!) and that good German soldiers would remember their duty. For men who probably imagined they could smell white bread baking, bacon frying, and coffee cooking across the lines, such wordage was nonsense. The Germans came on over to surrender.

Captain Blankenhorn's unit, without benefit of psychologists, developed a German morale analysis chart. This was made up before scientific polling had become a common technique, and was consequently based on a group of selected known factors given arbitrary weight and then averaged into a total. It was not, "number of German prisoners per hundred who express attitudes characterized by doubt" but "the U-boat situation," "unity in Germany," and other abstracted generalities which were used as controls. The chart was carefully kept, and sought to follow morale from its causative factors rather than by a percentage count of attitudes discovered in the newspapers or among prisoners.

The Bolshevik and Chinese Revolutions. The dynamic propaganda development of this period came about in Russia. The Russian revolution began as reaction to an adverse military situation, disesteemed leadership, economic hardship, and long overdue reforms. In its first, or constitutional phase, it had an inevitableness about it; there was little resistance to the revolution, and the popular mood was one of relief, joy, easement. However, the majority group of the Russian Socialists interpreted the Marxist philosophy to mean (putting it bluntly) that the end is justified by the means. They believed that they had developed a system of politico-economic forecasting which, while not always certain, was close to certain. And they further believed that no one else, lacking this system of forecasting, could lead the workers and peasants to their historically inevitable freedom. This philosophy may sound beside the point, but it is not. Such abstruse doctrines of Hegelianism and Marxism were used by the majority-Socialists (known by their Russian name, *Bolshevik*) to give themselves a sense of unconditional rightness. From the first phase of the revolution on, the Bolsheviks pitilessly sabotaged all other democratic groups. There was no point in helping other groups, when Bolsheviks alone had the inner secrets of history at their command.

In the geniuses Lenin and Trotzky, the Bolshevik movement found its leadership. Lenin had no use for democracy as it was known in America. To him it was a sham, a front for the great capitalist trusts, which—even though the capitalists themselves might not know it—were doomed to get bigger on a shrinking market, until international capitalist war, bankruptcy, and working-class revolution was the result. Lenin was as sure that this would happen as he was that the sun would rise the next morning. The only dispute was the matter of timing; a few Bolshevik pessimists thought that the capitalist world might last into the 1920's.

Such a frame of mind led to a very deadly kind of psychological warfare. The Bolsheviks despised their opponents, desiring to "liquidate" them (this meant breaking down a group and preventing its reforming as a group, but came above all to mean mass murder). They were so antagonistic to the "capitalist" world that they hated God, patriotism, national history, churches, money, private property, chastity, marriage, and verse that rhymed, all with equal

intensity. Moscow became the Mecca for the eccentrics and mal-
contents of the world and for some years Russia was in fact looser
in morals than any other civilized country.

Hatred for the capitalist world enabled the Bolsheviks to throw
Russian Czarist patriotism into the discard. They delighted in getting Russian troops to desert at the front; the Germans delighted
in this, too. But the Bolsheviks were certain they would have the
last laugh because they knew it was only a matter of weeks or
months before the revolution—the *inevitable* revolution, forecast
by Karl Marx's peculiar economics—broke out in Germany as well.
The Russian devil-may-care attitude toward all established forms
of society was perfectly characterized by Trotzky's flip but deadly
answer to the German military negotiators at the Brest-Litovsk
negotiations. When the Germans balked at some point, "All right,"
said Trotzky, "no war and—no peace."

The Germans insisted that if the Bolsheviks did not sign the
dictated peace terms the German army would make more war.

Fine, said Trotzky in effect, he didn't mind. Go ahead and make
war. It wouldn't worry him or his army. They would go somewhere
else and would refuse to play games with capitalists.

This stopped the Germans in their tracks. They did not want to
send their troops into a starving country that roared with subversive doctrines. They knew that while Trotzky wasted their time
quibbling over negotiations, his printing presses worked night and
day telling the German troops that the war was over, that capitalism was on its way out, that the workers' revolution was coming,
everywhere, for everybody, with food, peace, plenty, atheism and
all the other delights of the good Bolshevik life. The Russians
finally signed the surrender treaty but in point of fact, the German
divisions on the Eastern front were contaminated by Bolshevism,
and when they came back across Germany they brought the message of freedom and peace with them. Germany did have an abor-
tive Communist revolution—partly because of Russian operations—
though it was stopped by an alliance of the moderate Socialists
and the dependable remnants of the army.

The Russians went on merrily through a living hell. For five more years the Bolshevik leaders held their country together without industrial production, without food, without weapons. They had amazingly high morale among their own select Bolshevik group, and against the common people they had two weapons, propaganda and terror. (The terror was symptomatic of the first of the modern totalitarian dictatorships; its domestic police role is not a part of psychological warfare.)

The Bolshevik propaganda was probably the finest propaganda effort ever known in history down to that time—down, perhaps, all the way to our own time. The political limit was beyond reach; anything in the old world was fair game. Things the sober Soviet citizen of 1946 would regard with veneration were open to ridicule in 1919-1922: patriotism, religion, national sovereignty, international law, treaties with or between capitalist states. There flowed from Russia a world-wide stream of propaganda, mostly clandestine, some of it overt. In every nation of the world there was, to a greater or less degree, a "Red scare"; the propaganda of the Bolsheviks was regarded as having mystical subversive powers which no other operation could match. In retrospect it seems absurd that anyone could have worried about the Americans of the 1920's revolting against their own Constitution; but a lot of people, including the Attorney General of the United States, did indeed worry.

They had cause for alarm though not for the reasons they supposed. Much of the magic of Bolshevik propaganda arose from its taking up where British, French and American propaganda left off. The psychological warfare of the Allies had made the sad mistake of promising a new, a better world to everyone on earth. When the war ended, and conditions went back to normal, many people in the world did not consider "normalcy" the fulfillment of that better world. The Bolshevik propaganda reaped the harvest which the Allied propagandist had sown and then left untended. Expectations, whipped up beyond normal, turned to Bolshevism when the Western democracies abandoned both domestic and foreign propaganda operations. The strategic advantage of Bolshevik propaganda was overwhelming. The Allies had gotten the world ready for it, so that the wild Utopia of the Leninists temporarily made sense to millions.

This does not mean that the Bolshevik propaganda of the 1920s was not good. It was good, technically, psychologically, politically— but good in terms of achieving an immediate scare at the cost of long-range confidence. The eventual cost to the Soviet Union was terrible. The Soviet government isolated itself and declared a condition of open psychological warfare against every other government on earth, including the United States. (This so exasperated Presidents Wilson, Harding, Coolidge, and Hoover that they refused to recognize the Soviet Union.) The Bolshevik propaganda was carried by:

Russian government channels;
Communist "party" channels (the Communists not really being a political party, anywhere, but using the name "party" to designate the hierarchy of a dogmatic, ruthless and fanatical political religion);
trade unions;
individual subversive operators;
"cover organizations";
trade, consular and other official missions;
leaflets in the mails;
posters, books and other literature;
films;
radio.

The theme throughout was plain: the world revolution is coming, by inescapable economic laws discovered by our theory. The world revolution, which *will* come, will remove the *owning* classes from control of the productive capital, and will put all capital in the hands of the workers. "The expropriators will be expropriated." Thereupon the economic laws we have found in Marx's books will cease their bad influence and will guarantee world peace, world prosperity, happiness, human freedom. This is not an appeal (they said); this is *science*. This is *objective*. We *know*. Listen!

The Communists harped on these basic themes. They waged political warfare along with the psychological. Every attempt of the non-Communist countries to discuss the situation was termed "conspiracies of the warmongers." The word "democratic" was reserved to the Communists or to non-Communists who were certain to cause Communism no trouble. The Communists invented an entirely new vocabulary, which the Soviet and other Communist papers still use, with meanings that have the same emotional value (plus-value, or, "that's *good!*") as in America or Britain, but which have entirely different meanings in concrete practice. "Democracy" means "free elections"; "free elections" mean that the people elect "democratic leaders"; but "democratic leaders" are not the people who are elected in non-Communist countries. Non-Communist leaders are usually dubbed "tools" or "stooges" of something; they are "servile" or "reactionary." Real "democratic leaders" are only those people approved by the international Communist movement. It *knows.* By *science.*

What was the net effect of such psychological warfare? In the first place, much use of common terms without regard to ultimate fulfillment means that Communist propaganda is self-defeating. It can succeed only in situations of desperation, anarchy, or terror. That is satisfactory to the Communist leaders, because they think their *science* tells them that the capitalist states will lead to desperation, anarchy and terror anyhow. Secondly, Communist propaganda sacrifices all other values to the propaganda. One has to be a religious fanatic (of the Marxist sort) to turn it out; one has to be ready for a totally new creed in order to keep on accepting it. International understanding, patriotism, truthfulness, freedom of action, artistic conscience—all these are sacrificed to propaganda. In the end, *everything is propaganda* to the Communist. Nothing which hurts Communism can be true. They have their *science.* (If you would like to look at this fabulous *science,* read *The Communist Manifesto,* V. I. Lenin's *The Teachings of Karl Marx,* and Stalin's latest current compilation of speeches. You will be impressed by the crazy logic, the genuine but ill-informed zeal.) Third and most important, Communist psychological warfare is continuous. The themes may change—sometimes provocative, sometimes almost conciliatory—but the machinery, the operation, does not. Communist propaganda is therefore seasoned and professional, dependent on a powerful police-state at home and on uneducated or emotionally ill fanatics abroad, except for those few countries where Communism is so stable as to attract hard-headed or practical idealistic men.

This Bolshevik success, rather than the splendid but short-lasting accomplishments of the Allies in World War I, kept psychological warfare on the map. Modern Communism is permanent psychological warfare in action.

The Communist leaders unwittingly made a tremendous mistake between 1922 and 1927. They invited the military and political staff of the Chinese Nationalists (Kuomintang) to cooperate with them. Filled with their own Communist sense of certainty, it never occurred to them that anyone else could outsmart them. The Chinese did. Their military chief of mission in Moscow learned everything that the Communists had to teach about irregular fighting, subversive propaganda, revolutionary situations, mass agitation. He then went home and got more Communist aid to carry out the military phase of the Nationalist revolution, which started under way in the summer of 1922. The old war-lord armies were helpless in the face of agents, agitators, poster crews, student strikes, press propaganda and indoctrinated troops. The most sensational war in modern Asia involved relatively little combat. The Nationalist leader used all the Communist psychological warfare techniques, and added a few more of his own. His name was Chiang Kai-shek.

In 1927 the Communists began a debate in Moscow as to whether they had used the Nationalists enough or not. One group said they might as well liquidate the Nationalists, Sunyatsenism, Chiang Kai-shek and all; the other said they should use the Nationalists a little longer, to carry on the struggle against American, Japanese, and British "imperialism." Chiang Kai-shek displayed a keen interest in these formal theoretical discussions which, thanks to his Moscow training, he understood perfectly. While the Communists were still debating when and how to hijack him, he hijacked them. In the fall of 1927, he turned against them, using the weapons of terror and propaganda, and then shifting to the more solid ground of economic development. They have not forgiven him. Nationalist China to this day possesses a working duplicate of the Moscow propaganda facilities which the Communists, unconscious of the humor of it, call "fascist." (What is anti-Communist for whatever cause *is* Fascist, they say.)

The Russian revolution of 1917-1922 and the Chinese revolution of 1922-1927 represent the situations created by Communist psychological warfare. Since that time, except for Spain, Communist psychological warfare has failed in every single attempt to come to power outside Russia. Following World War II, Communist psychological warfare proved itself capable of holding countries only *after* the actual Russian army had occupied them. The magic has gone out of Communist propaganda; it can keep control only with heavy military pressure behind it. But in the far past, it has been capable of winning—as in Russia and China—without outside military aid. With a renovation of techniques, doctrines, and personnel, it may do so again.

NOTES:

[1] On World War I, see Harold Lasswell's *Propaganda Technique in the World War*, previously cited; George Creel's *How We Advertised America*, New York and London, 1920, the very title of which is an indication of its chief shortcoming; Lt. Col. W. Nicolai, *Nachrichtendienst, Presse und Volksstimmung im Weltkrieg*, Berlin, 1920, by the German general staff officer chiefly responsible for staff work on propaganda and public opinion, a very thoughtful though prejudiced book; Heber Blankenhorn's enjoyable little classic, *Adventures in Propaganda*, Boston, 1919 (Blankenhorn was the only American officer to see field service in propaganda in both wars, as a Captain

in I and a Lieutenant Colonel in II); and George G. Bruntz'
scholarly monograph *Allied Propaganda and the Collapse
of the German Empire* in 1918, Stanford, 1938. Readers
desiring further references should consult the bibliographies by Lasswell, Casey and Smith, cited above.

[2] Colonel Nicolai, book cited in footnote 1. pages 160-
161.

CHAPTER 6
PSYCHOLOGICAL WARFARE IN WORLD WAR II

Bolshevik accomplishments in psychological warfare were often regarded as part of the peculiar mischief of Marxism, not as techniques which could be learned and used by other people. Similarly, the history-making sweep of the Chinese Nationalist armies northward in 1922-1927 was considered to be specially and incomprehensibly Chinese; possible lessons which might have been learned from Chinese Communist psychological warfare were left unheeded by officials and students in the West. Meanwhile Germany, the greatest power of Europe, had been fighting bitter internal psychological warfare battles[1] which looked like heated internal politics. Not until Adolf Hitler assumed the Reich's Chancellorship and began using his Brown-shirt methods for foreign affairs did other people wake up to the existence and application of the new weapon.

(The War College files, for example, show that not one single officer was assigned full-time to study of these problems during 1925-1935. For the entire period 1919-1929, there are listed only two War College research papers on the subject. Yet the American Army was far from negligent. It was an excellent army, though crippled by outright poverty of personnel and materials. The Army was simply American, and like the rest of America for a while took the world for granted.)

The National Socialist German Workers' Party, as Hitler called his movement, was a conglomerate built up around a few determined fanatics. The Nazis do not appear to have believed their own

126

doctrines to anything like the degree to which the Communists believed theirs. From the first, the Nazis regarded propaganda very consciously as a new, fierce instrument which led to the accomplishment of *modern* power. The Communists had proclaimed that democracy was a fake; the Nazis agreed. The Communists had shown that a minority with a sacred mission of its own invention could get mass support for a government that claimed to be *for* the people, even though it was obviously not *by* the people nor *of* them. The Nazis took this as a model. The Communists had shown that a modern man-god could be set up and worshipped in a twentieth-century state, and called leader (*Vozhd* in Russian). The Nazis elevated the Soviet practice all the way into a principle, the principle of the leader (*Führer* in German).

The Communists had shown that an organization calling itself a *party*, actually a quasi-religious hierarchy with strong internal discipline, definite membership, and active organizational components, could control fifty times its own membership. The Nazis organized the same general sort of party, copying the Italian Fascists in part, but copying more from the direct example of the German Communists right in front of them. The Communists had shown that such a movement needed to have youth branches, women's organizations, labor sections, clubs of its own, and so on, calling this "mass organization." The Nazis copied this too.

The machinery of Nazism was in many ways a copy of Communism, applied to allegedly different ends (the Nazis had an Aryan myth; the Communists had their pseudo-economics). But the important thing about them both was the destruction of the *end* by the *means*; the problem of getting and keeping power despite the people was so obsessive that propaganda became all-important. Theoretically, the *end* (to the Nazi, German world rule; to the Communist, the fulfillment of history in universal communism) was the most important thing. But since any means at any time which led to that end was good, and since the Party bosses were the sole ones who could determine whether a particular action led to the very remote end or not, the outcome in both Russia and Germany became the conscienceless seeking of power for its own sake.

The new psychological warfare, a cause as well as a means of
World War II, arose from the subjection of other considerations
to *propaganda*. The propaganda addict takes everything with a ton
of salt; what he does believe is lost in what he doesn't believe. The
ordinary controls of civilized life—regard for truth, regard for law,
respect for neighbors, obedience to good manners, love of God—
cease to operate effectively, because the propaganda-dizzy man
sees in everything its propaganda content and nothing else. Everything, from a girl dancing on a stage to an ecclesiastic officiating
in a cathedral, is either *for* him or *against* him. Nothing is innocent; nothing is pleasurable; everything is connected with his dis-
eased apprehension of power. Before he gets power, he hates the
people who have power; he does not trust their intelligence, esteem
their personalities, believe in their good will, or credit their motives.[2] They must be scum, because they hold power when *he*, the
propaganda-infatuated man, is a member of the group that *should*
hold it. Yet when such a man comes to power he hates his colleagues
and comrades. Remembering the cold cynical way in which he himself sought power, knowing that his brother fanatics have the same
ruthless arrogance, the propaganda-using Party man cannot trust
anyone. Blood purges, mass trials, liquidations, removal of families, concealment of crimes—all these result from the establishment of propaganda in an overdeveloped role.

It is against such people that we—ordinary folk, Americans—
dared wage psychological warfare during World War II. Propaganda had grown into ideology; the world was convulsed with monstrous new religions. For instance: the greatest journalist of the
Soviet Union, Karl Radek, was placed on trial for treason. He was
asked by the prosecutor, Vyshinsky,

"These actions of yours were deliberate?"

Radek answered: "Apart from sleeping, I have never in my life
committed any undeliberate actions."[3]

This answer sums up the mood of the totalitarian who is obsessed by propaganda. He comes to believe that all activity, whether
his own or of other people, has meaning. He had developed the

sense of responsibility that made him violate tenets which Americans, in a free society, regard as fundamental to human nature: things like self-respect, kindliness, love of family, pity for the unfortunate.

This kind of mentality was found chiefly in the National Socialist and Communist states, and to a lesser degree in dictatorships such as Italy; by contrast, reactionary Japan was almost democratic. This mentality makes it possible for the ruler to control his own people enough to undertake "warfare psychologically waged." Without domestic fanaticism and domestic terror, governments have to fall back on "psychological warfare"—that is, the mere supplementing of politics and military operations by propaganda. It is vain to expect a free people in a free country to submit to such humiliating control, even for the purpose of winning a war. What made the psychological warfare of World War II peculiar was the fact that our enemies fought one kind of war ("warfare psychologically waged," or total war) and we fought them back with another. Theoretically, it is possible to argue that we had no business succeeding.

But we did succeed.

The Pre-Belligerent Stages. The propaganda-conscious Axis states had first to control their own people enough to wage aggressive war. They then had to split their possible enemies, to make piecemeal victory possible. They had to stay on good terms with the Soviet Union (Hitler till 1941; Japan till the last week of war). They had to frighten their immediate enemies while assuring their eventual enemies. This called for a great deal of propaganda.

Pre-belligerent operations required extensive use of "black" propaganda. Since their political systems aroused hostility and anger in audiences which they wished to address, the aggressors sought to disguise their propaganda. They used pacifist groups to keep the democracies from rearming. Militarist groups were encouraged to keep the democracies from undertaking domestic reforms or discussing military matters with Russia. Financial groups were contacted to preserve the fiction of normal international relations. Cultural groups were employed to preserve friendliness for their respective nationalities as such. The Japanese did a little global propaganda and for a while subsidized several magazines in this country, but in general they concentrated their main effort in the immediate area of their military operations.

It was the Germans who developed world-wide pre-belligerent propaganda to a fine art. They exploited every possible disunity which could contribute to the weakness of an enemy. They were not choosy about collaborators. If the Communist Party of the United States lent a hand (as it did between September, 1939 and June, 1941, terming the war "an imperialist war"; after Russia got in, the war was called "the democratic anti-fascist war"), the Nazis did not object. They willingly listened to men who had fantastic schemes for world peace and later used such men as aids in getting appeasement. They tried to rouse Catholics against Communists, Communists against democrats, Gentiles against Jews, whites against negroes, the poor against the rich, the rich against the poor, British against Americans, Americans against British— anyone against anyone, as long as it delayed action against Germany and weakened the enemy potential. They went to special pains to organize German-speaking minorities in non-German countries, but they never neglected using people who had no open connection with Naziism at all.

This work was performed, so far as the open propaganda itself was concerned, through the instrumentalities of the Reich's Ministry for Propaganda and Popular Enlightenment under control of that malignant intelligence, Paul Josef Göbbels. The broader program was not solely a publicity matter, and was operated chiefly through Party channels. The German capacity to learn was demonstrated by the contrast between World War I and World War II. In World War I the Germans lacked political motifs, professionalism, and coordination; in World War II they had all of these.

German Accomplishments. Three basic propaganda accomplishments were achieved by the Germans. First, in the political warfare field, they succeeded in making large sections of world opinion believe that the world's future was a choice between Communism and Fascism. Since they and the Communists agreed on this the point seemed well taken. Actually, there is no historical or economic justification for supposing that those two forms of dictatorship constitute a real choice in the first place, or that the civilized and truly free countries need ever depart from their ancient freedoms in the second place.

Second, in the strategic field, they made each victim seem the last. There was still hope that war would not arise, even while the Spanish Republic was being strangled before the eyes of the world. The British hoped that they could stay out even after Czechoslovakia fell. Astute though the Russians were, they hoped to stay out even after Britain and France fought. And as late as December 6, 1941, many Americans still believed that the United States would avoid war. This suited the Nazis' book; take them on one at a time.

Thirdly, in the purely psychological field the Germans used outright fright. They made their own people afraid of Communist liquidations. They brazenly showed movies of their blitzkriegs to the governing groups of prospective victims, just to lower morale. When one nation is really ready to fight, and the other knows it, the nation that doesn't want to fight can be reduced to something resembling a nervous breakdown by constant uncertainty. (The author was in Chungking during the summer of 1940, when the German propaganda agent, Wolf Schenke, showed these German movies to the Chinese leaders. The author asked for an invitation and did not get it; it was for Chinese only, said Schenke. But the Chinese were not awed, or made fearful of the power of Japan's ally. They simply said, "Nice movie . . . that's the kind of thing we used to do in the Ch'in dynasty," and let it go at that.)

The British-German Radio War. With the outbreak of war the British and Germans found radio at hand. Neither had to change broadcasting policies a great deal. Each could reach almost all of Europe on standard-wave; each could jam the other's wave lengths, never with complete success, and the struggle centered around a

Figure 14: Radio Program Leaflet, Anzio, 1944. These leaflets were dropped by the Germans on American troops at Anzio in April 1944. They show an interesting tie-in between two forms of propaganda. The counterpropaganda to the British Broadcasting Corporation is slight; chief emphasis is on entertainment value of the German radio programs. (From photograph taken by Signal Corps and released through War Department Bureau of Public Relations.)

contest for attention. Who could get the most attention? Who could get the most credence? Who could affect the beliefs, emotions, loyalties of friendly, neutral, and enemy listeners the most?

The Germans showed evidence of real planning. Their public relations facilities were perfectly geared to their propaganda facilities. When the Germans wanted to build the British up for a let-down, they withheld military news favorable to themselves. During the fight for Norway, they even spread rumors of British successes, knowing that if British morale went up for a day or two, it would come down all the harder when authentic bad news came through the War Office. When the Germans wanted to turn on a war of nerves, their controlled press screamed against the victim; when they turned it off their press was silent. The Germans thus had the advantage of not needing to make much distinction between news, publicity, and propaganda. All three served the same purpose, the immediate needs of the Reich.

The Germans put on the following types of news propaganda:

(1) Official OKW (*Oberkommando der Wehrmacht*, or *Wehrmacht* HQ) communiqués. (These rarely departed from the truth, though they naturally gave favorable situations in detail and unfavorable ones scantily.)

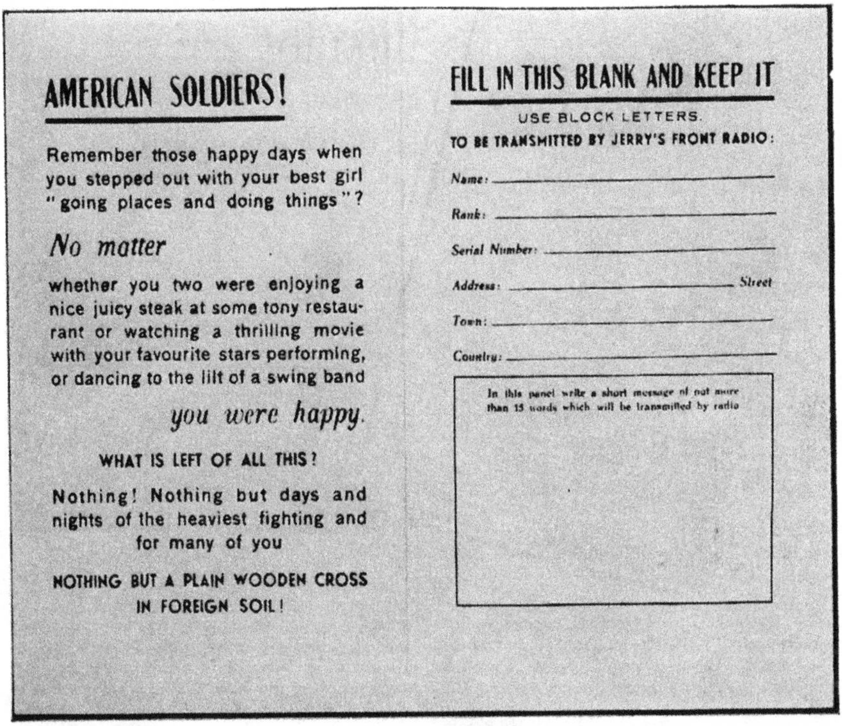

AMERICAN SOLDIERS!

Remember those happy days when you stepped out with your best girl "going places and doing things"?

No matter

whether you two were enjoying a nice juicy steak at some tony restaurant or watching a thrilling movie with your favourite stars performing, or dancing to the lilt of a swing band

you were happy.

WHAT IS LEFT OF ALL THIS?

Nothing! Nothing but days and nights of the heaviest fighting and for many of you

NOTHING BUT A PLAIN WOODEN CROSS IN FOREIGN SOIL!

FILL IN THIS BLANK AND KEEP IT

USE BLOCK LETTERS.

TO BE TRANSMITTED BY JERRY'S FRONT RADIO:

Name: ____________

Rank: ____________

Serial Number: ____________

Address: ____________ Street

Town: ____________

Country: ____________

In this panel write a short message of not more than 15 words which will be transmitted by radio

Figure 15: Radio Leaflet Surrender Form, Anzio, 1944. Willingness of prisoners to surrender sometimes involves speedy communication of their names to their families, as in the preceding illustrations. At other times, prisoners are very unwilling to be identified and want their faces masked. This leaflet combines radio program announcements with the standard surrender pass.

(2) Official government releases, marked by considerable dignity, possessing more political content than the military communiqués.

(3) News of the world, part of it repeated from the British radio, part plain non-controversial news (for stuffing), and part (the most important part) news of genuine curiosity value to the listeners but which, at the same time, had the propaganda effect of damaging belief in the Allied cause.

(4) Feature items, comparable to feature articles in newspapers, which tried to concentrate on a single topic or theme.

(5) Recognized commentators, speaking openly and officially.

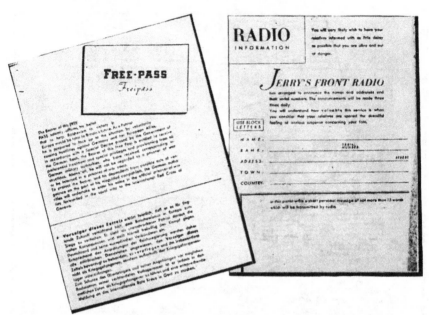

Figure 16: Invitation to Treason. Another German leaflet, also from Anzio, combines the radio surrender-notice form with a political invitation to Britishers to commit treason. The Germans had a few British traitors in their "Legion of St. George," and a few American civilian renegades, but in general this line of appeal was useless. The last paragraph of the appeal is such naïve trickery that it probably aroused suspicion in the minds of the men it was supposed to persuade.

(6) Pseudonymous commentators, pretending to speak from a viewpoint different from that of the German Government, but who were announced as being broadcast over the official German radio system. (Of these the British traitor William Joyce, since hanged, known as "Lord Haw Haw," was the most notorious. His colleagues were the American traitors Fred Kaltenbach and Douglas Chandler. At the end of the war Chandler was tried in Boston and sentenced to life imprisonment but Kaltenbach fell into Soviet custody and died.)

(7) Falsified stations, which pretended to have nothing at all to do with Germany. (The "New British Broadcasting Company" transmitted defeatist propaganda with a superficial anti-German tone. Others took a strong Communist line and sought to build up opposition to the British government within England.)

(8) Falsified quotations on the official German radio. (Sometimes it was easier to make up an imaginary foreign source, ostensibly quoted in the German program, rather than to set up a special fake program for the purpose.)

(9) "Planted" news sources quoted on the German radio. (A great deal of the German news was culled out of Swedish, Spanish and other papers which were either secretly German-controlled or which—as in the case of the United States papers involved—were so sympathetic to Germany that they voluntarily printed German-inspired news which the Nazis could then quote from a "neutral" or "enemy" source.)

(10) Open falsification of BBC (British Broadcasting Company, the official British agency) materials—at which the Germans were not necessarily caught by their ordinary listeners, but at which BBC caught them.

(11) Ghost voices and ghost programs, transmitted on legitimate Allied wave lengths when the Allied transmitters went off the air, or else interrupting the Allied broadcasts by transmitting simultaneously.

Of all these, it was soon found that the communiqués and government releases were the most important, although the bulk of the station time had to be diversified with other types of program. The Germans and British both found that radio was important as a starting point for news. It was more valuable to have the press (as in England) or rumor (as in Germany) pass along an item than it was to rely on the direct listeners. Each side sought to make opinion analyses of the enemy; some of the British studies were clever in technique. The radio propagandists had to ask themselves *why* they made propaganda. It is simple to make mischief, spreading rumors or putting practical jokes into circulation. Such antics do not necessarily advance a military-political cause. Sustained psychological warfare required—as both British and German radio soon found out—a deliberate calculation of the particular enemy

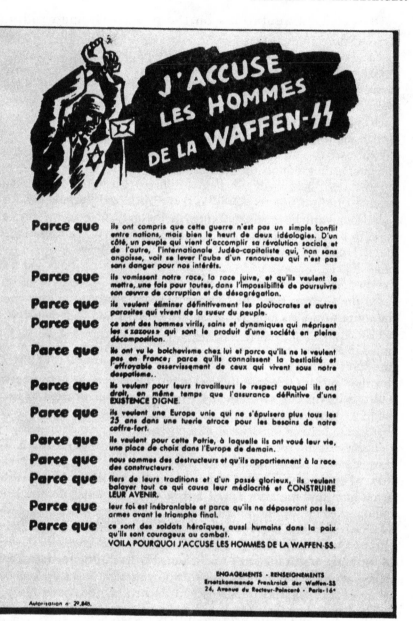

Figure 17: Anti-Radio Leaflet. Sometimes ground-distributed leaflets were used in an attempt to counteract enemy radio propaganda. This leaflet, circulated in France by the Nazis, uses the form of an Allied leaflet and accuses the Armed SS of wanting such things as a decent Europe, and end to atrocious killings every twenty-five years, and a worthy life. Allied broadcasters are identified as Jews.

frame of mind to be cultivated over a long period of time. When radio stations had to broadcast day after day whether anything happened or not, it became difficult to continue to circulate news without faking it and losing the confidence of enemy listeners.

On the German side, the German radio had the forced attention of the entire world. As long as the Germans had the strategic initiative for field warfare, they were in a position to make news scoops whenever it suited them. The security policies of the Allies often gave the Germans a monopoly of news on a given operation. There was never any danger that the Germans were not listened in on; the danger the Nazi operators had to worry about was disbelief. Hence the Germans tried to keep a moderate tone in their news, tried to prepare between crises for the news that would become sensational during crises.

The Germans soon learned a basic principle of war radio. They learned not to permit radio to run ahead of their military capacities. At first, when their spokesmen promised attainment of a given goal by a given time, and the army failed to live up to the schedule, the British radio picked up the unfulfilled promise and dangled it before the world as proof that the Germans were weakening. The Germans thereupon effected Army-radio liaison so that the radio people could promise only those things which the army was reasonably sure of delivering. When Allied propaganda analysis woke up to this fact, it added one more source of corroboratory intelligence to be checked. (See chapter 7.)

The British had their hands full getting news out in the languages of the occupied countries. It was immensely difficult for them to follow the politics of the underground. German counterespionage, under the deadly *Sicherheitsdienst*, made it difficult to keep track of opinion in the occupied countries. Work against Naziism depended on the temper of the people; propaganda against collaborators had to distinguish between outright evil collaborators and those public officials who stayed on out of a sense of mistaken or necessary duty. The British did not necessarily announce themselves at any time as anti-Communist, and collaborated for short-range purposes with Communists all over the Continent. Mr.

Churchill himself shifted his North Balkan political support from Mikhailovich to Broz-Tito. But it was vitally necessary to know just how and when to change support from one group to the other. Since the undergrounds had very few radio transmitters, and none of these was reliable during most of the war, the British faced the task of providing radio facilities for all of the occupied countries. The consequence was to make their radio warfare highly sensitive to politics; they had to address the right people with the right language at the right time, on penalty of failure.

To effect this end, the British set up an agency which never had an American counterpart, the Political Warfare Executive (known by its initials, PWE). This agency had representation from the War Office, the Admiralty, the Foreign Office, and the Ministry of Information. The PWE was the policy-servicing and coordinating agency for all British external propaganda, and left the execution of its operations to the Ministry of Information (MOI) and to the British Broadcasting Corporation (BBC). British radio propaganda maintained a high level of effectiveness. American officials and propagandists often complained that the British were running the entire war in their own national interest. The charge was unjust. The British had facilities for knowing exactly what they wished to do and when they wished to do it. If the Americans came along without clear policies or propaganda purposes, it was natural that the British should take the lead and let the Americans string along if they wished. Furthermore, the British were usually scrupulous in yielding to America's primary interest in areas they felt to be American problems—Japan, China, the Philippines. They were least cooperative when the OWI tried to spread the ideals of Mr. Henry Wallace in Burma or to explain the CIO-PAC to the Hindus.

No clear victor emerged from the Anglo-German radio war; the victory of the United Nations gave the British the last say. In the opinion of many, the British were one war ahead of the United States. They had profited by their World War I experience, and by their two years' operational lead which they had on the Americans. But side-by-side with the Germans, it is harder to appraise their net achievements. The British had immense political advantages; the resentment of a conquered continent worked for them. But they had disadvantages too. The enemy worked from the starting point of a fanatical and revolutionary philosophy; the British had the tedious old world to offer. The postwar interrogations of civilians in Germany showed that an amazingly high proportion of them had heard BBC broadcasts, and that many of the ideas and attitudes which the British propagandized were actually transmitted to the enemy. On the British side, it is almost impossible to find any surviving traces of the effect of Nazi propaganda. Had the war been purely a radio war this test might be conclusive. But if psychological warfare supplements combat, combat certainly supplements propaganda. The great British and American air raids over Europe unquestionably created an intense interest in British and American plans and purposes.

It is historically interesting to note that the Germans went on fighting psychological warfare even after the death of Hitler and the surrender of the jury-rigged government of Grossadmiral Karl Doenitz, which functioned 6-23 May 1945 at Flensburg under Allied toleration. This resulted from the inability of the 21st Army Group swiftly to initiate information control. The Flensburg radio, still under Nazi direction, emphasized Anglo-American differences with the Soviet Union in every possible way short of direct appeals. German naval radio also carried on propaganda for a while, using topics such as the sportsmanship of the German surrender, the hatred of the German Navy for atrocities committed by the Nazis, and the usefulness of the phantom government to the Western Allies.

Black Propaganda. Subversive operations formed a major part of the Nazi pre-belligerent effort. The Germans planted or converted quislings wherever they could, and when they failed to have time to prearrange stooges they converted them rapidly after arrival. (A major cause of the German defeat is to be found in the fantastic political policies followed in the Ukraine and neighboring Soviet Socialist Republics. In these areas, despite the Soviet

boast that Russia had no fifth columnists within her borders, the
Germans found thousands of helpers. The Nazis organized a large
army (General Vlassov's Russian Army of Liberation) out of Soviet prisoners, and these troops were usable and docile. But in the
political warfare field the Germans were too cocksure. They let their
men go wild in orgies of cruelty against the local population; the
economic system went entirely to pieces. The natives then became
convinced that the worst possible conditions of Sovietism were
infinitely better than the best that Naziism could offer.)

These subversive groups were formed by political means. Propaganda aid was offered to such an extent that it was often difficult to tell how much of the quisling movement was spontaneously
native, and how much mere cover for a purely German operation.

In the latter phase of the European war, the Russian Communists followed the German Nazi example of having tame natives
ready to take over the government of occupied areas. In Poland,
the so-called Lublin Committee took over the government from the
constitutional Polish Government-in-exile at London. In
Jugoslavia, the Russian-trained propagandist, Tito, seized the leadership from the recognized Minister of War, Draja Mikhailovich,
after the British and American governments had shifted their support to him; later Mikhailovich was put to death. The Russian army
brought along to Germany a considerable number of German Communists. In Czechoslovakia the strength of the constitutional regime was such as to compel the pro-Russians to allow the prewar
leadership a precarious toehold in the new government. The same
cadres of sympathetic persons who had been useful as propaganda
sources for psychological warfare during the period of hostilities
became useful instruments of domination after hostilities ended.
The British and Americans, with their belief that government
should spring from the liberated and defeated peoples, did not
prepare and equip comparable groups to rival the Communist candidates; only in Italy and Greece did the friends of the Western
Allies stay in power, and then only because they were the nearest
equivalent of *de jure* authorities. In the Scandinavian and Low
Countries the national leadership reemerged without prodding or

interference by the Western Allies; they passed from the sphere of psychological warfare (that is, of being someone's cover) to that of world politics.

Specific black propaganda operations were of considerable value. However, black propaganda is more difficult to appraise than overt propaganda. Analytical and historical studies, gauging the results obtained by Black operations in relation to their cost, are not yet available. (Certain particular operations are described later in this book, chapters 12 and 13.)

American Operations: OWI and OSS. Long after the outbreak of war in the Far East, and even after the coming of full war in Europe, neither the civilian nor military portions of the American government possessed propaganda facilities. This is not as serious as it may sound, for the United States is lucky in possessing a people well agreed on most fundamentals. The commercial press, radio, magazine, and book publishing facilities of the country for the most part expressed a national point of view without being prodded. (The isolationist issue never brought in the question of America's basic character.) Before the war, and even after the government entered the field, private American news and publishing continued to engage in operations which had the effect if not the intention of propaganda. OWI at its most vigorous could scarcely have reached the audience that had been built up by the *Time-Life-Fortune* group, not to mention the *Reader's Digest*, both of which became truly global in coverage during the war years. American movies already had a world-wide audience. The propaganda turned out unwittingly by such agencies may not have had the gloss and political smoothness of Dr. Paul Josef Göbbels' best productions but it had something no government propaganda had—the possession of a readership all of which was unmistakably voluntary, obtained by the appeal of authentic interest and entertainment—and proved by an ability to charm money out of people's pockets.

The American problem of propaganda was thus not a simple one. Total psychological warfare was out of reach if we were to remain a free people. Otherwise the simple-seeming thing to have done would have been to put a government supervisor in every newspaper, radio station and magazine in the country, and coordinate the whole bunch of them together in the national interest. Simple-seeming. Actually, such an attempt would have been utter madness, touching off a furious political fight within the country and meeting legal obstacles which would have remained insurmountable as long as there was a Constitution with courts to enforce it. The simplest official action which the United States could take was therefore hedged about by the presence of private competitors who would watch it enviously, jealous of their established rights and privileges, and by the operational interference which vigorous private media would have on public media.

The then Mr. or Colonel, later General, William Donovan had tasted the delights of political warfare when President Roosevelt sent him to Belgrade to talk the Serbs into fighting instead of surrendering. He was successful; the Serbs fought. He came back to the United States with a practical knowledge of what political warfare could do if qualified personnel operated on the spot. The outbreak of the Russo-German war lent urgency to American action in the political-intelligence field as well as in the propaganda field. On 11 July, 1941, President Roosevelt issued an order appointing Colonel Donovan as Coordinator of Information. The agency became known by the initials COI.[4]

The primary mission of COI was the collection of information and its processing for immediate use. Large numbers of experts were brought into its Research and Analysis Branch, designed to do for the United States in weeks what the research facilities of the Germans and Japanese had done for them over a matter of years. The inflow of material was tremendous and the gearing of scholarship to the war effort produced large quantities of political, sociological, geographic, economic and other monographs, most of them carefully classified SECRET, even when they were copied out of books in the Library of Congress. However, it was not the research wing of the COI that entered the broadcasting field.

Radio work was first done by an agency within COI called FIS— Foreign Information Service. In the few months before Pearl Harbor the group became organized in New York under the leadership of Robert Sherwood, the dramatist, and got a start in supplying the radio companies with material. The radio scripts were poorly checked; there was chaos in the matter of policy; little policing was possible, and the output reflected the enthusiasm of whatever individual happened to be near the microphone. Colonel Donovan had moved into this work without written and exclusive authorization from the White House; hence there followed a lamentable interval of almost two years' internal struggle between American agencies—a struggle not really settled until the summer of 1943, well into the second year of war. The occasion for struggle arose from lack of uniform day-to-day propaganda policy and from an unclear division of authority between the operating agencies. But the work was done.

Radio operations had to be coordinated with strategy on the one hand and foreign policy on the other, and we sought to develop methods for doing this. It is significant that all the major difficulties of American psychological warfare were administrative and not operational. There was never any serious trouble about getting the facilities, the writers, the translators, the telecommunications technicians. What caused trouble were problems of personality and personal power, resulting chiefly from the lack of any consensus on the method or organization of propaganda administration.

Military Intelligence Division had created an extremely secret psychological warfare office at about the time that the COI was established; this had broad intelligence and policy functions, but no operational facilities. It was headed by Lieutenant Colonel Percy Black, who began auspiciously by putting Dr. Edwin Guthrie in office as his senior psychological adviser. This ultra-quiet office was called Special Study Group; it and the COI developed very loose cooperative relations, consisting chiefly of SSG making suggestions to COI which COI might or might not use as it saw fit. Meanwhile, the Rockefeller Office was conducting independent broadcasts to Latin America; the Office of Facts and Figures was dispensing domestic information; and at the height of the psychological warfare

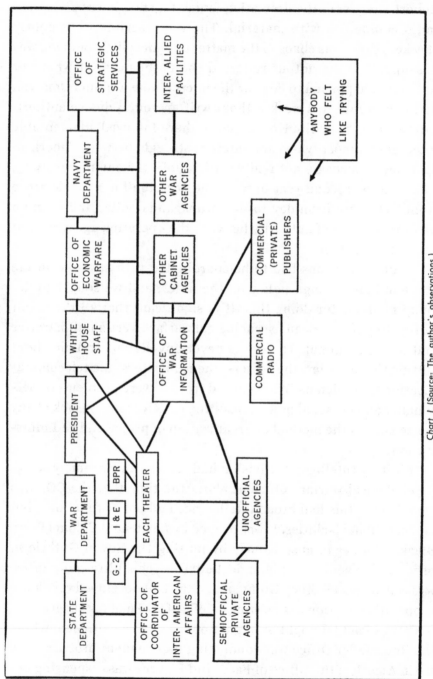

Chart I (Source: The author's observations.)

campaigning, there were at least nine unrelated agencies in Washington, all directly connected with psychological warfare, and none actually subject to the control of any of the others.[5]

A year of wrangling produced the solution, after a Joint Psychological Warfare Committee had been set up under the Joint Chiefs of Staff, and had failed to fulfill an effective policy-supervising function. On 13 June, 1942, the President created the Office of War Information. This agency was given control directly or indirectly over all domestic propaganda, and over white propaganda abroad, except for the Western Hemisphere, which remained under the Rockefeller Committee in the State Department. The FIS was taken from the COI, and the COI took on the new name of OSS—Office of Strategic Services—under which it retained three major functions:

(1) continuation of scholastic and informal intelligence;
(2) black propaganda operations (given explicit authority only in March, 1943);
(3) subversive operations, in collaboration with regular military authority.

The OWI was placed under Mr. Elmer Davis, a Rhodes scholar and novelist who had become one of the nation's most popular radio commentators. The FIS was perpetuated under the control of Mr. Robert Sherwood, who had a most extraordinary coterie of odd personalities assisting him: Socialist refugees, advertising men, psychologists, psychoanalysts (of both the licensed and lay varieties), professional promoters, theatrical types, German professors, a commercial attaché, young men just out of college, oil executives, and popular authors (novelists, slick writers, Pulitzer winners, pulp writers, humorists, poets and a professional pro-Japanese writer, fresh off the Imperial Japanese Embassy payroll).

The War Department agency, under the Military Intelligence Service of G-2, had been renamed Psychological Warfare Branch and had executed within the G-2 structure the equivalent of a knight's move in chess, ending up at a new place on the TO with no observable change in function or authority; it had passed under the authority of Colonel (later Brigadier General) Oscar Solbert, a West Pointer with wide international and business experience; he had been out of the Army as a top official with Eastman Kodak, after a cosmopolitan army career which sent him all over Europe and gave him one tour of duty as a White House aide. With the establishment of OWI, Colonel Solbert's office fissiparated like an amoeba; the civilian half of Psychological Warfare Branch, with a few officers, went over to OWI to be a brain-trust for the foreign broadcast experts, who failed to welcome this accession of talent; the military half remained as an MIS agency until 31 December, 1943, when OWI abolished its half and MIS cooperated by wiping out the other, leaving the War Department in the middle of a war with no official psychological warfare agency whatever, merely some liaison officers. Psychological warfare became the responsibility of designated individual officers in OPD—(the Operations Division of the General Staff), an outfit celebrated for conscientious overwork, as well as in MIS and the War Department got along very nicely. Meanwhile OWI and OSS fought one of the many battles of Washington, each seeking control of foreign propaganda. The D.C. and Manhattan newspapers ran columns on this fight, along with news of the fighting in Russia, Libya, and the Pacific. For one glorious moment of OSS, it seemed that the President had signed over all foreign propaganda functions conducted outside the United States to OSS, cutting the OWI out of everything except its New York and San Francisco transmitters; the OWI was stricken with gloom and collective indigestion. The next day, the mistake was rectified, and OWI triumphantly planned raids on the jurisdiction of OSS. Meanwhile, the following things were happening:

Highly classified plans for psychological warfare were being drafted for both the Joint and Combined Chiefs of Staff. These were discussed at various meetings and then classified a little higher, whereupon they were locked up, lest the propaganda writers and broadcasters see them and break security on them by obeying and applying them.

Broadcasts—thousands of words in dozens of languages—were transmitted to everyone on earth. They were written by persons

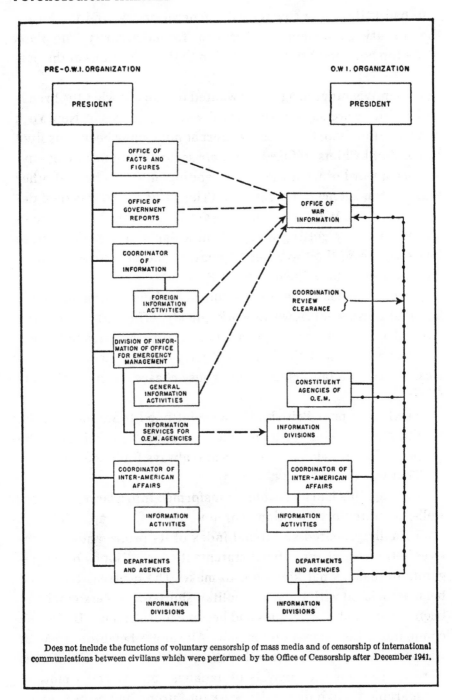

PRE-O.W.I. ORGANIZATION   O.W I. ORGANIZATION

Does not include the functions of voluntary censorship of mass media and of censorship of international communications between civilians which were performed by the Office of Censorship after December 1941.

Chart II (Source: Bureau of the Budget: *The United States at War,* Washington, 1947, p. 225.)

who had little if any contact with Federal policy, and none with the military establishment, except for formal security. The plans at the top bore no observable relation to the operations at the bottom.

When Washington agencies wanted to find out what the broadcasts really were saying, the actual working offices at New York and San Francisco, their feelings hurt at not having been consulted by the Joint Chiefs, refused (on *their* security ground) to let anyone see a word of what they were sending out. This baffled other Washington agencies a great deal. (The author, who was then detailed from the War Department to OWI, outflanked this move in one instance by getting a report on a San Francisco Japanese Broadcast from the Navy Department. It had been monitored by an American submarine out in the Pacific.)

Large overseas offices were set up at various foreign locations. Some of these went down to work quickly, efficiently, smoothly, and did a first-class job of presenting wartime America to foreign peoples; others, with the frailties of jerry-built government agencies, lapsed into inefficiency, wild goose chases, or internal quarrels.

Lastly, the poor British officials continued to wander around Washington, looking for their American opposite numbers in the propaganda field—looking for one and always finding a dozen.

That was in 1942-1943.

By 1945, this had all become transformed into a large, well run, well-integrated organization. Three weeks before Japan fell, the OWI finally prepared an official index of its propaganda "Directives"—that, is, of the official statement of what kinds of propaganda to make, what kinds not to make. The overseas units had been associated with the metropolitan short-wave. Personnel had been disciplined. Techniques had become more precise. Under the command of Lieutenant Commander Alexander Leighton, an M.D. who was also a psychiatrist and anthropologist, careful techniques were devised for the analysis of Japanese and German morale. Comparable though dissimilar work on Europe had been done by a staff associated with Harold Lasswell. The propaganda expert

Figure 18: Anti-Exhibit Leaflet. In the China Theater, we heard that the Japanese had organized a big exhibit in Canton, showing the starved and apathetic population some pieces of shot-down planes as demonstration of defeat of American air power. We made up this leaflet quickly, and dropped it on the city while the exhibit was still in progress. (China, 1944.)

Leonard W. Doob had been appointed controlling and certifying officer for every single order of importance.

The military relationship had been clarified. The War Department, acting through G-2, had reestablished a psychological warfare office under the new name of Propaganda Branch, under the successive commands of Lieutenant Colonel John B. Stanley, Lieutenant Colonel Bruce Bottles, and Colonel Dana W. Johnston. The new branch undertook no operations whatever, but connected War Department with OWI and OSS for policy and liaison, and represented one-half of the Joint Chiefs of Staff (an appropriate naval officer from a comparable office representing the other half) at the weekly policy meetings of OWI. Military needs in psychological warfare had been settled by regarding the Theaters in this respect as autonomous, and leaving to the respective Theater Commanders the definition of their relationships with OWI and OSS, and their use of each. OSS and OWI had passed the stage of rival growth, and consulted one another enough to prevent operational interference. Each had sufficient military or naval supervision to prevent interference with cryptographic security, communication and deception operations.

The Lessons. The major job of psychological warfare passed to the Theaters. In some theaters this was kept by the commander directly under his own immediate supervision, and OWI was used simply as a propaganda service of supply. In others, OWI was an almost independent agent. In some places, OWI worked with OSS as in the European Theater, in others independently, as in the China-Burma-India Theater. In one, it worked completely without OSS (SWPA), since General MacArthur did not let OSS into his Theater at all. (OSS got in the general area anyhow; with Navy permission, it turned up blithely, highly nautical on Saipan.) These Theater establishments were the ones that set up local standard-wave programs which the enemy could hear in volume. They provided the loudspeaker units which were taken right into combat. They serviced the ground and air combat echelons with leaflets as needed. They moved along behind the advances, opening up information booths and explaining to liberated natives why each did not get the four freedoms, the three meals a day, and the new pair of shoes he thought he had been promised by the American radio.

These military establishments are better described under operations, since it was their functioning which defined—down to the limit of present-day experience—American military doctrine concerning the conduct of psychological warfare in theaters of war. In concluding the historical summary of psychological warfare, it is interesting to look at three major points which emerge plainly from the experience of World War II—points which either were not discovered in World War I, or else failed to make an impact on the minds of the responsible officials and informed citizens.

The first of these is simple. It became almost a litany with Colonel Oscar Solbert, when he sought to indoctrinate civilian geniuses with military proprieties: *Psychological warfare is a function of command.* If command chooses to exercise it, it will succeed. If command neglects it, or if it is operated independently of military, command, it will either interfere with the conduct of war proper, or it will be wasted. It took us two bitter years to learn this lesson. Political warfare cannot be waged without direct access to the White House and the Department of State; field operations cannot be conducted unless they meet at some common staff point with field command. No one can succeed in improvising alleged policy and presenting that policy as United States policy, and get away with it. Sooner or later actual policy catches up with him. In the field, no civilian can write leaflets for air or ground distribution unless he has some idea of when, where, why, and how they will be used.

The second lesson of World War II, set forth by Colonel Solbert and Dr. Edwin Guthrie was simply this: *Atrocity propaganda begets atrocity.* Everyone knows that war is cruel, sad, shameful to the soul of man; everyone knows that it hurts, degrades, injures the human body; everyone knows that it is not pleasant to undergo, nor even to look at. If any particular war is worth fighting, it is

worth fighting for some reason other than the crazily obvious one—
the fact that it is already war. It is a poor statesman or general
who cannot give his troops and people an inspiring statement of
their own side in war. Atrocity propaganda reacts against war in
general; meanwhile, it goads the enemy into committing more
atrocities. The anti-atrocity rule was not lifted in World War II
(save for one or two notable exceptions, such as President
Roosevelt's delayed announcement of the Japanese having executed the Doolittle flyers) except for the specific purpose of preventing some atrocity that seemed about to occur in a known situation from actually occurring. Atrocity propaganda heats up the
imagination of troops, makes them more liable to nervous or
psychoneurotic strain. It increases the chances of one's own side
committing atrocities in revenge for the ones alleged or reported.
Furthermore, atrocity propaganda scares the enemy out of surrendering, and gives the enemy command an easier responsibility in
persuading their troops to fight with last-ditch desperation.

The third lesson was equally simple: *America does not normally produce psychological warfare personnel in peacetime, and
if such personnel are to be needed again, they will have to be
trained especially and in advance.*

Qualifications for Psychological Warfare. Effective psychological warfare requires the combination of four skills in a single
individual:

(1) An effective working knowledge of U.S. government administration and policy, so that the purposes and plans of the government may be correctly interpreted.

(2) An effective knowledge of correct military and naval procedure and of staff operations, together with enough understanding of
the arts of warfare, whether naval or military, to adjust propaganda

---

Figure 19: Propaganda Against Propaganda. As an occasional stunt, propaganda is directed against
propaganda. Hitler did so in his book, *Mein Kampf.* The leaflet, shown in the original and in
facsimile, was used by the Allies on the Germans in the West. A German leaflet, addressed to
their own troops ("defensive propaganda"), was picked up, X'd out, copied, and refuted.

utterance to military situations and to practical propaganda operations in forms which will dovetail.

(3) Professional knowledge of the media of information, or of at least one of them (book-publishing, magazines, newspapers, radio, advertising in its various branches), or of some closely related field (practical political canvassing, visual or adult education, etc.).

(4) Intimate, professional-level understanding of a given area (Italy, Japan, New Guinea, Kwangtung, Algeria), based on first-hand acquaintance, knowledge of the language, traditions, history, practical politics, and customs.

On top of these, there may be a possible fifth skill to make the individual perfect:

(5) Professional scientific understanding of psychology, anthropology, sociology, history, political science, or a comparable field.

The man who steps up and says that he meets all five of these qualifications is a liar, a genius, or both.

There is no perfect psychological warrior.

However—and the qualification is important—each psychological warfare team represents a composite of these skills. Some members have two or three to start with, the others virtually none. But all of the personnel, except for men with peculiarly specialized jobs (ordnance experts; cryptographers; translators; calligraphers), end up with a professionalism that blends these together. They may not meet professional standards as officials-officers-journalists-Japanologists-psychoanalysts when they return from psychological warfare operations against the Japanese, but they have met men who are one or more of these, and have picked up the rudiments of each skill—enough, at least, to suspect what they do not know.

The advertising man or newspaperman (skill 3) who goes into psychological warfare must learn something of the enemy, neutral

Figure 20: Re-Use of Enemy Propaganda. Leaflets sometimes develop an enemy pictorial or slogan theme and use it effectively against the original disseminators. Employing the colors and insignia of the U.S. Air Force, this Nazi leaflet for Frenchmen makes no attempt to minimize American bombing to the French. Instead, it uses the Allied heading, "The hour of liberation will ring. . . ." Then it adds the grim point, "Make your will, make your will."

or friendly groups whom he addresses (skill 4), something of United States civilian government procedures (skill 1), something of military or naval organization and operations (skill 2) and ideally something of psychology or sociology or economics, depending on the topic of his work (skill 5).

The psychological soldier deals with enemy troops in their *civilian* capacity; he addresses them as *men*, he appeals to their non-military characteristics in most instances, and he does not follow sportsmanship, as men did in other wars, by helping the enemy command maintain discipline. Furthermore, the soldier works with writers, illustrators, translators, script-writers, announcers and others whose skills are primarily civilian, and he takes his policy cues from the civilian authority at the top of the war effort. An infantry colonel does not have to worry about what the Secretary of State is saying, if the colonel is on the field of battle. But an officer detailed to psychological warfare must remain attuned to civilian life even if he has seen no one out of khaki for two months straight.

Personnel was probably the biggest field problem of the entire war. Should psychological warfare be needed again, it will take careful culling of personnel to obtain the necessary staff and operators. The continuation of psychological warfare techniques, in part at least, by both civilian and military agencies in time of peace will, it may be hoped, provide the U.S. with a cadre for the next time. Very little of the living experience of the Creel Committee was carried over into OWI. Walter Lippmann, who had worked with both Creel and Blankenhorn, was not a participant. Carl Crow, the advertising man and writer from Shanghai, worked on China for the Creel Committee in World War I and on China again for OWI in World War II. He was exceptional, and took no major part in setting up indoctrination. One of the OWI executives in 1946, shortly after his return to civilian life, read James Mock and Cedric Larson's account of the Creel Committee, *Words That Won the War* (Princeton, 1939); his interest was avid. When he finished, he said,

"Good Lord, those people made the same mistakes we made!"

He had forgotten that the Creel Committee record had been available all the way through.

Effects of American Operations. The net effects of the work of civilian-operated propaganda are hard to appraise because the radio broadcasts and leaflets for civilians were designed to have a long-range effect on the enemy. Statistical computations come to nothing. It would appear likely that some parts of our psychological warfare actually lengthened the war and made it more difficult to win. The "unconditional surrender" formula, the publicity given to proposals for the pastoralization of Germany, the emphasis on Japanese savagery with its implied threat of counter-savagery were not overlooked by the enemy authorities. It is certain that other parts of our psychological warfare speeded up the end of the war, saved lives, increased the war effort which was enormous when measured in terms of the expenditure of manpower, matériel and time involved.

One operation alone probably repaid the entire cost of OWI throughout the war. The Japanese offered to surrender, but with conditions. We responded, rejecting the conditions. The Japanese government pondered its reply, but while it pondered, B-29s carried leaflets to all parts of Japan, giving the text of the Japanese official offer to surrender. This act alone would have made it almost impossibly difficult for the Japanese government to whip its people back into frenzy for suicidal prolongation of war. The Japanese texts were checked between Washington and Hawaii by radiophotograph and cryptotelephone; the plates were put into the presses at Saipan; the big planes took off, leaflets properly loaded in the right kind of leaflet bombs. It took Americans three and a half years to reach that point, but we reached it. Nowhere else in history can there be found an instance of so many people being given so decisive a message, all at the same time, at the very dead-point between war and peace.

The Japanese had done their best against us, but their best was not enough. We got in the last word, and made sure it was the last.

Soviet Experience. Soviet psychological warfare used Communist party facilities during World War II, turning them on and off as needed. But Soviet psychological war efforts were not characterized by blind reliance on past experience. They showed a very real inventiveness, and the political policies behind them were both far-sighted and far-reaching.

The Soviet government was the one government in the world which could be even more totalitarian than Nazi Germany. Many Americans may consider this a moral disadvantage, but in psychological warfare it has very heavy compensating advantages. The Soviet people were propaganda-conscious to an intense degree, but the authorities took no chances. Revolutionary Communist themes were brilliantly intermingled with patriotic Russian items. Army officers were given extraordinary privileges. Everyone was given epaulettes. The Communist revolutionary song, the famous *Internationale*, was discarded in favor of a new Soviet hymn. History was rewritten. The Czars were honored again. The Church was asked to pray for victory. The Soviet officials were able to tailor their social system to fit the propaganda. They did so, even to the name of the war. They call it the Great Patriotic War. Outsiders may murmur, "What war is not?" But the Russian people liked it, and the regime used traditionalism and nationalism to cinch Communism in the Soviet Union.

In their combat propaganda the Russians were equally ruthless and realistic. They appealed to the memory of Frederick the Great of Prussia, they reminded the Germans of Bismarck's warning not to commit their forces in the East, they appealed to the German Junker caste against the unprofessional Nazi scum who were ruining the German army, and they used every propaganda trick that had ever been heard of. They turned prisoners into a real military asset by employing them in propaganda, and talked a whole staff of Nazi generals into the Free Germany movement.

Only in radio did the Russians retain some of their old revolutionary fire with its irritating qualities for non-Communist peoples. This was explicable in terms of the audience. The Russians could keep their domestic propaganda half-secret by imposing a censor-ship ban on those parts of it, or those comments on it, which they did not wish known to Communists abroad. The censorship was a permanent institution, in war and out, and therefore did not im-pose special difficulty. They could keep their front-line propaganda quiet, since they did not allow their Allies to send military observ-ers up front, and the Nazis could be counted on not to tell the world about effective anti-Nazi propaganda. But their radio propaganda had to be audible to everyone. Hence the radio propaganda was the least ingenious in using reactionary themes effectively. The Rus-sians and Germans both used black radio, but since each policed the home audience rigorously against the other, it is possible that the efforts cancelled out.

Japanese Developments. The Japanese invented little in psy-chological warfare. They made excellent and judicious use of news to the American audience. They actually got much more official Japanese news into the American press during the war years than they had succeeded in placing during peacetime, when they had offices in American cities. They did so by maintaining the regular Domei news service in English-language Morse wireless for the American press, ready-edited for the newspaper offices. They put by-lines on the stories and it is said they sometimes even told the American newspapers: "Please hold until nine AM Eastern War Time. Thank You. Domei." In dealing with Asiatic audiences, spe-cial Japanese *butai* did a great deal of black propaganda along with subversive operations, but they displayed little initiative as to the use of basic techniques. Their chief merits were industry, patience, and the delivery of a first-class news service.

Chinese Uses. The Chinese Communist forces broke all records for certain specialized aspects of combat propaganda. Japanese prisoners were given cordial welcome, better food than they had in the Army, the company of maidens, rich gifts, and political in-doctrination about the freedom of Japan. These soldiers then went with the Chinese Communists back to the front lines and talked

Japanese sentries out of their strong-points. The Yenan forces went
to great pains with this propaganda, and even "elected" a Japanese prisoner to the City Council of Yenan. The author talked with
the Political Director of the Chinese Communist authority at Yenan,
and with some of the Japanese in Communist China. There was
evidence of a real understanding of the problems of the Japanese
common soldier, and of real sympathy with him, which the Japanese enlisted men were quick to feel. The Communists went so far
as to throw gift packages into the Japanese lines—not booby-traps,
just nice gifts with the polite request for a reply. They learned the
names of Japanese field telephone operators, and then spliced into
the line and argued politics with them in a rough and jolly way.
When they had enough prisoners they kept the most promising
converts for political training. They fed the ordinary prisoners well,
entertained them royally, and sent them back to their own lines
with the suggestion that the Chinese Communists would appreciate it if their good Japanese brethren would in combat please shoot
their rifles in the air, thus making sure of not hitting Communists
while at the same time avoiding unnecessary trouble with the Japanese officers.

Under "Chiang the Chairman," the Chinese national government waged a dignified, humane kind of psychological warfare
against Japan. Few people remember an odd chapter out of modern history, the Chinese bombardment of Nagasaki, although it is
possible that Asiatic historians of the future will make a substantial contrast between the Chinese who struck the first blow at that
city and the Americans who struck the last. Shortly after the outbreak of the full quasi-war between China and Japan in 1937, the
Generalissimo ordered his bombers to attack Japan. American-
built Chinese bombers appeared over Kyushu, the first invaders to
show up since the shoguns repelled Kublai Khan 656 years earlier.
But instead of dropping bombs, they dropped leaflets denouncing
aggression and inferentially pointing out that while the Japanese
were uncivilized enough to bomb their fellow-Asiatics, the Chinese
were too civilized to undertake reprisals in kind.

The Generalissimo's troops also had fraternization and front-line propaganda, but not to the extent to which the Chinese Communists did. The Generalissimo himself followed a very liberal (not in the Leftist but the true sense) political line toward Japan. He uttered no threat of vengeance. He was the first leader of a great nation to say that the Japanese Emperor question was to be settled by letting the Japanese themselves choose their own form of government after the war was all over. He had Japanese on his political staffs—democratic persons whom his officials encouraged—and regular Japanese broadcasts were kept up throughout the war on the Chungking radio.

NOTES:

[1] For a pro-Hitler view of the world, see Wyndham Lewis' *Hitler*, London, 1931, if a copy is to be found. The author would probably prefer for the book to disappear. It is an eloquent, very pro-Nazi book, putting the Hitlerite terminology into the English language and—what is more important—infusing into the clumsy German pattern of thinking-and-feeling a lightness of touch which makes Naziism more palatable. The book converted no one in its time, and is not apt to do harm at this late date; but it will make the English-reading reader understand some of the novelty, the revolutionary freshness, the bold unorthodoxy which made millions of people turn to Hitlerism as an escape from the humdrum heartbreak of Weimar Germany. Much of the book is devoted to the problem of power—street-fighting, mass demonstrations, slogans, symbolisms—which so fascinated the Nazis.

[2] See Carl J. Friedrich, *The New Belief in the Common Man*, Brattleboro (Vermont), 1945. chapter III, "Independence of Thought and Propaganda," pp. 81-120, for a cogent discussion of this mentality. The present author, in *Government in Republican China*, New York, 1938, pp. 8-23, describes in epitome the method whereby the ancient

Confucian leadership of China, while propaganda-conscious, used ideology as an economical, stable method of
control and avoided its maleficent features. In one of the
few poorly argued passages of a great work, Arnold J.
Toynbee overlooks this peculiar characteristic of Confu-
cianism and merely equates the Confucian dogma with
those of other "universal churches" (*A Study of History*,
London, 1939, vol. V., especially pages 654-5).

[3] People's Commissariat of Justice of the U.S.S.R., *Report of Court Proceedings in the Case of the Anti-Soviet
Trotskyite Centre . . ., Verbatim Report*, Moscow, 1937,
page 111. These trials were themselves propaganda; in this
particular instance, propaganda of a rather poor order,
since they failed to convince the foreign public and presumably persuaded only those portions of the Russian
public who were so gullible that they needed no further
persuading. For a brilliant illumination of them in terms
of a readable novel, see Arthur Koestler, *Darkness at
Noon*, New York 1941; the same author also has a book of
essays on the totalitarian mentality under the rather fancy
title, *The Yogi and the Commissar*, New York, 1945. On
the same subject, see Louis Fischer's *Men and Politics*,
New York, 1942.

[4] This document establishing the COI, along with the
other major documents pertaining to American psychological warfare, may be found in J. P. Warburg's book
cited above, *Unwritten Treaty*.

[5] In the course of a routine day of work on overseas
propaganda in 1942, the author, who was then in SSG
of MIS, found it necessary to get in touch with Military
Intelligence proper, Naval Intelligence, the State Department, the office of the Assistant to the President, the
Office of Facts and Figures, the British Political Warfare
group (which was vainly seeking its American opposite
number), the Office of Civilian Defense, the Research
and Analysis Branch of the office of the Coordinator of
Information, the office of the Librarian of Congress, the
Foreign Information Service, and the Department of

Agriculture. Each of these either operated propaganda, or had policy or intelligence contributions to make. The Board of Economic Warfare naturally came into the field too. This was during a period of German and Japanese victories, so that even if propaganda had been coordinated, it probably would not have been much more effective than it was. From what could be figured out later, no real harm was done at this time. Nor was much achieved.

PART TWO
ANALYSIS, INTELLIGENCE, AND ESTIMATE OF THE SITUATION

CHAPTER 7
PROPAGANDA ANALYSIS

Opinion analysis pertains to what people think; propaganda analysis deals with what somebody is trying to make them think. Each form of analysis is a new and flourishing field in civilian social research; the bibliographies of Smith, Lasswell and Casey, and the current reviews in the *Public Opinion Quarterly*[1] demonstrate the existence of a large and growing literature on the subject. Each year, new textbooks in the field or current revisions of old ones can be counted on to bring scholastic and scientific findings up to date.

Technical writings on visual education, religious conversion, labor organization, practical politics, revolutionary agitation, and on commercial advertising have frequent bearing on propaganda analysis.

Propaganda cannot be analyzed in a logical vacuum. Every step in the operation is intensely practical. There is nothing timeless about it, other than that common sense which is based on the nature of man. The ancient Chinese three-character classic, from which several billion Chinese have tried to learn to read, says:

Jên chih ch'u
Hsing pên shan,
Hsing hsiang chin,
Hsi hsiang yüan.

Freely translated, this means, "When people are born, they all start good, but even though they all start out about the same, you

167

ought to see them after they have had time to become different from one another by picking up habits here and there!"[2] The common nature of man may be at the basis of all propaganda and politics, but incentives to action are found in the stimuli of varied everyday environments. Certain very elementary appeals can be made almost without reference to the personal everyday background ("cultural-historical milieu") of the person addressed. Yet in a matter as simple as staying alive or not staying alive in which it might be supposed that all human beings would have the same basic response—the difference between Japanese and Americans was found to be basic when it came to surrender. To Japanese soldiers, the verbal distinction between *surrender* and *cease honorable resistance* was as important as the difference between life and death. The Japanese would not survive at the cost of their honor, but if their honor were satisfied, they willingly gave up.

Propaganda is directed to the subtle niceties of thought by which people maintain their personal orientation in an unstable interpersonal world. Propaganda must use the language of the mother, the schoolteacher, the lover, the bully, the policeman, the actor, the ecclesiastic, the buddy, the newspaperman, all of them in turn. And propaganda analysis, in weighing and evaluating propaganda, must be even more discriminating in determining whether the propaganda is apt to hit its mark or not.

Monitoring. The first requisite of propaganda analysis is materials to be analyzed. In time of peace, it is usually enough to send a subscription to the newspaper, magazine, or pamphlet series, and to buy the books as they come out. Poster propaganda is more difficult to obtain, and frequently requires on-the-spot contacts. Dr. David Rowe brought back from Occupied China, in the early days of the Sino-Japanese war, a spectacularly well done and interesting series of Japanese and quisling posters. They were not hard to come by, once he was there, but he had to go about twenty thousand miles to get them and return.

In obtaining printed propaganda, better results will be achieved if the same sources are followed consistently over a period of time

		POSTERS	ADVERTISEMENTS	CITY DAILY PAPERS	LOCAL DAILY PAPERS	WEEKLY PAPERS	MAGAZINES	SPECIAL JOURNALS	GOVERNMENT RELEASES	MOTION PICTURE ANNOUNCEMENTS	REPORTS OF SPEECHES	RADIO PROGRAMS	OTHER MEDIA	
JANUARY					▓					▓			
FEBRUARY					▓					▓			
MARCH					▓					▓			
APRIL					▓					▓			
MAY					▓					▓			
JUNE					▓					▓			
JULY					▓					▓			
AUGUST					▓					▓			

Chart III.

than if one triumphant raid is carried through. The choice may look like this (*see Chart III*). If, in this instance the propaganda analysis is to be a one-man enterprise in a small country or area in time of peace, the one man can collect all the different kinds of samples in March and can then spend several months trying to see how they add up. By the time his analysis is ready, it will be badly dated and will necessarily be less interesting to the recipients than would a report which was up-to-the-week. Furthermore, unless the analyst knows the area very well indeed, he will risk mistaking transient issues for basic ones. If the Old Agrarians happen to be accused of Right Wing Deviationism during the week of 3-10 March, the analyst may falsely conclude that the Old Agrarian issue is tempestuous or profound.

Unless he has a large staff, faces a special crisis or pursues a scholarly purpose, the analyst does well to pick the alternative illustrated in the vertical column. He should pick his media carefully, accepting the advice of people who know the area intimately. In an opinion-controlled area, it is wise to take both a direct government propaganda paper and an opposition of semi-independent paper, if such exist. Local papers are often better guides to domestic propaganda than are big metropolitan papers. The propagandists of the country know that foreigners may watch the big papers, and they will reserve their most vicious, naïve, or bigoted appeals for the local press.

Along with the local press of one or two selected localities, the analyst should select several government personages and should follow every word of theirs he can find. The basic principle is for the analyst himself to determine the range of materials to be covered by deciding his own work-load in advance. This in turn depends on the time he has available for the task, his mastery of the language, his interest in the projects, probable interruptions due to semiofficial elbow-bending, and other personal factors.

The rule remains: *Consistent analysis of the same output with reference to basic topics over a sustained period will inevitably reveal the propaganda intention of the source.* (It must be pointed out that the expert analyst still is needed to select topics and to confirm interpretations.) To make a first guess as to whether the intended effect is being achieved or not, the analyst uses himself as a propaganda guinea pig. What does he think of the issues? What might he have thought otherwise? What would he think if he were a little less intelligent, a little more uncritical, than he is? And to complete the analysis, the analyst must go out to the audience that receives the materials and find out what effect the propaganda has had by asking them about it (see interrogation, chapter 8).

Printed Materials. The most readily available sources of propaganda are not printed ones. Especially in time of hostilities, it may not be easy to subscribe to enemy materials by the process of sending an international postal money order. Delays involved in transmitting the printed materials may make them useless for spot analysis, and valuable only for long-range basic studies of morale. The propagandist who is being analyzed may oblige by reading large numbers of editorials on the radio. (During the last war, officers and citizens occasionally exploded with alarm when Radio Tokyo quoted a *Life* or New York *Times* editorial several hours after it appeared. They naturally supposed that the Japanese had a secret short-wave transmitter running from New York City direct to Tokyo, and overlooked the fact that the OWI may have quoted long excerpts in slow Morse code on its trans-Pacific beam to China. The Japanese had picked it up, used subquotes, and beamed it back.)

Printed matter goes on the air in any major news operation. It is only a matter of time before telephoto facilities develop in line with the experimental New York *Times* edition printed in San Francisco during the United Nations organizational conference. This was sent, all in one piece, by wirephoto to Frisco and reprinted. The delay between the two editions was merely a matter of minutes. In the future, wireless telephoto may reduce this to seconds, so that all belligerents can simply tune in on each other's major newspapers.

Radio. For the present radio remains the biggest source of propaganda intake. Radio is convenient. It can be picked up illegitimately without too much fear of detection. For the cost per person reached, it is certainly the cheapest way of getting material to millions of people promptly. It lends itself to monitoring, and even standard (long) wavelengths can be picked up from surprisingly great distances.

The only defense against enemy use of radio monitoring or broadcasting consists of the application of wired radio—which means plugging all the radio sets in on the telephone circuit, putting nothing on the air, and defying the enemy to eavesdrop. If the radio sets are then policed, and are made incapable of receiving wireless material, that particular audience is effectively cut off from the enemy. (When the Red Army, with its acute propaganda-conscious security, moved into many Eastern European cities, the first thing it did was to round up all the radios which the Nazis had overlooked. This prevented the liberated peoples from being enslaved by the "filthy reactionary lies" of the American and British governments, and made sure that the peoples would stay liberated under influence of their local Soviet-controlled newspapers.)

Wired radio is expensive. Radio suppression is difficult; the successful concealers of radio receivers become two-legged newspapers and go around town spreading all the hot dope which the authorities are trying to suppress. Scarcity puts a premium on such news; rumor then becomes unmanageable. Except for strangely drastic situations, it is probable that the great powers will continue to tolerate radio reception even though it may mean letting foreign subversive propaganda slip in now and then.

It is therefore likely that radio broadcasts will be available for monitoring for the pre-belligerent stages of the next war, should war come again in our time, and that radio may last through a great part or all of the duration of the war. Factors which cannot now be foreseen, such as radio control of weapons, will affect this.

Radio propaganda analysis follows the same considerations as those which govern choice of materials for analyzing printed matter. It is a surer method to follow one or two programs on a station than to make wide random selections. A standard-wave transmitter to the home audience comes closer to revealing the domestic scene than would a global rebroadcast of ostensibly identical material. Radio has a further advantage over print. Few nations print out separate propaganda for each foreign-language area, while almost every large and medium-sized country has international facilities for broadcast. Since the programs are beamed to different language groups, the senders automatically make up propaganda lines for each audience.[3]

Attentive monitoring can provide material for distinguishing the various lines which any given nation is sending out to its friends, neighbors, or rivals. Frequently the differences between these lines make good counterpropaganda. If you hear the Germans telling the Danes that all Nordics are supermen and all non-Nordics scum, while telling the Japanese that the National Socialist idea of the world transcends pluto-democratic race prejudice, put the two quotations together and send them back to the Danes and the Japanese both.

Radio, unlike print, cannot be held for the analyst's convenience. It is physically unhandy to try to file actual recordings of enemy broadcasts for preservation and reference. When the analysis center is large, as it would be if near the headquarters of a government or a theater of war, the difficulties of monitoring involve problems of stenographic and language help. The monitors themselves can then be stenographers, taking verbatim dictation. They write down the enemy broadcast word-for-word, either right off the air or from records. The editor then selects the most important parts of the day's intake for mimeographic or other circulation. Important material can be put in a daily radio summary of enemy propaganda for the area monitored. The rest of it can be sent along by mail, put in files and classified (lest the enemy government find out what its own propagandists really were saying), preserved on the recording, or destroyed.

During World War II these basic verbatim reports played a very important part. The Foreign Broadcast Intelligence Service did the job for the United States, operating through the war years under the Federal Communications Commission. It has since been shifted from FCC to the War Department, and from the War Department to the Central Intelligence Group. Its materials sometimes are unclassified, although during most of the war they were marked *restricted*, and they are not available to the public except through microfilm copies of the Library of Congress file. These FBIS daily reports skimmed the cream off the enemy news broadcasts, and included editorial or feature material which might have intelligence or policy interest.

Monitoring by a Single Individual. Where monitoring must be done by a single individual or a very small staff, it is desirable to find a basic news broadcast and to take it down verbatim where possible. This gives the analyst the chance of a second look at his materials and keeps him from having to make snap judgments of what is important and what is not, right during the course of the broadcast. Selection of a basic news program, followed by reference to speeches, plays, lectures and other programs that indicate the over-all tone of the day's output, will make it possible for one person to do an adequate monitoring job on about one-eighth of his full-time work per station. This does not leave him time to do much fancy analysis, or to prepare graphs, but he can pass along the general psychological warfare situation so far as that particular beam on that particular transmitter is concerned.

The most likely situation for the isolated consul, businessman, officer, missionary, or amateur is one in which he can get a certain amount of stenographic help in taking down the broadcast material. The radio for monitoring varies in accordance with general reception conditions. Practically all the U. S. Army Signal Corps receivers will perform satisfactorily for local monitoring; so too will ordinary private sets, including the larger portables. An automobile radio can often be driven away from interference and from a hilltop or the edge of a lake can pick up a standard-wave station that cannot be distinguished on a much larger house set in the city. For transoceanic or world-wide reception, a short-wave receiver is of course necessary.

It is unwise to pick a sample that involves too much rapid speech, such as a foreign soap opera. The best reception is almost always the Morse code transmission of news or the slow dictation-speed reading of news from one central station to outlying news offices or substations. Selection of a program which usually comes in, arrangement for a verbatim copy of the program, daily checking of the news under standard analysis procedures—this gives a very fair cross-section.

One man sitting at Hankow could find out just what both the Generalissimo and the Chinese Communists were trying to tell the French-understanding and the Dutch-understanding listeners in the Far East. Another with pipe and slippers in Brussels could keep tab on the basic Russian lines to the Spanish-speaking world. Such monitoring obviously comes in handy for newspapers, commercial firms, governments, military establishments, speculators, and research institutions.

Identification: Propaganda vs. Truth. The point will invariably arise: "This tells me how to listen to a foreign radio. Okay, I'll get the news, the lectures, the plays—all the rest of it. But so what? How am I going to know what's the truth and what's propaganda? How can I tell 'em apart? Tell me that!"

The answer is simple: "If you agree with it, it's truth. If you don't agree, it's propaganda. Pretend that it is all propaganda. See what happens on your analysis reports."

Propaganda was defined (at the beginning of this book) as follows: *Propaganda consists of the planned use of any form of communication designed to affect the minds and emotions of a given group for a specific purpose.* Taking a lesson from Communist theory, we can say that any form of mass-communication is operated for propaganda purposes *if no other motive for running it is evident.* Human beings talk; they like to talk. Much private talk is idle—but only an imbecile would talk over a radio network just for the pleasure of hearing himself talking. Propaganda is presentation for a purpose; it is the *purpose* that makes it propaganda, and not the truthfulness or untruthfulness of it.

The collected news of any modern country contains more truth each day than any one man can could read in a lifetime. The reporters, editors, writers, announcers who collect truth not only collect it; they select it. They have to. Why do they select it? That is the propaganda question. If they select it to "affect the minds and emotions of a given group for a specific purpose," it is propaganda. If they report that a little girl fell out of bed and broke her neck—with the intent of frightening parents among their listeners into following the Safe Homes Week Campaign—that is propaganda. But if they report it because it is the only death in the community, and because they might as well fill up the program, it is not propaganda. If you put the statement on the air, "An American Negro workman in Greensboro, N. C., got eighty cents for a hard day's work last week," that can be presented and interpreted as:

(a.) simple news, if there is something more to the story, about what the man said, or how he spent the eighty cents on corn meal to feed his pet tarantula;

(b.) anti-capitalist propaganda, if you show that eighty cents is mighty little money for American business to pay its workers;

(c.) pro-capitalist propaganda, if you show that the eighty cents will buy more than two weeks' wages of a worker in the city of Riga, when it comes to consumer goods;

(d.) anti-White propaganda, if you show the man got only eighty cents because he was a Negro.

Figure 21: *Mockery of Enemy Propaganda Slogans.* Home-front propaganda was sometimes repeated in an inappropriate place, in order to achieve an effect contrary to that originally intended. These Nazi leaflets, dropped on American detachments in Europe, used modifications of the "It's Your Job!" posters and advertisements used by the U.S. for home-front purposes.

Figure 22: *Mockery of Enemy Propaganda Technique.* When the content of enemy propaganda cannot be attacked, the media themselves can sometimes be criticized. This German leaflet attempted utilization of potential suspicions of Hollywood. In so doing, it used three techniques: built up from a news item, suitably faked; raised suspicion of the movies which the Germans knew our Army showed for morale purposes; and spread racial hate.

And so on, through a further variety of interpretations. The facts—man, happening, amount, place, time—are *true* in each case. They could be sworn to by the whole membership of an interfaith conference. But the interpretation placed on them—who communicates these facts to whom? why? when?—makes them into propaganda.

And interpretation can no more be true or untrue than a Ford car can be vanilla or strawberry in flavor. The questions of truth and of interpretation are unrelated categories. The essence of motive is that it is ultimately private and impenetrable, and interpretation commonly involves imputation of motive. You can dislike an interpretation; you can kill a man for believing it; you can propagandize him out of believing it; but you cannot sit down and *prove* that it is untrue. Facts and logic are useful in propaganda, but they cannot be elevated to the point where you can say, "Is it propaganda or is it true?" Almost all good propaganda—no matter what kind—is true. It uses truth selectively.

There is no secret formula which, once applied, provides an unfailing test for propaganda. It is not possible for a person unfamiliar

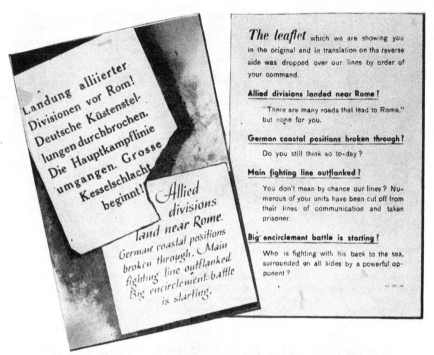

Figure 23: Direct Reply Leaflet. World War II propagandists often succumbed to the temptation of using the enemy materials and sending them right back. Sarcasm can be effective if the reader identifies himself with the speaker and not with the addressee. In this Nazi leaflet from the Anzio beachhead, the Germans probably antagonized more Americans than they befriended. A simple statement of the news would have been more effective. (Signal Corps photo.)

with the part of the world affected, with the topic discussed, with the interested parties, and with the immediate politics involved to put his finger on an item and say, "This Rightist charge is propaganda," and then to turn and say, "But that Rightist statement is not propaganda. It is fact." Untruthful statements are made at times for other than propaganda purposes; truthful statements may be propaganda or not. The analyst must himself be an interested party. He must determine ahead of time what he will regard as propaganda, and what not. And he must do so by delimiting the field of his analysis before he starts. No one person or staff of people could ever trace all the motives behind a single statement; even to attempt that, he would have to be a novelist of the school of Marcel Proust. (And he would end up feeling like James Joyce, Gertrude Stein, or Franz Kafka.)

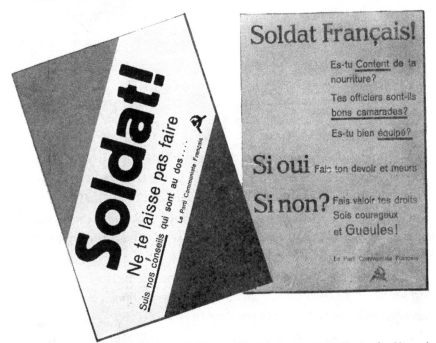

Figure 24: Black Use of Enemy Subversive Materials. This leaflet, printed in brilliant red, white and blue, was found in the printshop of a Nazi military propaganda company overtaken in Lorraine. It apparently dates from 1939-40, when the Soviet Union and Nazi Germans were at peace, with the result that Communists throughout the world opposed the ''imperialist war.'' The leaflet may or may not be duplicated from a French Communist original; the important thing is its reuse by the Germans. This constitutes black propaganda in one of its purest forms.

The analyst looks in the direction in which the message is going. He defines the *propaganda presentation* of the people who get the message in terms of *all the public information to which the persons addressed have access.* If he does not know the purpose of the message, he may divine it from the character of the audience and from the effect he presumes the message may reasonably be expected to have upon the audience. If he does not know the audience, he can at least follow the physical transit of the message. In what language does it move? Whence? Whither? When?

The Stasm Formula. The formula given earlier (chapter 3) was found useful in the spot analysis of German broadcasts, both open and clandestine, and Japanese materials, during the last months of the war. The formula reads:

S   ource (including Media)
T   ime
A   udience
S   ubject
M   ission

The neologism, *Stasm*, may serve a mnemonic purpose.

The formula works best in the treatment of monitored materials of which the source is known. First point to note is the character of the source. There are several choices on this: the true source (who really got it out?) and the ostensible source (whose name is signed to it?); also, the first-use source (who used it the first time?) and the second-use source (who claims merely to be using it as a quotation?). Take the statement: "Harry said to me, he said, 'I never told anybody that Al's wife was a retired strip-teaser.' Mind you, I don't pretend to believe Harry, but that's what he said, all right." What are the possible true sources for the statement of fact or libel concerning Al's unnamed wife? What are the alternatives on ostensible sources? First use? Second use? The common sense needed to analyze this statement is of the same order as the process involved in analyzing the statement: "Reliable sources in Paris state that the visit of the American labor delegation has produced sensational repercussions in Moscow, and that Moscow, upon the basis of the American attitude, is determined to press for unification of the entire German labor movement."

It is soon evident that the mere attribution of source is a job of high magnitude. A systematic breakdown of the STASM formula produces the following analysis outline, applicable to any single propaganda item, civil or military, in war or peace, spoken, visual, or printed. There are many other possible arrangements; the one given below is not represented as having official sanction or mysterious powers of its own. It has simply worked well for the author.

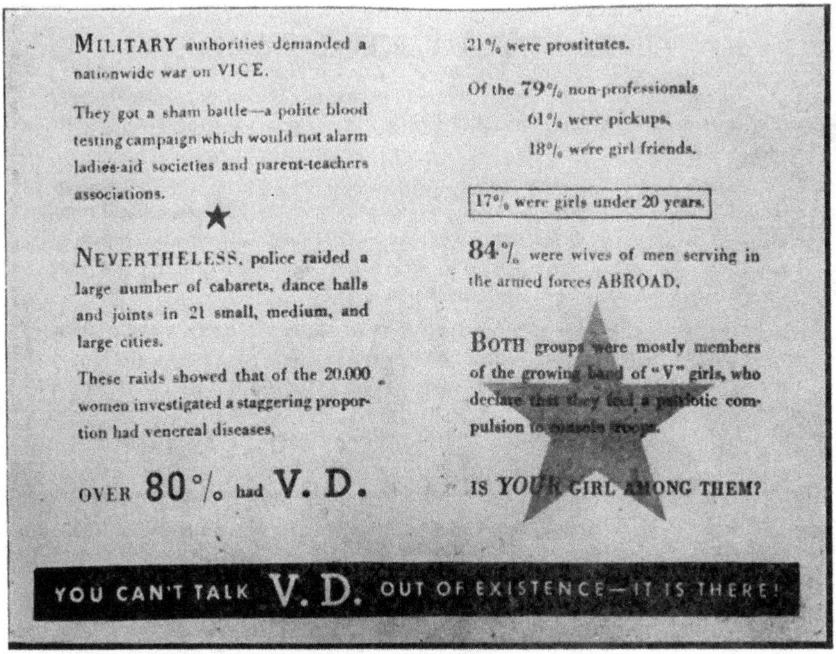

MILITARY authorities demanded a nationwide war on VICE.

They got a sham battle—a polite blood testing campaign which would not alarm ladies-aid societies and parent-teachers associations.

★

NEVERTHELESS, police raided a large number of cabarets, dance halls and joints in 21 small, medium, and large cities.

These raids showed that of the 20,000 women investigated a staggering proportion had venereal diseases,

OVER 80% had V. D.

21% were prostitutes.

Of the 79% non-professionals
61% were pickups,
18% were girl friends.

17% were girls under 20 years.

84% were wives of men serving in the armed forces ABROAD,

BOTH groups were mostly members of the growing band of "V" girls, who declare that they feel a patriotic compulsion to console troops.

IS YOUR GIRL AMONG THEM?

YOU CAN'T TALK V. D. OUT OF EXISTENCE—IT IS THERE!

Figure 25-A: Black Use of Enemy Information Materials. The Nazis used this leaflet on the Western Front. The real source was a German propaganda unit; the ostensible source was U.S. Army facilities. Note that the leaflet has nothing to do with stopping VD among troops, which is what the originals sought; instead, its effect is to depress American troop morale.

COMPLETE BREAKDOWN OF A SINGLE PROPAGANDA ITEM.

a. *Source*

(1) True source ("Where does it really come from?")

    (a) Release channel ("How did it come out?") if different from true source without concealing true source

    (b) Person or institution in whose name material originates

    (c) Transmitting channel ("Who got it to us?"), person or institution effecting known transmission—omitting, of course, analyst's own procurement facilities

(2) Ostensible source ("Where does it pretend to come from?")

    (a) Release channel ("Who is supposed to be passing it along?")

(3) First-use and second-use source (first use, "Who is said to have used this first?"; second use "Who pretends to be quoting someone else?")

GUARD AGAINST VENEREAL DISEASES

Lately there has been a great increase in the number of venereal diseases among our officers and men owing to prolific contacts with Filipino women of dubious character.

Due to hard times and stricken conditions brought about by the Japanese occupation of the islands, Filipino women are willing to offer themselves for a small amount of foodstuffs. It is advisable in such cases to take full protective measures by use of condoms, protective medicines, etc.; better still to hold intercourse only with wives, virgins or women of respective character.

Furthermore, in view of the increase in pro-American leanings, many Filipino women are more than willing to offer themselves to American soldiers, and due to the fact that Filipinos have no knowledge of hygiene, disease carriers are rampant and due care must be taken.

U. S. ARMY

Figure 25-B: Black Use of Enemy Information Materials. Compare this with the preceding leaflet. The real source in both cases is enemy. The ostensible source in both cases is the U.S. Army. The ostensible mission in both cases is the prevention of VD. But the mission is entirely different in the second leaflet. The first was addressed to *troops*—Americans—designed to make them feel bad. The second was dropped on *civilians*—Filipinos—whom the Japanese thus tried to stir up against the Americans. (Leyte Campaign. Courtesy of Mr. Robert Kleiman.)

    (a) Connection between second-use source and first-use source, usually in the form of attributed or unacknowledged quotation; more rarely, plagiarism

    (b) Modification between use by first-use and second-use sources, when both are known

        (i) Deletions

        (ii) Changes in text

        (iii) Enclosure within editorial matter of transmitter

        (iv) Falsification which appears deliberate

        (v) Effects of translation from one language to another

b. *Time*

    (1) Time of events or utterance to which subject-matter refers

    (2) Time of transmission (publishing, broadcasting, etc.)

    (3) Timing of repetitions

    (4) Reasons, if any are evident, for peculiarities of timing

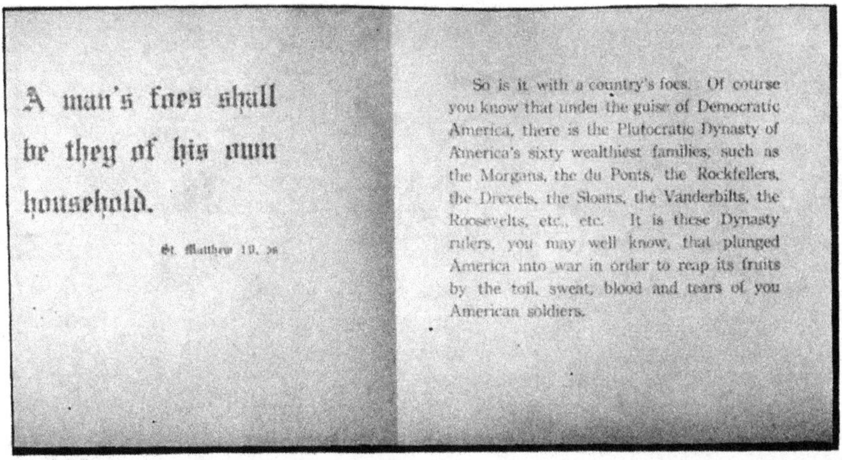

Figure 26: Religious Black. Perhaps because of their contact with Americans who happened to be missionaries, the Japanese overemphasized the effect of religion on Americans. They attempted crude appeals on religious themes. It is doubtful that leaflets such as this had any practical effect. (Philippines, 1944-45.)

c. *Audience*

　　(1) Intended direct audience ("in English to North America"; "a paper for New York restaurant operators")

　　(2) Intended indirect audience (program beamed "in English to North America" but actually reaching Hong Kong and Singapore by deliberate plan of the sender; "a paper for New York restaurant operators" being faked and sent to Southeast Europe in fact)

　　(3) Unintended audience (a Guadalcanal native studying *Esquire*; your aunt reading the *Infantry Journal*; a Chinese reading American wartime speeches against the "yellow devils" of Japan)

　　(4) Ostensibly unintended direct audience (such as an appeal to strikers in very abusive-sounding language, sent to businessmen to build up opinion *against* the strikers, or Hitler's black use of the forged Protocols of the Elders of Zion)

d. *Subject* ("What does it say?")

　　(1) Content listed under any convenient heading as

IT IS DANGEROUS TO READ THE
FOLLOWING:

1. Don't pretend lunacy. Your surgeon will detect such deception, and you are sure to be tried by court-martial. Or if you succeed in passing as a lunatic, you will be invalided home, without any more chance to rejoin your comrades at the front.

2. Don't spit freely. If you do, you will be obsessed with the habit of spitting. And remember, it is an early symptom of neurosis.

3. Don't think the reverse of everything you chance to hear. Or it will easily become habitual with you and develop into regular symptoms of neurosis.

4. Don't try to practise sleeping in a fixed posture. This is also one of the symptoms of neurosis. It is contagious to your comrades-in-arms.

5. Don't be so nervous as to feel your heartbeat from time to time. Such a symptom always appears in the early stages of lunacy.

6. Don't worry about the color of your urine or excrement. This is also an early symptom of lunacy.

7. One week's practice is enough to feign naturally the tremor of your hands, shoulders and legs. The tremor of the head, especially, is the most conspicuous sign of neurosis.

8. If you practise to quickly roll your eyeballs horizontally without moving your head, it will soon become habitual. This particular movement of the eyeballs preludes serious neurosis. Even without such a practice, your eyeballs will soon begin to tremor unwittingly if you are constantly worried about it.

9. Don't fall into the habit of glancing sideways at your comrades-in-arms. Your surgeon dislikes such a habit, as it predicts the approaching menace of neurosis.

10. Don't eat your own excrement or drink your own urine in the presence of others. If you do, you are sure to be branded as a lunatic however warmly you may protest.

11. Don't mumble the same words immediately after you have spoken them. If you practise it repeatedly, your surgeon's verdict will inevitably be neurosis.

12. Don't try to develop your imaginative power to the extent that all human faces look like animals. Or you are likely to see no more human faces even on your friends.

13. Don't imitate an epileptic fit. If you practise it for three days, you will certainly have a real one. Then you are on your way to lunacy.

Figure 27: *Malingerer's Black.* One of the favored targets of black propaganda is the malingerer. Suspicion of successful malingering inevitably hurts the morale of a unit. Even if the enemy's instructions are not followed, the troops may suspect genuine psychoneurotics of having faked their troubles. Almost all participants in World War II issued such instructions; the Allied samples are not available for publication. This is a Japanese leaflet from the Philippines, 1944-45.

though it were *straight news or intelligence*

(2) Content epitomized as demonstrating *new propaganda technique* (such as, "Now they're trying to get us out of Tientsin by appeals to our isolationists!")

(3) Content which may be useful in *counterpropaganda* (such as, "They said that the Greeks are our witless puppets, so let's pass that along to the Greeks")

(4) Significance of content for *intelligence analysis* (examples: When the Japanese boasted about their large fish catch, it was an indication their fishing fleet was short of gasoline again, and that the fish catch was actually small; when the Nazis accused the Jews of sedition, it meant that rations were short and that the Nazi government was going to appease the populace by denying the Jews their scanty rations by way of contrast)

e. *Mission*

    (1) Nation, group, or person attacked

    (2) Relation to previous items with the same or related missions

    (3) Particular psychological approach used in this instance (such as wedge-driving between groups, or between people and leaders, or between armed services; or demoralization of audience in general; or decrease of listeners' faith in the news)

    (4) Known or probable connection with originator's propaganda plan or strategy

Such an outline would be useful only if it were applied in commonsense terms, without turning each item into an elaborate project and thus losing the woods in the trees. In most cases, it would suffice to state the item briefly for reference and study in the order of the entries. When poorly trained help is available, it is of course necessary to print or mimeograph a form to be used.

It is as vain to prescribe a propaganda analysis procedure without knowing the user as to prescribe an office filing system while knowing neither the nature of the office nor the kind of files kept. In time of war, subordinate commanders in operational areas will need to keep files at a minimum, while rear echelon or national facilities may be able to keep files of enormous range and thoroughness. In the recording of a large number of propaganda items, however, the material becomes hopelessly unmanageable unless there is some standardized system for organizing it. Mere alphabetization leads inevitably to the question, alphabetization of what?, and the analysis function can be exercised more readily in terms of the sources of propaganda than in terms of its incidental topics.

Identification of Enemy Plans and Situations. Propaganda has its inevitable mirror image which gradually becomes plain to the analyst. If the analyst is careful, using shrewd judgment in appraising specific missions, he will gradually see forming in his files a record of the immediate and long-range aims of the propaganda orginators. This becomes possible only when enough material is available, over a period of time to make up a complete list of the probable enemy propaganda objectives for the period covered. The intent of propaganda is always a result observable as action, however remote the action may be from the date of operation. Much of the propaganda of the Communist Party in the United States is directed to the inculcation of correct *scientific* thinking (see chapter 5) which will be of decisive use only when the remote Day of Revolution arrives. Few of the Communist leaders, even in private conference, would venture to predict the exact year of the Day of Revolution; some may not even expect to see it; but they believe that if the propaganda is effective, the "proletariat" will be "militant" and its leaders will be conscious of their "historic role." From the propaganda of today, the action may be anticipated, no matter how distant it may seem; once the action is determined, the relation of other propaganda items to that action can be traced.

In war, the action sought is something militarily harmful to the enemy—strikes against his production, panic in his population, complaint from his consumers, mistrust from his newspaper readers and radio listeners (resulting in eventual subversive or negative action on their part), surrender of his troops, disunity of his political leadership to be expressed in deadlocks, and so on. In prebelligerent or peacetime propaganda, the action sought is against the war-making capacity of the audience—against war itself, if the propagandist feels that his own population is in no immediate danger of being infected by defeatism.

Estimating the Enemy's Propaganda Situation. In addition to presenting a picture of the enemy goals, and of the psychological means he considers to be useful in reaching those goals, propaganda analysis is also valuable in presenting the enemy's own propaganda situation. He avoids certain topics because he must. He talks about others because circumstances force him to do so.

For example, if the Germans stop talking about rations for Jews (in the World War II situation), it may be that their own people, filled with anti-Semitic poison, have been protesting the issuance of rations. Alternatively, it may mean that the Nazi authorities have just cancelled Jewish rations and are letting the Jews starve or are murdering them overtly. If the Germans follow this up with an item on the poor barley crop, it may be that they are preparing the sentimental and humane listeners in their own audience for the announcement of Jewish starvation. If they run Paris-quisling accounts of Jewish hoarding, and of Jews concealing large quantities of food, it means that they are almost certain to be under pressure to explain their Jewish policies and that, therefore, two factors face the German propagandist: first, he must get ready to announce the attack on the Jews; second, he thinks that the Jewish situation is going to arouse anti-Nazi sentiment even in Germany (if these are German-language programs) and he is therefore compelled to defend something because public opinion is believed by him to be against it. Out of a silence (no further news on rations), a domestic item (poor barley crop), and a foreign item (Paris Jews allegedly hoarding), it is possible to reconstruct a whole situation. The reconstruction may fall, if other interpretations arise, but it provides a starting guess.

The situation of enemy morale is often reportable through propaganda analysis long before it can be described by eyewitnesses. Omissions of attacks on the Church may indicate that the religious problem has become touchy. Failure to attack Communism may mean that the government is seeking a diplomatic deal with a Communist state. Mention of children may refer to the fact that parents complain of cold schools, bad food, absent doctors. Good morale is shown by a quiet tone in propaganda; bad morale is shown by extremes, whether of silence or of great vehemence. It is useful to know what the enemy propagandist thinks he is doing, what he considers the obstacles to his propaganda. Such considerations inevitably get to be embodied in the propaganda itself. A tone of extreme defiance, poor international cooperation, war bluster and so on may often spring from the desire to divert a hungry or discontented home public from its real worries at home to imaginary worries abroad.

Propanal as a Source of Military Intelligence. Propaganda analysis, or *propanal* for short, can serve as a very useful adjunct to military intelligence even if when not directly connected with counterpropaganda operations. In the first place, the enemy must give news, comment, opinion, entertainment in order to get attention. The incidental content and make-up of this propaganda is itself useful study material. If his ink is bad, his paper poor, his language incorrect, it shows shortages of supply and personnel. If he boasts about his victories, he usually gives his version of place names and aids cartographic reporting. In mentioning the names of heroes, he may supply order-of-battle. In making a good story out of his economic situation, he fills in missing statistics; even if the figures are falsified, they must be falsified for a purpose and can be used in conjunction with others in making up an estimate.

Nothing is as smart as a human being except another human being. What any one man can try to achieve in the way of deceit, another man can try to figure out. The bulk of propaganda, short of peremptory tactical leaflets, is filled with information about the enemy's personnel, his opinion of himself, his opinion of you, his state of mind, his order of battle, his economic system, and all the rest. The Japanese government, throughout the war, kept the United States informed *in English* of the changes of ministers and other high officials in the Japanese government. This gave us good political background. There was no use their trying to hide it over a long period of time, and presumably *Joho Kyoku* (the Imperial Japanese Board of Information) figured that the help it gave the Americans, in filling out their political intelligence files for them, would be more than counterbalanced by the fact that such news would make American newspapermen, officials, officers and others read the propaganda in order to get the facts.

Over and above the direct contribution to straight news or intelligence, enemy propaganda in times of war or crisis affords a clue to enemy strategy. If the coordination is not present the propaganda may do the enemy himself harm. But the moment coordination is present, and one end of the coordinate is handed over to us, we can start figuring what the coordination is for. Sometimes propaganda is sacrificed for weightier considerations of security; German propaganda gave little advance warning of a war with the U.S.S.R., and Soviet propaganda gave none. In other instances, the coordination does give the show away.

In 1941-1942, the Japanese radio began to show an unwholesome interest in Christmas Island in its broadcasts to Japanese at home and abroad. Christmas Island, below Sumatra, was pointed out as a really important place, and tremendously significant in naval strategy. Subsequently the Japanese armed forces went to and took Christmas Island. The home public was delighted that this vital spot had been secured. Of course, Christmas Island was not as important as the Japanese radio said it was, but the significant thing was that the radio talked about it *ahead of time.* For what little it was worth the Japanese had given us warning.

Enemy realization of an impending defeat may be preceded by disparagement of the importance of the area in which the defeat is to take place, or by description to the home audience of the enormous strength which enemy forces face at that particular place. Enemy action—when the enemy is security-minded—may be anticipated from his complete silence on something which he would normally talk about. It must have seemed odd that the Americans stopped talking about nuclear fission altogether, when prewar years had seen a certain number of news items on the subject in the New York press each month.

A nation getting ready to strike *à la* Pearl Harbor may prepare by alleging American aggression. A nation preparing to break the peace frequently gets out peace propaganda of the most blatant sort, trying to make sure that its own audience (as well as the world) will believe the real responsibility to lie in the victim whom he attacks. Hitler protested his love of Norwegian neutrality; then he hit, claiming that he was protecting it from the British. No hard-and-fast rules can be made up for all wars or all belligerents. The Germans behaved according to one pattern; the Japanese, another.

For example, the German High Command sought to avoid bragging about anything they could not actually accomplish. They often struck blows without warning but they never said they would strike

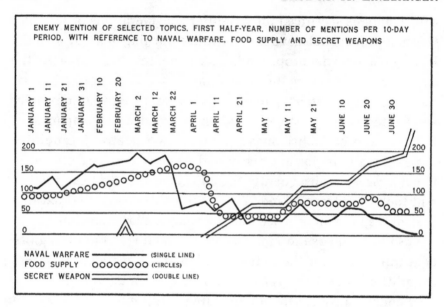

Chart IV.

a blow when they knew or believed that they could not do it. The British and Americans made up a timetable of this, and were able to guess how fast the Germans thought they were going to advance in Russia. Knowing this, the British and Americans planned their propaganda to counter the German boasts; they tried to pin the Germans down to objectives they knew the Germans would not take, in order to demonstrate to the peoples of Europe that Nazi Germany had finally bitten off more than it could chew.

Later, the Allies remembered this German habit when the Nazis on the radio began talking about their own secret weapons. When the British bombed the V-1 ramps on the French coast, the German radio stopped that talk. The British therefore had additional grounds for supposing that the ramps they had bombed were a part of the secret weapon the Germans bragged about. The British further knew that the Germans would try to counter the psychological effect of the announcement of Allied D-Day with some pretty vivid news of their own. When the German radio began mentioning secret weapons again, the British suspected that the Germans had gotten around the damage done to the ramps. D-Day came; the Germans, in one single broadcast designed to impress the Japanese and Chinese, announced that the secret German weapon was about to be turned loose, and that more such weapons would follow. One day later the first V-1 hit London.

In order to follow this type of propaganda, a quantitative chart is needed. A sample imaginary chart for a three-month period is given in chart IV. This chart reveals at a glance the fact that the enemy kept mentioning food supply and naval warfare until the middle of March, because he presumably thought his blockade runners would bring in more food. After March, food drops in emphasis but naval warfare continues to be stressed. In May, following enemy admission to himself of the hopeless naval situation, naval warfare drops almost altogether out of sight. Foodstuffs continue to be modestly mentioned as the enemy explained away minor difficulties, but the use of secret weapons propaganda shows that the enemy propagandists had to have something sensational to keep up the courage of the home audience. Whether the enemy really had a secret weapon or not, depends on the national character, past records, and so forth. The Germans and Japanese both said they had world-shaking secret weapons. The Germans delivered; the Japanese did not.

Such quantity records will also be useful in showing the enemy's propaganda statistically with reference to number of words uttered on each of his major subjects, number of inches of newspaper columns for specified kinds of news, and so on. Percentage charts show which major shifts his propaganda performs. Audience charts (that is, how much time he spends addressing workers, pacifists, mothers, minorities, etc.) show which groups he is really trying to reach. Emphasis charts for selected topics on which your own propaganda has been active show how much you force him to talk about something which he may not wish to discuss.

Such statistical use is possible only if usable records are maintained. A basic item-by-item file of all important or new items, combined with a worksheet of the amount of radio time or printed space the enemy put into use for a stated period, will provide the materials needed for propanal. Propanal is indispensable to psychological warfare. It sifts ordinary intelligence out from propaganda in one process, processing straight intelligence ready for the intelligence people to use, yet providing analysis for psychological warfare purposes.

For peacetime purposes, it is to be remembered that though enemies may hide their scientists, their launching ramps, or their rockets, they cannot hide the occasion for war, nor their own readiness measures. No government can afford to seem the plain unqualified aggressor. *Propanal* may prove to be one of the soundest war-forecasting systems available to us in a period of ultra-destructive weapons. Psychological mobilization may be disguised: it cannot be concealed.

NOTES:

[1] The bibliographies were cited previously. The journal comes out, as its title indicates, four times a year; it is published by the School of Public and International Affairs, Princeton University, Princeton, N. J. Every major library has it. The review section provides a good survey of new writing in the field. Journals such as *The American Political Science Review*, *The Annals of the American Academy of Political and Social Science*, *The Infantry Journal*, and *The American Historical Review* often have significant articles or book reviews in this field. *International Affairs* (Royal Institute for International Affairs, London) has excellent reviews of books arranged by geographic subheads. Opinion and propaganda topics are usually lumped together in academic studies; material on the one is apt to lead to the other.

[2] *San Tzu Ching*, translated and annotated by Herbert A. Giles, Shanghai, 1910, pages 2 and 3. The translation quoted is not by Giles.

[3] On the transmitting side, nothing could be more ruinous than mere translation, the more literal the worse,

of a single basic broadcast for all audiences irrespective of language or culture. For the text of war communiqués or of official documents, this is permissible, but for news or feature broadcasts, few things could be worse. It is not possible to *translate* subtle psychological appeals embedded in news or commentary; such materials by their nature must follow forms acceptable to the audience, building up confidence with familiar allusions and creating a sense of "we-ness" between the actual announcer and his listeners. Equivalents can be worked out. The same basic policies can be transposed. The same source of news and intelligence can be exploited. But the actual program cannot, be translated verbatim from one language to another; it must be transposed not only from one language but from one culture to another.

CHAPTER 8
PROPAGANDA INTELLIGENCE

The psychological warfare operator can usually count on two basic interests of his listener. In the field he can be sure that the enemy troops are interested in themselves. In the enemy homeland he can be sure that the civilians are interested in *their* enemy— himself. He has therefore a certain leeway in which he can be sure of doing no harm, and may accomplish good, if he confines his propaganda to simple, factual and plainly honest statements on these subjects. Pompousness, intricacy and bad taste will recoil against him; it is unwise to employ these even when the situation is well under control. In a developing situation the propagandist can remain safe by confining himself to simple statements as to how strong his country's armed forces are, how realistic and effective their leadership. Elementary information giving the favorable aspects of his economic, strategic and diplomatic situation may also prove valuable initial propaganda.

This interest can be counted on throughout the war. The enemy is always news. The wise enemy realizes this and keeps himself in the news, trusting that in the wider understanding of himself, his politics and culture there is the opening for a more favorable peace in the event of defeat, or for a more docile submission in the event of his own victory. Only unimportant enemies fail to become news. (Few Americans, for example, realize that we were at war with Bulgaria in World War II. Had the Bulgars developed sensational weapons, there would have been a sudden upswing of interest in them. People would have realized that Bulgaria, like Hungary and

194

Figure 28: Nostalgic Black. Soldiers in all wars have gotten homesick. Propaganda appeals to home-sickness in many ways. One of the simplest is the device shown in this German black leaflet, which shows the husband turning off the alarm clock while the wife wakes up. The printed message on the reverse makes out a discouraging case for the soldier's opportunity to return home, pointing out that the GI in Europe, even after victory, will face "that nasty jungle war . . . in the Far East." No identification of the leaflet is given.

long-lost Avaria, was once a fierce Asiatic state grafted onto the European system; the fabulous power of the Old Bulgarian Empire would have become known, and the names of Krum, Symeon and the Czar Samuel added to our calendar of hate. But Bulgaria never did enough against the United States to count as an enemy, and even succeeded, by diplomatic ineptitude, in getting into a state of war with all the Axis Powers and all the United Nations simultaneously; Bulgaria escaped the fame which goes with hostility. Contrast this with Japan: thousands of Americans have learned Japanese; Japanese national character is known to us; war has done in a five-year span what education could not have accomplished in a generation.) The wise propagandist can, when in doubt, play good music on the air, or he can—with equal prudence—give the enemy his own elementary-school history and language texts. These do no harm, and may achieve something.

News as Intelligence. Harmlessness is, however, a poor ideal for men at war; the propagandist who keeps out of mischief is doing only half his job. To make his message take effect he must convey to the enemy those kinds of information which tend to disrupt enemy unity, discount enemy expectation of success, lower the enemy will to resist. He cannot do so by means of recorded symphonies or tourist lectures, no matter how well done. He must turn to the first weapon of propaganda, the news.

The official propagandist is not a newspaperman. Since he speaks for an army or a government, his utterance is *officially responsible.* He must be as timely as the peacetime press, but must at the same time be as cautious as a government press agent. He is torn between two responsibilities: his responsibility to the job of propaganda, which requires him to get interesting information and get it out to the enemy quickly; and his responsibility to the official policies of his own government, which requires him to release nothing unconfirmed, nothing that could do harm, or that might embarrass or hurt the government. (A sort of institutional schizophrenia is common to all propaganda offices.)

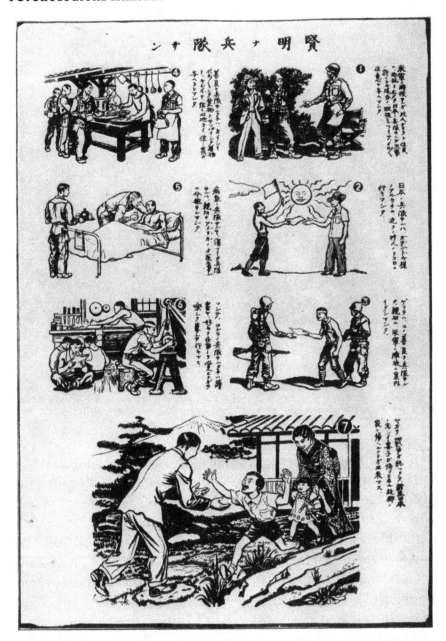

Figure 29: Nostalgic White, Misfire. Figure 30 was carefully adapted to Japanese customs. The mere fact that the Americans knew enough about Japan to celebrate a homey Japanese holiday was probably enough to make the Japanese reader examine the leaflet carefully. Here is a combined nostalgic and surrender leaflet showing how surrender leads the Japanese soldier back to his wife and children. The drawing looks American rather than Japanese, and it is not likely that a genuine Japanese could have been made homesick by use of this leaflet.

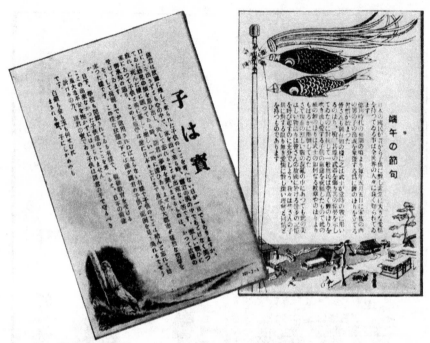

Figure 30: Nostalgic White. On March 5 of every year the Japanese celebrate the colorful custom of Boys' Day. Kites in the form of carp are flown over the cities and countryside and millions of families set out to give their little sons an excursion or some other treat. (It is characteristic of the Japanese that there is no Girls' Day.) This leaflet, from Psychological Warfare Branch, USAFPA, was designed for dropping on May 5. It ends with the appeal, "You must guard the strength of the new Japan, your treasure, your children." Thus it combines homesickness, patriotism, and pre-surrender indoctrination.

The sources of news are various. Classified incoming operational reports of the Army and Navy contain material of high interest to the enemy. There are obvious reasons for denying access to such information to the propaganda people. Propaganda men might think of their audience first and security second. If they do not know the secret information, but are advised by military consultants who do, security will be better maintained and the propagandist will not labor under the handicap of a double standard of information—what they know, and what they dare to tell.

In technically advanced countries, the regular commercial facilities of press and radio continue to do a normal news job, and usually do better work than the drafted amateurs in the government. (What intelligence agency in Washington could compile a weekly report as comprehensive, well edited and coldly planned as *Time* magazine?[1] The author often yearned to paraphrase *Time*, rearranging it and classifying it TOP SECRET, in order to astound his associates with the inside dope to which he had access.) The nature of news is not affected by its classification, and the distinction between news produced on the Federal payroll and news produced off it often consists of the superior professionalism of the latter.

The intelligence that goes into the making of propaganda must compete for attention with the home newspaper of the enemy. It must therefore be up-to-date, well put, authentic. There is no more space in propaganda for the lie, farce, hoax, or joke than there is room for it in a first-class newspaper. Even if exaggerations or nonsense appear in the commercial press of his own country, the propagandist must realize that he is Honorary G-2 to the enemy— a G-2 whose function consists of transmitting news *the ultimate effect of which should be bad* but which should go forth with each separate item newsworthy and palatable. (A little trick of the human mind helps all propagandists in this regard. Most people have a streak of irresponsibility in them, which makes bad news much more interesting than good. There is a yearning for bad news and a genuine willingness to pass it along. Bad news increases the tension upon the individual and tickles his sense of the importance of things; good news relieves the tension, and to that extent has the effect of a let-down.)

The palatability of news is not concerned so much with its content as with its trustworthiness to the enemy, its seeming to deal with straight fact, its non-editorialized presentation. (One of the reasons why Soviet Communist propaganda, after all these years, is still relatively unsuccessful, lies in the incapacity of the Communists to get out a newspaper with news in it. They put their editorial slant in all their news articles. "Man bites dog" would not make the front page in Russia unless the dog were Stalinist and the man reactionary.)

The Japanese who obediently hated the Americans when it was their duty to do so nevertheless could not help looking at maps that showed where the Americans actually were. Nazis who despised us and everything we stood for nevertheless studied the

Figure 31: Oestrous Black. Young human beings, especially young males, are apt to give considerable attention to sex. In areas of military operations, they are removed from the stimuli of secondary sex references which are (in America) an accepted part of everyone's daily life: bathing-beauty photos, magazine covers, semi-nudes in advertisements, etc. Our enemies tried to use the resulting pin-up craze for propaganda purposes, hoping that a vain arousal of oestrum would diminish morale. This choice Japanese item is from the Philippines. (The best collection of these is kept in a locked file—for experts only—at the Library of Congress.)

photographs of our new light bombers. The appeal of credible fact is universal; propaganda does not consist of doctoring the fact with moralistic blather, but of selecting that fact which is correct, interesting, and bad for the enemy to know.[2]

On the friendly side of the battle lines, the procurement of our own news is a budgetary matter. The propaganda office can subscribe to the news tickers, newspapers, telegraph services, and so on. How much is a matter of administrative housekeeping. In the field, the communications officer can frequently steal news from the news agencies of his own country or allied countries by the process of picking it out of the air. It would be highly unpatriotic of the news agency to send him a bill in the zone of operations, and he can classify his record copies of his material RESTRICTED so that the owners of the material would have no legitimate business acquiring copies that could later be taken into court to support a claim. (Americans would not do this, of course; the reference is to Byzantines.)

The Need for Timeliness. Some white propaganda and all black propaganda needs to be written so as to fit in with what the enemy is reading, listening to, or talking about in his home country. The use of antiquated slang, an old old joke, reference to a famous man as living when he died some time ago, lack of understanding of the new wartime conditions under which the listener lives and worries—such things sour a radio program quickly. In radio, the propagandist must be living in the same time as his listeners. Since the propagandist cannot shuttle between the enemy country and his own radio office (unless he is a braver and more elusive man than governments ever call for); he must try to get the up-to-the-minute touch by other means. Without it he is lost. He will be talking about something that happened a long time ago, not the situation which he is trying to affect.

This need may be called *timeliness.*

It can be served by obtaining all the most recent enemy publications that may be available, by listening attentively to enemy prisoners and captured civilians, and by carefully analyzing the enemy's current broadcasts to his own people. The Nazis made the unnecessary mistake of assuming that isolationism used the same old language after Pearl Harbor. They were right in assuming that there was considerable anti-internationalist and anti-Roosevelt sentiment left in the United States, but they were hopelessly wrong in using the isolationist language of mid-1941 as late as mid-1942. Pearl Harbor had dated all that and the isolationist-interventionist argument had shifted to other ground. When the Nazis went on using the old language, they were as conspicuous as last year's hat at a women's club. Instead of making friends and influencing people, they made themselves sound ignorant and look silly. They lacked the element of timeliness. They could have gotten it by procuring representative American publications in Lisbon and studying them.

SAM KNOWS WHAT HE WANTS

Two years ago, comely Joan Hopkins was still a salesgirl behind the ribbon counter in a New York 5 & 10 cts store getting 12 dollars a week.

To-day she is pulling down 60 bucks as the private secretary to Sam Levy. Business is excellent and Sam is making a pile of dough on war contracts.

FOR HIM THE SLAUGHTER CAN'T LAST LONG ENOUGH.

Sam has no scruples about getting a bit intimate with Joan. And why should he have any? Tall and handsome Bob Harrison, Joan's fiancé, is on the front, thousands of miles away, fighting for guys like Sam Levy.

Joan loves Bob, but she doesn't know WHEN HE WILL COME BACK.

Look for the other pictures of this series

To-day she is pulling down 60 bucks.......

SAM AT WORK

After his arrival in New York City, cigar-chewing Sam Levy, a steerage passenger from eastern Europe, used to live on the lower East Side not far from the Bowery. Soon he was able to move to upper Broadway. When President Roosevelt took those steps short of war, Sam had already leased a ten room apartment on Riverside Drive.

Slick-haired home-front warrior Mordecai Ezekiel, boss of a government department in Washington, saw to it that his chum Sam would be on the earning end of the war. Rich profits on war contracts let Sam climb up the social ladder, taking two steps at one time. He is now residing in a duplex de luxe apartment on swanky Park Avenue.

Why shouldn't Sam invite beautiful Joan Hopkins, his private secretary, former 5 & 10 cts salesgirl, up to his place to have dinner with him and cocktails.

Joan is feeling so lonely anyway. More than two years ago, Bob Harrison, the man she wanted to marry, had to leave her for the battlefields of Europe, thousands of miles away.

He is fighting there for Sam Levy and his kind.

Joan is hoping that Bob will return to her safe and sound. But she knows that many of her girl friends are already waiting in vain for their own to return.

Sam knows her predicament and he is trying his darnedest to cheer her up.

Why, Bob wouldn't know it anyway! And what's a little kiss among friends?

Joan is feeling so lonely anyway ......

Figure 32: Oestrous Grey. This and the succeeding illustration show a series of four leaflets which the Nazis used against American troops in Europe. Anti-morale in intent, they rely on the illustrations to get attention and then develop their malicious, salacious anti-Semitic story. The series illustrates the strength and weakness of Nazi propaganda.

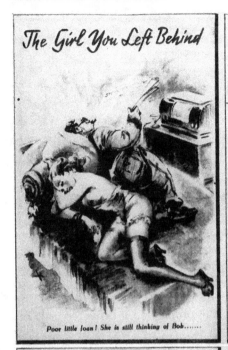

The Girl You Left Behind

Poor little Joan! She is still thinking of Bob.......

THE WAY OF ALL FLESH

When pretty Joan Hopkins was still standing behind the ribbon counter of a 5 & 10 cts. store on 3rd Avenue in New York City, she never dreamed of ever seeing the interior of a duplex Park Avenue apartment. Neither did young Bob Harrison, the man she loves. Bob was drafted and sent to the battlefields in Europe thousands of miles away from her. Through Lazare's Employment Agency Joan got a job as private secretary with wily Sam Levy. Sam is piling up big money on war contracts. Should the slaughter end very soon, he would suffer an apoplectic stroke.

Now Joan knows what Bob and his pals are fighting for.

Joan always used to look up to Bob as the guiding star of her life, and she was still a good girl when she started working for Sam Levy. But she often got the blues thinking of Bob, whom she hadn't seen for over two years. Her boss had an understanding heart and was always very kind to her, so kind indeed, that he often invited her up to his place. He had always wanted to show her his "etchings". Besides, Sam wasn't stingy and each time Joan came to see him, he gave her the nicest presents. Now, all women like beautiful and expensive things. But Sam wasn't the man you could play for a sucker. He wanted something, wanted it very definitely....

Poor little Joan! She is still thinking of Bob, yet she is almost hoping that he'll never return.

The Girl You Left Behind

It was a rude awakening for her........

THE MOMENT SHE DREADED

Forgotten are the days when shapely Joan Hopkins was still selling ribbons in a 5 and 10 cts. store in New York City. As private secretary to slick Sam Levy, big money maker in the war business, she rose to be a sugar daddy's darling.

Sam didn't have any cash when he got started, and he doesn't like to be reminded of his early days on the lower East Side. The war was just the right thing for him. Like many other home-warriors he made the grade piling up dough and growing fat on the sacrifices of those young American boys fighting on foreign battlefields.

At heart Joan is not a bad woman. For over two years she had not seen her fiancé, clean-cut Bob Harrison, whom she cares for very much. Bob was shipped to Europe to fight for the cause of Sam Levy and his kind.

Two years is a long time for any girl.

For more than half a year she had not heard from Bob. He seemed to be among the missing.

Some sunny afternoon, however, just when Joan and Sam were stepping out of fashionable Bonwit Teller's shop on Fifth Avenue, she was struck speechless by the sight of a man in uniform.

It was a rude awakening for her. And it was also a dreadful blow to Bob, for it was he who suddenly stood opposite her - on crutches, one leg amputated.

Two lives - lost to one another forever.

Figure 33: Oestrous Grey, Continued. Concluding the series begun in the preceding illustrations, these Nazi leaflets tried to lower American morale by combining oestrum, resentment, discouragement and inter-American hatred. The Dr. Mordecai Ezekiel mentioned in No. 2 is a real person, a splendid American and conscientious official. The Nazis used his name because it was so plainly Jewish, hoping that the ignorance of the American troops would permit their lies to spread.

Figure 34: Obscene Black. One of the wildest adventures of World War II concerns this now rare "Chinese Federal Reserve Bank" one-dollar bill. The bank was a Japanese puppet outfit in Peiping. The Japanese had banknotes engraved by Chinese artists, and only after the new pro-Japanese banknotes had been issued all over the city did they notice what the "ancient scholar" was doing with his hands. The engraver had disappeared and the Chinese enjoyed a rare, morale-stimulating laugh. Propaganda gestures such as this—spontaneous, saucy, silly—achieve effects which planned operations rarely attain.

Propaganda is like a newspaper; it has to be timeless or brand-new. In between, it has no value.

Opinion Analysis. In a favorable intelligence situation, espionage can succeed in running a Gallup poll along the enemy's Main Street. When this is done, the active propaganda operator has some very definite issues at hand on which he can begin work. When it is not possible to send the cloak-and-dagger boys walking up and down the Boulevard of the Martyrs of the Eleventh of July, propanal, properly handled, can produce almost the same result. The opinion of the enemy can be figured out in terms of what enemy propaganda is trying to do.

To be useful, opinion analysis must be systematic. For a while the author had the interesting job of interviewing all the latest arrivals from Tokyo at a certain headquarters. The travelers would usually be pumped up with a sense of their own smartness in having evaded the Japanese and arrived at Allied territory. You could almost hear them thinking, "Oh, boy, if Gendarmerie Chief Baka-yama could only see me now!" They were ready, in Army parlance, to spill their guts. The only item on which most of them maintained

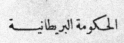

الحكومة البريطانية

BRITISH GOVERNMENT

الى كل عربى كريم

السلام عليكم ورحمة الله وبركاته وبعد ، فحامل هذا الكتاب ضابط بالجيش البريطاني وهو
صديق وفى لكافة الشعوب العربية فنرجو أن تعاملوه بالعطف والاكرام . وأن تحافظوا على
حياته من كل طارئ ، ونأمل عند الاضطرار أن تقدموا له مايحتاج اليه من طعام وشراب .
وان ترشدوه الى أقرب معسكر بريطاني . وسنكافئكم مالياً بسخاء على ماتسدونه اليه من خدمات .
والسلام عليكم ورحمة الله وبركاته

القيادة البريطانية العامة فى الشرق الاوسط

To All Arab Peoples — Greetings and Peace be upon you. The bearer of this letter is an
Officer of the British Government and a friend of all Arabs. Treat him well, guard him from
harm, give him food and drink, help him to return to the nearest British soldiers and you will
be rewarded. Peace and the Mercy of God upon you. *The British High Command in the East.*

SOME POINTS ON CONDUCT WHEN MEETING THE ARABS IN THE DESERT.

Remove footwear on entering their tents. Completely ignore their women. If thirsty drink
the water they offer, but DO NOT fill your waterbottle from their personal supply. Go to their
well and fetch what you want. Never neglect any puddle or other water supply for topping
up your bottle. Use the Halazone included in your Aid Box. Do not expect breakfast if you
sleep the night. Arabs will give you a mid-day or evening meal. Always be courteous.

REMEMBER, NEVER TRY AND HURRY IN THE DESERT, SLOW AND SURE DOES IT.

A few useful words

English	Arabic	English	Arabic
English	Ingleezi	Day	Yome
American	Amerikani	Night	Layl
Friend	Sa-hib, Sa-deck.	Half	Nuss
Water	Moya	Half a day	Nuss il Yome
Food	Akl or Mungarea	Near	Gareeb
Village	Balaad	Far	Baeed
Tired	Ta-eban		

Take me to the English and you will be rewarded.	Hud nee eind el Ingleez wa tahud Mu-ka-fa.
English Flying Officer	Za-bit Ingleezi Tye-yara
How far (how many kilos?)	Kam kilo ?
Enemy	Germani, Taliani, Sizlliani

Figure 35: Informational Sheet. This British leaflet combines a message for Arabs with instructions
for British pilots forced down in the desert. The propaganda content is closely associated with
the practical mission of the leaflet.

one-man security was the question, "Why, chum, did you yourself go to Tokyo in the first place?" Outside of that, they were eager to talk. (Some of them had frightfully good reasons to be eager; the adverb is literal.) With such sources of information, the author thought that he could find out in short order what the Japanese were thinking.

He found out, all right. He found out every single time. The refugee engineer said the Japanese were so depressed that there was a bull market in butcher knives. The absconding dairyman said the Japanese were ready to die with gloom. The eloping wife said she never saw happy Japanese any more. The military school deserter said the Japanese lay awake all night every night listening for American air raids. The reformed puppet said the Japanese had just gone to pieces. Then each of them grinned (the interviews were individual, of course), and expected to be patted on the head for bringing such good news.

Their comments were worthless. What the enemy thinks *in general* is worth nothing unless your troops are already in his suburbs. What an informant thinks the enemy thinks is worth even less. What do you, reader, think right now? What do you think you think? See? the question is nonsensical. To work, it has to be specific: What do you think about the price of new suits? What do you think about Senator O'May and Congressman MacNaples? Do you think that we will ever have to fight Laputa? Are you satisfied with your present rate of pay? Why?

What a person thinks—his opinion—is workable in relation to what he does. In practical life his opinion takes effect only when it is part of the opinion of a group. Some groups are formed by the common opinion and have nothing else in common: at a spiritualist meeting you may see the banker sitting next to his own charwoman. Most groups are groups because of things which the people *are* (Negroes, descendants of Francis Bacon, the hard-of-hearing); or things they *do* (electrical workers, lawyers, farmer, stamp collectors), or things they *have* (factory owners, nothing but wages, apartment houses) in common. The community of something practical makes the group have a community of opinion which arises

Nr. 77 O. U., den 22. 12. 44.

Skorpion
Informationsdienst

In den spärlichen Stimmen des Londoner Rundfunks zur Westfront spiegelt sich in zunehmendem Maße die Angst wieder, die deutsche Offensive könnte noch weitere ungeahnte und unübersehbare Ausmaße annehmen:

20. 12. 44. — 16.00 Uhr: Unser Korrespondent meldet, daß der Höhepunkt des deutschen Angriffes noch nicht erreicht ist.
17.00 Uhr: Es liegen keine Anzeichen eines Nachlassens des deutschen Gegenangriffes vor.
18.00 Uhr: Die deutschen Anstrengungen lassen darauf schließen, daß ein noch stärkerer Angriff zu erwarten ist.

21. 12. 44 — 12.00 Uhr: Man kann nicht verschweigen, daß deutsche Vorhuten noch immer im Vordringen sind.
16.30 Uhr: Aus den Frontberichten geht hervor, daß die Deutschen weitere beträchtliche Fortschritte machen.
21.00 Uhr: Die 1. Armee arbeitet Tag und Nacht, um Widerstandslinien zu errichten, aber dies dauert seine Zeit und die deutsche Offensive kann inzwischen weitergehn.
0.05 Uhr: Die deutsche Gegenoffensive nach Belgien und Luxemburg nimmt aufgrund jüngster Berichte, an Geschwindigkeit weiter zu.

22. 12. 44 — 7.00 Uhr: Der deutsche Vormarsch ist nicht zum Stillstand gekommen. Man muß mit einem weiteren Ansteigen der feindlichen Flut rechnen.

Stimmen zu den Fronten.

„Die gegenwärtige Schlacht im Westen ist die schrecklichste des ganzen Krieges. Es wird mit einer Erbitterung ohnegleichen gekämpft. Ehe man ein Urteil über die Lage geben kann müssen neue Nachrichten abgewartet werden". (Berichterstatter Eduard Beek, Radio London)

„Die deutsche Offensive ist gefährlich für uns. Es handelt sich um ein Unternehmen großen Stils, um unsere Pläne zu stören und unser Hinterland und seine Verkehrswege in Verwirrung zu bringen". (Radio London)

„Es ist nicht zu vermeiden, daß auch die Alliierten an manchen Abschnitten schwächer sind. Es ist normal, daß der Feind Boden gewinnt. Dieser Angriff zeigt aber deutlich, daß man sich, solange der Krieg nicht zu Ende ist, nicht in leichtfertigen Träumereien verlieren darf" — meldet der alliierte Kriegsberichterstatter Paul Levy aus Belgien.

„Die deutsche Gegenoffensive im Westen stellt nur einen Teil eines allgemeinen Planes des OKW. dar, der darauf hinzielt, die Vorbereitungen der Alliierten für entscheidende Kämpfe um die Ruhr- und Saar-Industriezentren mehr oder weniger auszuschalten". („Roter Stern", Moskau)

„Aus dem deutschen Schweigen und dem alliierten Geschrei läßt sich nur eines ableiten: Die völlige Verwirrung in den angloamerikanischen Befehlsstellen, die überrascht wurden und sich noch immer nicht von ihrem Schrecken erholt haben". (Span. Zeitung Informaciones)
Fliegende Bomben über der alliierten Front. „Das anhaltende Feuer der fliegenden Bomben liegt auf den englischen Truppen". (Radio London) — „Fliegende Bomben fallen so zahlreich in die Linien der 1 amerikanischen Armee als im letzten Sommer auf London niedergingen. (Radio London)

„Es ist klar, daß sich die deutsche Offensive noch in vollem Schwung befindet". (Times) — Es ist doch klar, daß die feindliche Offensivmaschine auf höchsten Touren läuft". (Radio London)

Tiefe Einbrüche in die amerikanischen Linien. „Tiefe Einbrüche des Feindes bleiben noch wieder gut zu machen". (Daniel Moore, Radio London) — „die deutsche Offensive erzwang größere Einbrüche". (Reuters Sonderkorrespondent William Steen) — „Es wird von weiteren vier Einbruchstellen gesprochen". (Radio London)

Figure 36: Counterpropaganda Instructions. The Wehrmacht in the West had a unit bearing the code designation *Skorpion.* This unit combined the functions of offensive and defensive propaganda, which remained separate throughout the war in the U.S. Army. The information service sheet shown provides clear, simple leads for counterpropaganda by selecting usable (usable for the Germans, that is) items from Allied sources. From this raw material, morale officers could make up their own leaflets, lectures, or broadcasts.

from the problems they think they face with respect to their common interests. Such groups are not only opinion groups, they are interest groups. It is these groups that do things *as groups*. It is these groups that propaganda tries to stir up, move, set against each other, and use in any handy way. (Few individuals belong to just one group at a time; the groups are almost illimitable in number.)

The propagandist should not get the idea that just because a group exists it is a potential source of weakness or cleavage. Workers are not always against employers, nor the aged against the young, nor women against men, nor shippers against railwaymen. In a well run society, groups have interest only for limited purposes. Railwaymen are not permanently hostile to truckers, shippers, fliers, canal operators. At the moment they may be maddest of all at the insurance companies because of some quarrel about insurance premiums and risks.

The poor propagandist tries to butt in on every fight, even when there is none. Often his propaganda is received the way an intervenor is received in most family quarrels, with the bland question, "*What* fight? We ain't mad." Sound propaganda picks only those group issues which are acute enough to stand a little help from outside. If outside help would be a kiss-of-death to the group that is helped, then black propaganda instead of white is indicated. In any case, sound operating intelligence is the first precondition to the attempted psychological manipulation of enemy groups.

Profile of Opinion. Opinion analysis can present a *profile of enemy opinion.* To make a profile, proceed as though assembling a photo-strip map taken by an aerial camera. Take the whole enemy country and divide, it into major groups by percentages. Select, particularly, those groups you are interested in addressing. If you have *kamikaze*-minded collaborators, send them in to the enemy country to ask a thousand enemies the same question, selecting the thousand the same way that the total population is made up. If the country is 32% Catholic, the thousand interviewees should include 320 Catholics. If the country is 36% urban and 61% rural

Nationalsozialistischer Führungsstab
der Wehrmacht

Januar 1945 Nr.
Zuschriften für die „Mitteilungen"
FP. Nr. 12 731

Mitteilungen für die Truppe

Die Mitteilungen dienen als Unterlage für Kompanie-Besprechungen

Gedanken zum Volkssturm

Vielen Soldaten ist das berühmte Defregger-Gemälde „Das letzte Aufgebot" bekannt. Es schildert den Aufbruch der Tiroler Bergbauern beim Eindringen der napoleonischen Heere in ihre Heimat. Als durch Führererlass der Volkssturm aufgestellt wurde, mag bei vielen der Gedanke aufgetaucht sein, ob es etwa mit diesem Volkssturm die gleiche Bewandtnis wie damals hätte, ob nun auch die Greise und Kinder als letztes Aufgebot unter die Waffen gerufen werden, ob auch sie nun mit primitivsten Waffen ausgerüstet sich als letztes Aufgebot an die bedrohte Grenze stellen wurden, um ihr geliebtes Vaterland zu verteidigen.

Dieser Gedanke findet seine augenblickliche Widerlegung, wenn man sieht, wie der Volkssturm aufgebaut ist, und wenn man darüber Klarheit gewinnt, welche Aufgaben dem Volkssturm zufallen. Zum Volkssturm wurden die 16- und 60-jährigen aufgerufen, und es hat sich gezeigt, dass die überwiegende Mehrzahl der Volkssturmmänner sich aus den Angehörigen unserer besten Männerjahrgänge zusammensetzt. Es sind dies die vom Uk-Gestellten aus der Rüstung, der Wirtschaft und dem Landvolk, die entlassenen Kriegsversehrten, die nicht einberufenen Körperbehinderten. Ueber die Altersgrenze der 60 hinaus haben sich viele Männer, alte gediente Soldaten, freiwillig gemeldet.

Der Aufbau des Volkssturms liegt in der Hand der Partei und ihrer Gliederungen, der SA und des NSKK.

Bei der Auswahl der Führer bis zu den kleinsten Einheiten wird von dem Gesichtspunkt ausgegangen, daß nur der in jeder Lage Bewahrte im Volkssturm führen kann.

Als die Volkssturmbataillone durch die Städte zur Verteidigung marschierten, konnte man auch die ausgezeichnete Bewaffnung unserer Volkssturmmänner beobachten. Vom neuesten Gewehr und Maschinengewehr bis zu „Panzerfaust" und „Panzerschreck" waren alle Waffen vertreten, und die Lüge vom Dreschflegel und der Sense und der altertümlichen Schrotflinte wurde a d a b s u r d u m geführt. Die Gesichter der Volkssturmmänner sahen absolut nicht wie ein letztes Aufgebot aus.

Der Gegner hat das Lachen über den Volkssturm schnell aufgegeben und sich zu der Erkenntnis durchgerungen, dass der Volkssturm eine sehr ernstzunehmende Tatsache darstellt. Wie sich der Volkssturm schlägt, das beweist sein erster Einsatz in Ostpreussen. Nur ein einziges Beispiel von vielen weicherausgegriffen, wo ein 16jähriger Hitlerjunge angesichts zweier einbrechender T 34 aus dem Deckungsgraben springt und beide mit der „Panzerfaust" erledigt. Kurze Zeit später wurden dem tapferen Jungen das EK 1 und zwei Panzervernichtungsabzeichen angeheftet.

Die Zeit wird beweisen, daß der Volkssturm kein letztes Aufgebot, sondern im Gegenteil die machtvollste Demonstration einer Stärke darstellt, die auch heute im sechsten Kriegsjahr immer wieder aus dem deutschen Volk erstrahlt. Je härter der Kampf, um so fanatischer die Entschlossenheit, unseren verhaßten Feinden die Stirn zu bieten, und daß der Volkssturm hierbei ein gewichtiges Wörtlein mitzusprechen hat, das liegt in dem harten Einsatzwillen der Volkssturmmänner begründet.

Die berühmten amerikanischen Freiheiten

Vor seiner vorigen Wahl hatte der amerikanische Präsident Roosevelt bekanntlich versprochen, kein amerikanischer Soldat werde außerhalb des Landes eingesetzt werden. Als er nachher das Gegenteil tat, begründete er seinen Wortbruch mit der Behauptung, er müsse der vom Nationalsozialismus geknechteten deutschen Menschheit die amerikanischen Freiheiten bringen, die Freiheit der Gedanken, des Wortes, der Schrift und des Glaubens.

Wie diese Freiheiten in Wirklichkeit aussehen, dafür gibt ein Bericht des Militärkorrespondenten im amerikanischen Europasender vom 20. November 1944 Aufschluß. In der kleinen Stadt Gangelt an der deutsch-niederländischen Grenze trafen die Amerikaner nur noch wenige Leute an. Aber folgende Maßnahmen, so berichtet der Korrespondent, sind getroffen worden:

1. Das Betreten der Straße wurde den Bewohnern nur zwischen 12 und 13 Uhr gestattet.

2. Für jeden anderen Ausgang ist ein besonderer Passierschein nötig.

3. An jedem Haus muß ein Schild hängen mit dem Verzeichnis aller Bewohner.

4. Die deutschen Zivilisten erhalten weder Nahrungsmittel, Kleidungsstücke, noch andere Versorgungsgüter usw.

Als Zweck der Militärverwaltung wird bezeichnet, zu beweisen, daß die Amerikaner als Eroberer gekommen sind.

Es ist das gleiche Bild überall. Aus dem Kampfraum Aachen liegen zahlreiche Meldungen vor, wie die Häuser ausgeplündert worden sind. Bei der Vernehmung der Kriegsgefangenen fungierten fast ausschließlich Juden. Die Behandlung der Gefangenen war miserabel, ihre Orden und Ehrenzeichen wurden ihnen geklaut, und man ließ sie tagelang hungern.

Erstaunen können diese Tatsachen niemand, der die amerikanischen Verhältnisse wirklich kennt und aus den vergangenen Jahren weiß, wie dieses reiche Land mit seinen eigenen Erwerbslosen umsprang. Erst kürzlich las man in einer amerikanischen Zeitung, es sei viel zu viel Aufhebens von den 12 Millionen Erwerbslosen gemacht worden. Warum man sie nicht habe „verrecken" lassen?

Kein politisch geschulter Soldat läßt sich mehr durch tönende Worte über angebliche amerikanische Errungenschaften bluffen. Wie die amerikanische Freiheit ist die Freiheit zu hungern den breiten Massen des Volks am vertrautesten geworden. Würde der eiskalte Dollarimperialismus von drüben je über Deutschland Macht gewinnen, so wissen wir, was dann die Uhr geschlagen hatte. Und darum wird das deutsche Volk das Aeußerste tun, eine Versklavung durch den amerikanisch-jüdischen Hochkapitalismus zu verhindern.

Ein gescheiter und nachdenklicher Brief über das Thema „Muss das sein?"

Ein Frontbrief bringt die folgenden Ausführungen, die uns alle angehen. „Der Krieg bringt zwangsläufig einen großen Verschleiß mit sich, aber wieviel wird sinnlos und leichtsinnig verschleudert! Vater, Mutter, Frau und Schwester stehen im Arbeitsprozeß, um die Abnutzung, die der Krieg nun mal mit sich bringt, wieder

Figure 37: Defensive Counterpropaganda. The "National Socialist Leadership Staff of the Wehrmacht" got out this *Communications for the Troops* as a guidance sheet for company talks. The content includes "Thoughts About the Volkssturm," "The Celebrated American Freedoms," and "Small Requests, but Important." This issue is dated from January 1945.

(3% unexplained), get 610 of your interviewees from the country.
The questions do not have to be asked in precisely the same form,
but they should bear on precisely the same issues. When your
agents come back you have a poll. If you do not have agents, then
use the percentages from reference books, and try to estimate how
many definite groups have what specific grievances. You are then
in a position to proceed.

Interrogation. When processing prisoners of war, it is an excellent idea to deal with them for morale intelligence as well as for
general and assorted military information. Questions should not
aim at what the prisoner thinks he thinks about God, his leader,
his country, and so on, but should concern themselves with those
things which most interest the prisoner himself. Does his wife write
that the babies have enough diapers? How is the mail service? Is
he worried about war workers getting his prewar job? How much
money is he saving? How is the food? How were the non-coms—
did they treat him right? Did he get enough furloughs? Does he
think that anybody is making too much money at home? Most men
carry over into military services the occupational interests which
they had as civilians. A carpenter in uniform, even though he may
be a good infantry top sergeant, is still a carpenter, and information can be obtained from him as to the problems of skilled labor,
of union members, of the poorer city dwellers, and so on.

The profile obtained from civilian polls or from propanal can
then be paralleled in the field. Set up a graph showing the entire
enemy army. Use several graphs if the army splits along racial,
national or plainly sectional lines. On each graph, enter the component groups. From the poll or from the interrogations, list the
dissatisfaction in terms of seriousness with which the dissatisfyee
attributes to it; it is not what you think he should worry about that
is important. It's what actually he does worry about. His weight-
ing counts. Make up a scale, quantitative on the actual count of
mentions of particular gripes. (For example, out of 699 prisoners,
of whom 167 were union members in civil life, there were 234 separate voluntary mentions of dissatisfaction with the enemy

government's labor union policy) When that quantitative count changes up or down, you have a definite guide with which to control your own propaganda policy.

Or you can proceed qualitatively. List enemy dissatisfaction under terms such as these for any one issue (shoe rationing, health facilities, minority rights, esteem for government leaders, etc.): Prisoner—

(1) is completely satisfied and has no complaints.
(2) has a few complaints but is generally satisfied.
(3) has many complaints and does not expect improvement.
(4) is despondent about the whole situation.
(5) is definitely antagonistic to home authorities in this matter.

Rate each prisoner or captured civilian according to your best judgment. Then make up percentage lists of the grounds for dissatisfaction of each component group in the enemy society. (This latter figure will be impressive in documents but will not mean as much for practical purposes as will the more specific percentages under each separate head.)

If you feel like showing off, average everything into everything else and call it the Gross Index of Total Enemy Morale. This won't fool anyone who knows the propaganda business, and you won't be able to do anything with or about it, but you can hang it on a month-by-month chart in the front office, where visitors can be impressed at getting in on a military secret. (Incidentally, if some smart enemy agent sees it and reports it back, enemy intelligence experts will go mad trying to figure out just how you got that figure. It's like the old joke that the *average* American is ten-elevenths White, 52% female, and always slightly pregnant.)

Specificity. Good propaganda intelligence provides:

(a) news;
(b) military intelligence which can be released as news;

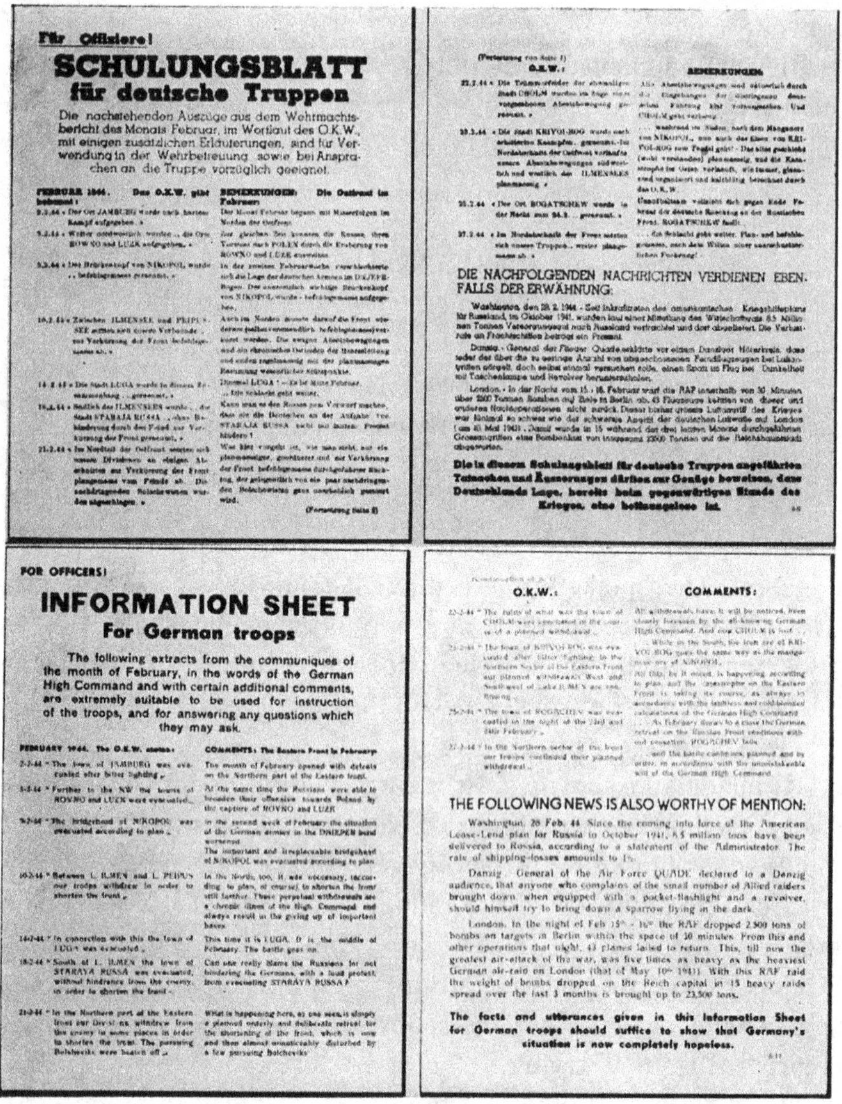

Figure 38: Black "Counterpropaganda." Seeing that the Germans had a good counterpropaganda medium, the Allies decided to use it themselves. They issued this "counterpropaganda" sheet, shown in original and facsimile in English. The "blackness" is not very black, since few Germans would consider this to be German in origin, once they had read it.

(c) military intelligence which cannot be released as news, but knowledge of which will prevent the propaganda operator from making mistakes or miscalculations in reporting the news;

(d) enemy news;

(e) up-to-the-minute enemy slang, hobbies, fads, grievances, and other matters of current public attention;

(f) specific grievances of specific groups and of the nation as a whole, should these arise;

(g) information about probable inter-group conflicts;

(h) types and forms of discontent with enemy authority;

(i) identification of unpopular or popular enemy personalities;

(j) all other information that will enable the psychological warfare operator to act promptly and sympathetically in taking the side of specific enemy individuals against their authorities or other enemy groups.

Enemy opinion cannot be manipulated in general. It must be met on its own ground—the current everyday thoughts of enemy citizens and soldiers. These thoughts do not usually concern grandiose problems of political ethics. They are practical like your own.[3] They must be appealed to in a way which makes the listener really listen, makes the reader stop and reread, makes them both think it over later. Getting the attention of the enemy is not enough. Most enemies will pay plenty of attention to you—too much, at times. Getting sympathetic attention is what counts.

This can be done only with specific grounds. With the news, you and he have a genuine common interest. Using his real troubles as a link, you must create that common interest. The force, the effectiveness of your argument may make him forget that it is the enemy who has brought his attention to this issue. You must leave him with the feeling, "By golly, that fellow is right!"

But to talk about his troubles, effectively, you must know what they really are. You must see it his way before you start showing him that his way is your way, that you think that he is really on your side, and that his bosses' side is wrong, incorrect and doomed to get whipped, anyhow. Propaganda can operate only on the basis of *specificity*. Real persuasion can be sought only on the basis of real sympathy with real troubles. Old, incorrectly guessed, or poorly described issues are worse than none at all.

NOTES:

[1] Free advertisement.

[2] Bad news about his side is not necessarily the only kind of bad news for the enemy to know. Gloomy news about our side can harm the enemy listener if his government is running a propaganda campaign to raise production, promote thrift, etc., by claiming things are worse on *their* side. In such a case, good news about us would be good for him. News must be fitted to the propaganda plan and to the propaganda situation.

[3] Walter Lippmann's book, *Public Opinion*, was first published in New York in 1922 but it is still clean-cut as a basic statement of the problems of public opinion. The author's own life an a commentator in remarkable in fulfilling the mission which he implicitly set himself when writing about public opinion: the job of lifting issues into emotional and psychological contexts in which the resulting judgment will be based on socially sound factors.

CHAPTER 9
ESTIMATE OF THE SITUATION

In physical warfare, the inherent instability of every situation is concealed by the apparent definiteness of the operation. Panic, revolt or dissolution of regiments is not normally figured into the situation. The assumption is made—and for professional military purposes must be made—that all identical units are of equal quality unless proved otherwise, that all men in a unit will respond with psychological uniformity unless they are reported out physically by medical reports, that the unit will be capable of doing tomorrow what it did yesterday. The terrain comes in as a constant factor and even such variables as weather can be calculated in terms of a predictable risk. Nevertheless, every experienced soldier knows that things do not always work out the way they should, that unexplained or unforeseen factors sooner or later complicate or frustrate the best plans, and that warfare is a huge gamble with a superficial but very necessary coating of exactitude.

In psychological warfare, these considerations apply even more sharply. Combat at least has terrain, order of battle, logistics, estimated capabilities and other concrete factors with which to figure. There is a known degree of difference between one enemy division and five enemy divisions. There is the possibility of computing the time which the enemy will need to fulfill this capability or that, and the equally good possibility of computing time on our side for counter-measures. Even in such very long-range operations as strategic bombing, economic factors can be figured out to give the operation at least the coloration of precision. With propaganda, none of this is possible.

The propagandist never knows the terrain, because his terrain is the enemy mind in its entirety—a factor beyond the understanding of any man. The enemy can have strongholds of faith to be shaken but the propagandist can never say, "This factor is finished. Therefore we proceed to the next." There is neither victory nor defeat, only the endless seesaw of probable accomplishments or probable blunders. The honest psychological warfare operative will admit that he does not know where he is at any given moment, how far from his start, how near to his goal. Even with surrender of the enemy, propaganda cannot be judged to have met with complete failure or complete success, because propaganda is an interminable stream going on into international affairs and carrying over to the next war. Psychological warfare can be given apparent certainty only by the creation of assumptions on the part of the planner. The assumptions will not stand up if questioned by a clever philosopher, any more than did the basic assumptions of the German General Staff when questioned by the sardonic Trotzky at Brest-Litovsk. Nevertheless, the assumptions can work for planning purposes.

Definiteness of the Goal. The first assumption to make is this: goals can be sought with some hope of success. The propaganda planner uses the intelligence available to him. He consults with knowledgeable persons. He defines (1) specific kinds of demoralization and discord he wishes to create, (2) the particular enemy audiences in which he wishes to create them, (3) the types of argument he proposes to use, and (4) the media through which he intends to project his propaganda. He assumes that the kind of discord, depression or surrender which he seeks will hasten the end of the war. In so doing, he is on ground only a little less sure than that of the strategic bombing planner, who also seeks results indirectly.

For field operations, the goal of the propagandist is normally surrender of the enemy troops. If the troops are moving forward and are not likely to be in a mood to surrender, then other goals, such as conflict between officers and men, encouraging desertion, informing enemy troops of bad news elsewhere in the war, or morale-depression may be sought. In each case, the propaganda must be aimed at a goal, and a goal is as essential to the operation of psychological warfare as is definition of a target for artillery or bombing. No one ever accomplishes anything shooting "somewhere or other"; no one propagandizes successfully unless he seeks the attainment of a state of mind or series of actions which may actually happen. Most times, it is thus impossible to aim at the total surrender of the enemy armies or state. One can aim for concrete operational purposes only at specific enemy troubles or effects. For the field, troop surrenders; for the home front, interference with the enemy war effort—these are about as general as goals can be made.

They can be made very specific indeed. A situation reported by intelligence may provide an almost perfect opening for psychological warfare. If the enemy press reports that twenty-three embezzlers have been detected in food supply and have been shot, it is a perfect opening for the black propaganda goal, "to conduce to enemy mistrust of food control, to increase food spoilage, to lower efficiency of enemy food consumption through enhancing misuse of food supply." Some of the means might be these. An alleged enemy leaflet could be prepared warning quartermasters to destroy canned foods that have lost labels; another leaflet describing diseases that come from partly spoiled food; an "enemy" allegation (from your side or, better, from neutral territory) that the political chiefs of the enemy country are the biggest food embezzlers of all; getting a black-radio and rumor campaign under way describing the seven hundred and eighty-three people who died last month as a result of eating musty food (even though your own doctors say the mustiness may not interfere with the wholesomeness of that particular food); describing common diseases that actually occur in the enemy country, such as arthritis, stomach ulcers, sinus headaches or infectious jaundice, and blaming them all on the foods the enemy government distributes to the enemy people. On white radio, features could be put on describing the unhappy plight of your own side, where people may get their rashers of bacon for breakfast only every other day, and where nobody can have more than three eggs at a time; point out that the government is worried that food prices have risen 5.3%, without mentioning at that time the fact that enemy prices have gone up 45% or more. The definite goal gives the propaganda boys something to work on. Propaganda to the allies or satellites of the enemy can point out that the enemy government is apt to dump the spoiled food onto the foreign market, that food spoiling in territory of the big enemy will make him requisition more food from his little allies, et cetera.

When the topic has been worked for a while, stop; keep it up only if actual news from the enemy country shows that they are having enough real trouble with food to make your *improvements* on the fact thoroughly credible.

Propaganda cannot function in a vacuum framed by moral generalities. The goal must be defined in the light of authentic news or intelligence. The operation can be sustained only if there is enough factual reality behind it to make the propaganda fit the case known or credited by the majority of the listeners, counted one by one.

Since no trouble-free, wartime country has been known to exist, the goals should be tailored to the troubles of the particular enemy, and should aim at increasing real difficulties, building up pre-existing doubts, stimulating genuine internal hostilities. Propaganda which invents pure novelty gets nowhere. The Russians did not hesitate to appeal to Bismarck in order to show the professional German soldiers what a rotter Hitler was, and how stupid the Nazi strategy. But if Bismarck had actually said nothing on the subject of the army in general or an Eastern war in particular, they would have been wise to leave him alone. If the Japanese had tried to make the ex-Confederate States secede all over again, they would not have gotten anywhere because they would not have started with a real grievance. But if they had alleged that the Negro units were used for stevedoring because Whites regarded Negroes as unworthy of carrying weapons, they might have hit on a real grievance. The goal must be deeply bedded in reality.

The Propaganda Man. It has been pointed out that the true terrain of psychological warfare—the private thoughts of the enemy people, one by one—is known only to God. There is, however, a way of finding approximate terrain. That consists of setting up a hypothetical enemy listener or reader, and then trying to figure things out from *his* angle.

The first thing to do with the hypothetical man is to make him fit the kind of person who does get propaganda. In dealing with China, for example, it would be no use to take a statistically true Chinese, who lived on a farm 1.3 acres in size, went to town 5.8 times a year, had 3.6 children, and never read newspapers. The man to be set up would be the *reachable* man, the city, town or village dweller who had an income 2.1 times greater than that of the average in his county, who owned 1.7 long coats, and who shared one newspaper with 6.8 neighbors. Take this lowest-common-denominator of a man who can be reached by enemy propaganda and by yours. Name him the Propaganda Man. (Realistically speaking, modal and not arithmetical classes should be set up.)

Make up the prewar life of the Propaganda Man. Use your regional experts as informants. What kinds of things did he like? What prejudices was he apt to have? What kind of gossip did he receive and pass along? What kind of words disgusted him? What kind of patriotic appeal made him do things? What did he think of your country before the war? What things did he dislike you and your people for? What myths did he believe about America—that all Americans drove sports convertibles while drinking liquor? that all had blonde sweethearts? that all exchanged gunfire periodically? Of what American things did he think well—food, shoes, autos, personal freedom, others? What is he apt to be thinking now?

To this add what the enemy propaganda is trying to do to its Propaganda Man. That is, size up the domestic propaganda of the enemy in terms of the concrete individuals at whom it is aimed. This may reveal the enemy's vital necessities and his concealed weaknesses. What *are* the leaders trying to do? Are they trying to make the Propaganda Man get to work on time? Are they trying to make him give up holidays willingly? Are they trying to make him think that your side will kill him if you win? Are they trying to keep him from being worried about his city going up in an incandescent haze? Are they trying to make him believe that the concrete shelters are good? Why are they harping so on the safety of the shelters? Has the Propaganda Man been muttering back about the flimsiness of the shelters? Does he want to be evacuated from target cities? Are the police being praised for their fairness and speed in issuing leave-the-city permits? Are illegal évacués being treated as scum and traitors and cowards?

Then go after the Propaganda Man yourself. He is your friend. You are his friend. The only enemy is the enemy Leader (or generals, or emperor, or capitalists, or "They"). How is the Propaganda Man going to hear from you? Leaflets? Short-wave—and if so, why is he listening to the enemy in the first place? Standard-wave? Speaker planes? Rumors? Get things to him that you know he will repeat, things which will interest him. Make up a list of the things he worries about each month, a list of the things which the enemy propaganda is trying to do to him currently, a list of the things your propaganda is trying to do. Do the three lists fit? Would they work on an actual living breathing thinking human being, with the prejudices, frailty, nobility, greed, lubricity, and other motives of the ordinary human being? If your list fits his real life, if your list spoils the enemy propaganda list, if your list builds up a psychological effect of confusion, gloom, willingness-to-surrender which accumulates month after month, the terrain is favorable. It is in your Propaganda Man's head.

There are no maps of the human mind, but in certain special cases sociology and psychology can provide leads which even the most acute untrained observation would otherwise overlook. During World War II, for example, Mr. Geoffrey Gorer, a British anthropologist, was able to provide character analyses of the Japanese that stood up under the rigorous analysis of experts long resident in Japan. Gorer took as base data the experience of the Japanese infant in the first forty-odd months of life. How was the baby given toilet training? how was it weaned? how was it disciplined into the family life? how did the small child learn what it was? Gorer found that Japanese domestic life started the child out with a mixture of uncertainty and defiance—that the infant soon learned he was in a definite position in the human queue, where all above him had to be respected on the threat of immediate and condign reprisal, while all below him could be mistreated almost with impunity—that the Japanese had sad dirty little private thoughts about himself to a degree unknown to ourselves or the Chinese— that the Japanese was in adult life the inevitable fulfillment of what he had been made in infancy: arrogant, timid, insanely brave, deferential, fearful of foreigners and overtly cruel to them.

Furthermore, the Japanese identified persons, nations, or institutions as Female (peaceful, possessing enjoyments, subject to bullying) or as Male (fierce, counteraggressive, superordinate). The U.S.A. of Admiral Perry seemed Male; that of Cordell Hull, Female. These findings, applied to propaganda, gave British-American operations an audience unlike the Japanese whom missionaries, soldiers, diplomats, businessmen, and journalists had portrayed in such varied and inconsistent terms. This Japanese Propaganda Man (analyzed at a distance, since Gorer had never been nearer Japan than Indo-China) became a believable person. It was uncanny to see Japanese propaganda movies after reading the Gorer analyses, and to find the Japanese government propagandists, by hunch and instinct, appealing to the same Propaganda Man whom Gorer, by bold but permissible extrapolations, had revealed to Allied propaganda planners.

The Attribution of Motive. One of the least factual elements in human life is motive. Motive is hard to discern, even in one's own life, and it is difficult if not impossible to prove. It must frequently be attributed. Motive is therefore easily interpreted; "falsification" is almost impossible because no matter how much probable motive is twisted, it still might fit the case. Motive is therefore excellent material for psychological warfare. (Those propaganda veterans, the Communists, have a formula for showing that the motive of every person opposed to them is unprogressive, illiberal, and greedy, even if the person himself does not know it. Their own motives are always pure because they are "objectively" and "historically correct" according to *science*, that is, according to the historical rigmaroles of Karl Marx. The formula is a poor science, but a superb propaganda weapon.)

War eases the motive-switching operation because the leaders and people on each side derive moral exhilaration from the common effort. Ostensibly, politicians become statesmen; all higher-ranking officers become strategists; ordinary men become heroes, martyrs, adventurers. The lofty process of war is one which psychologists will not explain in our time; it transposes ordinary persons and events to a frame of reference in which individuals are less self-conscious and also less critical. Among European and American peoples, particularly, there arises the assumption that because of war men should be brave and unselfish, women kind and chaste, yet alluring, officials self-sacrificing, and so on, even though the facts of the case in the particular country involved may be very much to the contrary. The cruel futility inherent in war is so plain to all civilized men that when war does come men overcompensate for it. They set up illusions.

This need not be taken as a criticism of war or of mankind. The world would be a more inspiring place in which to dwell if people generally lived up to the wartime standards they impose on themselves. That these standards are felt to be real is attested by the distinct drop of the suicide rate in wartime, and the increase in suicide, murder, and crimes of delinquency after every war; that the change of role is largely illusory is attested by the fact that no nation appears to have undergone permanent sociological change as a result of improvement during war. Many wartime changes carry on, of course; but they rarely comprise, by the standards of the people concerned, improvements. The upswing is genuine, when it occurs, but it is rarely permanent, and it seldom affects all levels of the entire population with the same degree of exhilaration.

The propagandist thus has an ideal situation. In the enemy country everyone is trying to be more noble, more unselfish, more hard-working. Everyone applies a higher standard of ethics and performance than in peacetime. Businessmen are not supposed to make too much money, politicians are supposed to work around the clock, officials are supposed to cooperate, housewives to save, children to scavenge, and so on. Yet a certain percentage of the enemy population is not taken into this. Sometimes minorities feel themselves emotionally excluded; at other times private temperamental differences make some persons skeptic while others remain believers. The ground is ready for rumor, for tearing down inflated personages, for breaking the illusion by the simple process of attributing normally selfish motives in wartime.

It is easier to attribute bad motives to civilian leaders than to military. The ceremonialized discipline of modern warfare makes the military figure a little mysterious; his normal peacetime obscurity shielded him and his family from exposure, cheap publicity, gossip. The civilian leader does not have this protection. The very process of becoming prominent has involved his seeking publicity, for the one part, and his pretense of avoiding it, for the other. Furthermore, the man who serves his nation serves himself. It is not possible for a man to lead a large country without benefiting himself, since the act of leadership is itself intensely pleasurable. Also, prominence possesses a characteristic of vice; even when it loses its value for positive enjoyment it retains withdrawal pains. The once-prominent individual hates to leave prominence though he may be genuinely weary of it. He is willing to be tired of the country, but not willing for the country to be tired of him. In wartime old leaders remain and new ones come in. Fame and obscurity shift with even greater rapidity than before. The personality-politics condition of the country is highly mobile. Personalities are tense with interpersonal conflict.

Then comes the propagandist.

First, he attributes normal human motives to the leaders who so obviously possess them. In this job, he is doing what the famous little boy in the Hans Christian Andersen story did when he said of the Emperor, "Mamma, he hasn't any clothes on!" The propagandist need only say what everyone knows: that this man is notoriously fond of money; that another one has been a poor sportsman;

that a third has betrayed some old friends; that a fourth has sought power in a selfish, vindictive way. The response which the propagandist seeks is a simple "That's so."

The next step in propaganda is to show that these persons do not measure up to the tragic, heroic, historic roles war has imposed on them. That too is not difficult, especially if the war is not going decisively one way or the other. Defeat or victory serves equally well to make leaders into heroes; Churchill and MacArthur were never more splendid than when they were whipped, the one after Dunkirk, the other after Bataan.

The final approach is the total discrediting of leaders. If the internal politics of the country have been bitter enough, some of the leaders may even come over voluntarily to the enemy. Quisling in Norway; Wang in China; Doriot and Laval in France; Vlassov in the U.S.S.R.; Laurel from the Philippines—such men all possessed a certain amount of standing in their own countries but through capture, impatience, or seduction decided to continue their careers with enemy backing. The propagandist can now pretend to be tolerant. It is he who believes in peace, in reconciliation, in easygoing live-and-let-live attitudes. He describes his protegés, the quislings, in warm complimentary terms; he lightens the tenor of his attack on the non-quisling enemy leaders. He takes the attitude that war continues because of private stupidity, vengefulness, greed, unreasonableness on the other. For his part, he is willing to let the politicians, both quisling and patriot, "settle it between themselves." Let them form a coalition government.

Personal smearing is effective. If the war situation runs in the enemy's favor, the easing of the enemy position permits the population the privilege of backbiting, and even within the leader-group some leaders may feel more free to destroy the positions or reputations of the others. The impossible and foolishly heroic stances which the leaders have taken in time of strain now make most of them look a little silly. Conversely, in a downgrade situation, the leaders may gain stature in the first tragic weeks of defeat, but soon the ignobility of defeat sweeps over them all. The propagandist need only be a good reporter, and the leaders of the defeated country will provide him with good propaganda material.

In estimating the propaganda situation, the vulnerability of the leaders to personal attack is one of the major elements. Properly handled, it can be of real value. In the American Revolution, the personal character of George Washington was a very substantial asset. A very rich man, he could scarcely be accused of a gutter revolution. A slave owner, he could not be accused of wanting the overthrow of the social order. An experienced soldier, he could not be attacked as a military amateur. A man of patience, correct manners, and genuine modesty, he was not easily described as a bloody empire-builder, an immoral sycophant, or a power-drunk madman. British propaganda accordingly went after the Continental Congress, of which there was a great deal to be said. On the other side, the Americans had duck soup when it came to George III and most of his Cabinet—personalities which included boors, fuddy-duddies, too-little-and-too-laters, and conspicuous nincompoops.

A Written Estimate of the Situation. If, as indicated above, the terrain of Psychological Warfare consists of the private thoughts and feelings of each member of the audience reached; if the mission of Psychological Warfare is the accomplishment of anything from entirely unknowable results (such as an imperceptible change of mood) all the way through to complete success (such as organized mass surrender); if the capabilities of the enemy have virtually nothing to do with one's own Psychological Warfare commitments; and if the decision consists of choices of means and theme— if these peculiarities all apply, the usual "estimate of the situation" has almost nothing to do with military propaganda.

Roughly speaking, this is the case. An attempt to apply the outline given in FM 101-5, Appendix I, would produce only a lamentable parody of a military document.

The *situation* of the military unit possessing Psychological Warfare facilities has relatively little to do with the *capabilities* of the Psychological Warfare unit. The morale of one's own men should have no effect whatever on the output of the radio script writers and the leaflet writers.

In combat operations, military forces *meet*. In Psychological Warfare, they do not. In combat operations, it is impossible for two hostile units to occupy the *same* territory for any length of time without both of them degenerating into a chaos of armed mobs. In Psychological Warfare operations, both sets of operations can be conducted in the same media, can address themselves to the same basic human appeals, can use the same music, the same general kind of news account, and so on.

Furthermore, no modern army ever went into operation with certain units designated as wholly and exclusively defensive, and certain others as wholly and exclusively offensive. (The Great Wall of China is the world's most celebrated example of purely defensive planning, yet it protected Chinese offensive bases for twenty-one hundred years.) But in Psychological Warfare, the Japanese-language short-wave broadcasts from San Francisco had no imaginable effect on the American forces in the Pacific. The only people who could understand them were the Japanese-language officers in G-2 and ONI offices; their personal vexation did not matter.

The offensive operations of combat troops are predicated upon finding the enemy, effecting contact, and either destroying the enemy or making him yield terrain. The defensive operations of combat troops, contrariwise, are planned with a view to resisting an enemy who has been met.

In Psychological Warfare, operators and enemy do not effect contact. The audience cannot strike back through a radio set; the enemy reader cannot throw a leaflet back at the bomber which has dropped it on him. When American planes bombed German radio stations, they did not do so because the flight commander was trying to get German propaganda off the air; they did so because the Americans were trying to break up the entire German communications network. It is almost impossible to pinpoint radio transmitters and printing presses with such accuracy as to deny the enemy all chance of talking back. In a purely physical sense, there are only two sets of measures whereby an actual defense can be set up against Psychological Warfare. Each is a measure of desperation; neither is considered effective; the Americans did not bother with either in World War II.

The first physical defense consists of radio jamming and of the planned interception of enemy leaflet raids. Radio jamming is ineffectual except in the case of an enemy possessing hopelessly inferior signal equipment. (The Japanese tried to jam our radio at Saipan, just as the Germans tried to jam BBC. They impeded reception, but they never succeeded in blocking it out altogether.)

The second physical defense consists of destroying reception facilities. It is possible to sweep an occupied territory and to sequester *almost* all the radio sets in use. It is possible to issue a military order that any soldier or civilian found in possession of enemy printed matter will be court-martialed and punished. These measures are useful to dictators having secret police, and among armies having the Prussian level of discipline, with the enlisted men regarded as robots. It is not to be expected that they would work against Americans.

Therefore, propaganda does not meet propaganda. Combat forces *meet*; Psychological Warfare forces pass one another in opposite directions.

In American practice, the forces which countered enemy propaganda were those pertaining to troop information and education—morale or special services. These did not concern themselves with propaganda to the Germans and Japanese. In the German and Russian armies of World War II, but not in the American, British, French or Japanese, there were *political officers* attached to the units under a variety of titles; these often took charge of propaganda to the enemy (offensive) as well as indoctrination of their own troops (defensive), but the unrelatedness of these two functions let them split apart.

Even here, the parallel between combat operations and propaganda operations breaks down. Rarely does it occur that there is a simple juxtaposition of forces, thus:

Enemy Propagandist ⟶ *Audience* ⟵ *Own Propagandist*
(Troops)

The issue is more commonly one in which the propagandist on each side attacks those troops which are retreating, cut off, suffering heavy losses, politically disaffected, or otherwise psychologically promising material for him. Of the factors which can affect troop or enemy morale, the presence of friendly propaganda is a minor one. The result then becomes complicated:

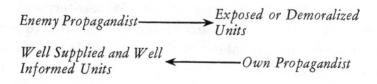

Troops who are starving or are subjected to inordinate losses will not have their propaganda-resistance heightened by pep talks. A chopped-up unit has no means of enjoying USO facilities.

Propaganda vulnerability depends most commonly on the objective situation of the audience. If the objective situation is good or neutral, one's own propaganda can supplement the good morale conditions, but even here, it does not and should not meet enemy propaganda frontally.

In so far as it can be tabulated, the visualizable propaganda situation at any given time would be something like this.

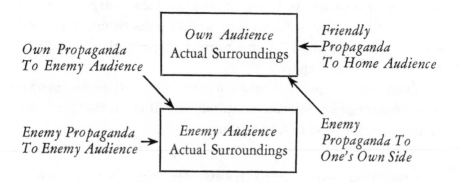

In each of these instances, the propaganda operators are themselves members of an audience. Furthermore, propaganda leaks, as it were, out of the channels into which it is directed. Additionally, propaganda in all countries has to compete with the normal day-to-day preoccupations of the listener—his food, his health, his hour-by-hour activities, his tangible interpersonal relationships. Save for rare moments of intense crisis, propaganda can expect to occupy only a small fraction of the audience's attention. In dictatorships, the range of propaganda can be widened by polluting all news, all theater presentations, all churches, etc., with the "Party line," but visitors to totalitarian capitals—of both the Fascist and Communist varieties—report that most of the common people have become calloused with apathy, over-all disbelief, or skepticism as a result of overexposure to official indoctrination.

Hence a written estimate of the situation follows *not* from some special Psychological Warfare situation, but from the practical measures available. If desired, it can summarize the following points:

1. Definition of the Audience
    a. Medium through which reached
    b. Anticipated attention (including means of getting attention)
    c. Pertinent characteristics (from propaganda intelligence report)

2. Psychological Goals to be Sought
    a. Attention of the enemy
    b. Present goal (if strategic, opinion or sentiment; if tactical, action)
    c. Ultimate goal (applicable to strategic only)

3. Limitations of Policy
    a. National political limitations
    b. Limitation by adverse factual situation
    c. Limitations arising from one's own security

4. Media Available
   a. Kind and quality of media to be used

5. The Propaganda Man
   a. Descriptive appreciation of a typical audience member

6. Competitive Factors
   a. Listener's non-propaganda preoccupations
   b. Continuation of adverse indoctrination
   c. Effect of news available both to one's self and to listener
   d. Competitive effect of hostile propaganda

7. Relation to General (Military) Estimate of the Situation
   a. Timing relationships
      1. Contingency plans
      2. Contingency prohibitions
   b. Contribution of Psychological Warfare to operations planning
      1. Combat operations psychologically advisable
      2. Combat operations subject to propaganda exploitation
      3. Operations providing adverse propaganda with opportunity
   c. Correlation of Psychological Warfare with
      1. Public relations programming
      2. Information and education plans
      3. Medical plans and reporting
      4. Countersubversive functions

Such papers might be of use, gathering together in a single document all pertinent facts. In most tactical situations, the situation would have obsolesced before the author of the estimate had finished his document. In strategic situations, it could not normally be made specific enough to be practical—at the operational level—without becoming hopelessly unwieldy. Each skill represented in the estimate does prepare other reports, and the practice of most modern armies indicates that it is better to conduct routine propaganda planning, supervision, and appreciation through liaison than to prepare elaborate documents gathering together the multifarious factors which actually affect Psychological Warfare.

In most American Psychological Warfare facilities—especially in the theaters—the estimate of the situation consisted of a brief résumé of home propaganda by the enemy (taken directly from propaganda analysis), comment on the audience by appropriate representatives from the State Department or other Federal agencies, and discussion of the audience by some kind of Psychological Warfare operations-planning and intelligence board. Some of the most valuable suggestions came from persons not concerned with propaganda—such as target-intelligence people who could anticipate enemy civilian or military shortages, or economic-warfare people who suggested vexations which the enemy listener was probably experiencing.

The Question of Choice. An estimate of a combat situation is something like a diagnosis and prognosis in medicine. The estimate sets forth the situation, presenting the difficulties to be faced and the general range of pertinent fact, all in orderly array, like a systematic diagnosis. The plans are then drawn up in the light of the estimate; they are limited by the harsh, immediate facts of the situation; they resemble a doctor's prognosis, which may have room for several choices, but which does not open the way to speculative, creative action. Psychological Warfare situations are usually fluid, save at times of specific tactical emergency (the appeal to an enemy unit, when it is surrounded, to surrender; pre-invasion propaganda for specific points).

Therefore the psychological estimate should not be presented as a propaganda-*versus*-propaganda analysis; if it does, it will end as an productive and meaningless duel between the propagandists on the two sides. Nor should the estimate pretend to present

choices with the pretense that these choices are definitely prescribed by the situation itself. In any field, an expert can hoax or
befuddle a layman. A Psychological Warfare officer should present
choices for what they really are—options open to him and his staff
as creative writers. Policy issues, in specific cases, can be answered
yes or *no*. This is not true of propaganda as a whole. The task of
the propagandist is to create something which will arouse attention, will induce attitudes, and will eventually lead to action. It is
a task of permanent offense. Its variations are as infinitely diverse
as the imaginations of mankind can make them.

Choice is perpetually before the Psychological Warfare propagandist. But it is the wide choice of what he can think up, not the
narrow choice dictated by fixed terrain, by specific enemy capabilities, by concrete physical necessities. Adolf Hitler himself, in
the near-delirium of his last days of life, recognized this. He told
his followers to hold out; German propaganda might still provoke
the "inevitable" American-Soviet clash which would save Germany.
He said he would choose one side or the other—he didn't much
care which. Thus, at the end, the range of propaganda possibilities
deceived even the arch propagandist, despite the bold shrewdness
he had shown in the past. He knew, as his generals did not, that in
the realm of the psychological, the "factor of the unexpected" is
always a large one, and hoped to the last to turn it to his ends. His
premises were right, even though his conclusion was fatal for him.

Allied Operations. Estimates become more complex when several nations fight on the same side.

In a particular type of instance, estimates of the antagonist's
propaganda capacity form a part of normal military operations.
This occurs in the instance of allied operation: when the outside
ally fears that the local ally may be subverted. Such was the state
of France in relation to Britain in 1940, of Central China in relation to the Americans in 1944, of the Balkan states in relation to
the Third Reich in 1945. In such instances, estimate of the enemy
propaganda becomes a vital part of the total military estimate. The
principles stated below can be applied by changing the direction

of their application. Propaganda analysis can, in situations like this, provide cues for effective action and correct timing. In this type of situation, the outside ally cannot afford to sit by and hope for the best. By black operations he too must prepare to re-subvert the local ally if the local ally goes over to the enemy. In Roumania, Bulgaria and puppet Serbia the Germans were not successful; in Italy they created the Fascist Italian Social Republic and brought a large part of Northern Italy back into the war. In China, Allied pro-Communist sympathizers hoped that the Japanese would subvert the Generalissimo so badly that America would build up Yenan as a precautionary measure; but the Generalissimo stood firm, and the Yenan maneuver lingered on as an unpleasant memory between certain Americans and certain Nationalist Chinese. This type of situation mixes politics, economics, propaganda and warfare to such a degree that no sound estimate can appraise one factor without including the others.

Estimate of One's Own Capacity. In preparing a routine estimate of one's own capacity, militarily speaking, the measurable factors of space and time provide guides for projecting plans into the future. It is possible to plan, "At 1830 hours, D day plus 8, the Smithforce will have arrived at Tenallytown," meaning that 8 days after the start, this result can be expected. Psychological warfare can be estimated in a loosely comparable way, provided the terms of reference are different.

Naturally, no sane Theater commander would rely on psychological warfare alone for the accomplishment of a military result. It is possible, nevertheless, to allow for planned good luck—good luck which one has created with many months of hard work. When psychological warfare is used in conjunction with invasion, its planned use (to judge by the results found in World War II) might often justify commanders in using minimum rather than maximum allocations of troops for the protection of lines of communications against guerrilla or civilian attack. If the Nazis had chased the Soviet peasants through the woods with soup kitchens, free movies, and mittens for the babies, they would not have had so many furious partisans sniping at them.

Psychological warfare can be relied upon to a considerable degree to step up enemy panic in the application of a rapid forward movement. The Japanese in China panicked whole regiments of local volunteers plumb out of existence by the use of fast-marching Chinese-speaking plainclothes troops, some of whom may have been air-dropped. In the Nazi establishment of the first salient through to Abbeville, the psychological aspects of the blitzkrieg helped prevent the British and French from re-forming a continuous line and led eventually to the pocketing of the British at Dunkirk.

Psychological warfare can also be counted on, tactically, to speed up the reduction of isolated enemy positions when these positions are clearly beyond hope of rescue. All the psychological warfare people need to do is to go in with map leaflets, surrender leaflets, loudspeakers and a near-by radio. The unit may not give in instantly, but the unit would be superhuman if it fought as well in the face of persuasion as it would have fought without psychological attack. In the mopping-up of Japanese in the Pacific island fighting, psychological warfare teams and techniques undoubtedly eased and speeded the process.

These references are to tactical estimates. Strategic propaganda is beyond estimate. All it can do is to weight the probabilities a little more favorably than would be the case without it. If the United States had not dropped the Japanese surrender proposal in Japanese all over Japan, the Japanese government leaders might have been more inclined to resist surrendering. If the Germans had not softened up the French before the Great Western Blitz of 1940, they might have needed more time, days or weeks more to reduce France, and thus might have faced a united French overseas Empire even after France-in-Europe fell. The success of a strategic propaganda operation cannot be guaranteed in any plan. It would be foolhardy optimism to think that psychology can assume a major portion of responsibility for direct military results. It would appear that the Soviet Red Army, despite its propaganda-conscious

Communist background, never passed the whole buck to psychological warfare. The Russians never appeared to leave the artillery at home in order to take the loudspeakers or leaflet mortars along. They made brilliant, almost terrifying use of pre-belligerent propaganda; they used propaganda tactically with immense success in the taking of prisoners; they used psychological warfare, with a heavy infusion of political warfare, more drastically for consolidation and occupation purposes than did any of the other United Nations. But like everyone else, they seem to have used strategic propaganda for whatever it might bring in—immediate generalized effect, and the ultimate production of windfalls.

Tactical psychological warfare can be estimated, though to a limited extent, as part of a tactical potential of either the enemy or one's own side. Strategic propaganda can be planned and evaluated only in terms of the diffuse general situation, with the reasonable and fair expectation that if properly employed it will better the position of the user. It sometimes achieves results which astound even the originators, but these results cannot be calculated (except by hunch) in advance. Nevertheless, the operation is well worth trying since it has incalculable possibilities and is quite inexpensive in relation to the gross cost of war.

PART THREE
PLANNING AND OPERATIONS

CHAPTER 10
ORGANIZATION FOR PSYCHOLOGICAL WARFARE

Big jobs require big organizations. Eight *billion* leaflets were dropped in the Mediterranean and European Theaters of Operations alone under General Eisenhower's command. That is enough to have given every man, woman and child on earth four leaflets, and this figure, large as it is, does not include leaflets dropped in all the other theaters of war by ourselves, our allies, and our enemies. It does not include the B-29 leaflet raids on Japan, in which hundreds of tons of thin paper leaflets were dropped. Huge American newspapers were developed, edited, printed and delivered to our Allies and to enemy troops. One of these, *Parachute News* (*Rakkasan*), attained a circulation of two million copies per run; this was in the Southwest Pacific. In parts of the upper Burmese jungle and the Tibetan borderland where no newspaper was ever distributed before, the Fourteenth Air Force distributed a Japanese newspaper, *Jisei*, along with picture sheets for illiterate tribesmen.

In getting at the enemy, the United States printed leaflets, cartoons, pamphlets, newspapers, posters, books, magazines. In black operations enough fabrications were perpetrated to keep the FBI busy for a thousand years. Movies in all forms (commercial, amateur, all known widths, sound and silent, even lantern slides) went out all over the world. Radio talked on all waves in almost every language and code; loudspeakers, souvenirs, candy, matches, nylon stockings, pistols you could hide in your mouth, sewing thread, salt, phonograph records and baby pictures streamed out over the world. Much of this was necessarily waste. In the larger

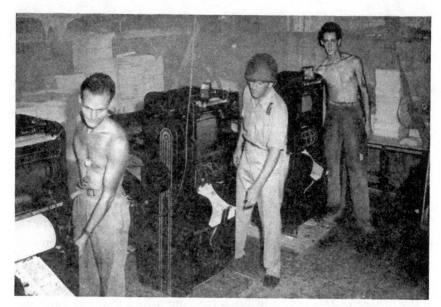

Figure 39: Leaflet Production: Military Presses. The machines shown are Davidson presses, widely used by the Americans in all theaters of war. The unit shown is Psychological Warfare Branch during the Leyte operations. The leaflet being run off is addressed to both Filipino guerrillas and Japanese troops, facilitating a difficult three-way operations whereby Japanese are told to surrender to Filipinos, Filipinos told not to kill surrendering Japanese, and Americans instructed to receive prisoners from Filipinos.

Figure 40: Leaflet Production: Rolling. When round bombs were used, the leaflets had to be rolled into round packages to fit. Forty thousand leaflets could be packed into one bomb, and a Mitchell bomber could carry seventeen such bombs. (Photo by Ninth Air Force Combat Camera Unit.)

Figure 41: Leaflet Distribution: Attaching Fuzes. Packaged leaflets must spread out. Bundles of paper which fall intact make little impact on the enemy unless they hit him on the head. Their subsequent employment is rarely related to propaganda. To be effective, leaflets must scatter. World War II saw the adaptation of various scattering devices, of which the most effective was the barometric fuze, shown here. The others included self-timing packages, slip-strings which unwrapped the package in the air, and a belly-tank which fed leaflets out at any desired speed, either in a continuous stream or in bursts.

waste of war it appears almost frugal when taken in relation to the results thought to have been achieved.

Every American theater commander, given the choice of using psychological warfare or not, as he chose, did choose to use it. Every major government engaged in the war used psychological warfare, along with a number of assorted private characters, some of whom later founded governments. (The sacred government of the Dalai Lama, in forbidden Lhasa, undertook a neat little maneuver in limited overt propaganda when it printed a brand-new set of stamps for presentation to President Roosevelt; the Inner Mongols were propagandized by the Outer Mongols; the Grand Duchy of Luxembourg

Figure 42: Leaflet Distribution: Packing the Boxes. Sometimes boxes were used instead of bombs. These, being square, facilitated the packing process, since the rectangular packages could be used just as they came out of the printshop. The fuze is attached to the package, not to the box.

broadcast against the Reich.) Psychological warfare proliferated so much as to change the tone if not the character of war. General Eisenhower wrote, at the end of the European operations, that psychological warfare had developed as a specific and effective weapon of war.

The organization of psychological warfare was as much a problem as the operation. It overlapped military, naval, diplomatic, press, entertainment, public relations, police power, espionage, commercial, educational and subversive operations. Almost every nation involved had extreme difficulty in fitting these new powers and unknown processes into the accepted frame of government, and almost every national solution was different. The British and the Japanese achieved a considerable degree of unification. The Americans, Nazis and Russians were hampered by the number of competing agencies. The French were burdened through most of the war by an excess of governments. The Chinese did things in their own formal but offhand manner; the Nationalist party carried on information functions for the Chinese government, while the Communist guerrilla authorities carried on functions for the Communist party.

The lower down the echelon, the nearer the armies of the world came to standardizing psychological warfare organization. They did this for the same reason that they all organize into regiments instead of centuries, cohorts, or tribes. Modern war is a self-standardizing process if the enemy experience is to be copied, enemy techniques improved, allied assistance accepted, and military practice kept up to world standards. Psychological warfare units needed printing and radio sections; to service these sections they all needed intelligence and analysis offices; to distribute their materials they all needed agents and liaison. Black propaganda organization varied more than did white, but it was amazing to Americans, uncovering Japanese subversive-operations units, to see how much the Japanese organization resembled their own.

National Propaganda Organizations. At the national level, the psychological warfare facilities were parts of their national governments. Neither the Axis nor the United Nations developed

Figure 43: Leaflet Distribution: Loading the Boxes. Boxes were built to fit the bomb bays. Boxes were opened, one after the other, by a trip lever, shown above at left. Each box can be emptied in turn, giving the pilot the opportunity to select more than one target.

Figure 44: Leaflet Distribution: Bombs at the Airfield. Leaflet bombs, filled with rolls such as those shown in figure 40, are delivered to the bomber. The scene shown is somewhere in England. Officers and men picked up British slang for leaflet operations, and called such missions "nickelling."

Figure 45: Leaflet Distribution: Loading the Bombs. The bombs were loaded as shown. The entire bomb dropped out of the plane and was disintegrated in the air by a small explosive charge. No illustration can do justice to the sight of such a bomb in the actual dropping, since the leaflets tend to look scattered or to disappear under normal flight conditions. Army motion picture films preserve the process for the official record, however.

Figure 46: Leaflet Distribution: The Final Result. Search of prisoners provided a fair, accurate test of how the leaflets took effect. Sometimes surrender leaflets actually came to have black-market value. Enemy officers prohibited the carrying of Allied surrender leaflets, since they knew that a soldier who had one in his pocket or hidden in his clothes was halfway or more through the psychological process of surrendering. Here a German hands in a leaflet to his American captor.

super-national psychological facilities. The closest thing to international agencies were the American-British coordination facilities under authority of the Combined Chiefs of Staff, along with that mysterious force which in the latter part of the war impelled Russian-occupied countries to sound amazingly much like Moscow. Short of preparing a textbook for political science study, explaining each of the governments and the location of its intelligence and informational functions, it would be impossible to explain in any detail how each of the systems worked. Even between governments having the same general political orientation, the improvised war agencies were different, and in the same government, the practices of World War I were not carried over into World War II. Some description of the American psychological warfare may be warranted, chiefly as a means of showing how a simple task can be accomplished even with intricate and confused organizations, and the Japanese system (on paper, the best of them all,

Figure 47: Consolidation Propaganda: The Movie Van. Consolidation of friendly, neutral or hostile civilians in an area of operations can become a vitally important function. During the North African operations, this movie van showed newsreels and documentary films to the local people. Similar vans were used in Italy, France, Holland, Belgium, Germany, Austria, and other areas.

though weak in field operations and control) may be outlined for the sake of contrast.

American Psychological Warfare Agencies. The American Army failed to establish its authority and leadership in the field of psychological warfare despite its creation of the Psychological Warfare Branch under G-2. In large part this was a matter of practical politics and of personalities. The United States government as a whole, in the successive administrations of President Roosevelt, acquired tremendous administrative vitality but at the same time permitted the older "constitutional" agencies to lose ground to their newly founded rivals. Had an administrative purist and traditionalist been in the White House, instead of a bold governmental experimenter, the logical creation of a psychological warfare facility would have paralleled the later creation of SWNCC (State-War-Navy Coordinating Committee).

From the purely theoretical standpoint, it would have been far sounder to put national policy formulation (White House and Congress), foreign policy formulation (State), strategic propaganda

Figure 48: Consolidation Propaganda: Posters. An American soldier pastes American posters over Nazi ones while a French crowd looks on. (The crowd is pretty typical as to size and content, but a thousand such crowds will cover an entire town.) The poster operation shown was conducted by Psychological Warfare Division of SHAEF. (OWI-PWD photo.)

(State, War, Navy) into a single administrative entity than to create a new federal agency with improvised procedures, improvised security, and an improvised staff. However, the State, War and Navy Departments (at the very opening of our war) were overworked and understaffed. Many of the senior personnel regarded psychological warfare with downright suspicion and propaganda was regarded as a dirty name for a dirty and ineffectual job. Hence the old-line agencies let pass the opportunity for establishing initial control.

Subsequent experience suggests that the use of existing facilities and existing agencies wherever possible instead of new ones imparts stability, discipline, and morale, and lowers the organizational friction common to all new political agencies, especially to instrumentalities in so controversial a field as propaganda. On the chart shown, for instance, it would not have mattered whether the Psychological Warfare Facility (whatever its name) were put for housekeeping purposes under the State, War, Navy Department, or the Office for Emergency Management. The essential requirement would have been to use State Department men for jobs that involved determining foreign policy, military men for tasks of a military nature and naval for navy work, and to recruit only after cadres had been established. The sponsorship of psychological warfare by one—any one—of the old-line departments might have slowed down the feverish tempo of reorganizations, quarrels, cabals, internal struggles for power and clashes with other Federal agencies which were so characteristic of OWI and its colleague organizations.

The actual conduct of psychological warfare was shown in Chart I. (No official authority exists for such a chart; the author bases it on his own observation and experience.) Only agencies themselves originating psychological warfare materials are shown. Relationships between State, War and Navy were stable, but were frequently

Figure 49: Consolidation Propaganda: Photo Exhibit. When newsprint is short, a photo exhibit has great appeal to civilians. In backward countries, people sometimes waited their turn to get a chance to see the American pictures. Even in Cherbourg, the French city shown, these passersby are showing a very real interest in the picture display.

by-passed; for example, the Zacharias broadcasts, which were our biggest political warfare experiment, did not go to the State Department until after they had started. Relationships between OSS and other agencies were erratic and cloaked in extraordinary but irregular security. The OWI ran for most purposes as an autonomous group, with occasional reference to State, Navy, and War Departments. The President in his individually official capacity was apt to improvise psychological warfare operations of high importance, without warning his subordinates of what was coming (paper knife made of human Japanese bone; the "unconditional surrender" formula). The White House staff sometimes worked through channels, sometimes not; the Harvard professor who advised on inflation was simultaneously involved with psychological warfare on continental Asia. The Secretary of the Treasury openly discussed what he would like to do with Germany in terms which the Nazi radio naturally conveyed to its own people. Within the OWI itself, the overseas operation was separated from the domestic, the broadcasters from the planners, the outposts from everybody else, during much of the war. But the job was done!

Success was not due to the formal structure of the Office of War Information (see charts V, VI). No administrative formula could have transcended such governmental confusion. It was owing to the fact that all the people just described—who went around, with the best will in the world most of the time, minding one another's business—did in the end achieve effective results. The common denominator behind them was not the authority of the President, the discipline of the Democratic Party, or the casually designed, casually overlooked formal lines of authority. The common denominator was American civilization itself. Had we been deeply disunited, this ramshackle structure would have collapsed into chaos. But there was broad concurrence, a sense of cooperativeness, good will and good temper. A German, Russian or Japanese bureaucrat would have gone mad in the wartime mazes of the Federal system; a Chinese would probably have felt very much at home, but would have polished up the titles and honorifics a little.

The difference between our governmental organization and that of our enemies lay in the fact that to us the T/O were something that could be used when convenient, and could (without breach of faith or law) be short-circuited when convenient. Word was passed around, material exchanged, coordination effected in ways which could not be shown on any imaginable chart. It was neither a merit nor a defect, but simply an American way of doing things.

This characteristic has the effect, however, of making after-the-fact studies quite unrealistic. There is not much from the formal records and the formal charts which conveys the actual tone of governmental operations in terms of propaganda. Study of World War II organization for the sake of research and planning against possible future war would not be very profitable unless it delved into the concrete experience of individuals. The formal outlines mean nothing; they are positively deceptive unless the actual controls and operations are known. (Mr. Warburg makes it plain in his book that he thinks little of Mr. Elmer Davis' conception of his job; but he does not mention that Mr. Sherwood, theoretically Mr. Davis' subordinate, ran foreign operations without much reference to Mr. Davis or to any other part of the Federal government. Since Mr. Sherwood was closer to the White House than was Mr. Davis, this important consideration escapes being recorded on the chart: foreign operations were actually autonomous.[1]) Examples of how things really worked—as opposed to how they looked as though they worked—could be multiplied forever; but the soundest way of finding out sober, judicious opinion will necessarily await the writing of autobiographies and memoirs by the people concerned.

With these sweeping reservations in mind, it is worth noting the organization of OWI (internal). The Domestic Operations Branch can be dismissed with brief mention. It proved to be the object of profound suspicion on the part of many members of Congress, and its function was to stimulate and assist inward media of public information in support of the war effort. The Domestic Operations Branch never superseded other U. S. government informational services (State, Agriculture, Treasury, War, and so on), so that it was the wartime supplement to the governmental supplement to the regular news and information system, which remained private. This precluded intimate coordination of domestic and

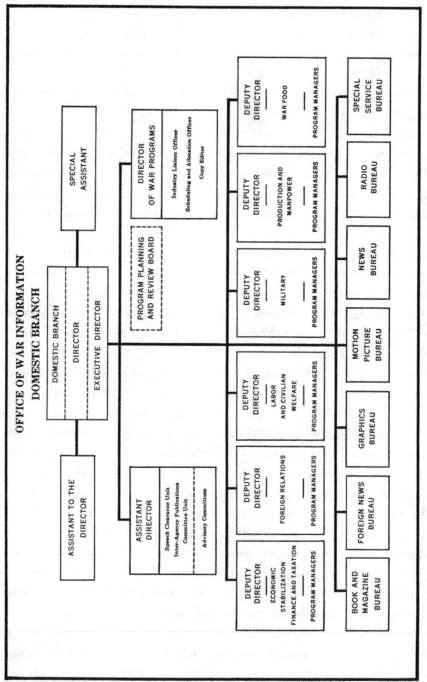

Chart V (Source: OWI administrative memorandum. Courtesy of Dr. E. P. Lilly.)

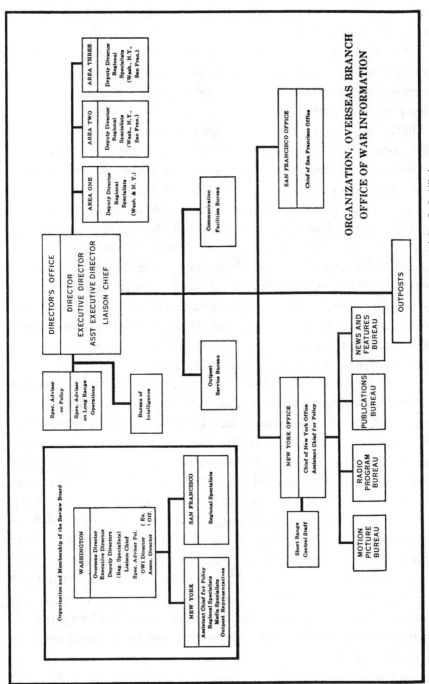

Chart VI (Source: OWI administrative memorandum. Courtesy of Dr. E. P. Lilly.)

overseas propaganda and rendered illusory any hope that domestic propaganda, as eavesdropped by our enemies, could be used as an instrument of war.

The Overseas Operations Branch had two basic missions. Within the United States it was the operating and controlling agency for government-owned or government-leased world-wide short-wave. For actual overseas purposes, it was the rear echelon of both the Navy and Army theater facilities and of its own OWI Outposts. The Outposts were themselves under OWI for certain purposes; for other purposes they were subject to the chief of mission (ambassador, minister or chargé) of the U. S. in the foreign country, and still other purposes under the American military commander having local jurisdiction. (OWI-Delhi, for example, was under the office of the American High Commissioner in India; also under the Rear Echelon Headquarters of the Commanding General, United States Army Forces, China-Burma-India Theater; also under OWI-New York for supply of its printed materials, most personnel and needed presses; under OWI-San Francisco for supply of its wirelessed news; and under OWI-Washington for general policy, hiring and firing, and everything else.)

In terms of its own global radio, OWI prepared planning and control materials in Washington and relayed these to New York and San Francisco. The radio facilities in these cities then transmitted the material overseas. Through the first three years of the war, the precise nature of the Washington controls was in question, enforcement remained a perplexing problem, and coordination between planning and execution remained unsolved in part. By the spring and summer of 1945, OWI had solved most of these problems, chiefly by means of circulating the Area I, II, and III chiefs to the operating offices. When personal relations were satisfactory (as in the instance of Mr. Owen Lattimore, chief in OWI San Francisco, Mr. George Taylor, chief of Far East in Washington, and Mr. F. M. Fisher, chief of China Outpost in Chungking, all of them China experts) coordination might be difficult but was never exasperating.

In terms of supply, the materials gathered by the other agencies went to the Outpost Service Bureau, which ran a virtual informational

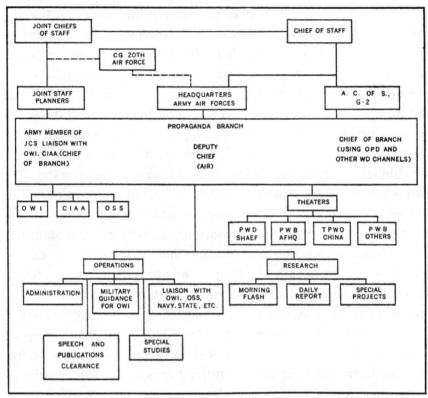

Chart VII (Source: Chart prepared for Colonel John Stanley in Propaganda Branch, G-2.)

Sears Roebuck for the outposts. Foreign demands for American materials were unpredictable. The OWI learned rapidly and effectively, and the material going out of the outposts to foreign audiences very soon reached a high level of quality.

Other psychological warfare agencies at the national level were the CIAA (Coordinator of [later the Office of] Inter-American Affairs) which conducted propaganda exclusively to Latin America and the Caribbean, and the OSS (Office of Strategic Services), which serviced the Joint Chiefs of Staff with intelligence and policy materials, and served as a home base for its own units which operated abroad under Theater authority. No U.S.-based black propaganda operations were reported to the public.[2]

Reduced to the concrete terms of definite policy execution (as opposed to the making of policies that might or might not ever reach their supposed executors) and the routine working of operations, the national level was not important except for the two functions stated above, global short-wave, and source of supply. The decisive choices were made in the theaters or at the outposts, half the time in ignorance of what Washington policy-makers had decided in conclave on that particular topic. (When the author was in China, he found that the OWI China outpost decoded its week-to-week propaganda instructions only after they were hopelessly obsolete; they were then filed.) The theaters were able to use psychological warfare as and when they pleased. Between the ETO and Washington close politico-military coordination was possible. Between Washington and the others it was impracticable.

The War Department participation in the control and planning of psychological warfare is shown by Chart VII, which represents the situation as of 1945. The Propaganda Branch, attached to G-2 as a staff agency and not to Military Intelligence Service as an operating agency, served to carry out the psychological warfare functions of the War Department.[3] The Chief of the Branch represented the Joint Chiefs of Staff at OWI meetings, along with his Navy confrere; he took care of official messages to the Theaters pertaining to psychological warfare matters, and his office itself performed a few limited functions. (One of these functions required the author to get up at four-thirty mornings in order to digest the overnight intake of enemy propaganda. He was joined in this by Teheran-born, Columbia-trained Edward K. Merat. It was with real relief that he saw the Nazi stations go off the air. He was then able to pass the early-bird business to his Persian colleague.) The Branch also made up propanal studies whenever these were warrantable at the General Staff level. The Deputy Chief (Air) was the vestigial remnant of a short-lived Army Air Forces propaganda establishment; he had direct access to the air staff, and took care of things having a peculiarly air character. (The abbreviations under Theaters are explained below, since Theater nomenclature for psychological warfare was never standardized.)

With the termination of hostilities, though it was not the juridical finish of the war, both OSS and OWI were swept out of existence. By executive order of 20 September 1945, effective ten days

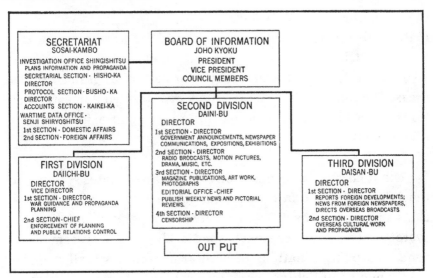

SECRETARIAT SOSAI-KAMBO INVESTIGATION OFFICE SHINGISHITSU PLANS INFORMATION AND PROPAGANDA SECRETARIAL SECTION · HISHO-KA DIRECTOR PROTOCOL SECTION · BUSHO · KA DIRECTOR ACCOUNTS SECTION · KAIKEI-KA WARTIME DATA OFFICE · SENJI SHIRYOSHITSU 1st SECTION · DOMESTIC AFFAIRS 2nd SECTION · FOREIGN AFFAIRS	**BOARD OF INFORMATION** JOHO KYOKU PRESIDENT VICE PRESIDENT COUNCIL MEMBERS	

SECOND DIVISION
DAINI-BU
DIRECTOR
1st SECTION · DIRECTOR
GOVERNMENT ANNOUNCEMENTS, NEWSPAPER
COMMUNICATIONS, EXPOSITIONS, EXHIBITIONS
2nd SECTION · DIRECTOR
RADIO BRODCASTS, MOTION PICTURES,
DRAMA, MUSIC, ETC.
3rd SECTION · DIRECTOR
MAGAZINE PUBLICATIONS, ART WORK,
PHOTOGRAPHS
EDITORIAL OFFICE · CHIEF
PUBLISH WEEKLY NEWS AND PICTORIAL
REVIEWS.
4th SECTION · DIRECTOR
CENSORSHIP

FIRST DIVISION
DAIICHI-BU
DIRECTOR
VICE DIRECTOR
1st SECTION · DIRECTOR,
WAR GUIDANCE AND PROPAGANDA
PLANNING
2nd SECTION · CHIEF
ENFORCEMENT OF PLANNING
AND PUBLIC RELATIONS CONTROL

THIRD DIVISION
DAISAN ·BU
DIRECTOR
1st SECTION · DIRECTOR
REPORTS FOREIGN DEVELOPMENTS;
NEWS FROM FOREIGN NEWSPAPERS,
DIRECTS OVERSEAS BROADCASTS
2nd SECTION · DIRECTOR
OVERSEAS CULTURAL WORK
AND PROPAGANDA

OUT PUT

Chart VIII (Source: Chart prepared before VJ-day in Propaganda Branch, G-2.)

later, OSS was broken up; the scholastic portions were dismembered and reassembled into the Department of State, where they presumably helped collate material for the new interdepartmental Central Intelligence Group (CIG). The operational parts were handed over to the War Department. For all the author knows, some distressed colonel may have a desk full of fountain-pens which explode, transmit radio messages, or can be used for invisible tattooing, along with an edible blotter, a desk telephone which is really a hand grenade and a typewriter which is a demountable motor scooter; such speculations are delightful topics on which to dwell, but the day of black propaganda is over. Obsolescence reduces all things, even OSS, to absurdity.

The OWI perished a more lingering administrative death. It was transferred to the Department of State as an operating unit under the name Interim International Information Service (IIIS) and a new Assistant Secretary of State, Mr. William Benton, took over its sponsorship. Later, under the abbreviation OIC (Office of International Information and Cultural Affairs), it was coordinated on January 1, 1946, with preexisting State department offices and with certain leftovers from the Office of Inter-American Affairs (OIAA). It retained the global broadcasts on a limited budget; it still served the surviving outposts, which were being integrated with diplomatic and consular offices overseas; and for Korea, Japan, Germany, Austria, and Venezia Giulia, it acted as the supplying service for the Military Government information programs in those areas. The Bureau of the Budget took over limited domestic functions when the OWI passed out of independent existence on 31 August 1945.

The Joho Kyoku. Comparison of this United States system with the Japanese Board of Information (*Joho Kyoku*), as outlined in chart VIII, shows the difference between integrated and disparate systems. The Japanese developed a close-knit system which combined public relations of both army and navy, all domestic government publishing, complete control of book-publishing, magazines, press, radio, and film, propaganda intelligence and over-all psychological warfare. The progress of an item through the Japanese psychological warfare system may look intricate when followed on the chart, but it was in fact much less intricate than the comparable American processing of an item.

The only aspect of psychological warfare that does not show on the chart is the Japanese political warfare system—by the test of success, the best developed by any belligerent during World War II. The Japanese very early learned the simple rule: *Political warfare cannot convert a sub-subsistence economy and government into a satisfactory system, but political warfare can convert a subsisting area into one that has the illusions of prosperity and national freedom.* To succeed in the face of economic difficulty, political warfare must be shrewd, simple, insistent, and backed up with a touch of terror. The Japanese moved into the Western colonial areas of the Far East between 1940 and 1942 (Indo-China, Malaya, Indonesia, the Philippines, parts of China, Burma, and areas inhabited by substantial Indian minorities). They organized the following "independent" governments:

The Imperial Government of Manchukuo;
Federated Autonomous Inner Mongolia;

The Reorganized National Government of China, superseding earlier puppets;

Malai (under Japanese military control but promised ultimate independence);

The Republic of the Philippines;

The Empire of Vietnam (later the Vietnam Republic);

A dictatorship in Burma of the Adipadi;

Republic Indonesia;

Azad Hind (Free Indian government-in-exile) and the Azad
Hind Fauj (quisling Indian National Army, which put
large forces into the field against British-controlled
Indian troops and helped to neutralize the entire military potential of India);

The independent Kingdom of Cambodia (made independent
by telling the helpless King that he need not let the
French come back).

These Japanese-sponsored governments flew their own flags,
had enough troops to help Japan police their home areas, developed psychological warfare facilities with intensive Japanese
assistance, and went through all the motions of independence. In
1944, some of them even held an international conference at
Tokyo, thanking Japan for liberating all the non-White States and
adopting high-sounding resolutions. (The Siamese puppet ambassador to this meeting had the unforgettable name of His Excel-
lency, the Honorable Witchit Witchit Watakan!)

Behind the pageantries of Japanese political warfare, economic
and social realities were horrid. The Japanese printed money which
had far less backing than cigar store coupons. They bankrupted all
non-Japanese business so that Japanese carpetbaggers could buy
their way in cheap; businesses owned by white foreigners were
expropriated out of hand. They cut off communications, spread
terror, raised the price of food, put hospitals out of business, de-
graded schools—and received the devoted loyalty of large parts of
the cheated populations. It did not matter to millions of Burmese
whether they had lived well under British rule or not; the British

did not let them have their own flag, did not let them send ministers and ambassadors, did not let them run a scow up and down the river with a mortar on it, calling it a navy. The *miranda*, the pageantry of politics, was what mattered—not law-and-order, democracy, security, education, health.[4]

The same story might have been repeated on a larger scale throughout the Far East, perhaps ultimately leading to something like Lothrop Stoddard's old nightmare, *The Rising Tide of Color*. Countervening factors included the presence of Chinese agitation both Kuomintang and Communist in leadership, guerrilla operations throughout Southeast Asia, and the ruinous economic effects of American submarine and Fourteenth Air Force anti-shipping operations. Shipping losses drove the Greater East Asia Co-prosperity Sphere below subsistence level and created a condition where even the most fanatic patriot realized the disadvantages of the situation.

The Japanese put all the captured radios to work. They had traitors of all kinds on their side including, it is shameful to admit, Americans, Russians, British, Australians, and French. (Despite the fact they occupied all of Guam, they never used a single Guamanian traitor—testimony to the simple loyalty to the U.S. of the Chamorro people and to the popularity of the long-established U.S. naval government on the island.)

Japanese psychological warfare failed because the real warfare behind it failed. The Japanese could not whip their over-docile troops into a fighting frenzy without allowing those troops to behave in a way which made deadly enemies for Japan among the peoples she came to "liberate." The Japanese did not have sense enough to be satisfied with 100% return per year on their money, but wrecked the conquered economic systems with inflation, poor management, and excess exploitation. Even the quislings became restless under the poor occupation policies of the Japanese, and before the war was over a considerable number of the Japanese quislings re-quislinged back to the United Nations side.

Theater Psychological Warfare. The Japanese had superlative close-knit psychological warfare staff organization within metropolitan Japan. They possessed many first-class field operators, first among them the true-life master-mind Major General K. Doihara, whose dinner guests often woke up the next morning with bad hangovers and high treason on their consciences. But the Japanese did not have adequate channels of communication, supply, and control between their smooth system at the top, and the working propagandists at the bottom. The *Kempeitai* (military-political gendarmerie) structure got in the way; Japanese propaganda lines lost touch with the strategic realities of their slow defeat. They did, instead, what any propaganda system does on the downgrade; they turned to repression instead of counterpropaganda with the inevitable result.

In contrast, the American psychological warfare structure included Theater operating units, usually called PWB (Psychological Warfare Branch), although it became PWD (Psychological Warfare Division) in SHAEF and did not grow beyond TPWO (Theater Psychological Warfare Officer) in China Theater. The supreme authority was, of course, the Theater Commander, on whose responsibility the operation had to be carried out. When propaganda bungled and got into the field of political trouble, it was the Theater Commander and not the subordinates who took the blame. Every theater was under the command of a general, except for Central Pacific (under Admiral Nimitz, and he used an Army colonel as his propaganda chief). In most theaters, the Political Adviser was the buffer between psychological warfare and the commander himself; in Southwest Pacific and later the Headquarters of the Supreme Commander for the Allied Powers, Japan, General MacArthur instituted the office of Military Secretary and made this officer responsible for reporting to him personally the developments in the propaganda field.

Subject to local variation, the Theater agencies faced similar problems. They had to serve in turn as a rear echelon to service the needs of combat propaganda, while working as the actual operating agencies for the bigger radio programs and the preparation of

strategic leaflets. As the areas behind them became more consolidated, displays and films took their place beside news and leaflets as chores that had to be performed. Communications facilities were a problem. Purely military facilities could not, of course, be overloaded by the lightly coded transmission of hundreds of thousands of words of political and other news and guidance; the psychological warfare establishments had to jerrybuild communications facilities out of what they could borrow from Army, or obtain from OWI supplies in the United States, or buy locally.

In most Theater organizations, the chief was a military man and the staff was partly military and partly civilian. Under General Eisenhower, PWD was not only Army and OWI but included OSS, on the American side, along with British partnership, French participation, and other Allied personnel as well. Under General MacArthur, OWI participated under strict Army control. Under General Stilwell, no Theater organization as such was set up; the G-2, the Political Adviser or the General himself handled propaganda matters when they turned up. Under General Wedemeyer, there was a Theater officer. Under General Sultan, the OWI ran itself; the Outpost serviced the Theater. Under General Clay, Information Control Service, OMGUS, became an integral part of military control. The same thing happened in General MacArthur's reorganized PWB—an organization termed CIES (Civil Information and Education Section) had the organization and personnel not only of the American structure, but the usable purged parts of the *Joho Kyoku* obedient to its command and liaison. Other Theaters had comparable arrangements, each suited to the Theater.

The common features of all Theater establishments were:

Figure 50: Consolidation Propaganda: Door Gods. One of the most unusual consolidation propaganda operations was the distribution of "door gods." These were small good-looking posters which traditionally displayed figures from the Chinese Pantheon. During the war, farm families who had been accustomed to putting up new door gods each lunar New Year found that they could not afford them. China Division, OWI, then run by F. M. Fisher, Richard Watts, Jr., Graham Peck, and James Stewart, made up new door gods which showed American aviators, thus familiarizing the Chinese peasantry with our insignia and preaching the cause of inter-Allied cooperation.

←

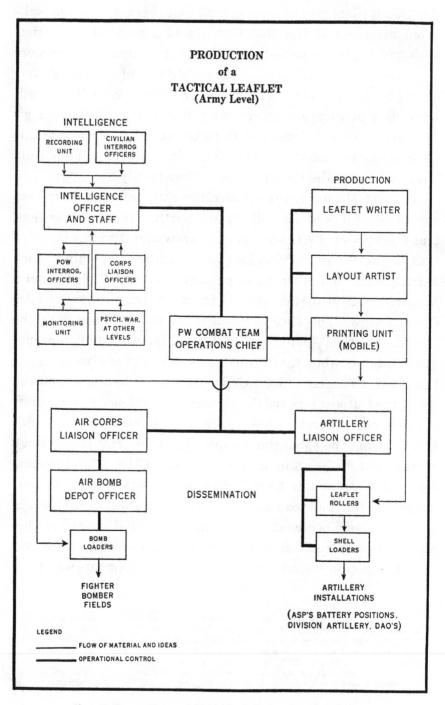

Chart IX (Source: *History of 2d Mobile Radio Broadcasting Company.*)

(1) Liaison or control from Army, State, and OWI, sometimes including OSS.

(2) Responsibility to the Theater Commander.

(3) Direct operation of strategic radio.

(4) Preparation of strategic leaflets, and sometimes of tactical leaflets as well.

(5) Use of local, native, or allied personnel.

Within the Theater staffs, the psychological warfare facilities were to a great extent assimilated for control and movement of personnel, supply, and so on. The G-3's and G-4's of the Theaters normally serviced the PWB's along with the rest of their work. The OWI and other civilian persons were put into uniform and given simulated rank, sometimes wildly disproportionate to their Army counterparts. The Army G-2's naturally worked with the PWB intelligence facilities; in some Theaters the G-2 was *ex officio* the chief of psychological warfare, as was the Assistant Chief of Staff G-2, War Department General Staff, himself at home. G-1's usually kept out of the way of psychological warfare and the housekeeping of the units was in most cases autonomous.

Responsibility for financing psychological warfare was never established as doctrine. The State Department kept most of it off its budget, leaving the actual payments up to the War Department and the OWI to figure out. Oftentimes this resulted in a curious sort of neo-capitalism within the U.S.-owned socialism of the Army. The two agencies would hold on to property as though it were private property, on the basis of immediate title, without reference to the plain fact that all of it was paid for in the end by the United States Treasurer. (OWI once murmured threateningly about bringing its radio material home from Manila rather than let General MacArthur's people highjack it. Such talk ended when the material was declared surplus or stolen.)

Field Operations. Field operations were most highly developed in the Mediterranean and European Theaters of Operation. Combat propaganda units came into being, carrying fully equipped mobile radio stations, and high-volume printing presses, along with them. Later, under SHAEF, these units developed further and Army-level organizations were set up which duplicated the Theater organizations on a reduced scale. (See Chart IX for chart of an Army unit.)

The tactical leaflet (page 211) came into its own with such units. It was possible to develop high-speed routines for using intelligence swiftly. Maps were dropped on the enemy in unfavorable situations. Order of Battle became highly important for psychological warfare purposes when enemy units could be addressed by their proper unit designation or by the name of their commanders. Intelligence was brought into play: bad food, bad supply, poor command, or mishandling of enemy forces in any way brought prompt propaganda comment.

Radio was the least useful for tactical operations simply because enemy troops do not carry private portable radio sets around with them. Radio was of high value in consolidation operations, passing along instructions to liberated populations, and telling civilians in the line of approach about measures which they could take for the common benefit of themselves and of the Allies.

A constant problem, never completely ironed out, was the use of airplanes for dropping purposes. The leaflet producers had, in all Theaters, a tendency to prepare excellent leaflets, bale them, and send them along to the airfields in the expectation that an overworked, unindoctrinated air force staff would automatically pick up the leaflets, develop dropping mechanisms, pack the leaflets into planes, take them out and drop them to the right language-groups at the right time in the right place. This was of course as absurd from the aviators' side as it was, to the civilians, to let their brain-children accumulate in hangars or warehouses. For strategic droppings, systematic arrangements could be made through proper official channels, and a regular air operation detailed to do the job. Tactical dropping did not allow enough time for elaborate staff work in each instance, and recourse was had to psychological warfare liaison officers (either Army officers or civilians with the approximate status of Tech-rep, technical representative, a familiar sight on World War II airfields) to get in touch with the units, help them install dropping facilities, explain the leaflets to the actual pilots and bombardiers, and thus obtain a high degree of cooperation. In almost every theater, this policy succeeded, and a wide variety of leaflet bombs, leaflet dispensers, and other leaflet-circulating gadgets was developed.

Artillery distribution also played a significant part. For frontline situations artillery could do the job better than planes, without risking aircraft in a quasi-combat operation. Leaflet bombs of considerable scope appeared, and could be made to fit almost any appropriate weapon. Circulation was also effected by means of clandestine operations to friendly civilians, frequently combined with air-drop of weapons, medicine, and other essentials.

The organization of all these new functions has changed military organization. A whole new series of units were attached in echelon, each fitted to the appropriate level for its work. The rear-area functions and strategic propaganda work always required a considerable proportion of civilian aid, since some of the best workers in this line were persons who either did not wish to join the Army or whom the Army did not wish to have join it. These psychological warfare organizations were unbelievably cheap, even if measured by the most conservative estimates of their success. It is impossible that the army of the future, whether American or foreign, will overlook this source of assistance. Psychological warfare nowhere replaced combat, but it made the impact of combat on the enemy more effective.

NOTES:

[1] The American newspapers between 1942 and 1945 carried intermittent accounts of these personal and political problems, frequently in the columns of commentators rather than in the regular news sections. (The book by Warburg is of course *Unwritten Treaty*, mentioned above.)

[2] For popular histories of the OSS, see *Sub Rosa: The O.S.S. and American Espionage* by Stewart Alsop and Thomas Braden (New York, 1946) or Corey Ford and Alastair MacBain, *Cloak and Dagger* (New York 1946). An exciting thriller novel by Darwin Teilhet gives an oblique and guarded description of black propaganda and clandestine polling: *The Fear Makers* (New York, 1945) Teilhet was himself in OSS. For an interesting description of OSS field operations, see Nicol Smith's *Into Siam* (New York, 1946). OSS was picturesque from the very start, and it is likely that other participants in OSS work will from time to time bring out books on their adventures.

[3] Bureau of the Budget, *United States Government Manual*, 1946, First Edition, Washington, 1946, says of the Military Intelligence Division, "It has charge of propaganda and psychological warfare" (page 198). The fiat may be a little more precise than circumstances warrant, but it at least shows where, for the record, psychological warfare belonged.

[4] See Charles E. Merriam's study, *Political Power*, Chicago, 1933, and his later works for suggestive approaches to the political setting of propaganda problems. He developed the terms *miranda* and *credenda* for modern political science usage.

CHAPTER 11
PLANS AND PLANNING

With most military planning, it is feasible to work from the top down, define the strategic objective and then work out the actual requirements of the operation in advance. This is not true of psychological warfare.[1] The objectives may be defined, and in the process of definition the general needs of a propaganda agency may be clarified. If a plan calls for a press or a radio, somebody can requisition a Davidson Press or a Hallicrafter radio and get ready to use it. But the plan cannot define goals, set time limits for the achievement of the goals, relate the goals to one another in a scheduled pre-fixed program of success, establish terms whereby psychological victory can be told from psychological defeat.

Psychological victory exists only in terms of the military victory which it is designed to assist. Psychological defeat, no matter how much critics or the enemy propagandist may allege it, can be proved to exist only when an actual defeat makes it real. Psychological plans are always contingency plans for the assistance of military operations. They are dependent on the military operation and they cannot be checked against fact except in terms of the military operations they ostensibly support.

Unfortunately, they were not always written with these reservations in mind.

Needs of the Operator: Materials and Guidance. American officers, assisting foreign troops, could not plan logistics until they found out what the foreign troops actually required. How much

269

did they eat, and what? How much could they carry, and for how long? How much tonnage had to be sent them, and how often? Such questions had to be asked about the needs of the individual men before unit planning, not to mention national planning, became possible at all.

Similarly, in psychological warfare, planning can be made realistic if it starts with the individual operation for the control of which the planning is done. Define the operator as anyone having a task in the actual preparation, production or transmission of propaganda materials, whether through electric communications or by print. The operator is not usually a person with a high security classification, yet he plays his indispensable part in fulfilling the highest and most secret strategy of the war. How can a plan be written that will be useful in carrying out the actual (and highly secret) strategy of the war while meeting the needs of an inexpert individual way down at the bottom of the control system? The answer is, of course, that no such plan can be prepared. Different plans are needed for successive phases.

The operator needs simple but basic materials. If he is a producer of some kind—such as a creative writer, an artist, a singer, a program arranger, a newscaster who does his own scripts and so on—he is likely to be a person with ideas of his own. Individual creativeness cannot usually be turned on and off like a faucet. Low-ranking and disciplined though the hired writer may be, he is still subject to the inward frailties of authors if he is any good. (This particular author sympathized deeply with some poor American Japanese who were given unbelievably dull outlines and told, "Turn this into exciting Japanese material! Give it pep! Make it rock them off their *tatami!* But don't get away from that outline one damn inch!" The *nisei* rolled their eyes; they did a poor job, as they knew that they would.)

The person who has to be told day in and day out how to operate is no operator at all. Psychological warfare is no place for unsuccessful short-story writers or would-be radio commentators. It demands professional standards, and it has more than professional difficulties. Therefore what the operator needs is not technical instruction but general guidance.

He must be told what he can say, what he cannot say. He should whenever possible be given some reason for perplexing or cryptic instructions. He should be helped to become familiar with what we are trying to tell the enemy. There is nothing classified about that, since the enemy is to be told it as soon as possible. The guidance given the operator should be:

(1) Plain.

(2) Feasible. (This sounds superfluous, but was not so during World War II when operators were sometimes told to attack such-and-such an enemy institution without referring to it directly or indirectly.)

(3) Organized. (The material at OWI was not organized until the last several months of the war, with the result that hundreds of thousands of words of propaganda commands remained in force, technically, but un-indexed and arranged only by weekly form.)

(4) Specific in showing timing. (General controls should not be issued at the beginning of operations; when revised, the revision should supersede the revised section, and not be placed beside it. Other provisions should be given expiration dates, after which they pass out of effect.)

(5) Mandatory. (Control should be expressed in *do* or *don't*; personal advice is better conveyed through informal channels.)

(6) Non-security or low-classified. (This material, for the operators, should be accessible to the operators. Often the most important operator—the best newsman, the most effective leaflet artist—may be a rather doubtful citizen, an alien, or even an enemy volunteer. He cannot follow guidances unless he knows them, and it makes a farce of security for his superior to be able to tell him the guidance, so that he can memorize it, but not able to give him the document itself.)

These rules, though simple, are not always easy to follow. Here is an example of a bad guidance:

CLASSIFIED

Without superseding instructions concerning religion, we may use the occasion of the Sacred Banyan Tree Festival to needle the Provisional President. Make a dramatic story of the President's life. Undermine his use of religion to bolster the dictatorship.

Caution: do not mention religion. Do not indulge in scurrilous personal attacks. Material concerning our information of the President's biography is highly classified and must not be used.

The exaggeration may seem apparent, but it is a fair sample of the worst directives as actually issued and many, though not quite so bad, were near it. The same guidance in more acceptable form would read:

UNRESTRICTED

(Expires 24 September, week following Festival.) Standing instructions make Banyan Tree Festival difficult topic with which to deal. If operators can suggest means of referring to Festival without violating prohibitions against religious offense, encourage them to try. Monitoring and diplomatic sources show that Provisional President is utilizing Festival to consolidate his position. If he can be attacked, do so.

The other need of the actual operator is material. The script writer needs actual texts of everyday enemy speech in order to keep his slang and idiom up to date. The artist needs correct photographs of enemy cities in wartimes so that the leaflet picture he makes will not look as outmoded as a crinoline or a Model T. All of them need all the information they can get about their own country—good handbooks, dictionaries, elementary histories, textbooks in fields which they may not know. It is amazing how hard it is to explain America to foreigners; the American soon finds out how little he knows his own country, and needs information about his own background along with current materials concerning the enemy.

Where radio propaganda is in question, the script-writers and broadcasters will read the enemy radio propaganda if they do not get enough fresh non-propaganda material concerning their audience. Sooner or later this will degenerate into alternate soliloquies of the radio men on each side, each watching the other to see if he got a rise out of him last time. OWI people frequently expressed idiot glee at having made Radio Tokyo frantic. The OWI men were the first to admit that their glee was pointless, since it was the Japanese broadcaster and not the Japanese audience who responded. But for lack of current information about the enemy the propagandist will refer to his own professional opponent. There is, of course, a very substantial difference between a change in enemy propaganda occasioned by a real inroad which one's own propaganda had made in enemy opinion, and a change that consists simply in angry or smart backtalk. Finding that difference is the responsibility of propanal, not of the operator.

Pre-Belligerent Planning. Pre-belligerent planning differs from regular planning in that it does not have the substantial context of actual military operations to make it realistic and urgent. Like all plans, the pre-belligerent plan should enumerate the facilities available, the basic course of action to be followed, and the limits within which offensive propaganda will be permitted. In fairness to the planners themselves, as well as to the authorities who will fit this plan into related military, economic, or political plans, the plan should define the proper scope of propaganda as applied to the contemplated situation.

One of the most useful functions of the pre-belligerent plan lies in the periodic exercise which it gives in propaganda discipline.

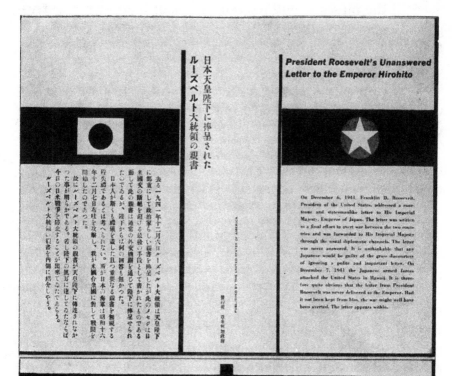

Information and intelligence agencies frequently see their jobs so technically that they lose sight of the need for coordination within the mechanism of an entire government. Press relations people try to get stories in the papers. Radio people try to maintain listener interest. Educational officers are concerned with the teachability of their materials. Spokesmen of the different agencies in related fields (such as shipping, air transport, currency control, social welfare) are apt to comment on a particular situation without reference to the needs of an inclusive national policy. How much advice was handed out on the occasion of the ultimatum to Tito? The Jugoslav authorities plainly risked politico-psychological pressure from us; they came prepared for the consequences; but both American official and private opinion expressed a wild medley of recommendations, suggestions, and analysis. Federal officials showed no better discipline than did the private citizens. Pre-belligerent planning may be forced on the United States by eventual international crises, but before that stage is reached, private and governmental persons working in the informational field might do well to consider how readily they could offer or enforce cooperation in the event of a real emergency.

Psychological Warfare Plans. A general plan for psychological warfare expresses the aims of the portion of the war (either in point of time, or with respect to a stated area) to which it refers. It states the maximum goals which psychological warfare can, with honest realism, be counted on to accomplish if all goes well. It indicates the minimum effect, which (unlike combat operations) can fall precisely at zero.

The general plan then goes on to state the conditions which will govern the operating agencies. The important part of this section lies in guessing where the operating agencies are likely to need

Figure 51: Basic Types: Start of War. This leaflet embodies almost all possible mistakes in psychological warfare. It was prepared to explain why war came between America and Japan, but was not even begun until many months after Pearl Harbor. The heading and style are official and formal. The message is no more than a footnote to history. Its last fault redeemed it; no arrangements were made for dropping it.

←

coordination and where not. If the plan is to reveal highly important and therefore secret strategy, it should merely sketch the broad outlines of the processes intended, leaving to experts the responsibility of determining specific *do's* and *don'ts*. In such a case, however, the plan should not leave room for inter-agency or inter-personal doubt as to where the interpretive function lies. Too often, highly formal agreements are interpreted out of existence by propagandists who are interested in adding their own proposals to those set forth and agreed upon in the plan. When definition of the plan in operational terms[2] is needed, the location of the sub-definer should be made very plain unless the propaganda establishment itself happens to be remarkably well organized and in no further need of definite prescriptions of function.

The inclusion of actual political and military goals in a propaganda plan is an exceedingly ambitious undertaking. The goal, "To foster a spirit of nationalism and independence among the Eastern Arachosian people to the end that they may revolt and set up their own pro-Allied government," is a commitment beyond the reach of normal propaganda. It comes closer to requiring all the facilities of the operating state, financial, diplomatic, covert, and paramilitary, to put it into effect. The goal, "To give sympathetic circulation to Eastern Arachosian autonomist sentiments so as to promote interference with the occupying power," is much more nearly attainable. Military goals are often described by propagandists as attainable by means of propaganda alone, but there is no known example of psychological warfare having attained a strictly military goal without assistance by other means of warfare. Goals such as "the defeat of—," "the surrender of—," or the "destruction of—," have no place in practical propaganda planning, since they are pretentious or deceptive. More legitimate are the goals actually obtained by propaganda, such as "encouragement of a spirit of factionalism which may assist defeat . . ." "promotion of war-weariness that will make the process of surrender more easily accomplished . . .," and "appeals for the destruction of—." Such points may appear minor, but it is the overstatement of the propaganda

case that has many times goaded disinterested outsiders into becoming skeptics or opponents.

Political and military goals can be described only in terms of
hopes; effective psychological goals—goals resting in the form of
opinion which it is desired to create—are very concrete. If enemy
surrender is desired, propaganda leaves to the operator no further
scope for revenge themes which will frighten the enemy away from
surrender. If the enemy leader is to be discredited on the basis of
having poor military judgment, the contrasting good judgment of
the enemy general is a necessary ingredient. The psychological
goals have to be framed in terms of how much the enemy listener,
the Propaganda Man, can stand and can believe. (See chapter 9.)
Since he listens irregularly, furtively, and half-antagonistically,
propaganda will defeat itself if it shifts from goal to goal with logical but finespun dexterity. Psychological goals are attained only
by sustained, consistent patterns of propaganda; they have to be
plain, repetitive, and insistent. Political and military goals can be
anything the planners feel like including as a pious wish. They
might as well consist of a current re-statement of political and
military aims for the subject or area at the time of planning. They
are beyond the reach of practical psychological warfare.

National-level and general staff level plans have to be made up
in much the same way. If the plan is good it will provide for its
own circulation to all government instrumentalities which do in
fact conduct propaganda in the particular field involved. It does
no good to adopt a plan for the encouragement of the Filipinos
and the inducement of cooperation among the Filipino officials of
the Japanese-sponsored Republic (which means a tone of concili-
ation toward Filipino leaders or officials who hold puppet titles) if
a cabinet member keeps calling publicly for the immediate execution of any Filipino who ever had dinner with a Japanese. It is useless to try to cooperate with Communist guerrillas in West K'tai
on the argument, "We all oppose the Axis together! Ideologies don't
matter when brave men fight side by side"—if at the same time the
guerrillas know we have a strong domestic campaign on against
Communism. Telling a Communist that ideologies don't matter is

like saying to a Jesuit, "Let's skip the superstitions, Father, and leave religion out of it. Get down to business." To some kinds of people, ideology *is* business. The broad propaganda plan should make choices that reflect the judgment of the reviewing officers. If they are made in a vacuum, without taking into consideration the actual opinion of the audience group, they might as well not be made at all.

Propaganda plans must be circulated to non-propaganda agencies in order to make sure that routine public relations or announcements of current or contemplated action, and statements of basic policy do not contradict or neutralize the plan once it is put into effect. Frequently months of propaganda work can be undone by a tactless speech from somebody in the same government but in an unrelated agency. Authoritative circulation of the plan—which means that the plan must be neither long nor over-secret—can help forestall such mistakes. Speech clearance, requiring review of all official and policy-making speeches in advance of delivery, is the surest safeguard against overt collision between different spokesmen. In World War II it was applied with some success, but the exceptions were so conspicuous that the effective coordination passed almost unnoticed.

Strategic and Consolidation Plans. Advance psychological warfare plans for concrete military operations not only require a statement of the propaganda operation to be performed with facilities and personnel who are expected to remain static, but demand that the psychological warfare personnel, together with the needful gear, be moved right along with the advancing forces. This makes planning more definite, and those parts of the plans that do not require psychological or political prescription of content can be written in standard military form.

Wise consolidation plans give urgent priority to the restoration of the home-grown informational media and recreational facilities of the occupied territory. Definite anticipation of shortages in radio facilities, newsprint, ink, paper, and other supplies can ensure prompt reopening of consolidated facilities under way.

The propaganda operators may tell higher echelons that the local people are not competent, cannot be trusted, and so on, but General MacArthur's experience in Japan would seem to indicate that no army can carry on consolidation propaganda as efficiently as the conquered civilians themselves can, provided the civilians have:

(1) Reasonable though restricted freedom of utterance, so that they can know what they may or may not say;

(2) Prompt liaison for security and policy clearance, so that they can get an authoritative yes-or-no answer on proposed projects, enabling them to maintain operation without intolerable delays;

(3) Friendly professional assistance in meeting material and staff shortages;

(4) A series of phases, marking off the forms and methods of control so that the controlling staff can plan for a first phase of doing its own publishing and broadcasting, a second phase of letting the local people work under license with close supervision and technical help, and a third phase of permitting them freedom within the normal censorship limits of military government. The American DISCC's (District Information Services Control Commands) in the American Zone of Germany did an excellent job in moving rapidly from phase one to phase two in 1945 and 1946.

Contingency Plans. Frequently the chiefs of government and services know of an operation or danger that may arise, which will change the character of the war. Such were the North African landings, the Italian surrender, D-day itself, the joining of the American and Russian forces in Germany, Hitler's death. For such contingencies, it is desirable to have plans ready stating the reaction of the government to the event. Such plans can be prepared and distributed to select personnel, and downgraded or released, together with any needed last-minute change, when the first word comes through that the event is officially to be recognized.

Profoundly secret contingencies—such as Hiroshima day—do not lend themselves to such treatment.

It must be repeated that plans are effective only when transposed into plain, simple, usable guidances for the actual operatives. When a plan is so secret or so involved that the only people who could carry it out are not allowed to know anything about it, it becomes a sad self-defeating effort.

Notes:

[1] While this statement is plainly a matter of individual opinion, the author considers that his own experience supports his opinion in this instance. He wrote plans on almost every operating level in the governmental and military hierarchy during World War II, all the way from drafting plans for the Joint (American) and Combined (British-American) Chiefs of Staff down to helping field agents in the China Theater work out practical little propaganda plane for their own missions, or planning the writing, use, and classification of leaflets one by one, in collaboration with OWI operators. He found planning to be fascinating at the top, and worthwhile at the bottom of the pyramid, but he found no significant correlation between the top and the bottom, save in the sense which he makes plain.

[2] In the pseudo-technical propaganda slang of the OWI people, this was called "spelling out." The same people "stockpiled" "campaigns" to "needle" the enemy.

CHAPTER 12
OPERATIONS FOR CIVILIANS

Plainly, psychological warfare operates against civilians with as much effect as it does against troops. Indeed, under the rather high standards set for modern warfare by The Hague and Geneva conventions, psychological warfare is left as one of the few completely legitimate weapons which can on occasion be directed against an exclusively civilian and noncombatant target. Even though World War II erased most of the distinctions between military and civilian, leaving civilians in the vertical front line of all air war, psychological warfare gained. It became a more useful instrument for bettering war. Civilian interest in propaganda became no mere matter of emotional loyalty or philosophical preference, but a life-and-death matter to its recipients. After fire raids it would be a madman who would disregard an enemy bomb-warning leaflet without trying to figure out its application to himself and his children.

Short-wave Radio. Short-wave radio is the chief burden-bearer of long-distance psychological warfare. It is more useful as a means of connecting originating offices with standard-wave relay stations than as a direct means of communication. Even in free countries, short-wave sets are not often plentiful. The conditions of reception, from a purely technical point of view, are often undesirable; recreational material does not go through since a short-wave listener will put up with the static when he is receiving vital, vividly presented news, but often will not try to make out soap opera or

281

music over the squawks of the ether, and the use of short-wave reception in wartime implies a deliberate willingness on the part of the listener to do something which he knows to be disloyal or dangerous.

Short-wave does make it possible for advanced standard-wave propaganda stations to pass along material which has been prepared in the homeland. Large staffs can do the work. The news can be put through a large, alert, well-organized office. Features can be prepared by real professionals, acted out by a number of actors, put on records, reviewed, and then relayed to the standard-wave station whenever needed. The Americans at Radio Saipan thus broadcast right into Japan, and were able to transmit materials which could not possibly have been put on the air with the staff working on the island. The people at Saipan were mostly telecommunications technicians, engaged in picking up the short-wave from Hawaii or San Francisco and in passing it on into the enemy country on the standard wave length. Millions of Japanese heard our Saipan standard-wave broadcasts, in contrast to the dozens or hundreds who had heard our short-wave previously.

The use of homeland facilities makes possible the advance preparation of a large collection of material ready for broadcast. In security-sensitive or otherwise dubious situations, four or five alternate programs can be worked out for the same amount of program time. On wire recorders or disc records, the proposed material can be passed around in finished form, reviewed, selected, censored, and approved. This would not be true of a hurried station working far forward in the zone of operations.

Short-wave has its own advantages, however, apart from its utility as a means of getting program material to the relay stations. Short-wave can and will be picked up by the enemy monitors and enemy intelligence systems. It will also be heard by persons of power, wealth, and influence, irrespective of the economic or political system of the enemy. The big shots of any system know how to transcend limitations that awe or defeat the ordinary man. The short-wave transmitter speaks therefore to the enemy government, to the groups which compose the enemy government, and to the individuals in or out of the enemy government who are leaders in their own country. We found that the *Joho Kyoku* and the *Gaimusho* (Foreign Office) in Tokyo were mimeographing a daily summary of our San Francisco broadcasts, and we thus knew that anything we said over San Francisco would be heard by the most influential men in Japan. Captain Ellis Zacharias, U.S.N., spoke Japanese and had known most of the Japanese leaders personally before the war; with government monitoring known to exist he felt free to address the Japanese leaders personally and directly with assurance his words would reach them, and his broadcasts are confessed by the Japanese themselves to have played a contributory part in bringing about the Japanese decision to surrender.

Standard-wave. The most effective use of radio is that which falls within the receiving capacity of the ordinary receiving sets owned or used by the enemy population. This means the establishment of transmitting facilities close enough to the enemy territory for the programs to get through. As between the United States and Japan from 1941 through 1944, this was very difficult. No Americans ever dared join the Shantung guerrillas, whether Kuomintang or Communist, with transmitters; and as long as we broadcast from the safety of our side of the ocean, we could only hope that occasional freak conditions would echo programs into Japan two or three times a month. With the British and the Germans, it was altogether different; the two countries were virtually touching, and each could cover the entire enemy territory.

With short-distance standard-wave broadcasting to an enemy known to have millions of radio receivers, strategic radio becomes effective. The chance is provided for building up a consistent group of listeners, for influencing their morale and opinions, and for circulating rumors that will reach almost every single person in the enemy population. The temptation to perform tricks, to lapse back to peacetime standards of radio-as-entertainment or radio-as-advertising, is a constant one. The propagandist knows that he is being heard, and he fears that his audience will lose interest if he does not stimulate them with a brilliantly variegated series of programs.

Black radio comes into its own on standard wave. The British could put the mysterious anti-British, anti-Hitler broadcaster *Gustav Siegfried Eins* on the air, with his rousing obscenities, his coarse but believable gossip, his wild diatribes against the Allies and against the Nazi scum who got in the way of the glorious German army. He was so good that for a while even American propanal thought he might be a spokesman for the saucier members of the *Wehrmacht* general staff. The Germans could broadcast proletarian propaganda on the *Lenin Old Guard* station, foaming at the mouth whenever they mentioned the crazy vile Fascist swine Hitler, and then going into tantrums because the Communist party needed all the brave glorious leaders who had been murdered by the fat bureaucrat Stalin. Ed and Joe could talk out of Bremen and pretend to be scooting around the American mid-west, one jump ahead of the G-men with their trailer and concealed transmitter, telling the rest of the Americans the low-down about "that goof Roosevelt and his Jewish war," but Ed and Joe were not good enough to fool anybody. Black radio is great fun for the operators, but its use is often limited to a twisted kind of entertainment designed to affect the morale of dubious groups. It leaps to sudden importance only in times of critical panic when it can add the last catalyst to national confusion, precipitating chaos.

The beginning and end of standard-wave transmission is news. News (see chapter 8) uses standard appeals. It should be factual but selectively factual. Repetition of basic themes is much more important than the constant invention of new ones. The propaganda chief has nothing to do, day in and day out, but to think of his own programs. He becomes familiar with them and bored by them. He visualizes his Propaganda Man as a person who hears all transmissions and is understandably bored by them, overlooking the interruptions that listeners face, the long gaps between the programs they hear, the weather interference, the static, the police measures.

Even with peacetime facilities tremendous simplicity and repetition are needed to convey advertising on the radio. In wartime repetition is even more necessary. It serves the double function of driving the theme home to listeners who have heard it before, while broadening the circle of listeners with each transmission. A point of diminishing returns is soon reached but even diminished returns are often rewarding. The hardest-to-reach people are sometimes the ones it is most important to reach with a simple, basic, persuasive item. Repetition thus ensures depth of response in the core audience, while adding to the marginal audience with each additional application. What is deadly monotonous to the propagandist himself may, on the thousandth repetition, merely have become pleasantly familiar to the Propaganda Man on the other end. The author has talked to any number of clandestine listeners to our propaganda who have almost wept with rage as they told of listening to jokes, novelties, political speeches and other funny stuff when they hoped to get a clean-cut announcement of the latest military news.

Communication Through the Mails. In World War II, propaganda was not able to make use of the mails the way that the propagandists of World War I succeeded in doing. The mails were much more intermittent. The channels into Germany through Scandinavia were not kept open except for Sweden, which was reachable, rather perilously, by air alone; Iberia was an inhospitable base. German counterintelligence was more than ruthless; it was effectively savage and made the Germany of Kaiser Wilhelm seem rustic by contrast. With Japan, anything would have had to go through Soviet censorship to get there in the first place, and then meet the traditional intricacies of Japanese red tape. Mail propaganda was therefore not heavily developed.

Something was accomplished, however, by use of the Portuguese, Spanish, Swiss and Chinese press. Enemy officials and private persons were known to read these, and it was possible to do a great deal toward influencing editorial content.

Major mail-propaganda operations were conducted against us, however. The Nazis, as part of their pre-belligerent planning and operations sent enormous quantities of propaganda through the United States mail—sometimes postage-free under the frank of

Congressmen. The Japanese, down to the time of Pearl Harbor, kept large public-relations staffs running at full speed in New York, Washington, and other American cities. They helped their American friends with money and by heavy purchase of copyright material friendly to Japan—thus making it unnecessary for any author to report himself as a Japanese paid agent, and they offered Japanese "cultural and educational" information to interested persons. It really was cultural and well done. By talking about Japanese poetry, religion and cherry blossoms, and omitting all war propaganda, the handsome little booklets kept alive the memory of a hospitable, quaint, charming Japan. Some of this material was mailed directly from Japan to the United States.

Since mail propaganda depends on the freedom of the mails, it is much more apt to be used by a dictatorship against us than by us against a dictatorship.

Leaflets. The types of leaflets are described in the next chapter, in the course of discussing leaflets addressed to troops. Each leaflet designed for a military group has its civilian equivalents. In addition to the military types, overt propaganda leaflets for civilians should include:

(1) Communications from the legitimate authorities (whether government-in-exile, underground, or friendly quisling) of the civilians addressed.

(2) Newspapers in air format, reduced in scale, but with a heavy proportion of the normal peacetime features of the audience's own press.

(3) Novelty materials appealing to children, who are apt to be among the most industrious collectors of leaflets, disseminating them far and wide with less danger of reprisal from the occupying power or the police than adults might face. (Good adult leaflets are as interesting to children as are leaflets especially designed for them. The use of color printing, vivid illustrations, pictures of air battles, how-it-works diagrams of weapons,

and so forth, may reach the teen-age audience best if it gives no indication of being aimed at them.)

(4) Gifts—soap, salt, needles, matches, chocolate and similar articles dropped to civilian populations. (This demonstrates the wealth and benevolence of the giver. Countermeasures to enemy use of this type of propaganda consist of dropping a few duplicates of his gifts, containing poison-ivy soap, nauseating salt, infected-looking needles, explosive chocolate, etc. The Germans are reported to have followed this procedure against the American air gifts dropped to Italy and France. With the avoidance or the spoilage of gifts, the propaganda effect becomes so confused that both sides find it worth desisting for a while.)

(5) Appeals to women. Women, statistically, are around 50% of the population of any country. With the diversion of men to fighting operations the percentage of women in the home population rises and in wartime it may become 60% or 70%. They face social and economic problems much more immediately than do men because the responsibility for maintaining homes and children normally falls on them. Evidence of humane intentions, of reluctance to wage the most cruel forms of war, of attempts to help civilians escape unnecessary danger, can bring women into the participating enemy group for relaying propaganda.

Pamphlets. Where air-dropping facilities are plentiful, leaflets can be supplemented by pamphlets. Pamphlets have the advantage of giving the propagandist more space for texts or pictures, enabling him to tackle enemy arguments in detail or in depth. Pamphlets can present sustained arguments, and thus come closer to meeting the domestic propaganda facilities of the enemy on even ground. They are especially useful in countering or neutralizing those enemy arguments which depend either on formal argument or on misapplied statistics, and which therefore require point-by-point confutation.

The pamphlet shown in figure 6 is an excellent example of the medium. Though it carries a complex message, it can be read by persons at the lowest educational level. It meets enemy propaganda over a whole range of themes. It is apt to be disseminated farther, whether initial distribution be by ground or by air.

Unlike the leaflet, the pamphlet is sometimes hard to conceal. For well policed areas, it must be supplied with a protective disguise if it is to be passed along. One ingenious pamphlet made up by Dennis McEvoy and Don Brown at OWI for dropping on the Japanese, started out with a warning: "*Enemy!* Warning! This is an Enemy Publication, issued by the United States Government. Finder is Commanded to take this to the Nearest Police Station Immediately! *Enemy!*" The pamphlet gave a general statement of Japan's bad war position, and *was addressed to Japanese policemen and police officials*. The cover urged the policemen not to keep the pamphlet, nor to destroy it, but to pass it on up through channels to their superiors as an instance of enemy propaganda. (We never found out what the Japanese police actually did when they got these.)

One Japanese black leaflet assumed the proportions of a book, and was made up in the familiar format of the pocket-sized twenty-five-cent volumes. With a New York dateline, a copyright notice, and even a printers' union label all neatly falsified, the book expressed opposition to Roosevelt's war. It was circulated by the Japanese as a captured enemy book, presumably, in order to convince their own people and their Asiatic associates that opposition to World War II existed within the United States itself.

Almost all belligerents issued malingerer's handbooks during the war. These started out with statements that the medical control system was inadequate, that each man had to look out for himself, and that feigned sickness was often the only alternative to real sickness. Disguised as entertainment booklets, "instructions" accompanying medicine, or even as official handbooks (of the enemy government) for this and that purpose, the leaflets gave detailed instructions on how to fake tuberculosis, heart trouble, and other diseases.

Subversive Operations. Propaganda to friendly civilians whose country has been overrun by the enemy can be effectively promoted by collaboration with local patriots—unless political considerations prevent such collaboration. This type of operation requires careful cooperation between propaganda (overt), subversive facilities, and intelligence personnel. World War II saw the type used on all fronts. The Japanese made especially bold use of it during the conquest of Malaya, the occupation of Burma, and the Chinese Railway Campaigns of 1944. Natives on the enemy side were regarded by us as quislings; the Japanese honored them as patriots and duped them effectively.

Bold black propaganda operations can often embarrass the enemy. The dropping of a few hundred tons of well-counterfeited currency would tend to foul up any fiscal system. Peacetime counterfeiters operate with poor materials, secretly, and in small shops. When instructed, a government agency can do an astoundingly good job of counterfeiting. The United States is on the vulnerable side of this operation, because our money happens to be the most trusted and most widely hoarded in the world. Various governments are believed to have run off substantial numbers of United States twenty and fifty dollar bills. A less offensive operation consists of giving the enemy populace sets of ration cards, along with simple suggestions on how to finish the forging job so as to make it convincing. The Nazis were especially subject to this kind of attack, since German methodical bookkeeping required a large number of documents to be in the possession of each citizen. Falsification of any of these made the German officials go mad with confusion.

To a country suffering from too much policing, the transmission by black propaganda of facsimile personal-identity cards in large numbers would be welcomed by many common citizens and would keep the enemy police procedure at a high pitch of futile haste. The essence of this, as of all good black propaganda, is to confuse the enemy authorities while winning the thankfulness of the enemy people—preferably while building up the myth within the enemy country that large, well-organized groups of revolutionists are ready to end the war when their time comes.

If white propaganda is to be compared to incendiary bombing, in that it ultimately affects the enemy armed services by disorganizing the homeland behind them, black propaganda may be compared to the tinfoil strips used in anti-radar. Black propaganda strikes directly at enemy security. It gives him too much to do, and thus increases the chances for agents down on the ground to succeed in their lonely, dangerous work.

Motion Pictures. In consolidated areas, allied or neutral territory, and the home jurisdiction, motion pictures for civilians can be employed as a major propaganda instrument. The combination of visual and auditory appeal ensures a concentration of attention not commanded by other media. In both World Wars, the U.S. made extensive use of film.

Procurement can be either through direct governmental manufacture of the finished product, or by subcontracting to nongovernmental agencies. Propaganda films normally make a point of displaying the military prowess and civic virtue of the distributor.

Officially distributed films are, however, almost always overshadowed by pure entertainment films. The wartime official movie can penetrate no deeper than can the unofficial picture. Financial and commercial control, plus censorship, limits the periphery into which motion-picture showings can be extended. Often the private film will be shown when a public one would be suppressed. And in time of peace, the propaganda movie has ever sharper competition from its private competitors. Few propaganda movies have ever achieved the spectacular impact of some private films in portraying the American way of life. Tahitians, Kansu men, Hindus and Portuguese would probably agree unanimously in preferring the USA of Laurel and Hardy to the USA of strong-faced men building dams and teaching better chicken-raising.

Only rarely does the cinema penetrate enemy territory or reach clandestine audiences. Its direct contribution to critical-zone psychological warfare is therefore slight. Perhaps television may in course of time combine attention-holding with transmissibility.

CHAPTER 13
OPERATIONS AGAINST TROOPS

In every instance of systematic American use of psychological warfare against enemy troops during World War II, affirmative results were discerned after the operation had been in effect for a short while. Figure 46 shows the consummation of the troop propaganda program; these Germans are surrendering and they carry the Allied leaflets with them. By the latter phases of the liberation of France, 90 per cent of the enemy prisoners reported that they had seen or possessed Allied leaflets and the most famous leaflet of them all, the celebrated *Passierschein* (see figure 4) came to be as familiar to the Germans as their own paper money.[1] Since every enemy who surrenders is one less man to root out or destroy at a cost of life to one's own side, the sharp upswing of enemy surrenders was a decided military gain.

Two separate types of psychological reaction are to be sought in the enemy soldier's mind. The first consists of a general lowering of his morale or efficiency even when he is not in a position to perform any overt act, such as surrendering, which would hurt his side and help ours. This may be called MO, or morale operations. The second type of action is overt action (surrendering, deserting his post of duty, mutinying) which can be induced only if the appeal is expertly timed.

Operations against troops must be based on the objective military situation. Suffering and exertion increase realism; plain soldiers are not apt to be talked over by propaganda unless the propaganda is carefully cued to their actual situation. All propaganda should be based on fact; propaganda to troops must be based not

Figure 52: Basic Types: Troop Morale. Leaflets may be aimed at (1) morale, (2) news, (3) action. Morale leaflets neither communicate news nor call for specific action. Rather, they pave the way for action. Many of the previous illustrations have been of this type. This one is a troop morale leaflet used by the puppet Free India Army on their own men, who were discouraged by the self-evident lack of matériel and numbers. (Singapore, about 1944.)

merely on fact, but must show shrewd appreciative touches of understanding the troops' personal conditions. Propaganda is not much use to a nation undergoing abject defeat, for the troops on the victorious side will be buoyed up by the affirmation of victory from their own eyes.

Troop propaganda must therefore aim at eventual willing *capture* of the individual—not at surrender by his individual initiative. It must implant the notion that he may eventually be trapped, and that *if* that happens he should give up. The propaganda must not meet the soldier's loyalty in a head-on collision but must instead give the enemy soldier the opportunity of rationalizing himself out of the obligations of loyalty ("true loyalty requires survival and therefore surrender"). The steps, therefore, needed for good propaganda to actual combat troops include the following:

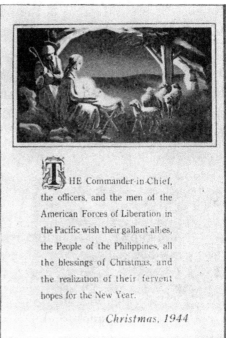

HE Commander-in-Chief,
the officers, and the men of the
American Forces of Liberation in
the Pacific wish their gallant'allies,
the People of the Philippines, all
the blessings of Christmas, and
the realization of their fervent
hopes for the New Year.

Christmas, 1944

Figure 53: Paired Morale Leaflets. The Christmas card showing the Nativity was dropped by General MacArthur's psychological warfare people on the Filipinos. The Christmas cards with bells were prepared by the Japanese for the U.S. Army. The former were designed to cheer on the Filipinos; the latter, to depress the Americans with the defeatist messages inside the cards.

first, the notion that the enemy soldier may have to surrender as his side loses or retreats ("other [named] units
have surrendered, with so-and-so many men; you will
have to, too");

second, themes which make the enemy soldier believe that
an all-out effort is wasted or misapplied;

third, the idea that he or his unit may find themselves in a
hopeless situation soon;

fourth, identifying the next authentically bad situation with
the "hopeless" situation;

fifth, concrete instructions for the actual surrender.[2]

Morale Operations. Morale operations in the black field are,
for the American record, still a closed book. German black operations against the French included such enterprises as sending

French soldiers letters from their home towns telling them that their wives were committing adultery or were infected with venereal diseases, or calling out names and unit designations to French troops facing them in the Maginot Line, or giving away mourning dresses to women who would wear them on the streets of Paris, or intercepting telephone communications in the field and giving confusing or improper orders.

Morale operations on the white side included such items as the following:

Sending mournful poetry leaflets to Japanese units which were known to be demoralized for lack of home furlough (China Theater);

Dropping beautiful colored pictures of luscious Japanese victuals on starving troops (North Burma);

Showing the Japanese Sad Sack in a cartoon, fighting everywhere while his officers get all the liquor, all the food, all the girls, and all the glory, while the common soldier ends up cremated (Southwest Pacific);

Demonstrating that the Nazi pets on the German High Command have disrupted the splendid German military tradition and have thrown out the really competent professional generals (Soviet-German front);

Pinning the nickname, *Der Sterber* (roughly, "Old Let's-go-get-killed!"), on a German general who had boasted of his willingness to expend personnel (Anglo-American and Soviet radio);

Telling the German troops they were dying for a cause already lost (Italy)

Reporting back to the Germans the statements made by prisoners, to the effect they were damned glad that they were out of the fighting (France);

Telling the Japanese on Attu and Kiska that just as surely as the *kiri* leaf, symbol of death, would fall in the autumn, they too would fall (North Pacific);

Figure 54: Troop Morale Leaflet, Grey. This German leaflet from the Italian front attempts to remind American troops of the bonus troubles of 1932—a year in which most of the American soldiers were still in school. Only to older men could the appeal carry much weight. The drawing and typography are distinctively German. In terms of source, this leaflet is grey.

Telling the Japanese homeland and troops that the Japanese Emperor had loved peace but that the militarists had dragged the Sacred Empire into war ("Peaceful is Morning in the Shrine Garden" leaflet; designed for Aleutians, used over Japan);

Telling the Chinese in China that the Americans would soon cut the Japanese conquered empire in two with Asiatic landings, and then dropping the leaflet, written in simple Chinese which could be figured out by Japanese, on the Japanese troops (China);

Congratulating imaginary agents in ostensible code over the voice radio for the excellent work they have allegedly done in the enemy home country (all theaters).

The category "morale leaflets" covers all leaflets which neither call for immediate action, nor are designed primarily to convey news as such.

Figure 55: Chinese Communist Civilian Morale Leaflet. This leaflet attempts to raise peasant morale while calling in general terms for economic action. It shows a peasant family welcoming home the father, who has been made a Hero of Labor. (Given the author by Political Department, Border Area Government, at Yenan in September 1944.)

Figure 56: General Morale: Matched Themes. The American leaflet and Japanese one both show the same map with the same event—cutting of the enemy lifeline. In each case, the event is alleged to be news. However, the purpose of the leaflet is to depress the morale of all enemies who see it and to raise the morale of all friends.

News Leaflets. Figures 1, 7, 59, 60 and 65 are news leaflets. The propaganda purpose is evident, even to the enemy. But in the best of these leaflets there is a tendency to let the facts speak for themselves, and to show the enemy just what the actual situation is.

Tactical Defensive Psychological Warfare. Morale operations are designed, therefore, to obtain responses other than immediate action. Several possible goals can be sought, singly or jointly. The commonest is preparation of the enemy soldier's mind for the actual physical act of surrender, the moral act of doing no more for his own side. Whenever surrender requires nothing more than passivity, morale leaflets are even more promising; in such cases all that is asked of the enemy is that he sit tight, fight inefficiently, and put up his hands when he is told to do so. Other purposes of morale operations include the irritation of enemy groups against each other, the general depression of enemy morale, the discouragement of enemy troops, officers or commanders.

Morale operations, to be effective, must be aimed at the actual, specific morale with which they are concerned. Well fed troops cannot be frightened by the remote prospect of starvation. Well officered troops cannot be induced to mutiny. Troops with good mail service cannot be made homesick. However, weak points in the enemy organization can and do provide targets for morale operations. The defeat situation imposes tremendous strain on both the individual soldier and on officers in positions of responsibility. At such times, disunity rises to the surface, rumors spread more readily, and propaganda operations against morale can have devastating effect. (Allied psychological warfare against Germans in 1944-45 was aimed both at general officers and at the mass of the German troops—operations against the officers being founded on the common-sense premise that if large-scale German surrenders were sought, they could best be obtained by influencing those Germans who had the authority to surrender.)

A curious point developed. German morale in the higher grades was worse than in the lower. In the very last year of the war, despite the terrible air raids on their homeland behind them, the

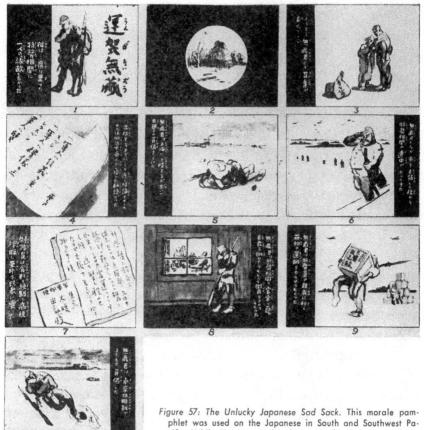

Figure 57: The Unlucky Japanese Sad Sack. This morale pamphlet was used on the Japanese in South and Southwest Pacific. While it never produced any startling results on them, it did no harm. The pictures are done by a qualified Japa-

German troops on the Western front underwent only slight morale deterioration—in comparison with what they should have undergone had their morale borne a direct relationship to the strategic position of Germany as a whole. On the other hand, the morale among general officers and staff officers became wretched. The *putsch* of the generals the previous summer was merely a foretaste of the demoralization of the German higher command.

This unusual situation arose from the fact that the National Socialist propaganda machinery was still working on the masses of the troops. The political officers still made speeches. The troops were given pep talks, information about the war (hopelessly distorted information, but information none the less), and promises of privileges and comforts which—while they rarely materialized—

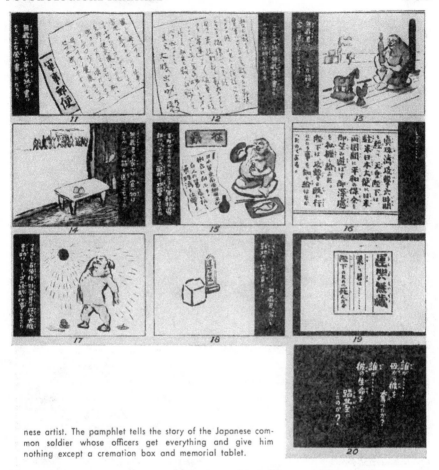

nese artist. The pamphlet tells the story of the Japanese common soldier whose officers get everything and give him nothing except a cremation box and memorial tablet.

were cheering. Simultaneously, German army discipline in the Prussian tradition, never known to be wishy-washy or weak, was sharply stiffened. Furthermore, the plain soldiers carried over to the months of defeat those propaganda attitudes which they had been taught in the prewar and war years by Hitler's incessant domestic propaganda.

In contrast with common troops, the officers had the professional skill to understand the advantages possessed by the Allied armies. The officers knew enough about global and continental strategy, about the immediate strategy of the Western front, about economic factors and so on, to see that the situation was genuinely bad. Furthermore, the officer class had been less indoctrinated in the first place—many of them having personally despised the Nazis

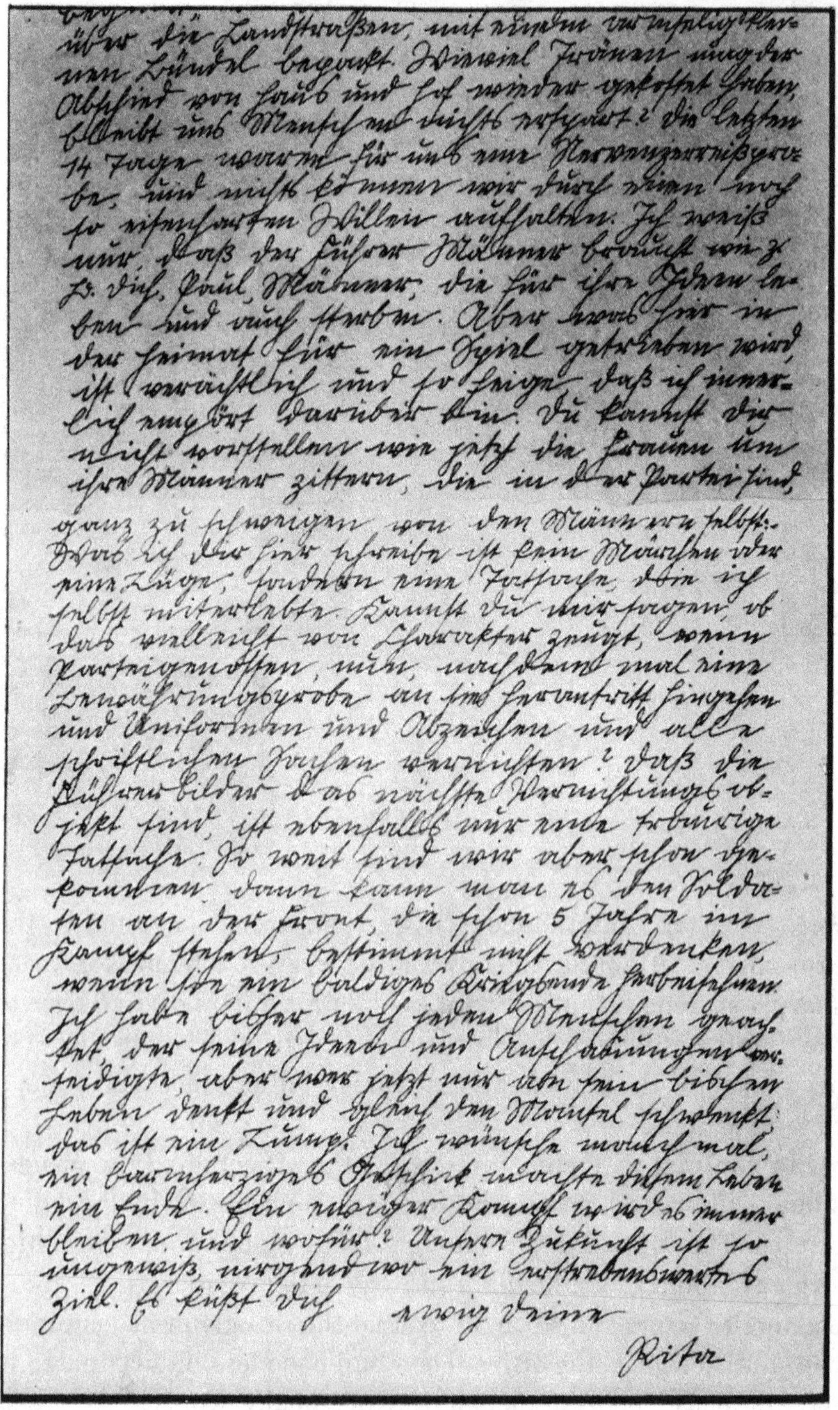
über die Landstraßen, mit einem armseligen Klei-
nen Bündel bepackt. Wieviel Frauen mögen den
Abschied von Haus und Hof wieder gehofft haben,
bleibt uns Menschen nichts erspart? die letzten
14 Tage waren für uns eine Nervenzerreißpro-
be, und nichts können wir durch einen noch
so eisernen Willen aufhalten. Ich weiß
nur, daß der Führer Männer braucht wie z.
B. dich, Paul Männer, die für ihre Ideen leben und auch sterben. Aber was hier in
der Heimat für ein Spiel getrieben wird,
ist erbärmlich und so feige, daß ich inner-
lich empört darüber bin. Du kannst dir
nicht vorstellen wie jetzt die Frauen um
ihre Männer zittern, die in der Partei sind,
ganz zu schweigen von den Männern selbst.
Was ich dir hier schreibe ist kein Märchen oder
eine Lüge, sondern eine Tatsache, die ich
selbst miterlebte. Kannst du mir sagen, ob
das vielleicht von Charakter zeugt, wenn
Parteigenossen, nur, nachdem mal eine
Panzerfaustgruppe an sie herantritt hingehen
und Uniformen und Abzeichen und alle
schriftlichen Sachen vernichten? daß die
Führerbilder das nächste Vernichtungsob-
jekt sind, ist ebenfalls nur eine traurige
Tatsache. So weit sind wir aber schon gekommen, denn kann man es den Soldaten an der Front, die schon 5 Jahre im
Kampf stehen, bestimmt nicht verdenken,
wenn sie ein baldiges Kriegsende herbeisehnen.
Ich habe bisher noch jeden Menschen geach-
tet, der seine Ideale und Anschauungen ver-
teidigte, aber wer jetzt nur eben sein bischen
Leben denkt und gleich den Mantel schwenkt,
das ist ein Lump. Ich wünsche manchmal,
ein barmherziges Geschick machte diesem Leben
ein Ende. Ein ewiger Kampf wird es immer
bleiben und wofür? Unsere Zukunft ist so
ungewiß, nirgendwo ein erstrebenswertes
Ziel. Es küßt dich ewig Deine

Rita

...camps, ...ded with their pitiful little bundles. How many tears must be shed at leaving house and home. Is no mercy to be shown to us human beings?

The last fortnight has been a nerve-shattering trial for us, and however we steel ourselves we can't stave off anything. All I know is that the Führer needs men – men like you, Paul, for example. Men who are ready to live, and also to die, for their ideas. What's going on here is so contemptible and cowardly that I'm seething with rage! You can't imagine how the women are quaking with fear for their menfolk in the Party – not to speak of the men themselves! What sort of people are they? Can you tell me? – Party members who, once they have been put to a little bit of 'testing', go off and destroy their uniforms, badges and all documents?

The fact that the pictures of the Führer are the first things to be destroyed is just one additional sad fact. Things have come to such a pass that one can't think ill of the soldiers at the front, who've been in the war for five years, if they wish for a speedy end to it.

Until now I respected any man who defended his ideas and views, but a man who at this time simply clings to his little bit of life and at once becomes a turncoat – he's a scoundrel.

I wish merciful fate would put an end to this life. It will never be anything but fighting. And what for? Our future is so uncertain. Nothing anywhere is worth striving for.

Love and kisses,

Eternally yours

Rita.

←↑

Figure 58: Civilian Personal Mail. A common stunt in black or grey morale propaganda is the printing of facsimile personal letters. The letter shown at left is given in the original German form, along with its English twin which was—as usual—prepared for administrative clearance, records, and information. (Europe, Allied, 1944-45.)

Figure 59: Basic Types: Newspapers. Newspapers were prepared by almost every belligerent for almost every other. The examples shown above are *Luftpost* (SHAEF for Germans) and *Rakkasan News* (USAFPA for Japanese). Each newspaper copies the form of enemy civilian newspapers. The gross circulation of these airborne papers reached in some cases up into the millions.

while welcoming Naziism as a means of getting the "cattle," the common people, into line behind the Wehrmacht—and those of them concerned with propaganda naturally became critical of all propaganda, including their own government's, and communicated their criticisms to their brother officers.

German defenses against Allied psychological warfare worked. The German troops fought on when they had no business fighting, when their own generals thought it was time to quit and held out only because the S.S. and Gestapo promised ready death to any high officer who even whispered the word, "Defeat!"

This German defensive success was based on two factors:

(1) The good condition of the German troops in terms of food, supply, communications, and weapons;

(2) The coordination of all morale services for the purpose of defensive psychological warfare.

Figure 60: Basic Types: Spot-News Leaflets. Spot news often makes better propaganda if handled while still fresh than if carried in newspapers or morale leaflets later on. The examples above were used against the Germans. News is given on one side of the leaflet, and is dropped while the news is still news; the other side has a propaganda appeal reading, in effect, "You must choose for yourself. Die for the Party or live for yourself!"

A common *Landser*, tough and ready in a whole division full of well fed, well armed men, could not be expected to undergo despair because freight-car loadings hundreds of miles away had dropped to zero. He might see that the Luftwaffe was less in evidence; he might grumble about mail, or about having to use horse transport, but as long as he could see that his own unit was getting on all right, it was hard to persuade him that defeat was around the corner. In World War I, the German troops at the time of surrender *were* much better off than most of them thought they were;

Figure 61: Basic Types: Civilian Action. Desired civilian action can often be obtained by the use of clear instructions transmitted in leaflet form. This leaflet calls on the people of Alsace, Lorraine and Luxembourg to stay away from German communication lines, not to work for the Germans, and to make careful notes of atrocities which the Germans may commit.

in World War II, they *thought* they were better off than they actually were. The Germans may not have been in perfect shape, but they were incomparably better off than the starving scarecrows with whom Generalissimo Chiang was trying to hold back the Japanese in West Hunan or the Americans who had fought despair, fever and Japanese—all three at once—on Bataan.

Along with their relatively good immediate condition, which masked and hid from them the strategic deterioration of the Reich to their rear, the German troops had the services of morale officers who were actually defensive psychological warfare operators.

In some units (more on the Eastern front than the Western) the Germans had PK units—*Propagandakompanie*, or propaganda companies. These were organizationally very interesting. They combined the functions of a combat propaganda company—printing, radio work, interrogation of prisoners, etc.—with the job of morale builders. Their services were available not only for use against the enemy, but for aid to the German troops themselves. Since they were currently informed of Allied propaganda lines, they were able to distribute counteracting propaganda at short notice and were even capable, on occasion, of forestalling Allied propaganda themes in advance.

Defensive psychological warfare in the Wehrmacht and, so far as it is known from Russian articles and fiction, in the Red Army as well, depended on unit-by-unit indoctrination with contempt of the enemy, mistrust of his news facilities, fear of his political aims, and hatred for the whole enemy mentality. Propaganda officers, counter-subversive operatives, public relations men, and information-education officers were either in the same office or were in fact the same men. Combination of functions made possible the use of flexible counteracting propaganda.

Most of this counteracting propaganda was not counter-propaganda, technically speaking. It was not designed against *Allied* propaganda, but for *German* morale. Morale-building was not left to occasional recreational facilities, newspapers for troops, USO entertainment and the like, but was compelled through the use of internal espionage, affirmative presentation of the German case, and unified informational operations. This German tactical defensive psychological warfare was neither a total success nor a total failure; insofar as it helped the Wehrmacht hold out, it aided the last-ditch Nazi war effort.

The American army did not employ defensive psychological warfare in World War II. Troop indoctrination was extremely spotty. American morale remained good, not because it was *made* good by professionals who knew their job, but because Providence and the American people had brought up a generation of young men who started out well and—since the situation never approached hopelessness—kept on going with their spirits high.

For the future, the American and British armies face the problem of devising arrangements whereby within the limits of a free society soldiers can be affirmatively indoctrinated in the course of operations. USO, Red Cross, public relations, information and education at home, morale staffs in the theaters, Armed Forces Radio Service, OWI, the American press and the overseas military papers—these went their separate and uncorrelated ways without doing any

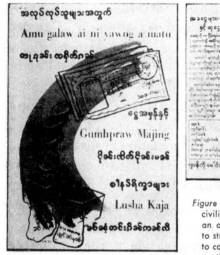

Figure 62: Basic Types: Labor Recruitment. On occasion, civilian labor becomes a highly critical factor even in an area of active operations. Leaflets can urge labor to strike against the enemy; they can also induce labor to come over and get to work. This leaflet was dropped on the Burmese, Shans, and Kachins, showing all the good things of life, promising high wages and bonuses and adding that, anyhow, it was patriotic. Come work for the Allies!

harm, *last time*. If the next war starts, as it may, with an initial interchange of terrifying strategic bombardments, the morale situation may be inherently less healthy. Wise planning would provide, perhaps, a single chain of command for public relations, military propaganda and morale services—extending this all the way down to the platoon, if necessary—to make sure that the "national line" on any given topic is explained, presented, repeated, and (if necessary) enforced.

Such defensive psychological warfare might work against sensational enemy black operations, against attempted political division, and against fabrication of the news—provided it was carried out in an expert fashion. It could not change morale deterioration resulting from practical deterioration within the troop unit itself, except to decelerate the rate of decline. It would not make up for poor leadership. Nothing makes up for poor leadership.

Defensive psychological warfare at higher levels remains a self-contradiction. As pointed out above (chapter 9), good psychological warfare is never directed merely against other psychological warfare. It is directed at the mind of the target audience, at *creating* attitudes of belief or doubt which lead to the desired action. Getting and keeping attention is one of its major missions, and psychological warfare which starts by fixing attention on the enemy presentation is doomed from the start. One of the most conspicuous examples of this was President Roosevelt's sensational message of 15 April 1939, addressed personally to the German Chancellor, Hitler, asking that Hitler promise not to invade 31 countries which Roosevelt listed by name. Defensive in tone, the message gave Hitler the chance to answer over the German world-wide radio while his Reichstag laughed its derision and applause. President Roosevelt's message was decent, sane, humane; it was inspiring to the people who already agreed with him; but it created no attitude in the Germans to whom it was addressed. A sharp, bullying, implicitly threatening speech from President Roosevelt might have penetrated the German mentality of the time, even Hitler's; reasonable reproach did not work. It was not aimed at creating any specific emotional reaction in the *German* mind.

Finally, it must be mentioned that defensive psychological warfare must include countersubversion and counterespionage. The Cheka—Soviet secret police in its first form—once boasted that "capitalist trouble-makers and saboteurs" could not long function in Russia because the countersubversive police were over a hundred million strong. What they meant was that they had trained and bullied the population into reporting anyone and everyone who seemed out of line. An attitude of popular cooperation with countersubversive agencies can be achieved only when those agencies are efficient, respected, and properly presented to the public. Psychological warfare can defend its homeland against enemy operations in kind only if it creates an awareness of propaganda and makes the public critical of attitudes or opinions adverse to national policy. Inexpert official tactics, or the general denunciation of dissent, makes the citizen believe, with Mr. Bumble in *Oliver Twist*, that ". . . the law is a ass, a idiot."

Role of Small-Unit Commanders. Unless a small-unit commander happens to command a unit which includes a Psychological Warfare team, he will have no active Psychological Warfare role. Psychological Warfare operations require the services of experts, and it would be easy for a small-unit commander to jeopardize the propaganda effort of an entire front by well meant but ill-conceived interference in Psychological Warfare operations.

Where the unit does include a Psychological Warfare team, a duality of control arises. This requires good sense to keep in balance. The commander possesses absolute command and responsibility for the movement, protection, and operations timing of the team which happens to be attached to his unit. He should not presume to interfere in the special propaganda instructions flowing down to the team from superior Psychological Warfare echelons. Because of the pressing needs of propaganda operatives for news and for order-of-battle intelligence, it is normally desirable that they have their own signal facilities and that their routine operational communications short-circuit normal military channels. Otherwise, the unit's signal facilities will be overloaded with messages important to the Psychological Warfare team, but useless to the unit as a whole. Such absurdities as the encipherment and decipherment of routine enemy news digests should by all means be avoided. On the other hand, the command and administrative messages should go through normal military channels. In the Galahad operation against the Japanese in North Burma, in which Merrill's Marauders participated, such a double set of communications channels took a long time to develop.

Where the small-unit commander does not possess professionally trained and equipped Psychological Warfare facilities, he should no more expect to engage in offensive Psychological Warfare than to undertake chemical warfare with improvised materials. It becomes his responsibility to turn to liaison.

Field Liaison. One of the new roles developed within the Army during World War II was that of "Psychological Warfare Liaison Officer." Such men were either commissioned officers, usually of company grade, who had been given appropriate training, or were uniformed civilians detailed from OWI or OSS. It is the job of the liaison officer to become acquainted, as far down the echelon of command as may be necessary, with the commanders whom he is to service. He must at the same time retain an intimate knowledge of the personnel, procedures and facilities of the Psychological Warfare unit from which he is detached. His position must be compared to that of a salesman, who should know his product, his company, his sales manager, and his customers, all equally well. The liaison officer should be able to explain to small-unit commanders what Psychological Warfare can do for them, and he should learn to discriminate between high-priority and low-priority requests for PW materials.

For example, a well-trained liaison officer might receive a call from a regimental or battalion commander. He would find that the commander desired leaflets to be used in a particular tactical situation. He should be able to explain what standard ready-prepared leaflets were available, what delay would be involved in making up special leaflets, and what quantities of leaflets would be advisable. Turning back to his home headquarters, he should be able to present the commander's case to the leaflet printers or the public-address team, and should help the propaganda people in understanding the commander's problems.

Mechanics of Liaison. The mechanics of liaison depend in each case on the Psychological Warfare unit. Some had extensive networks of liaison officers; others had virtually none. In China during 1943-44, the most minor tactical request for a leaflet had to be channeled all the way back to Theater Forward Echelon Headquarters, because the political situation was so touchy, the Chinese language so difficult, printing facilities so scarce, and qualified personnel so rare that there was no point in having channels cut across lower down. In France and Belgium, during 1944-45, Psychological Warfare units were established on a considerable scale at the army level, and liaison officers were widely scattered; it was possible for regimental or battalion commanders to make direct requests of liaison officers.

Radio Support. On rare occasions, it becomes possible for radio support to be given a specific unit. The American standard-wave broadcasting station was set up in the vicinity of Lorient while that French port, still held by the Nazis, was under American siege. *The History of the 2d Mobile Broadcasting Company*[3] describes the operation as being

> . . . the first attempt to coordinate artillery, leaf-
> let and radio propaganda. The station had learned
> the location of the billets of various [Nazi] units in
> the town, together with the names of their key per-
> sonnel. With this information, a "game" was arranged
> with the artillery. One day, at a certain time, these
> units were addressed by name and their members
> were told to go outside their buildings and five min-
> utes later they would receive a message. Precisely,
> five minutes later, leaflet shells released the mes-
> sages advising surrender. The ability of the Ameri-
> cans to do things like that impressed the German
> soldiers with their hopeless position more than
> words.

Obviously, such an operation required close contact with the enemy, plus known possession of standard-wave radio receivers by enemy personnel.

Air Support. Normal communications channels, such as might be used for air-ground combat liaison, form one of the most valu-able aids to the small unit. From time to time it is possible either for the unit to make up the leaflets (if it has a PW team) and to request their dropping by the associated air unit, or else to make a direct request to the appropriate higher Psychological Warfare headquarters, asking that the headquarters not only make up the leaflet but arrange for its dropping at a stated time.

Leaflet-Discharging Weapons. The airplane was far and away the most important leaflet-distributing device. In the CBI Theater, there was developed a leaflet belly-tank of local design for use on pursuit planes. The belly-tank was converted to a leaflet-throwing machine. Adjustment of the controls could regulate the speed at which leaflets were discharged, so that the pilot could give enemy units or installations bursts of leaflets in precisely the same way that he would strafe them with machine guns. This, however, was exceptional, owing to the tremendous dispersion of the Japanese in the jungle and the need to conserve leaflets. In most instances, the leaflet bomb or leaflet box was the standard Air Force method of distributing leaflets.

Among the ground weapons used for discharge of leaflets, there are the following:

chemical warfare shells converted to leaflet use, especially smoke shells;

almost every variety of available artillery shell (howitzers having proved especially useful)

rifle grenades converted for leaflets;

leaflet bundles with a small quantity of explosive, attached to a quick fuze, packed so as to be thrown in a manner similar to the manual throwing of a grenade.

Mortars were probably the chief leaflet-throwing device on both the European and Asiatic fronts; the Germans went so far as to develop a special propaganda mortar. Smoke shells proved particularly easy to adapt.

The firing of leaflet shells is a responsibility of the unit possessing the guns. Psychological Warfare teams were not issued their own guns, save for unit protection. The actual distribution of leaflet shells was effected, taking the Fifth Army as an example, in the following manner:

The Army Combat Propaganda Team planned, cleared, printed and packed leaflets suitable for the occasion.

The Team cleared with the Artillery Officer, Fifth Army, an agreement for an order to use the leaflets.

The Team's own liaison officers transmit the order to the appropriate divisions and lower echelons. The order itself prescribed the times for picking up the leaflets from the ammunition dumps.

The Team procures the empty shells and packs them with leaflets.

The Army order allots 150 leaflet shells per division.

The Team specifies, in the order, the time-limit within which the shells are to be used.

Corps and/or division selects the specific targets, the general target being all enemy concentrations within range.

In smaller units, the propaganda unit would often be placed in direct communication with a specific artillery unit, which would be charged with the responsibility for discharging the leaflet shells at opportune times. When a requesting unit asks for leaflets, and itself possesses the guns which could fire leaflet shells, it is entirely possible for the supplier to send leaflets ready-packed in the shells. However, even the most rapid shell-packing job takes considerably more time than the readying of aircraft for leaflet distribution. When it is considered that the plane not only discharges the leaflets, but delivers them from the supply point, all in one operation, it will be seen that close air-ground coordination will often do a quicker, bigger job of leaflet saturation than could be achieved by the requesting, preparing, transporting and firing of leaflet shells.

Contingencies of the Future. This text refers to known experience. Short of turning to the field of futuristic fiction, it is impossible to provide discussion of situations which have not been known in the American Army. The experiences of the Nazis and the Japanese cannot be taken by ourselves as wholly parallel, since those peoples, under dictatorship and rabid indoctrination, produced a different kind of army from the American. What should a small-unit commander do if his men thought they had been contaminated by airborne disease germs distributed by enemy bacteriological warfare planes? How should he act if his men were told by an enemy broadcast that they would be exposed to radiation which would cause anemia, cancer, or death—if they did not surrender immediately? What should he do if he finds himself cut off from all American supplies, operating a lonely unit in contaminated or dangerous areas, and then discovers that his own men are the victims of enemy black propaganda? How should he behave if his men get the idea that they are never going to be replaced, and if they suspect (either spontaneously or because of enemy action) that the unit has been abandoned by the American government and people?

What could a commander do if a delegation called on him, right out in a zone of operations, and demanded a right to be heard? Suppose that he knew their complaints about food, rotation, danger, etc., to be justified, and knew at the same time that the enemy had subverted some of his men into being either dupes or traitors. Suppose his men protested a lack of deep lead-lined shelters the day after enemy leaflets instructed the American soldiers to ask for such shelters. Should he treat all such enlisted men as traitors? Suppose he is faced with the specter of political treason, subversion, and revolution? American officers have not faced such problems since the days in which George Washington was Commander in Chief. War after war, we have gone into the fight with a profound confidence in our ability to win. Future war may hold forth no such assurance. If America is injured, her troops decimated, their homes exploded or poisoned by foreign atomic attack, brand-new questions of psychological warfare will be posed. No living American has ever had to face such problems. This is no assurance that they will never occur. Upon the manhood, the fairness, the sheer intelligence of small-unit commanders there may fall the unexpected task of holding their units together in the face of disastrous psychological attack.

Surrender Leaflets. Surrender leaflets are the infantry of the propaganda war. They go in and finish the job to which the preceding years of radio broadcasts, the demoralization of the home front, the campaigns of news and morale materials to troops, and the actual air, ground, and sea attacks have led up.

Sudden use of surrender leaflets on a victorious or unprepared enemy is not likely to take effect. The Japanese surrender leaflets dropped on the Americans in Southwest Pacific were issued without previous materials readying the Americans. Furthermore, they were dropped when the American situation was plainly improving, and when American soldiers were not likely to be thinking about surrender in order to get individual escape from the war.

The preparation of surrender leaflets calls for the tactical use of printing facilities. This is the job of the combat propaganda unit, with its high-speed press, its liaison with both ground and air forces, its up-to-the-minute intelligence on enemy movements, situation, and order of battle. The enemy should be given leaflets showing him how clearly he is pinned down, identifying him, generally stripping him of the sense of secrecy and the trust in his commanders that make it possible for him to go on fighting. When surrender can be effected, he should be given the simplest, plainest command the circumstances allow. In the case of the Japanese, there were difficulties on the American side about letting the Japanese come over to surrender; too many of them were suspected of having tucked hand grenades into their *fundoshi*. Many a Japanese started out for the Allied lines and failed to make his peaceful intentions plain enough. The result was a strong deterrent to other Japanese who may have been trying to decide whether they wanted to surrender or not.

It was found that the bright white leaflet with the identifying stripes on it (figure 69) would be shown to our troops, who could be taught to hold their fire when they saw Japanese carrying that type of leaflet. To the Japanese, the plainness of the surrender formula was a considerable help in coming over.

Variations on the surrender leaflet include the following devices:

Letters, with signatures blacked out, of prisoners of war who
   have found conditions decent and who are enjoying rest,
   good care, and good food;

Figure 63: Action Type: Air-Rescue Facilities. These leaflets from China Theater were designed to help the work of the Fourteenth Air Force. Action called for from the civilians included the assistance of hurt flyers, the identification of Americans as allies and not as Japanese when they parachuted to the ground, the avoidance of bridges and other bomb targets.

Photographs, with the faces blocked out when security procedures or the rules of war so require, showing enemy prisoners actually enjoying the benefits of being out of the war;

Political arguments to the effect that the highest duty of the soldier is to his country (or Emperor) and that if he dies for the sake of some general in a foolish war, he will be denying his country a fine postwar citizen like himself, needed for reconstruction and progress;

Figure 64: Pre-Action News. Psychological warfare facilities can be extremely helpful in favorable situations. One of the most important ways of developing a favorable situation is to predispose enemy soldiers toward the idea of surrendering. News of surrender, emphasis on the comforts and relief of prisoners of war, and above all, emphasis on their numerousness can contribute to the actual act of surrender. This newspaper looks like a newspaper, but its chief emphasis is on the extent of surrenders.

A list of the foods available to surrenderees (see figure 13, from World War I);

A statement of the conditions of military imprisonment, reaffirming the rules of the Geneva convention;

The promise that the potential prisoner will be allowed mail communication with home;

Anger-motif, showing scum and profiteers at home, and attempting to induce surrender by telling the soldier that he is being made a sucker;

Obscene pictures, showing naked women, designed to make the involuntary celibate so desirous of women that he surrenders out of bad nerves. (Japanese idea, and did not work; the troops naturally kept the pornography but merely despised the Japanese as queer little people for having sent it. This type cannot be illustrated; the Library of Congress has copies in a locked file.)

Figure 65: Direct Commands to Enemy Forces. As the situation develops against the enemy, it becomes possible to use leaflets to force the surrender of enemy troops by direct command. This kind of appeal is lost when enemy morale remains irrationally high because of a beloved commander or some other unpredictable factor, but in normal situations it either forces the enemy commander's hand or leaves him with a deteriorating force.

BEFEHL

AN DIE VERSPRENGTEN DEUTSCHEN TRUPPENTEILE

Das schnelle Vordringen der Alliierten hat es mit sich gebracht, dass zahlreiche deutsche Einheiten versprengt und aufgelöst worden sind und daher von zuständiger deutscher Seite keine Befehle mehr erhalten können.

Um nutzlose Opfer an Menschenleben zu vermeiden, ergeht daher folgender Befehl:

1.) Deutsche Soldaten, die abgeschnitten oder versprengt wurden, sowie Einheiten, die vom deutschen Kommando keine Befehle mehr erhalten, haben sich beim nächstliegenden alliierten Truppenteil zu melden.

2.) Bis dahin ist der Einheitsführer bezw. rangälteste Unteroffizier für die Disziplin seiner Mannschaft verantwortlich. Die umstehenden Verhaltungsmassregeln für versprengte Einheiten treten mit sofortiger Wirksamkeit in Kraft.

DWIGHT D. EISENHOWER
Oberbefehlshaber der Alliierten Streitkräfte

Figure 66: Basic Types: Contingency Commands. Leaflets can be made up in advance to govern typical situations which may arise. This "Command to the Scattered German Troop Units" orders all isolated German remnants to surrender to the nearest Allied force.

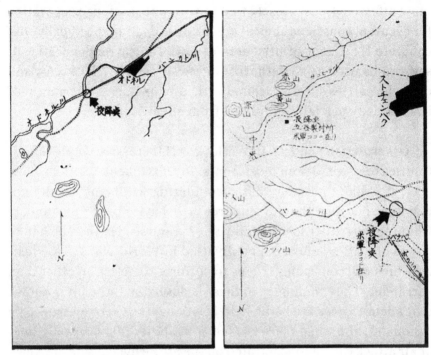

Figure 67: Tactical Surrender Leaflets. Enemy troops often fail to understand why they should surrender. Under such circumstances, it is useful to send them a map, showing them plainly what their situation is. If misrepresentation is done at this point, it will be at the cost of loss of credence later on. These leaflets were prepared to prevent Japanese units in the Philippines from staging last-ditch fights after surrender of Japan. Similar maps had been used for tactical purposes earlier.

The effective surrender leaflet frequently turns language difficulties into an asset. Whole series of leaflets will teach the enemy soldier how to say, "I surrender," in the language of the propagandist. The words, "Ei sörrender," were made familiar to every German soldier; it is simply the phonetic spelling of English for Germans to pronounce. Surrender is not merely a case of transferring loyalties; it is a highly dangerous operation for most infantrymen. It takes nerve if done deliberately. The voluntary surrenderee risks being shot by some exasperated officer or comrade on his own side; he risks court-martial for treason if his surrender is wilful and his side wins the war; he may run into a trigger-happy enemy who will shoot him; he may fail to make himself understood to the enemy. Therefore surrender leaflets try to catch some simple procedure, to indoctrinate the enemy soldier with routine things which he can do when the opportunity arises. Of all leaflets, those most effective (most closely tied in with unconscious preparation for eventual conscious choice) are the ones dealing specifically with concrete treatment of prisoners of war. The surrender leaflet itself can be used as an authorization to surrender. The enemy soldier who carries a leaflet around with him, just in case he may need it, is already partially subverted from enemy service.

Other Action Leaflets. In World War II there were ample opportunities to surrender on most fronts. In subsequent conflicts, however, it is quite possible that surrendering will be physically unfeasible, because the surrenderee will have no one at hand to whom to surrender (see chapter 14). Recourse may then be had to a type of leaflet only occasionally used in World War II—the leaflet which calls on enemy troops to perform some action other than surrender. The commonest of these is desertion—when it is known that enemy forces are being held in a dangerous spot by their own command, and when there is a fair probability that heavy artillery or air attack can be concentrated on the area which has been strewn with leaflets. (A bluff normally fails, and moreover discredits later operations of the same kind, whereas a successful and fulfilled threat builds up cumulative credibility among the enemy audience.) When long range weapons are used, it may be possible to address troops by leaflet before the attack, suggesting that they remove themselves, as individuals, to places of safety; such an operation would assist enemy disorganization. The author knows of no case where the Germans did this with their V-1 or V-2 bombs, but figure 3 applied to both civilians and troops in the cities marked for destruction by incendiary B-29 raids.

Black action appeals may teach the enemy troops how to malinger, may present political or ethnic arguments to troops known to be members of minorities or satellite nationalities (for example,

Figure 68: Basic Types: Surrender Leaflet. The surrender leaflet shown was not welcomed by the Japanese because it indicated that the Japanese soldier using it wished to surrender. This was very vulgar and depressing indeed, and few Japanese soldiers would accept such a humiliation. Except for its wording, the leaflet is good. As large as a big magazine cover, it is white with red and blue trim and can be identified readily.

此ノ勸降狀ノ内容ハ諸君ハ人道的
待遇ヲ受ケ好シ食物 清楚ナ兵食且又
手厚キ醫師ノ看護ヲ受ケルヲ證明スルモノ
デアル米國兵士ニ此ノ勸降狀ヲ
持參スレバ可ナリ.

I
SURRENDER

ATTENTION
AMERICAN
SOLDIERS

THIS LEAFLET GUARANTEES HUMANE
TREATMENT TO ANY JAPANESE
DESIRING TO SURRENDER TAKE
HIM IMMEDIATELY TO YOUR NEAREST
COMMISSIONED OFFICER

BY ORDER C.G. U.S. FORCES

Poles in Nazi service), with the intent that these mutiny, or may—at the very end of a war—call upon enemy troops as units to cease resistance and to await a later opportunity for organized surrender.

Loudspeaker Units. The use of the amplified human voice developed slowly in World War II. Improvised units were set up in North Africa, in the Italian landings, at Anzio, and in the Normandy operations. At times these talked over valuable groups of enemy prisoners, but their range did not go beyond two hundred yards, which sharply limited their utility. The Navy was simultaneously experimenting with Polly Planes in the Pacific, which flew at considerable altitudes over islands and talked to the Japanese troops on the ground.

Ultimate success came with the development of loudspeakers on tank mounts. These developed a range of two miles with the result that they had real value in combat operations. In April, 1945, a loudspeaker tank with the XIX Corps made an average of twenty broadcasts a day during action. Short talks were given to the enemy troops just before attack. Attacks were then withheld long enough to permit prisoners to come in. The attacks were then launched, lifted after a pause to permit more prisoners to come in, and finally pushed through. This tactic worked particularly well at road blocks where enemy troops were flanked. In the Teutoburger Wald a whole platoon was persuaded to surrender. At Hildesheim two hundred and fifty prisoners came over together. Elsewhere in the drive into Germany, the Germans came over in even greater numbers, but the situation was then so obviously at its best for us that they probably would have responded similarly to command banners, black words on white background, such as the ancient

Figure 69: Improved Surrender Leaflet. The new leaflet which did bring the Japanese in was better phrased. It did not mention the nasty word, *surrender,* but said, "I Cease Resistance." It also showed the Japanese how to carry the leaflet so as to persuade the triggery Americans that he was not holding a hand grenade behind it. The back of the leaflet, instead of being left blank, showed happy Japanese prisoners enjoying American captivity, their faces left identifiable as Japanese but blanked out enough to head off individual identification. Compare this with figure 4, the *Passierschein* we used on the Germans.

←

Chinese imperial forces used to carry around for tactical communication with bandits and rebels.

On Okinawa tank-mounted loudspeakers were ingeniously hooked up. The American tank officers and crews obviously could not speak good colloquial Japanese. The Japanese troops were dug in like rodents, and in a condition of desperation that made them fight cruelly and suicidally. Even if the Americans shelled the openings of their cave mouths or ran armored bulldozers over the holes, burying Japanese alive, there was the chance that the Japanese would run through long underground passages and pop up later, possibly at night, to cause more damage before they were killed. With Americans and Japanese unable to talk to one another, this condition might have led to a severe loss of American life in mopping up hundreds upon hundreds of such minute Japanese strongholds. The American tanks had loudspeakers mounted on many of them; they had radio telephone communication, that could be used between the different tanks on a tank team, or—it was an alternative, and could not be used simultaneously—could be employed for the commanding tank to communicate back to headquarters.

At headquarters, American Japanese, whose American accents had been trained out of their voices in special public-speaking classes, sat ready and waiting.

The tank team would come into the valley, and the American commander would look the situation over. He would cut his radio telephone into communication with headquarters, and would then say:

"Hillside ahead of me. No characterizing features. Five or six holes, but I can't tell which ones have Japanese in them. I can get up the hill. There are two trees at the crest of the hill, and a bunch of these native graves over on the left."

The American-Japanese at headquarters would say: "Regular announcement, sir? Do you want them to assemble by the graves or at the trees?"

"Tell them to stand in front of the graves. That way they'll be coming down hill. Want to be cut in?"

"Yes, sir," says the headquarters man.

The tank commander would then cut his radiophone into a relay, and the tanks which had loudspeakers would automatically connect the loudspeaker units direct with the radio telephone. A voice, loud as the voice of a god, would fill the entire valley, coming from everywhere at once and speaking good clear Japanese:

"Attention, Japanese troops, attention! This is the American tank commander calling. I am going to destroy all resistance in this valley. Attention! I have flame-throwers. These will be used on all dugouts and caves. Attention! Flame-throwers will be employed. Gunfire will close the cave mouths. No Japanese personnel can expect to escape. Japanese personnel commanded to cease resistance. Japanese personnel commanded to cease resistance. Japanese personnel must assemble in front of native burial place, to American left flank, Japanese right flank."

The tank commander would watch, while the loudspeakers blared. First one Japanese, then more would come in small knots to the assembly place as directed. The commander would then cut the American-Japanese back in and say,

"I think they're holding out on the hill crest. Try that. Just a minute or two. If they don't start coming, I'll go after them and cut you in just when I reach the top. . . ."

"Yes, sir. Which part of the hill crest, sir?"

"I can't tell. Anywhere."

The speakers would be cut back in: "Attention, Japanese forces remaining on hill crest. Japanese forces just behind us under command of Colonel Musashi surrendered last night and are now well taken care of. You are being given the same chance. Attention, I will soon come up the hill. . . ."

A few more Japanese figures, small as ants on a sand dune, would come into sight on the hill and begin clambering down to the point of surrender.[4]

NOTES:

[1] So far as he knows, the author was the first—about May of 1942—to urge that a surrender Pass be made to look like an official document, with banknote-type engraving and with formal style. Unfortunately, it was printed in green, instead of the old-fashioned orange-gold of the U.S. Treasury yellowbacks, and was sent to the jungle areas of the South and Southwest Pacific, where everything was green to start with.

[2] These suggestions are based on the comment of Major Martin Herz, who prepared the leaflets at Anzio beachhead and subsequently was leaflet expert at SHAEF.

[3] No author, publisher, place or date. Issued by the unit. The reference is to page 55.

[4] The Department of the Army is understood to be preparing a Field Manual and Technical Manual for Psychological Warfare which will describe the doctrines and the equipment, respectively, to be used in combat propaganda situations.

CHAPTER 14
PSYCHOLOGICAL READINESS AND DISARMAMENT

Psychological warfare is not alone in facing an uncertain future. The entire world is governed in accordance with political customs, ideas, and structures that were developed long ago to meet the needs of European Christendom. The sovereign state itself is not an immutable factor in human affairs but an organization of a particular kind. World Wars I and II demonstrate what happens when the capacity to make war rests with political agencies responsible to just one nation at a time. War arises, and no one state or one man can help it.

With the development of psychological warfare in World War II, we are in a sense *reactionary*. We go back behind the modern, formal assumption that the enemy soldier is a lawful armed agent of the enemy state; we approach him as a man and a brother, unmindful of the fact that we induce this man and brother to commit high treason. Psychological warfare is in this sense the affirmation of the human community against the national divisions which are otherwise accepted in war. Furthermore, psychological warfare—though it can and must torment, weaken and tempt—is among weapons of war one of the most humane: if supplements violence, and by the economy of violence it saves lives on both sides. Thousands of Japanese live today because they surrendered to the Americans on Okinawa, after they read leaflets or heard loudspeakers. And thousands of Americans are alive today, who themselves might be dead and their families grief-stricken because the Japanese surrendered instead of fighting it out. Psychological warfare is good for everybody.

327

Nevertheless, there are unpleasant and immoral things about psychological warfare which the citizen must heed and the officer remember. In the hands of the wrong persons, systematic psychological warfare is capable of being converted into a drastic instrument of domestic confusion; certain techniques of it could even be used for crime. On the broader, international scale, "warfare psychologically waged" by a total state against a free one can be an instrument both vile and effective, achieving its victories by exploiting the peacefulness, indecision, and disunity of its victims. It is a shameful thing to see a proud and brave people reduced to such a state of humiliation that they can be easily enslaved. "Warfare psychologically waged" with a long, sickening, uncertain prebelligerent stage of intimidation and appeasement could suck the vitality even out of America before the next aggressor got ready to release real weapons against us.

Countermeasures are nothing that can be applied at the moment. There is no simple formula to restore a disheartened people. No one "black" operation can undo the effects of partisanship and bitter disunity. The most powerful countermeasure to hostile pre-belligerent attack is high national morale, and morale in turn depends on the mental, emotional, and physical health of a people. (If it were not impious, in so secular a book, one might say it depends on their spiritual grace.) If the people themselves are well behaved; if they live without strain; if they think hatred is silly and fury a waste of time; if they trust one another's good will; if capital does not expect a Red purge from labor, nor labor a Fascist massacre from capital; if the high officers of state and army use moderate language for everyday business, so that when true crisis comes they can cry "Wolf!" and be believed—if such conditions are fulfilled in part, the people will withstand psychological attack.

Ostentatiously chasing fifth columnists, repressing ineffectual sedition, exciting people with counteraccusations—such measures, by working on the nerves of the people, are sometimes more apt to help the enemy than to hurt him. The enemy can be stopped best by such things as good food for children, new cars and gadgets for adults, wholesome public recreation, and a fair-minded press.

Improvement of the economic, social, and educational condition of the people as a whole is the surest guarantee of disciplined sobriety in time of strain. All these things maintain business as usual and fortify the calmness so necessary in times of international crisis.

It is not enough to consider the time of a possible attack. It is necessary to plan and prepare counterattack. When it comes to intimidating other nations, the United States is poorly organized. We are not a nation of slaves led by blackmailers. If our government tried to commit filthy, violent or dishonest acts against a foreign people, it could and would be stopped by the force of domestic public opinion. Sometimes, when our government is merely applying counterpressure to a foreign pressure, some of our citizens are over-eager to protect the rights of the Yenanites, Jugoslavs or Albanians at the cost of our own substantial interests. Such meddling from within may irritate statesmen and generals, but it is a small price to pay for the privilege of self-government, security, and personal freedom.

It is not unlikely that, if war forces gather against us overseas, we shall find ourselves once more in the difficulties we encountered in 1939-1941, when both citizens and leaders called one another bad names until the Imperial Japanese authorities settled all issues for us. It cannot be expected that the next enemy will oblige us by making a blunder like Pearl Harbor, electrifying our people with fury and unity. A more artful aggressor will know how to force us into untenable positions without taking responsibility for the showdown himself or he may win by making his first blow so deadly that it can safely be his last. Each step of aggression will be compensated by the illusory offer of a final settlement which, if accepted, will prove final only till the next aggression. Each period of waiting will be accompanied by monstrous military threats, hints of rockets, radioactive poisons, disease, torment, world suicide. The Americans who stand up to the aggressor will be called Reds or reactionaries or Fascists or tools of monopoly capital. The aggression will be represented as the unanimous wish of all the foreign peoples involved, which only swine and warmongers in

America would dare to question. And within our own home cities voices will be raised:

"They're right. . . ."

"It's democratic!"

"Ya see, it's like the Panama Canal. We got a right to the Canal, haven't we? This place here means just as much to them."

"They won't attack America."

"The President wants to be reelected for sure."

"Don't send my boy overseas to die."

"This time it's world suicide."

"There must not be war."

Each of these voices will be genuine; but behind each genuine voice, amplifying it into a nerve-shattering shriek, there will be the instrumentalities of hostile propaganda.

It will not be easy for the government to stand firm in such a time. It will be too late to reconsider a thousand little acts of improvement, prosperity, progress that might have fortified our people and our forces against the time of crisis. Psychological readiness will be something which will have to emerge from the spirit and the character of our people.

The General Staff cannot plan morale. The President cannot issue an executive order and make morale when it is needed. Our form of government prevents anyone from using the schools, the press, or the normal communications of this country for a nation-wide half-concealed propaganda campaign. Under the American Constitution and laws, the American government is incapable of indoctrinating its people with an effective peacetime domestic propaganda campaign. But neither the Constitution nor the laws can protect us from the psychological ravages of international strain, assisted by a well-organized, half-legitimate fifth column!

Psychological Readiness. In such a situation of pre-belligerent propaganda which moves both ourselves and our antagonist in the direction of war, we will find ourselves well equipped in one respect. If psychological warfare skills and organizations developed in World War II are not destroyed, but maintained in cadre, it will be possible for the government and services to apply counter-sanctions in kind. The American form of government prohibits this government from terrorizing or regimenting its own citizens, but it does not say anything about what we may or may not do to foreigners who are hostile to us. Profound psychological readiness can be accomplished only by good national politics and good national morale. But short-range psychological readiness in a short-range way can be found in the maintenance of propaganda instrumentalities.

A bold and inventive people such as ourselves can find ways of evading foreign censorship and oppression, and of communicating to enslaved nations those messages which their despots would prohibit them from receiving. When the alternative is wholesale death, it should not be felt improper to miss a few foreign customs or censorship regulations in order to propagandize a potentially hostile audience. (The State, War, and Navy Departments unquestionably have no such intention in mind; it is this author himself, looking to a war-haunted future, who advocates that our overt propaganda should prepare to violate foreign municipal law.) The British failed to send bombers over Berlin in July 1939 to let the German people know that Britain really would fight if Poland were attacked. The Russians were unable to tell the German people in 1940 how mighty the Red Army had become, how pitilessly uncompromising Soviet leadership would be if Hitler provoked war. The Japanese people were as surprised by Pearl Harbor as we were! In each of these cases, there is a superlative demonstration of failure to exploit psychological weapons.

Psychological readiness and psychological disarmament, curiously enough, have the same net effect—the opening of international communications all the way down to the common people of the world. If you sometime hear the American government called Fascist by a critic or if an American president is called a Bolshevik tyrant, ask yourself these questions:

"Can I, myself, possess a short-wave radio receiver and listen to Moscow, London, Paris, Leopoldville, Mexico, Shanghai, Tokyo? May I subscribe to the foreign press? May I own a printing press without a government license? May I write letters without having them opened in the mail in time of peace? May I leave the country, complain to foreigners, or seek refuge abroad, and then change my mind and come back without being shot dead for it?"

If you can do these things in peacetime, you are as free as any rational man can expect to be in our troubled time.

The difference between psychological offensive readiness and psychological disarmament lies in the fact that with readiness we must be prepared to communicate the truth—our truth—to a foreign people whether the government concerned likes it or not, whereas with psychological disarmament this government and all others remove legal and financial barriers to free speech, free publication, and the free travel of individuals.

Psychological Disarmament. Governments are conditioned by the public opinion prevailing within their jurisdictions. A fanatical, oppressive, unproductive, or reactionary government has no choice but to control opinion lest the impact of unmodified fact destroy popular faith in the oppressors. Real life is the biggest propaganda of all, and no propagandist has been able to disprove (by theory or demonstration) the Lincolnian dictum that you can fool some of the people all of the time, all of the people some of the time, but not all of the people all of the time. Even the most-regimented illiterate on earth will change his mind if he can see things happening in contradiction to his previous faith or opinion. It is the essence of peace that this happen—this mind-changing—by natural, private processes all over the world, and that the influence of non-private propaganda (whether by business, by cliques, or by governments) be kept to a minimum.

The acid test for psychological disarmament is not the circulation of books, the possession of radios, the toleration of the press, the functioning of churches—though each of these helps. The ultimate test lies in the free movement of people. If ordinary people can go from one country to another, come home, report what they have seen while abroad, having told what lies or truths they please about themselves to the foreigners, it will be difficult for any propaganda system to build up toward a war of fear—and a war of fear, on the "They will hit us first!" line, is the only kind politically practicable in our own time. We need not fear that if foreign people visit us, or we them, our political doctrines will be overthrown. For a thousand years and more, Orthodox Christian Greece and Islamic Egypt have lived face to face without much mutual respect, but without converting one another to strange doctrines. The British have been in India for centuries, and few of them have turned Hindu; and in proportion to the opportunities offered, mighty few Hindus have turned Christian. Conversion proceeds rapidly when it is assisted by the knout, the sword, the firing squad, or the political prison. Anybody can convert children to anything by removing the parents. But mass violence would not come into question if free travel, free speech, free reporting would be encouraged.

In relation to those of our brother nations in the United Nations which are abnormally sensitive to public expression, it would help if the American Congress and the judiciary gradually developed a body of legal doctrine to prevent the malicious and wanton libel of foreign peoples, religions, leaders, or governments. Political persons are not protected against abuse of speech, if they are foreigners, by the laws of this country. Stalin, Chiang, Tito, Franco, Neville Chamberlain, Winston Churchill, T. V. Soong and Molotov have one time or another been reported or described in ways for which they could theoretically seek redress. Under our law it is not practical for them to do so. There is no reason why a man should be prohibited from calling an individual Jew a criminal, and yet be permitted to call all Jews criminal; or why a man should be sued successfully for libel if he says that Mr. Smith, a Communist, is a degenerate and a murderer, and yet escape scot-free if he calls the Russian government one of degenerates and murderers. No such legal doctrine could be defined *ad hoc* in such a way as to protect the interests of international decency on the one side, and the freedom of fallible citizens (who have a right to be fallible) on the other. It is not too much to expect that such a doctrine could grow if the temper of the country and the world were inclined that way.

Pending an approach to real psychological disarmament,[1] there are a great many concrete, small projects which the State, War and Navy Departments, the colleges, press, and private citizens of this country, and friendly foreigners, together or singly can accomplish. Opinion, like life itself, is a continuous process; there are no right angles in it; no now-or-never occasions save in the employment of war. The finding of historic turning points is an interesting game after history has happened, but few turning points can be proved at the time or even identified beyond doubt later. The important thing about psychological disarmament is the persistence of the effort, the sustaining of pressures that really make for peace.

Organizational formulas often look like real solutions; they rarely are. Psychological disarmament, for example, requires a concentration of propaganda responsibility so that a government which pledges itself to restrain propaganda will have the means to do so. One method—suggested by the author and a few colleagues at the end of World War II—would be to provide central national propaganda facilities in each national government. In the United States this might have taken the form shown in chart X. If disarmament had been agreed upon, the Psychological Warfare facility could have effected the necessary intragovernmental clearances; had disarmament failed, the facility would have provided a central agency for further development. But neither this nor any other administrative reshuffle can make peace mechanically, whether in propaganda, economic, political, or military fields.

Ultimate peace-building forces are beyond the province of the propagandist to define, but in practice we all know the difference between friendliness, unexcitedness, patience, and reasonable trustfulness on the one side and their opposites on the other. Buying and reading foreign books, making foreign trips, speaking moderately and justly of foreign leaders, remaining patriotic with good taste and good nerves—things like these unquestionably help international understanding. And behind all these there lie massive forces of commerce and finance and statecraft which, properly used, can bring about peace no less certainly than they can lead to war.

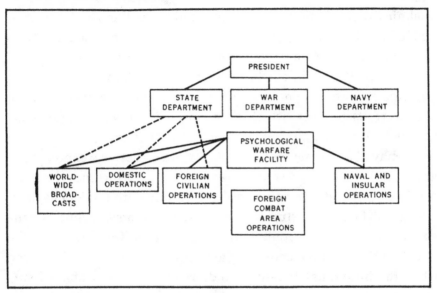

Chart X.

Psychological Warfare and Ultra-Destructive Weapons. The bombing of Hiroshima and Nagasaki was not the sole demonstration of the use of ultra-destructive weapons. Incendiary raids, depopulation facilities, and the development of rockets and gases point the way with equal certainty. The possibility of weapons which possess both high speed and extreme detonation makes the use of strategic psychological warfare much more important for the future than it ever was in World War II. Indeed, one of the most eminent atomic scientists regards surprise and terror as being just as much a part of the military function of the bomb as its physical destructiveness.[2] The mere existence of new weapons has changed the potentialities of any future war almost beyond recognition. There are, however, a few assumptions which now appear persuasive.

It may be assumed that the pre-belligerent stages of psychological warfare will become almost chronic as soon as ultra-destructive weapons are possessed by more than one nation. The fact that the United States has the atomic bomb has scared or sobered American opinion already. It will be much worse when we know that the danger we dread has become a real danger against us.

Technically competent propaganda analysis will most certainly be needed to distinguish genuinely pre-belligerent propaganda from the propaganda of universal international bad nerves. It will indeed be worth our while to become familiar with the domestic propaganda lines of all potential enemies, so that the psychological preparations for war, which an enemy government might make among its own people, can be detected as such.

It may also be assumed that if ultra-destructive weapons have anything like their presently dreaded capacity, ordinary tactical warfare will be sharply circumscribed along with tactical psychological warfare. Opportunities for taking prisoners or for lowering enemy morale will become scarcer. (In China, we found that the Fourteenth Air Force could not accept Japanese surrenders even when the individual Japanese soldiers might have preferred surrender to strafing. The planes simply had no way of picking the men up.)

Strategic and consolidation propaganda will assume new importance, because any initial application of ultra-destructive weapons will require some kind of consolidation procedure, at which point the consolidating troops may run into old-fashioned warfare of the World War II kind. Persons subjected to intensive attack by ultra-destructive weapons, if found alive, should prove highly receptive to strategic propaganda; faced with effective forces able to remove them from further danger, survivors may and probably will prove suggestible to consolidating or occupational propaganda. Their own side is not likely to bomb them deliberately, and the danger from our side is removed by our presence. Occupied areas may seem safe.

If ultra-destructive weapons of either the atomic or other types do substantial damage out of proportion to the accomplishments of weapons hitherto known, there is the very real possibility that the structure of civilized society will begin to pull apart.[3] In this case, the militant group in each fighting country may need to use psychological warfare methods on its own people in order to convince them that the country still exists as a nation, that the war must still be fought, that the enemy is still the enemy, and so on.

An die überlebenden
Soldaten und Offiziere der

7. Armee!

Alliierte Panzer stehen jetzt h i n t e r E u c h . Während Ihr gegen die überwältigende Übermacht an Soldaten, Panzern, Artillerie und Flugzeugen gekämpft habt, haben alliierte Panzerkolonnen Eure Flanke umgangen :

Argentan, der Verkehrsknotenpunkt hinter Euch, ist in alliierten Händen. Der Grossangriff auf Eure rückwärtigen Verbindungen hat nunmehr begonnen.

WAS IST ZU TUN?

Rückzug wäre daher unvermeidlich — aber Ihr habt keine Rückzugslinien. 6 000 alliierte Flugzeuge belegen die schmale Rückzugspforte hinter Euch mit Bomben, Bordwaffen und Raketen. Jeder Rückzug über diese Strassen bedeutet Rückzug ins Verderben.

Euch wird von den Kriegsverlängerern befohlen werden, den selbstmörderischen Kampf fortzusetzen — weiterzukämpfen ohne Luftunterstützung, ohne Reserven, ohne zureichende Transportmittel, ohne Hoffnung.

NUR EINE RETTUNG:

DIESES FLUGBLATT GIBT EUCH GELEGENHEIT, EUER LEBEN F Ü R D E U T S C H L A N D ZU ERHALTEN. JEDER VON EUCH MUSS FÜR SICH SELBST ENTSCHEIDEN. JE FRÜHER IHR EUCH ENTSCHEIDET, ZURÜCKZUBLEIBEN, DESTO WAHRSCHEINLICHER IST ES, DASS IHR DEN FRIEDEN NOCH ERLEBT.

To the surviving
officers and men of the

7th Army

Allied tanks now stand behind you. While you have fought against an overwhelming superiority of men, tanks, artillery and aircraft, Allied tank columns swept around you .

Argentan, the communications hub in your rear, is in Allied hands. The big attack on your rear has now begun.

WHAT IS TO BE DONE?

Retreat, therefore, is unavoidable — but you have no lines of retreat. 6,000 Allied planes are pounding the narrow escape gap behind you with bombs, machine-guns and rockets. Any retreat over those roads is a retreat into disaster.

You will be ordered by the war-prolongers, to continue the suicidal fight — to go on fighting without air support, without reserves, without sufficient transport, without hope.

ONLY ONE WAY OUT:

THIS LEAFLET GIVES YOU AN OPPORTUNITY TO SAVE YOUR LIVES FOR GERMANY. EVERYONE OF YOU MUST DECIDE FOR HIMSELF. THE SOONER YOU DECIDE TO STAY BACK, THE MORE PROBABLE IT IS THAT YOU WILL LIVE TO SEE THE PEACE.

Figure 70: End of War. This leaflet helped the war to end, just as did the great leaflet which submitted the Japanese surrender terms back to the Japanese people. On one side the leaflet carries news from the Wehrmacht's last defeats; on the other it takes up the future of Germany as determined by the Crimea Conference.

Contrary to them, the superseding group may have recourse to psychological warfare techniques in order to convince the people that the old international war is over, that the only good war is the war against the warmakers at home, and that one more victory will bring peace. (This general situation was foreshadowed by the propaganda conflicts within Russia in 1917.)

Lastly, as an extreme possibility (but a real possibility as it has never been before in the time of man), there is the chance that ultra-destructive weapons will destroy war itself by destroying the good death. Civilized men die for their countries when they believe that their fellow-citizens live after them to profit by that death offered as free sacrifice, to honor the fallen soldier, to support and protect the wife and children whom the soldier loved. The soldier may not be ready to die; he may have an intense aversion to dying.

But the colossal fact of World War II shows that the common men of all nations go more or less willingly toward death if not straight into it. If, however, the ultra-destructive weapons tear down cities, countries, populations, civilizations so fast that the soldiers themselves know the old world to be lost, the war can be expected to degenerate into armed chaos. No man will fight when the context of loyalty is destroyed. In that final situation, it will be the strange mission of psychological warfare to persuade the soldiers of a ruined or well-nigh extinct nation that their country still exists, that war still has meaning, that even though they may die they will not die altogether without purpose.

Psychological warfare cannot outlast war. Neither can it be prohibited before war itself is gone. Its mission is the improvement of the function of war. For the peaceful citizens of a free country, this is perhaps not good to think about. But if we have bad tasks let us at least do them well. Our forefathers have trained us to be good, decent people, and we can be sure that in the face of such international responsibilities as we now have we shall not err in the direction of violence, dishonor, or crime, as did the Germans. If we fail, we shall fail for decent reasons—because we were easygoing, because we loved freedom, because we were inattentive—because we wanted to mind our own business.

But we have no right to fail.

NOTES:

[1] Mr. J. P. Warburg, ex-OWI, whose book *Unwritten Treaty* has been mentioned, states that he thinks we should have four things in order to promote psychological disarmament: an American cabinet officer for the peacetime legitimate propaganda function; an international act to promote free movement of informational communications; another act to mark out the limits of permissible propaganda, and therewith to permit it; and an act which will define and prohibit bad forms of propaganda. It must be pointed out that the three proposed

international acts would be indefinable as between ourselves and the Soviet government, since there is no common ideological ground into which we could define
"information," "propaganda," "injurious," "harmless," or
"free." As between ourselves and most of the other
governments of the world, such acts or agreements are
not necessary.

[2] See J. R. Oppenheimer's remarks quoted in Bernard
Brodie (editor), *The Absolute Weapon: Atomic Power and
World Order*, New York, 1946. This book is a levelheaded
frank discussion, by authorities of recognized eminence
and common sense, of the character of war and international relations in the light of the atomic bomb.

[3] The wartime chief of the Psychological Branch of the
Dutch War Ministry warned, in a letter published in the
New York *Times* on June 8, 1947, that the presence of
ultra-destructive weapons provided the impetus for an in-
advertent war of nerves which was already undoing us.
In the first place, we might find that continued stress
shocked us into passivity; secondly, it might rouse aggression as an escape from suspense; third, it might stir up
an unconscious craving for doomsday which—though consciously rejected—would have the effect of driving us more
and more toward war. The letter is worth study in its entirety. The author, whose name is given as A. M. Meerloo,
does not appear to have published these comments elsewhere.

PART FOUR
PSYCHOLOGICAL WARFARE AFTER WORLD WAR II

EXPANDED MATERIAL FROM
THE SECOND EDITION

PREFACE TO THE SECOND EDITION

The present edition of this work has been modified to meet the needs of the readers of the mid-1950s. The material in the first edition following Chapter 13 has been removed; it consisted of a chapter hopefully called "Psychological Warfare and Disarmament." A new Part Four, comprising three fresh chapters, has been added, representing some of the problems confronting students and operators in this field. . . .

This edition, like the first, is the product of field experience. The author has made nine trips abroad, five of them to the Far East, since 1949. He has profited by his meeting with such personalities as Sir Henry Gurney, the British High Commissioner for the Federation of Malaya, who was later murdered by the Communists, meetings with Philippine, Republic of Korea, Chinese Nationalist, captured Chinese Communist and other personalities, as well as by association with such veterans in the field as General MacArthur's chief psywar expert, Colonel J. Woodall Greene. To Colonel Joseph I. Greene, who died in 1953, the author is indebted as friend and colleague. He owes much to the old friends, listed in the original acknowledgment, who offered their advice and comment in many instances.

Many readers of the first edition wrote helpful letters of comment. Some of their suggestions have been incorporated here. The translators of the two Argentine editions of this book; the translator of the Japanese edition, the Hon. Suma Yokachiro; and the translator of the first and second Chinese editions, Mr. Ch'ên

343

En-ch'êng—all of them have made direct or indirect improvements in the content or style of the work.

The author also wishes to thank his former student, later his former ORO colleague, now his wife, Dr. Genevieve Linebarger, for her encouragement and her advice.

The author hopes that, as U. S. agencies and other governments move toward a more settled definition of doctrine in this field, a third edition—a few years from now—may be able to reflect the maturation of psywar in international affairs. He does not consider the time appropriate for a fundamental restatement of doctrine; he hopes that readers who have suggestions for future definitions of scope, policy, or operations can communicate these to him for inclusion in later printings of this book.

P. M. A. L.

3 August 1954

CHAPTER 15
THE "COLD WAR" AND SEVEN SMALL WARS

The period after 1945 has turned out to be considerably more turbulent than most Americans expected. Though the victory over Fascism and Japanese militarism has proved to be psychologically and historically complete, the struggles between the victors have developed such mistrust and bitterness as to create a present-day equivalent of the Thirty Years' War, rather than a period of peace as it was understood by educated men of the nineteenth century.

Along with many other military and political phenomena, psychological warfare has been thrust into a period of "no war and no peace" which has proved to be extraordinarily difficult for Western men to deal with either emotionally or intellectually.[1] Such phrases as Churchill's term, "the Iron Curtain," and Walter Lippmann's coinage, "the Cold War," have become a part of civilized speech throughout the world. They have obscured almost as much as they have explained. It is entirely conceivable that an adequate description of the present historical period will only be written after the forces now operating have ceased to be significant; at that future time it may be possible for serious and reflective men to determine what happened in the middle of the twentieth century.

Recognition and Delay. One of the preeminent factors in the psychological and opinion aspect of the turmoil in the mid-twentieth century has been the very sharp contrast between the time on which a given event occurred, the delay between the occurrence of the event and the final understanding of that event in their own

345

terms by the strategic policy-makers affected, and the successful recognition of the event in policy papers looking toward a further future. The political and strategic character of much recent military history has therefore been a grotesque comedy of errors—ridiculous if it were not so deadly serious—involving the lives of the major urban populations of the world.

An event such as the liberation of Indochina from Japanese military occupation in 1945, met competently and reasonably by the standards of an anticipated "world of 1946," which unfortunately never materialized, led to the frustrations, bloodshed, deceit, and warfare of the late 1940s, and by 1954 became partially intelligible as a facet of the free world's struggle against Communism.

New Interpretations of Policy and Propaganda. Polemic writing has been done concerning the role of propaganda, psychological warfare, psychological strategy, and comparable operations. In many instances the polemics have involved the presentation of two sides, each of which was right—one side maintaining that the old-fashioned world of free, sovereign nations, meeting in a parliament of man as constituted in the United Nations, could and should use the "realities" of traditional power politics as a guide to the present and the future, and should avoid the hopelessness, terrorism, and fanaticism of chronic ideological war; the other side with equal merits has often argued that the ideological war is here, that its deniers are the witting or unwitting sympathizers or appeasers of Communism, that their "realities" are outmoded, and that the United States must face up to a crusade which will end in annihilation or death for either the Communist system or the constitutional democratic group of states.

What such polemics overlook is the terrifying probability that events may happen so rapidly that no one on either the Communist or anti-Communist side is capable of assimilating a new datum, such as the development of the hydrogen bomb, the death of Stalin, or the appearance of Israel among the nations, *until well after the event has occurred.* The occurrence of public events in all past civilizations has involved a considerable number of public agreements on the major hypotheses concerned; as pointed out earlier in this book, the antagonists in older wars usually, though not always, knew what the war was about. Today the spiritual, psychological, logical, and scientific inconsistencies and paradoxes within each system are so deep as to make the definition of long-range goals almost impossible. Any one goal, such as the establishment of peace, the appreciation of an international system of alliances against aggression, the maintenance of national sovereignty, the protection of a free-enterprise economy, the assurance of self-determination to non-self-governing peoples, or the like, may, *if emphasized*, contradict the concomitant goals which support it.

Communist and Anti-Communist Psychological Events. Each of the two major systems has strengths of its own. The Communist strengths are sometimes too apparent to Americans, so much so that Americans exaggerate Communist power and overlook serious deficiencies in the economies and the political character of the Communist group of nations. The Communists can suppress dissidence with a fanatical party line: the price they pay is the abrupt shifting of that line as international situations change. The Communists can appeal to youth by their dogmatic faith that they are the masters of the probable future of the world: they risk much if this faith does not pay off and if the world's youth sometimes turns against them because they promise too much and deliver too little. The Communists operating from an allegedly material basis offer psychological and spiritual values of a perverted kind, but have very considerable propaganda value; they give people a chance to sacrifice themselves, to work for causes greater than their individual personalities, "something to die for," and an apparent understanding of history: yet the Communists also risk psychological exhaustion and cynicism among their elite cadres as well as among their mass followings.

In the next chapter, concerning strategic information operations of the United States Government in the foreign field, there will be further discussion of the psychological strengths of the free world; we will say at this point that in the light of the strategic and military contexts of the postwar period the free world has had the advantages of modesty, relaxation, and elasticity. Among Americans, even among intelligent Americans, it is frequent to find the assumption being made that the chief strength of the free world consists of its legal rights and its democratic political processes, rather than in its actual (not merely formal) toleration of many points of view and its actual relaxation of the populations under its control.

Since the free world is not committed to victory as much as is the Communist world, it can afford more defeats without a corresponding loss of morale. Since the free world has not promised a utopian future, it can go from the reality of the 1950s to whatever realities the 1960s or the 1970s may bring without a sharp letdown in morale or widespread heartbreak among its most gifted advocates. In Cold War terms the free world is committed to fighting, but not to victory, while the Communists are committed to the actual though remote promise of triumph for their system throughout the world. The citizens of the United States can therefore contemplate the survival of the USSR or its annihilation and replacement by a democratic Russia with equanimity; their Soviet opposite numbers, group for group and class for class, cannot be as detached from the struggle.

Over all of us there hangs the entirely uncertain future raised by possible use of atomic bombs, hydrogen bombs, and other novel weapons—a future about which former Governor Adlai Stevenson felt so gloomy that he said another war would end civilization. (The rejoinder can, of course, be made that if another war would end civilization anyhow, win, lose, or draw, the United States might as well disband its defense forces now and enjoy life for the few short years that remain.)

The Cold War. In some respects the Cold War is not novel. It resembles the intercivilizational wars of the past in which competing civilizations with definite moral and political foundations fought one another for final survival. This kind of warfare is very different indeed from struggles waged between nations which have a common civilization and which have a common interest in the preservation of that civilization. The Americans of the 1950s are waging a struggle much more like that between the Protestants and Catholics in the years 1618-48 than they are to the Civil War of 1861-65 or the Revolutionary War of 1775-81. In some respects we Americans are back all the way to the fight between the Aztecs and Cortez or the struggle between Chinese and Chams in ancient Annam. What Mr. Lippmann calls merely a Cold War is something deeper, bigger, and worse than any war Americans have ever known before. The only parallel to it was the struggle between settlers and Indians on our own frontier: our battles with the Indians at least had the advantage of never leaving us with the hideous dread that the American Indians might sweep a White and Christian civilization from this continent.

Nature of the Cold War. The Cold War is therefore a struggle, the beginnings of which can be found at any one of several dates (1848, 1917 and 1943 are some of those given) which is now being waged between non-Communist states and a Communist group of nations. No one now living can speak with assurance of the outcome. Only the most foolhardy of optimists could visualize a world in which the better aspects of each system would be developed and the factors common to each would be underscored and strengthened as supports for a peace-seeking international system under the UN. The struggle is larger than a war because it comprises pre-belligerent, belligerent, and post-belligerent activities both in global wars and in a possible general war. On the Communist side the techniques include sabotage, revolution, conspiracy, and fanatical organization. On the anti-Communist side a family of paramilitary weapons is gradually being developed and may or may not be thrown into the struggle. No war was ever as bitter or uncertain as this one because war, whatever its demerits, at least commits the nations to combat and to victory. War has the supreme merit of *decision.* The Cold War does not: people have to fight it without knowing what it is or what they would get out of it if they could obtain the advantage.[2]

Origins of the Cold War. In retrospect it is easy to argue that
the Communist system has been fighting all non-Communist systems ever since 1848; that the Soviet system has been in a moral
condition of war with all other governments since 1917; that the
democratic-Soviet alliance against the Fascist powers during 1941-
45 was a sham and a fraud covering a three-cornered war; and that
therefore attempts at a good alliance between non-Communists and
Communists were shams, mistakes, or frauds. This is easy to say
in the 1950s; it was not so apparent in the 1940s.

It can even be argued that Yalta, and everything for which Yalta
stands, was a tragic mistake and yet a blessed one. If the Western
powers had not attempted to deal amicably with the Soviet Union
at Yalta the Western peoples, already hypersensitized in matters
of conscience, might have attributed to themselves and to their
posterity an unbearable burden of guilt. We and our children might
have gone down fighting while wondering in our innermost hearts,
"Why didn't we make a *real* try to avoid war with Soviet Russia?"

Though the Teheran and Yalta agreements have been violated by
the USSR almost from the moment they were concluded, it can be argued that the Western world was wise in experimenting with appeasement because it liberated our consciences for future struggle. No one
can possibly argue that we did not try to get along with the Communist system, that we failed to offer the Communists a reasonable share
in the world of power politics, or that we threatened the Communists
with aggression during the course of our antifascist struggle. For better or for worse, we *did* try to get along with them. We have failed.

Why have we failed?

The failure seems to be much more on the side of the Communists than on the side of the free nations. Though it is possible for
Left-liberals or hypercritical intellectuals to find fault with the U.S.
and British position in this respect or that, short of extreme nit-
picking it must be argued that the Communists jumped the gun on
the Western powers in almost every case. Tito, while still in agreement with Moscow, proved implacable toward the constitutional
Yugoslav government and the Church as they had existed before
1941. While Roosevelt was still living the Lublin Poles prepared a

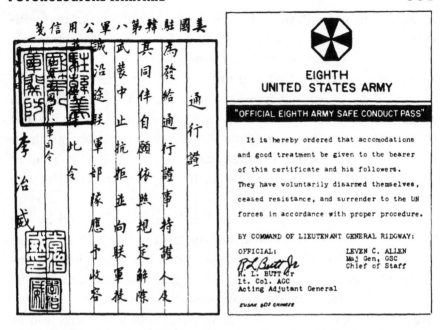

Figure 71: Official Chinese Letter. This surrender pass from Korea shows intelligent American use of materials from another culture – the ancient format, in this case, of the traditional Chinese bureaucratic letter.

savage double-cross of the London Poles, Whether Communist action arose from a lamentable fear of our own aggressiveness, or a Machiavellian plan to conquer the world does not, at any time, matter very much; what matters is the almost indisputable fact that in many parts of the world the Communists undertook the initiative against the anti-Communists.

(The first edition of this book, *Psychological Warfare*, was written in 1946 and published in 1948; the second edition is being completed eight years later, in 1954. Any reader who contrasts the two editions will see at a glance that the author, although suspicious of Communism, had no real anticipation of the fury or seriousness of the Communist attack upon the non-Communist world, nor of the strategic arguments and responsibilities which the free world would therewith be forced to accept.)

The Cold War and the Actual Fighting. As late as 1948, when the talented and bold-minded Lt. Gen. Albert C. Wedemeyer was

Deputy Chief of Staff, the U.S. Army's psychological warfare facilities at the General Staff level consisted of a few paper assignments to colonels in operations and in training together with your author as a part-time consultant and one girl stenographer to keep the files. By 1953 these numbers were multiplied by the hundreds. Each of the military services has accepted its responsibility so that by 1953 there was not merely one Army PsyWar system, but there were at least five separate organizations in the U.S. Government in different places and at five levels directly concerned with these problems.

A curious division of responsibilities not anticipated by the Creel Committee of World War I or the OWI of World War II arose in the Washington of the Cold War period. While the military establishments were given jurisdiction over propaganda activities connected with actual combat, other propaganda activities were kept largely in civilian hands, though simultaneously the direction of civilian policy at its very highest level became para-military through the influence of the National Security Council.

In other words, most of the national foreign-policy decisions at the highest level have been dictated in recent years by strategic considerations. They have been National Security Council decisions, not Cabinet-type decisions of the kind which might have been made in the years of William McKinley or Warren G. Harding. Yet, even though the decisions have been strategic in type, the propaganda implementation of these decisions has fallen for the greater part on the State Department and on the economic aid program facilities, not on the military. The military have been pretty strictly confined to those aspects of propaganda which directly pertain to combat areas. By 1953 U.S. leaders had begun to understand the situation with which they had been dealing since 1947 and in light of that necessarily belated but correct appreciation of their own position, the William Jackson Committee began to recommend that propaganda policy be written not as something self-contained, but be considered an integral part of every other U.S. Government decision possessing world situation or news impact.

The Cold War and the Home Front. Among editors, professors, officers, officials, and other experts concerned with foreign affairs, there has been frequent lamentation that the American people did not take the great struggle of our time more seriously. The contrary should be argued, at least by way of contrast.

If it is true that the United States is engaged in a major struggle, if it is further true that this struggle has no visible end, if this struggle threatens all of us and our children as well with lifetimes of tension and violent deaths under ultra-destructive weapons, one may quite reasonably ask the question, *Which is the better reaction for the bulk of the American population: normality, emotional health, mild irresponsibility, and the stockpiling of nervous and physical strength for a time of trial which may lie far ahead; or, alternatively, tension now, worry now, responsibility now, fatigue now, all the way through from the uncertain present across the bitter and perilous future to the months of near-Armageddon which may lie fifteen, twenty, or thirty years ahead?*

Sadly and seriously, with no attempt at cleverness or mockery, a staff officer could argue today that the American people should leave their worries to their leaders so as to be strong when the time of trouble comes. In the field of civil defense, for instance, it is grotesque to spend billions on offense and little on the saving of American lives. On second glance, this may not be so grotesque after all. The technological advance of fissionable and thermo-nuclear weapons is so rapid, the development of guided missiles and other carrying instruments so swift and so unpredictable, that a 1955 model civil-defense system might become a fool's paradise by 1960. If this be true, it is better to live as well as we can to maintain the profession of arms at an adequate level, to hope (quite irrationally) for the best, and to let the dead of the future bury their dead as best they may.[3]

Alternatives to Victory and Defeat. In a cold war, as opposed to a war, the role of the armed services is to deter the enemy, not fight the enemy, and the purpose of the government is to achieve an accommodation (in the sense of an arrangement satisfactory to both sides), not a victory. If this is correct, serious reappraisal must be made of the U.S. PsyWar position as well as of our strategic thinking.

The alternatives to victory and defeat are forms of survival of the competitors. The entire health of each competing civilization matters. It is obvious enough to Americans that we must remain prosperous, free, constitutional, democratic. It goes without saying that we must, as far as our individual fortunes permit us, retain our belief in God and derive from religious beliefs those spiritual strengths not available to the Communists. What is not often raised is the equally important factor of *the conquest of probability*.

Wars are much more often won by people who are sure they are going to win than by people who know that they would *like* to win, but who think at the same time that they *will* probably be defeated. The overconfidence of a Cortez or a Mao Tse-tung may seem insane to many of us. With the passion for security so prevalent in individual and national lives, both the Western powers and the individuals comprising them grotesquely exaggerate the margin of safety which they need in which to survive.

Part of this springs from the fact that much of our civilization is not forward-looking, that neither young Americans nor old Americans have a clear-cut or hopeful picture of what the world should be, will be, and must be, by A.D. 2055. On the Communist side it is frequent, but not universal, to discover that the best Communist cadres are made up of men who are dead sure that Communism will win, who are equally sure that Communism does not have to be right in order to win, and who are sure that "objectively and scientifically" (whatever that may mean), the Communist system is almost certainly destined to succeed. If Communism cannot get out of succeeding, the responsibility of the individual Communist becomes bearable; he is still seriously and tragically responsible for the expediting or the delaying of the inevitable, but he does not take the mantle of God or Karl Marx and state that this is the world as he wishes it to be and that the world of his desires will come into existence if, and only if, he fulfills his personal responsibilities to the utmost.

In Asia, perhaps more than in Europe, there are many persons who are turning toward Communism, not because they think it is good or just, or even because it is powerful, but simply because it is *likely*. Every individual in his own life has known that he cannot undo the passage of time, the aging of his body, the death of his loved ones, the loss of opportunities which might have been seized, or even his own death; in their individual lives men of all nations perform the feat, characteristic of the human being and apparently shared by no other species of life, of living from day to day in a constant reconciliation of the past and present with their own estimate of the probable future. At times in history, *that which should happen* seems to be unleashed like spiritual lightning and men rally in frenzy around causes which for the year or the decade seem inspiring, terrifyingly beautiful, and within human reach; through most of history, *that which is apt to occur* provides a more sober guide to the future and men prepare to live in accordance with its standards.

In the battle of the probabilities the PsyWar of the Western powers has been weak, high-pitched, and uncertain, while the insistence of the Communist themes has been as monotonous and hypnotic as a jungle drum. For better or for worse, the Communists have broken a path through to what they think to be the future; we of other nations have not.

The chief element of anti-Communist victory—practical, sober expectation of a certain and final downfall of the Soviet system— has thus far been lacking on the anti-Communist side.

The Communists, on the contrary, have unreasonably, provocatively, and untruthfully raved, screamed, shrieked, and lied to bring about that better world which, curiously enough, their most effective cadres considered to be an inevitable world. Thus the UN prisoners held by the Communists during the Korean war were subjected to a constant bombardment of Communist propaganda concerning their personal responsibilities before history and the opportunities which they would have to serve peace and mankind, as these noble concepts are set forth on the Red side.

The End of the Cold War. If the hypothesis set forth above, namely, that the Cold War may turn out to be unendable war except in terms which no living man can visualize, it may be true that appreciation of the role of psychological warfare (whatever it may later be called) in this struggle may have to wait a few more years. One factor often overlooked on the American side has been the *limitation of the originators.* Propaganda, to be effective among foreign peoples or foreign armies, cannot and should not outrun the strategic capabilities or the political intentions of the issuing power.

It does no good for an American propaganda radio to pledge battle to the death while the U.S. press services amiably discuss an accommodation with the Communists. Comparably, an official propaganda plan to make the people of France feel that the Americans love and admire them is not very realistic if, in terms of column-inches of French press material, unofficial American utterances are related to France to the effect that the French are washed up, their cause in Indochina hopeless, their economy unviable, and their political goals foolish. The years 1950-54, during which the Korea struggle took place and in which NATO and the European Defense Community (EDC) came to prominence, often showed a proclivity on the part of U.S. official propagandists to go far beyond that which their home public would support. Need it be said that the effects on foreign public opinion were possibly deflationary?

An imaginable end to the Cold War may lie in neither victory nor defeat, in neither accommodation nor reconciliation, but in the development of more, newer, and different quarrels. Hostility of Protestant and Catholic faded out in Europe when the hostility of French, Germans, Spaniards, and other nationalities came to be more important. It is a problem for the psychiatrist and sociologist to answer if they can. Is it possible that semantics of war-causing quarrels can be superseded by anything other than *different* quarrels? A tension-free civilization is imaginable; given the characteristics of most present-day cultures it is scarcely more than merely *imaginable.*[4]

If within the limits of practical possibility one were to list the hypothetical requirements for an end of the Cold War, the following might stand forth:

(1) General war leading to destruction of either the Communist or non-Communist systems; *or*

(2) Prolongation of the present Cold War atmosphere until new and more interesting quarrels arise which make the present ones obsolete; *or*

(3) Reconciliation of the Communist and anti-Communist systems, by some process not now imaginable, along the general lines of Franklin D. Roosevelt's "Grand Design;" *or*

(4) Collapse of all major civilizations under impact of fissionable and thermonuclear weapons; *or*

(5) Gradual erosion of the anti-Communist world and an eventual Communist victory by sustained Communist successes short of war—or the alternative of gradual erosion of the Communist world and the creation of a constitutionalist and libertarian probability of victory, also without the outbreak of general war.

It would be a brave and foolish man who would say which of these the world should expect, but it would be a stupid staff officer who did not anticipate at least one of them and who did not as a military officer or government official do his best to bring about "victory" in a form which his side could define, recognize, welcome, and achieve.[5]

The Seven Small Wars. The foregoing extensive discussion of the Cold War has been included because it explains a great deal of the apparent contradictoriness, irresoluteness, and uncertainty of the small wars which have occurred since the end of World War II. The seven small wars fall into a threefold pattern, if China is excluded (China is taken up in the next section). This is the first pattern; five of the seven wars were Asian struggles against the Western powers: Korea, Indochina, the Philippines (in which Communist Filipinos regard the United States as their ultimate enemy), Malaya, and Indonesia. In Korea and Indochina the struggle came to be Communist-controlled. In Indonesia the struggle ended in a

nationalist victory. In the Philippines the struggle degenerated into petty skirmishes between a native constitutional government and Communist extremists. One war was an expression of European nationalism on the soil of Asia, with the creation of the new state of Israel. The third category is, of course, the special case presented by the Indian-Pakistani fighting which is a struggle between Asian nationalisms without much intervention from either European colonialism or Communism.

The most important of these wars were the five in Korea, Indochina, the Philippines, Malaya, and Indonesia. The Israeli struggle appears pretty well settled as a fighting war and the India-Pakistan issue appears not to be one which will lead to general war between those two countries. The predominant group of wars shows variations of the same components in different quantities.

Each was a reaction to the fall of Japan's short-lived East Asia military empire. Each involved partial or complete resistance to economic affiliation with the capitalist world. Each had an ingredient, though these differed in stress and direction, of local Asian nationalism. Except for Indonesia, each eventually became a part of the world-wide front between Communism and anti-Communism. These wars deserve consideration one at a time for their PsyWar content.

The Special Case of China. None of the wars mentioned above was as bloody or as tragic as the Chinese civil war between Communists and Nationalists which ended with a Red victory in 1949. The China situation is too complicated to be summed up in a single paragraph. The political, economic, and propaganda components on each side of that war are as yet not completely assessed.

For instance, one of the major factors in the defeat of the Nationalists consisted of the withdrawal of the Japanese managers and technicians from China as well as of those Japanese troops who had been maintaining a degree of law and order in Manchuria

---

Figure 72: Intimidation Pattern. A Korean-language leaflet maximizes the threat to enemy ground personnel of U. S. air operations. The enemy dug in.

and North China. This withdrawal was not only sought by such "progressives" in the State Department as John Stewart Service and Alger Hiss; it was also enthusiastically endorsed by conservatives such as General Wedemeyer, who shipped the Japanese out and General MacArthur, who received them. No American, right-wing or left-wing, seriously proposed replacing the Japanese with United States or United Nations personnel until the Nationalists had enough trainees to manage a modern, capitalist China. By withdrawing the Japanese the Nationalists and the Allies destroyed the political and economic system under which the Nationalists proposed to operate and were then astonished when the Nationalists met defeat.

In the China policy situation the contribution of Communist covert propaganda within the United States in preventing aid to Chiang in the crucial years of 1947, 1948 and 1949 should not be overlooked; neither should it be overestimated nor considered the sole determinant of events which took place within China.[6]

PsyWar in the Indonesian-Dutch War. A rapid and talented command of propaganda was shown by the Indonesians in their retention of power in the face of a Dutch landing in the islands in 1945-46. The Indonesians were readily alert to the necessity for obtaining U.S., British, Australian, and other foreign sympathizers. They opened propaganda offices abroad and did an excellent job of presenting their own case. While Indonesian combat propaganda against the Netherlands troops is not recorded as having had much effect on Dutch morale, their use of global strategic propaganda to support a local war was excellent. Netherlands ships were refused docking and loading services by Australian stevedores. American press and public sympathy ran very largely in the Indonesian favor. Indonesian acceptance of the political concept, "United States of Indonesia," which was dropped as soon as

←

Figure 73: Communist Wall Propaganda. Wall messages have been ubiquitous in China for many years, leading one wit to accuse the Chinese of "mural turpitude." Here the ancient Chinese device has been turned against English-reading personnel.

independence was won, may have played a significant role in winning American sympathy.

Dutch military and strategic propaganda in their war with the Indonesians suffered from uncertainty on the Dutch side as to the goals of the war, the suspicion that a Netherlands victory would be nothing more than a triumph of colonial capitalism, and the insistent interference of United Nations and United States observers. The Dutch were never able to put across the point that Indonesia derived its nationhood from Imperial Japanese sponsorship and the Netherlands withdrawal was dictated as much by the practical necessity of reconciling world opinion and balancing the home budget as by the militarily untenable nature of the Dutch enterprise.

The Philippine War Against the Huks. By contrast, the Republic of the Philippines faced a very serious military situation in the challenge of the Huk armies—tough Communist troops concentrated in central Luzon—who waged a cruel and bitter war, rather like the struggle of the Irish Republicans against the Black-and-Tans. By 1950 the Philippine Government was in a serious position. There was at least the remote possibility that if the Government continued to falter, the city of Manila might have fallen to a Communist *coup*.

In this situation Ramón Magsaysay, as Secretary of Defense, developed some of the most provocative and audacious anti-guerrilla operations of the postwar period. To meet the Communist claim that the struggle was one of the landless against the rich, he offered all surrendered Huks resettlement in a new land project; he visited the project himself frequently enough to make sure it remained a valuable demonstration area. To allow the common people to help the Government, without their suffering from Communist reprisals against themselves or their families, he disseminated secret methods whereby the people could communicate with the Government forces. He established a psychological warfare office under Major José Crisol. This office was doing as good a job of tactical PsyWar with leaflets, mimeographs, loudspeakers, light planes, and other field and headquarters equipment as any army installation which the author has seen, Most of the doctrine and procedures for the operation of the office were American, but the content of the materials was Filipino. Catholicism, Filipino patriotism, Malayan nativism and peasant common sense were some of the factors used to underscore the Philippine Army's appeals. In the following three years the Huks shrank seriously although the danger could not be said to have been eliminated altogether.

Indochina and Political Warfare. With devotion, often with heroism, frequently with brilliance, the French military forces in Indochina fought a Communist-captured nationalist movement known as the Viet Minh; they fought despite the accompaniments of a wretched and vacillating home policy, incredibly poor psychological relationships with the native elite, and security situations which pass all American belief. (One Vietnamese recently told the author that the pro-Communist Viet Minh soldiers fought as long as they could against the French and then came back to French territory to eat good food, visit their families, rest and relax before returning to the field to murder more French sentries, blow up more French patrols, or attack more French outposts.)

It ill becomes an American to criticize the French for their policy in Indochina since it was by virtue of a U.S. strategic decision and a U.S. logistical action that Indochina was turned first from Japanese hands into the hands of the British in the south and the Chinese Nationalists in the north. The British did not care much about the local situation. The particular Chinese Nationalists in northern Indochina were mildly sympathetic with local nationalism, but chiefly preoccupied with stealing everything that could be put on a truck. After this ill-fated liberation the Americans then assisted the French in transporting forces back to Indochina. This was after much of the U.S. press and many U.S. leaders had indicated their disapproval of French colonialism and had given indirect but powerful encouragement to Viet Minh's rebellion against the French. Having helped foul up the situation for the French hopelessly, the United States then observed their return (a return which was definitely, though indirectly, made possible only by U.S. aid to France) with uncertainty and disquiet. It took the Americans four years to decide that they were on the French side and even then they were not very much on the French side.

Neither were the French.

The "French side" was an indefinable amalgam of old-fashioned French colonialism, the membership of three small Asian states in a French Union, and anti-Communism. The French made the mistake which the Americans repeated when they invited the Chinese Communist general, Wang Hsiu-ch'üan, to New York to defame the United States through the courtesy of the United States Government, or when they tried dealing with the Chinese Communists, fighting them, dealing with them, and fighting with them again. When the French finally decided to seek an all-out military victory against the Communists they set up local governments which they themselves promptly dishonored, giving them neither prestige nor authority enough to combat the Communist menace in local Asian terms.

That the French should have held the Asian anti-Communist front under these strange political circumstances is a credit to France. The Indochinese war has been dirty, discouraging. It has often verged upon the hopeless. The French have been criticized by the Americans in the early period of the reoccupation of Indochina for not turning the country over to Communist "nationalists" lock, stock and barrel; later the Americans criticized the French because the French did not annihilate the same "Communist nationalists" whom the Americans had previously lauded. In the end, Dien Bien Phu and Geneva were the inevitable concomitants of Panmunjom. Once we made "peace," the French had to make an equally bad "peace" too.

The United States was adroit enough to obtain the immense psychological leverage of getting the Korean war recognized as a UN war. The Indochinese war was not made a UN war even though it was the same enemy who was being fought—Asian Communists underwritten by Peking and guaranteed by Moscow—in each case.

Amazing though it may seem, practical psychological warfare was almost completely neglected by the French until the Americans supplied the French with printing facilities for French Annamite leaflets in 1950. By 1952 the French had assigned staff officers to carry out psychological warfare responsibilities and were making a serious effort to link up with the other anti-Communist forces in East Asia for the purpose of obtaining psychological warfare know-how. A considerable improvement in tactical psychological warfare was made between 1950 and 1952. The strategic psychological warfare position of the French in the area must be referred back to the "battle of the probabilities," mentioned earlier in this chapter. So long as French, Americans, and Annamites all feel that a French defeat is quite probable and say so both publicly and privately, it will be difficult for the French to make the Indochinese believe that Viet Nam, Cambodia, and Laos are here to stay as French-protected and anti-Communist nations.[7]

Malaya and the MRLA. The MRLA, or Malayan Races Liberation Army, is a Chinese Communist guerrilla army operating in the jungles of Malaya. Malaya (minus the island of Singapore, which is a separate Crown Colony to itself) has been constituted in the postwar period as a federation of Malay sultanates. The British have talked a great deal about the self-government of Malaya, the eventual end of their own rule, and the progress of the people. Everything, or almost everything, which the British say is true—except for the fundamental fact that the Chinese in Malaya can, under British rule, enjoy anything except life, purpose, and honor.

What are "life, purpose, and honor" in basic human terms?

They are the rights to belong to something, to be a part of history, to make one's own world move, to be a human being superior to other human beings, to be vain, to be proud, to be self-sacrificing.

After years of war against the Chinese Communist guerrillas who have small components of Malayans and Indians with them, the British have not yet found a single British brigadier or major general of the Chinese race. The world at large on the anti-Communist side has yet to hear of a Chinese-Malayan hero who served mankind by falling martyr to the Communist terror or by emerging as victor in valiant heroic combat.

The Chinese in Malaya, as the author has observed at first hand, are probably more prosperous than any other Chinese have ever been anywhere in the world. Under capitalism today the Chinese communities in Malaya have achieved a degree of wealth, health, and education which Communist China will be remarkable to have achieved if it survives and succeeds for the next hundred years.

Does this not give the lie to the great Communist myth concerning Asia—the myth accepted by many Western politicians, intellectuals, and newspaper men—that the struggle between Communism and anti-Communism is a struggle for living standards? that the issue is an issue of "who will provide the best livelihood"?

On the pro-Communist side in Malaya, Chinese who are not religious and who are known for their practicality and secularism, struggle for the chance to go forth and suffer, to serve in an army with bad medical service and no pensions, to face an almost certain death in the jungle, to lose life and property (which they could keep on the British side) in order to gain that other kind of life— life with honor and purpose, on the Communist side.

The British meanwhile progress, no doubt. In many respects the British administrations in Singapore and Malaya are more enlightened than some of the local governments in the United States. But whatever the reason, they do not seem to belong to the Chinese who live there or even to the Malays. They are governments for the people, and not (so far as the local people seem to judge) governments of the people.

Is it reasonable to ask in the mid-1950s that decent British officers and civil servants convert themselves into apocalyptic fanatics of a weird composite Asian nationalism? Can the British make revolution in Malaya when they are rather fatigued with their own Labor revolution at home? Can we Americans, who have made nothing, absolutely nothing, out of the heroism and romance and tradition that might have been reconstituted as the ancient kingdom of Ryukyu (Okinawa), be in a position to chide the British for not doing that which we ourselves do not undertake?

The Communist magic is strong, bad magic. In North Korea it created officers in an unreasonably short time, developed fanatics while we were trying to develop gentlemen, and came close to defeating us in the perilous weeks of the Pusan perimeter. In China soldiers of whom many Americans despaired when they fought on the Nationalist side became desperate assault infantry under Communist training. The timid and quarrelsome Annamites who had given the French so little trouble before Communism organized them, fought like leopards once they read Marx, Lenin, Mao Tse-tung and Ho Chi-minh.

Was this why the Communists were able to continue in Malaya? No one has ever accused the British Army of a lack of ingenuity. The forces who developed desert raiders, coastal commandos, air-dropped *banditti*, and a plethora of amusing, shocking, and audacious innovations cannot be accused of a lack of imagination.

The British *did* use psychological warfare in Malaya strategically, tactically, in the field, in the cities, by radio, and by print. When Carleton Greene was directing the British PsyWar effort from the headquarters of that redoubtable gentleman, Malcolm MacDonald, British Commissioner General for South East Asia, he even resorted to the device of writing individual letters to known Communists and leaving these letters scattered through the jungle. The British used white propaganda, black propaganda, grey propaganda; if there had been a purple propaganda they certainly would have tried it. Alex Josey came close to it when he shocked the planters in Malaya by delivering socialist speeches over the Malay radio in an attempt to pull the Left wing off the Communist bird.

Sir Henry Gurney, the High Commissioner of the Federation who was murdered in 1952, was a veteran of irregular warfare. He had faced the Zionist terrorists in Jerusalem and was a man without fear. His approach to the problem of confronting Communism was *hopelessly sane*. The Communists were offering young Chinese the intoxication of craziness, of a mad and heroic righteousness to justify the misspending of their lives. Sir Henry's answer was decency, goodness, security, prosperity, authority, liberty under law. He offered everything except glamour, terror, inspiration, and romance—

Everything except the chance to join the British side.

What kind of British side?

A British side which, like the Communist side, would welcome the makers of the future, the builders of the next civilization, the arbiters of history.

The Communists have presented a high bid against the U.S. and Britain as well as the other Western powers. We have not yet overbid them. The high bid is the opportunity to join, to belong, really to be equal, not just legally equal, and, above everything, to share, to struggle, and to work under conditions of heroism for a common goal.

The Right to Join. The West has lost a lot of the Cold War in Asia because the Communist side could be joined and the Western side could not be joined. There is no American party in India, but there is a Communist party. There is no anti-Communist army to which cadres of men from either Soviet-occupied or Soviet-free territories can be made welcome. There is no command point for the anti-Communist struggle. There is the promise of immense U.S. help, even the promise of British, Colombian, Ethiopian, and other help, for Korea or other Koreas. Is there much willingness *to be helped?* Is there any way that we can let ordinary Asians in on our side?

The top levels of this problem are, of course, political. They must be solved in the light of a U.S. home public which eschews crusades and dreads adventures. At a lower level the problem becomes one for the military staffs of the future. How can the United States, the United Nations, or other anti-Communist forces recruit native leaders and native followers under circumstances of dignity and honor? How can we either learn to love the allies we have or to find allies whom we can love? Until then much of the spiritual and organizational advantage in Asia will fall to the Communists. We may have the better ideals, but if people who are determined to illuminate their own lives with the splendor of risky,

Figure 74: Divisive Propaganda, Korean Model. In this leaflet an attempt is made to show the Asians-die-for-the-Kremlin theme.

heroic, or self-sacrificing action (and who insist on doing something desperate somewhere somehow, so as to relieve the ignominy, poverty, and monotony of their existences) cannot learn how to join us, they will perforce join the other side.

A slight or even a substantial increase in economic welfare in the Asian states seems to the author to favor a sharp increase in Communist strength. When people are desperately poor or sick they cannot worry about causes. When they become moderately well off—well enough off to know that they are despised, poor by our standards, ignorant by our standards—then the point of psychological frenzy comes in.

Propaganda Techniques in the Seven Wars. Neither in the Chinese civil war nor in the seven other wars listed has there been much refinement of propaganda techniques over World War II. As a matter of fact, it took the Korean war two years to come up to the standards of Normandy. It is amazing how many propaganda techniques had become lost arts between 1945 and 1950. The author himself flew under the Chinese Communist forces along the Han River in March 1951 when the voice plane in which he rode as an observer had to hug the valley bottoms in order to get its message to the Chinese ground forces past the sound of its own propellers; instead of ingenious, up-to-the-minute gadgets to dispense leaflets the author joined the young officers in the plane in throwing the leaflets out of the plane door by hand. He thought ruefully about the leaflet bombs and leaflet dispensers which had been used in Europe and in Burma, and when he returned unharmed to Taegu he submitted one more red-hot memorandum recommending the obvious.

The strategic PsyWar self-limitations imposed by the United States on the United States in the Korean war were also crippling. The United States did not desire anything which a professional soldier would recognize as victory. U.S. opinion was divided as to whether all of Korea should be liberated by UN forces. At the policy-making level—certainly among our allies—there was pretty general agreement to remain at peace with the supply dumps and high command of the Chinese Communist forces in Manchuria and China while fighting the forward echelons of those forces in Korea. The United States would not accept defeat nor would it seek a decisive victory because victory might have involved the risk of war.

Under these conditions it must be pointed out that General MacArthur had the first and only PsyWar establishment ready to operate the moment the Korean war began. Col. J. Woodall Greene ably managed the Tokyo headquarters for most of the period of the Korean war. The Department of the Army showed great good judgment in bringing back Brig. Gen. Robert McClure, who had been Eisenhower's PsyWar chief in Europe, to the new Department of the Army's PsyWar establishment which was created on 15 January 1951 in the Pentagon as a part of Special Staff, United States Army, with the title of Office of the Chief of Psychological Warfare (OCPW). When General McClure departed for Teheran, he was succeeded at OCPW by Brig. Gen. William Bullock. The last period of the Korean war found Korean local PsyWar at the headquarters of Eighth U.S. Army in Korea (EUSAK) under the command of Col. Donald Hall, who had probably seen more continuous PsyWar service than any other officer in the U.S. Army.

NOTES:

[1] In the postwar period a great many reflective publications began to appraise what had happened in the PsyWar field. One of the best of these is Daniel Lerner's *Sykewar: Psychological Warfare Against Germany, D-Day to VE-Day* (New York, 1949) which covers the European operation in detail. This was followed by *Propaganda in War and Crisis*, edited by Daniel Lerner (New York, 1951). A heavier work, covering many of the same problems is *The Language of Politics*, by Harold D. Lasswell, Nathan Leites and associates (New York, 1949). Leonard Doob's work on propaganda, long the leading American text in the field, was issued in a revised, postwar edition (New York, 1948); the postwar book does much to put "psychological warfare" in perspective. A simpler text than Doob's, useful for less advanced students, is Frederick C. Irion's *Public Opinion and Propaganda* (New York, 1950). A manual directly pertaining to psychological warfare is *America's Weapons of Psychological Warfare* edited by Robert E. Summers (New York, 1951); this also contains a bibliography which is helpful to the layman. Three outstanding works summarize the postwar propaganda position of the U.S. Government: Charles A. H, Thomson's *Overseas Information Service of the United States Government* (Washington, 1950) shows the continuity of the problem from war to peace; Wallace Carroll's *Persuade or Perish* (Boston, 1948) argues the necessity of maintaining an opinion offensive; and Edward Barrett's illuminating discussion, *Truth is Our Weapon* (New York, 1953), brings the story down to the Eisenhower Administration.

[2] New insights into the nature of the Soviet antagonist were presented by three related monographs originally prepared inside RAND Corporation, the research facility which often works with the U.S. Air Force. Nathan Leites, *The Operational Code of the Politburo* (New York, 1951) digests Soviet fundamentals of international behavior. Margaret Mead's *Soviet Attitudes Toward Authority* (New York, 1951) applies anthropological and psychiatric methods of analysis; this book, to the military or general

reader, should be prefaced by reading her distinguished work, *Sex and Temperament in Three Primitive Societies*, which is now available in an inexpensive, paper-bound reprint (Mentor Books, New York, 1952). Philip Selznick makes the point that organization is itself a Communist power-achieving instrument in his *The Organizational Weapon* (New York, 1952), the third of the RAND group. Lt. Col. William R. Kintner, a Regular Army officer, prepared the challenging study of the specific military content of Communist thinking in *The Front is Everywhere* (Norman, Oklahoma, 1950). Among the many good recent books about the Communist challenge, R. N. Carew Hunt, *The Theory and Practice of Communism* (New York, 1951), is outstanding for its dispassionateness while James Burnham's *The Coming Defeat of Communism* (New York, 1951) is a ringing appeal to our side to meet the challenge. Stefan T. Possony, in *A Century of Conflict* (Chicago, 1953), presents the most coldly damning and most far-ranging critique of Communist operations which this writer has seen. Willmoore Kendall rendered Americans a service with his careful translation, editing and introduction of A. Rossi, *A Communist Party in Action* (New Haven, 1949), while Bob Darke, in a British counterpart, gives a less intellectual and much abbreviated description of the British Communist set-up and operations in *The Communist Technique in Britain* (London, 1952). Communist revelations of "capitalist" conspiracies which tell more about the haunted, anxious, nasty minds of the Communists than about our own operations are, among others, L. Natarajan, *American Shadow Over India* (Bombay, 1952), and Jean Cathala, *They Are Betraying Peace* (Moscow, 1951).

[3] Paul M. A. Linebarger, "Communism as a Competing Civilization in Southeast Asia," a contribution to *Southeast Asia in the Coming World*, Philip W. Thayer, editor (Baltimore, 1952).

[4] For a contrary point of view, see the works by Harry Stack Sullivan, Brock Chisholm, and others.

[5] Problematical in all such attempts of working officers to define "victory" is the serious intellectual issue of
avoiding means which by themselves defeat the ends
which are sought. If the means are "dangerous" or "immoral" by the standards of the society which applies them,
their value becomes low indeed. For the covert side of U.S.
operations, see the breezy and popular volumes on OSS:
Lt. Col. Corey Ford and Major Alastair MacBain, *Cloak
and Dagger: The Secret Story of OSS* (New York, 1946);
Stewart Alsop and Thomas Braden, *Sub Rosa: The OSS
and American Espionage* (New York, 1946); and the most
vividly concrete narration of the group, Elizabeth P.
MacDonald, *Undercover Girl* (New York, 1947). For an
astonishing work which seems to violate security on every page, see Commander Roy Olin Stratton, *SACO—The
Rice Paddy Navy* (Pleasantville, N. Y., 1950); this is the
description of a Navy group in China which the author
shows to be more covert than OSS itself. A dry, German
view of Anglo-American espionage in Holland is given in
that superb true-life adventure story, H. J. Giskes, *London Calling North Pole* (London and New York, 1951).

[6] See the works of Freda Utley, Herbert Feis, the Linebarger–Djang–Burks political science text (New York,
1954), and others, not to mention the contributions by
Mao, Liu Shao-ch'i, and other Communist leaders.

[7] The author himself pleads guilty to having criticized
the French unduly without accepting a reasonable share
of U.S. responsibility for the situation in Indochina (Paul
M. A. Linebarger, "Indochina: The Bleeding War," *Combat Forces Journal*, March 1951), and was deservedly re-
buked from some French readers for his denigration of
French imperialism. The author cannot endorse as wise,
shrewd, or kind the French political decisions in Indochina, but he can say that the Americans who made (or
failed to make) basic policy concerning that area have
been as irresponsible and foolish as the French. He trusts
that, by the time this note reaches print, a more effectual
Franco-American understanding will have replaced the
previous difficulties.

CHAPTER 16
STRATEGIC INTERNATIONAL INFORMATION OPERATIONS

From 1776 to 1945 the U.S. system of government managed to survive in a world comprising many types of government without setting up its own propaganda and agitational forces. Propaganda through most of the twentieth century was pretty clearly limited by the U.S. conception of propaganda as a weapon auxiliary to war. "Psychological warfare" became proper, in conventional American terms, only when there was a war to be won. With the coming of peace in 1945 there was considerable uncertainty as to whether the United States should have a propaganda establishment at all.

Even at the time of writing (1954) there is still some doubt as to whether the United States needs propaganda facilities. The William Jackson report of July 1953 indicated that the terms *propaganda* and *psychological warfare* were unsatisfactory. Of course they were. They still are. The world itself is unsatisfactory—in terms of the traditional, humane, rational U.S. point of view.

The story of U.S. "peacetime" propaganda since the end of World War II is a very complicated one. Quantity, direction, purpose, and quality have shifted with the various turns of the international situation. The subject has become much more difficult to write about since the time the first edition of this book was written in 1946.

In the first place, governmental secrecy has been very sharply restored. Even very routine State Department operations for putting across the U.S. point of view have been shrouded in masses of classified documents. For reasons not always evident to the

374

outside observer, the assumption has become prevalent that the normal operations of the United States Government should be kept confidential, secret, or even top secret. Often it would seem that the attempt to maintain secrecy in non-sensitive functions is not worth the security effort at all or, contrariwise, may even reassure the antagonists of the United States by not letting them realize how serious and how unfriendly our plans or policies with respect to them may be. (This is not the time or place to discuss the problem of secrecy as a protection against domestic criticism—which secrecy, of course, has often become, to the detriment of both the government and the citizens of the United States.)

In the second place, not only have information activities become more hush-hush: they have also become more complicated. It is difficult to do justice to an intricate moving panorama of activities, some of which may not be mentioned or described under existing law.

Demobilization and Remobilization. The ending of the OWI and the installation of the International Information Service, mentioned before, in turn changed into the information activities of the Department of State. These were headed from 1945 to 1953 by an Assistant Secretary of State for Public Affairs. In 1953 a Director of the United States Information Agency, *not* under the Department of State but mysteriously attached to the National Security Council, was inaugurated. The overseas operating component of USIA remained the United States Information Service (USIS), transferred from State Department control.

In other words, there were eight years in which the Department of State had primary responsibility for the conduct of peacetime propaganda of the United States. This was the first and only time that the United States Government had in a period of relative peace undertaken a sustained propaganda effort.

The effort had ups and downs because neither the citizenry nor the officials knew whether the country was in a condition of peace or at war and, if at war, at war with *whom*. To some the enemy was Communism, the ideology; to others, Communism the movement;

to still others, the USSR; to others, the Korean Communists, but not the Chinese Communists; to others, the Chinese Communists in Korea, but not the Chinese Communists in China; and so on, *ad infinitum*.

The general history of these eight years was, by and large, a first phase in which the United States demobilized or destroyed propaganda facilities which had been built up with great skill and at great cost during World War II, and a second phase in which those facilities were partially rebuilt and the skills rediscovered. The low point in this development was probably the winter of 1947-48.

For a while, the rumor went around Washington that the Secretary of Defense, Louis Johnson, would not tolerate the utterance of the words *propaganda* or *psychological warfare*, and that the Secretary of the Army, Kenneth C. Royall, refused to have the topic mentioned to him. That may be the exaggeration characteristic of newspapermen, but it epitomized the spirit of that time.

While "psychological warfare" almost disappeared from the Department of Defense and the three services during this low point, the State Department never quite demobilized. For one thing, the State Department had inherited the OWI facilities and the Army facilities in the occupied countries—Austria, Germany, Korea, and Japan. As the heir to substantial informational facilities the State Department kept a certain minimum activity going. Facilities such as American Broadcasting Station in Europe (ABSIE), Radio in the American Sector—of Berlin—(RIAS), the Information Control Commands in the American Sector of Germany, Information and Education (I&E) Section of the General Headquarters of the Supreme Commander for the Allied Powers (SCAP) in Japan—these (though sometimes renamed) represented going propaganda concerns which required a Washington command post.

Meanwhile, it became standing operating procedure in the U.S. diplomatic establishment to attach some kind of an informational facility to every diplomatic establishment and to most of the major consulates.

Since there were always advocates of complete propaganda dismantlement, as well as enthusiasts for the maintenance of information programs, the issue of remaining in the propaganda business or getting out was always more or less in doubt. The economy and the demobilization phases of 1947 and 1948 were stimulated by evidence of Soviet bad faith in Europe during 1949 and brought into sharp focus by the outbreak of the Korean semi-war in 1950.

It is not possible to do justice to all these different systems in a single phrase. Even as late as the present, it is sometimes difficult to determine why the U.S. need have an information program operating in such entirely friendly countries as Cuba, Haiti, Ireland, or Australia. There is some point to the argument set forth by ultraconservatives that what was good enough for Theodore Roosevelt ought to be good enough today; that, in other words, the United States should be known for what it is and not by what a few hired promoters can say about it.

As in so many other fields of activities, however, the past is irrecoverable. The United States can no more return to the pre-atomic age in propaganda matters than it can in defense matters. The world we have built is with us and the only alternative to survival seems death. With respect to the specific field of propaganda, this leads to occasional curious political alliances. Sometimes the conservatives in U.S. politics are so conservative they want no propaganda at all; at other times these same conservatives are so anti-Communist that they want more propaganda. On occasions the Left within the USA has viewed U.S. propaganda with alarm and at other times has demanded that there be more of it and that more of the content be Left.

Assistant Secretary of State for Public Affairs. The Assistant Secretary of State for Public Affairs has been the principal officer of government responsible for the conduct of U.S. propaganda during 1945-53. His successor, the Director of the United States Information Agency, faces very closely related problems. Fortunately, one of these Assistant Secretaries of State has written an excellent book relating his experiences and the problems of his office in detail. Edward W. Barrett in his *Truth is Our Weapon*

(New York, 1953), describes his own experiences with two years in that position. The Assistant Secretary had the help of an interdepartmental committee which, under various labels and with various degrees of secrecy, attempted to coordinate the foreign informational activities of the various departments of the United States Government to common goals.

Later, as will be described, the Assistant Secretary of State for Public Affairs was supplemented by a Psychological Strategy Board outside of the Department of State and still later by a White House assistant in charge of informational policies at the highest level.

What can be said of this first U.S. peacetime performance in the propaganda field?

The Assistant Secretaries themselves have been men of varied capacities and interests. Mr. Barrett was an OWI veteran and a journalist of high standing. George Allen was a tough-minded career diplomat. Howland Sargeant was a distinguished government official. William Benton was the founder of the most successful "canned" music system for restaurants and the most vigorous promoter which the *Encyclopedia Britannica* ever had; later he became a Senator. Men such as these can scarcely be called tight-lipped fanatics emerging from the hidden recesses of a U.S. "Politburo." They and their colleagues did a surprisingly good job.

American travelers overseas were often amazed to find that the U.S. propaganda effort was far more polished and purposeful than an observer within the United States could expect it to be. The activities of the Assistant Secretary of State for Public Affairs consisted of supervising the domestic origination of broadcasts directed to the Soviet Union, the satellite countries, neutrals, and friends. The radio system was generally known as the Voice of America. To this degree he had charge of a propaganda system operated within the United States by Americans, but speaking to foreigners, sometimes by transmitters located within the USA and more often with relay transmitters which picked up programs originating in the continental United States and rebroadcast overseas.

One echelon removed, there were installations attached to the diplomatic and consular establishments of the United States which were usually known as USIS although in some particular cases quasi-private facilities were sponsored instead. In each foreign country there was at the embassy or legation level a Public Affairs Officer (PAO) who was the information specialist for the diplomatic mission and—in theory at least—in charge of all U.S. propaganda or informational activities, whichever one preferred to call them, in the country to which he was accredited.

A complex hierarchy of officials routed, relayed, screened, and coordinated programs from headquarters to the PAOs in the field and proposals or requests from the PAOs back to headquarters.

Other U.S. Facilities. A complicated element in the State Department's conduct of propaganda was the fact that at no time did the State Department enjoy even a monopoly of the *governmental* mass communications of the United States abroad. (It goes without saying that at no time did the State Department achieve or seek control of private U.S. mass communications such as the international editions of *Time* and *Newsweek*, the circulation of American books and magazines on a commercial basis, commercial American-owned publications abroad, or the like.) At the very least level of competition the State Department had the Armed Forces Radio Service (AFRS) broadcasting to most of the countries in which the State Department was active—often broadcasting in quite a different tone of voice and with very different content. In many instances, foreigners who understood English preferred to listen to the lively radio programs transmitted for the edification of U.S. service personnel stationed abroad, rather than to listen to "canned" programs made up for the benefit of themselves as a foreign target. (The author has seen Chinese shopkeepers in Singapore listen very seriously to a sergeant giving the news of the day at dictation speed from an armed services transmitter somewhere in the Pacific Ocean area.) In 1948 there was virtually no coordination between the armed services and the Department of State. As time went on, the two sets of U.S. broadcasts took a certain amount of note of each other. Coordination was not as easy as it might seem on paper.

After all, what is one to do? Is it valid to "propagandize" our innocently cherubic service personnel abroad whom so many domestic purity leagues and local pressure groups are anxious to defend? After all, these service people possess fearful weapons. Each has a Congressman to whom he might write. But if service personnel in a foreign country are to be given nonpropaganda materials, how can the same area be given propaganda materials for the benefit of the indigenous personnel? The propaganda from the United States Government must not be too much at variance with the "nonpropaganda" of the United States Government. If the two extremes of communication were too far apart, the United States Government might look like an ass. That would be most unhappy.

Over and above the contradictions and difficulties involved in the operation of at least two governmental systems and many private systems of U.S. news communication and dissemination systems in foreign areas, there is the further problem of additional U.S. facilities. Sources such as *The Washington Post*, Joseph Alsop, James Reston, and other well-informed Washington journalists often hinted gloomily and darkly that U.S. cloak-and-dagger operations are still going on; Dorothy Thompson was often troubled by what she regarded as the feckless successors of the wartime OSS. Many times Americans resident in local areas concerned seemed never to have heard of the hush-hush operations in their own overseas homes, operations which were denounced with purple prose in Washington; we can say that covert operations, when they have been really uncovered, as in the case of the *Time* story about overzealous U.S. support of a German nationalist resistance group, turn out to be much more pale than the lurid columnists or inside stories from Washington would lead one to believe.

More serious have been the duplication, and triplication, and occasional quadruplication of *official* informational activities. The overseas economic and military aid program, known successively as Economic Cooperation Administration (ECA), Mutual Security Administration (MSA) and Foreign Operations Administration (FOA) has not only supplemented the existing leaflet, broadcast, and other informational activities of the State Department and the armed forces with a third set of information programs; it has itself had a fourth rival in the Point Four administration, the Technical Cooperation Administration (TCA), which was both a part of State and not a part of State, depending upon the particular situation overseas.

Radio Free Europe and Radio Free Asia. Over and above the Government's operations in this field there have been the quasi-private undertakings of the Committee for a Free Europe and the Committee for a Free Asia. These have been privately sponsored and privately financed by altruistic organizations dedicated to broadcasting those things which the State Department finds it impolitic to put on the air. The degree of governmental contribution or participation is not known, although it is often touched upon in the U.S. press; that the organizations are to a definite extent private is evident in their ability to broadcast local and controversial news to particular Iron Curtain countries and by the fund drives which they have waged with little contribution boxes inside the USA.

The advantage of the RFE and RFA type of operation is that by giving voice to independent nongovernmental resistance to Communism it has often been possible to go far beyond the limits which intergovernmental protocol would impose upon U.S. official broadcasts. That is, the United States can scarcely describe a deputy minister in the Rumanian Government as a scoundrel, thief, pervert, or renegade; Rumanian exiles allowed access to Radio Free Europe stations need have no such limitations. On the other hand, there is the difficulty that Radio Free Europe, because of its U.S.-based finance and management might lend an unnecessary U.S. sponsorship to genuinely independent anti-Communist undertakings. Here again, as in the case of the reconciliation of the State Department and Defense broadcasts, it is impossible to draw a doctrinal rule which would prescribe on one hand that all propaganda broadcasts should be unofficial or that they should all be official. One cannot even say that they should all be coordinated.

The Psychological Strategy Board. Coordination was nevertheless attempted—at least for the governmental side. In 1951 President Truman created the Psychological Strategy Board, bringing the versatile and judicious Gordon Gray back to Washington for the purpose. The prescribed role of the Board was to coordinate, plan, and phase all United States information policies so as to achieve maximum effect from the governmental effort; not once did the Board dare reach out for a penny's worth of jurisdiction over private U.S. facilities. The Psychological Strategy Board was only originally under the chairmanship of the Director of the Central Intelligence Agency, then General Walter Bedell Smith, with the members of the Board consisting of the Under Secretary of State, the Under Secretary of Defense, and the Deputy Director of what was at the time known as ECA, later MSA. The Board had a series of able staff directors and small staffs detailed from other Government departments on a permanent basis to serve as a working secretariat. The precise operations of the Board were cloaked in extraordinary secrecy. It cannot be said that U.S. propaganda worsened in the two years following the establishment of the Board; neither can it be said that U.S. PsyWar operations scored any coups so striking as to deserve a position in the annals of international affairs.

William Jackson Report. After the Republicans came into office in 1953, President Dwight D. Eisenhower moved to overhaul the information establishment. He appointed a committee under the chairmanship of William Jackson, a former OSS official and investment banker, and under the secretaryship of Abbott Washburn, who had headed the superlatively successful advertising department of General Mills, Inc., which had successfully given away millions of prizes for millions of box tops from cereals consumed by American youth or flours relished by the American housewife. Some of the liberal press commentators eyed the committee gloomily as it went to work. Nevertheless, that portion of its report which was made public turned out to be a document of remarkable finesse and sophistication.

The report, released in July 1953, pointed out the Psychological Strategy Board had erred in trying to plan informational activities in its own light instead of considering the *informational aspects* of every single U.S. Government activity possessing international significance. The report recommended the replacement of the Psychological Strategy Board by a more realistic policy-coordinating organization which would coordinate not merely propaganda policies, but all policies and, having coordinated all policies, would then resolve upon maximum psychological exploitation of the policies which had been decided.

In a sense this is rather like saying that the United States should have a President, since the powerful chief executive of this government has, since 1789, been the final arbiter of executive matters, both foreign and domestic. In another sense it can be interpreted to mean that the responsibilities of the Presidency are so great that no one man could perform in his head all the staff work necessary to see through the opinion-reactions which might develop abroad to U.S. executive decisions made here at home. If the latter supposition is true, it means that the United States is saddled with one more intricate governmental process made necessary by the closeness, dangerousness, and importance of international affairs in the lives of Americans and their government.

Operations Coordinating Board. On 3 September 1953 President Eisenhower, then at Denver, Colorado, issued an Executive Order abolishing the Psychological Strategy Board and creating the Operations Coordinating Board. According to informed press comment at the time, it was the intention of the White House to carry out the recommendation to this effect made by the President's Committee on International Information Activities. The new Board was located immediately under the National Security Council. C. D. Jackson was a significant member of the Board, but not as chairman; the chairman was Walter Bedell Smith. Besides General Smith, then Under Secretary of State, the Board included Harold E. Stassen, Director of the Foreign Operations Administration; Allen W. Dulles, Director of the Central Intelligence

Agency; and Roger M. Kyes, Deputy Secretary of Defense. The President also directed that Theodore C. Streibert, Director of the U.S. Information Service, make himself available.

In so far as this development represented an attempt to coordinate the framing of U.S. Government policy in such a manner as to achieve maximum impact on the rest of the world, it represented a major step forward. The de-emphasis of "psychological warfare" or "psychological strategy" as operations which could somehow or other be efficacious *without* a context of material support through the real-life behavior of the Government issuing the propaganda was a healthy sign indeed.

Psychological warfare is at best a cumbersome and pretentious label for an important modern political and military weapon, the use of mass communication. The definition of empirical "psychological warfare" given in Chapter 3, and reproduced as it was originally written in 1946, makes it perfectly plain that the term acquires specificity which is made plain by the particular individualities involved undertaking the operation at any given time: psychological warfare is not an ancient term which is so well defined by the usage of centuries that modern men would be ill advised to redefine it or to sweep it aside.[1]

Indeed, the basic weakness of the term *psychological warfare* is its pretentiousness within American civilization of the 1900s. No one now knows whether the United States of the 1960s will turn out to be dynamic, forward-looking, insistent upon its own view of the world. It is difficult in the 1950s to see how the next decade or so could bring forth anything as explosive or violent in the social and political field as the atomic bomb has been in the field of fission. The United States certainly does not seem to be on the threshold of a new Islam. For better or for worse, the U.S. strengths are the strengths of sobriety, calmness, health. They are the strengths of *living* as opposed to the strengths of *revolution*. Revolution may be strong; it may even be pleasurable to some persons involved, but as Denis W. Brogan has pointed out in his *The Price of Revolution* (Boston, 1952), revolution has a cost factor which must be weighed against the results expected from it.

In the context of mid-twentieth century affairs it is almost piti-able and endearing to see us Americans of this time, who are so little given to the drama of fanaticism or the salvation of the world through cruelty, attempting to dramatize our own modest and rea-sonable operations by giving them melodramatic and pretentious labels. If the Communists torment us long enough they may make us into alert brutes; this seems doubtful now. It seems probable that we will continue to be brave without becoming fiendish in combat, strong without becoming ferocious in peace.

Varying definitions of PsyWar are adopted by official agencies from time to time. The current (1953) Joint Chiefs of Staff defini-tion runs as follows:

"Psychological warfare comprises the planned use of propa-ganda and related informational measures designed to influence the opinions, emotions, attitudes, and behavior of enemy or other foreign groups in such a way as to support the accomplishment of national policies and aims, or a military mission."

This definition differs from the one given in Chapter 3 in the following important respects: it stresses the *planned* character of PsyWar; it restricts the pertinent measures to those of an *infor-mational* character; and it makes clear the operational goals. It is not clear why it is necessary to stress the element of planning of PsyWar as distinguished from other sorts of war, unless it is a hom-ily to the PsyWar operator to keep his functions in line with those of other national activities. The question of restriction to infor-mational character is more serious; it excludes the interpretation that in essence, psychological warfare depends upon warfare psy-chologically waged. Thus, substantive operations of a noninfor-mational character, adopted and executed primarily for their psychological effect, could properly be called PsyWar. Finally, the specification of goals is chiefly important for the control of the function, and can largely be taken for granted. Therefore, to pre-serve an inclusive view of the function which will comprise the range of variation in official definitions—including those of one's enemies—the author stands by the definition stated in 1946.

Limitations of the American Originators. There are illusions about psychological warfare—illusions spread, in many cases, by the overenthusiastic friends of this kind of operation. Excessive claims have been made for the efficacy of propaganda. Sometimes psychological warfare has even been offered as a substitute for war or for diplomacy. On other occasions Americans have asked that their government do "as well as" this or that foreign government in the propaganda field, forgetting that the United States is a republic and a democracy, and therefore subject to the sharp limitations which republican, democratic governments possess.[2]

A republic cannot impose a purpose upon mankind.

A democracy cannot denounce a policy and then stick to it for years and decades.

Americans are not Messiahs. The limitations of American civilization over and above our specific political institutions are such as to make it impossible for Americans to lead a fanatical countercrusade against Communism, or to guarantee to the human race at large that Americans of 1955 promise that Americans of 1975 will perform this or that specific action.[3]

American propaganda is always limited precisely because it is American. Even in an age of atomic weapons, to be American means, to some degree at least, to be *free*. The people of this country, or at the very least an awful lot of them, *do* have something to do with operating the government. A new election and a hostile House of Representatives can cut off the funds for any project no matter what its merits may be in the eyes of the top-secret planners. The outside world knows this even if Washington politicians and bureaucrats sometimes forget. One can even contradict the title of Archibald MacLeish's famous poem, *America Was Promises*, and state categorically that in the propaganda field, America certainly is not promises. The promise of a tsar or a dictator is usually good for his lifetime, whereas the promise of the United States is good only within the letter of the law—a specific treaty, a definite commercial agreement, a very sharp and very narrow commitment.

There is an American strength in international affairs. This strength does not lie in a propaganda capacity to promise, to threaten, or to commit the United States Government to future courses of action. It lies, rather, in the immense probabilities of American life, in the virtual certainty that the American people will react in such and such a fashion to a new aggression, that the American people will (if attacked) in all probability destroy their attackers, whoever those attackers may be, and that the American people, despite their occasional shortcomings in matters of racial tolerance, political freedom, and economic injustice, will in the long run be solidly ranged behind whatever policies seem to promise equality, prosperity, and freedom for all mankind.

The limitations of the United States as a source of propaganda are sharp. There is no U.S. party line; it is virtually impossible to imagine that within our civilization as we now know it there could be one. There might be an official U.S. line, unanimous and binding upon all federal departments, but the federal government itself is, after all, only one among the forty-nine separate governments operating within the continental USA. The state governments, the cities within them, and the people at large are free to contradict what the federal government may say at any given point.

American strength cannot be sought in unanimity. U.S. propaganda is incapable of pulling the Sudeten rabbit out of a Munich hat. Short of an intimate and extreme danger of war itself, the U.S. Government cannot threaten a foreign government very successfully; too many U.S. citizens would immediately shout at one another, at their own government, and to the foreigners concerned: "Those Washington officials don't really mean it! We don't want war. We're not going to go through with it." If the USA moved against Spain, there are friends of Franco in Washington who would tell him to sit tight; if the USA moved too rapidly against the Communist world, there are plenty of Americans, both in and out of government, who would say privately, through the press, or by letters that the Indian Government or some other should assure Moscow and Peip'ing that the U.S. would not dare carry through.

Exploitation of U.S. propaganda strength must therefore always be developed from *the probable or apparent "center" of American opinion at that moment*. It is impossible to find a U.S. policy which can be made compulsory and unanimous upon all Americans both public and private. It is not impossible through an adroit combination of the skills of leadership, foresight, and a keen awareness of intra-U.S. politics to devise foreign-policy programs which will command the decisive assent of the American people.

War and Unanimity. The less peaceful the world is, the more effective a peacetime information program can be. The attack of the Communist aggressors in Korea, which involved the U.S. armed forces, pushed the U.S. public into line behind the U.S. Government in a way which no degree of propaganda manipulation from Washington could have contrived. In times of danger the American people stick together. In times of relaxation they scatter about. One should not plan a crusade for the American people to carry out unless one is sure that someone on the outside will goad the American people with repeated stings of danger or trouble.

Once war breaks out, the American people have in the past shown a very good capacity to unite in winning and finishing the war. There is no reason to suppose that the situation will be different in the future. What is perplexing, and for the present insoluble, is this: how can the American people, short of getting involved in war, become so purposeful, so decisive, so nearly unanimous, as to take actions which will prevent a war? The situation in the early 1950s is on the Communist side a major crusade against what the Reds regarded, or pretended to regard, as "aggressive" U.S. capitalist power.

In other words, the Communists of the world had a crusade against the USA. The USA had a crusade against no one. A prominent Washington official long displayed the sign in his office: *I Ain't Mad at Nobody.* In a very real sense this epitomized one of the very real moods of the American people. How do we defend ourselves against a crusade, especially if we have no desire to have part in a counter-crusade?

U.S. propagandists sometimes forget that they are not speaking for a mere nation, but are the representatives of something which is far bigger than any single nationality—they are the spokesmen, whether they like it or not, for a way of life which is new in the world, for a kind of freedom which, though coarse, is real. Characteristic American strengths have been, are, and will be the strengths of patience, endurance, versatility, and curiosity. It is foolish to ask Americans to be strong in bitterness, strong in hatred, strong in a cruel or proud self-righteousness. We are not Japanese, or Prussians, or Russians; we are not Irish, or English, or French; we are mostly European and yet un-European. Our propaganda will be effective only if it springs from the simplest and strongest aspects of our life at home. Our material prosperity is beyond doubt; what is not so evident to the outside world is the frugality, the kindliness, and the humble foresight which drove so much of that prosperity into being.

The Propaganda of Friendship. U.S. limitations are nowhere more evident in peacetime propaganda than in the oft-repeated phrase of "winning friends for America." The desire for having a friend is a deep necessity amid the crowded loneliness of U.S. urban society. The necessity to "be liked" leads to grotesquely exaggerated inferences as to what "being liked" may involve. Americans in and out of government often argue that America should "make friends" on the naïve assumption that "friends" are useful to nations in time of trouble.

This is, of course, not true.

The Swedes were very good friends of the Norwegians. Nevertheless, the Swedes saved their Swedish skins by sitting back when the Nazis overran Norway.

Did Lithuania have an enemy? Did Latvia have an enemy? Did Estonia have an enemy? These countries were the good friends of all the Western powers. These countries have disappeared.

The United States was a friend of China, a friendship boastfully and sentimentally proclaimed for more than a hundred years, from the days of Daniel Webster to the finale of George C. Marshall. What use was it to the Chinese to have the United States as a friend? When they fell upon trouble, a U.S. Secretary of State denounced their government as corrupt and told the Chinese how good the United States was.

Friendship does not usually lead to war or peace. War and peace depend upon survival. Any veteran will remember men whom he disliked intensely in his own wartime outfits: he never day-dreamed of turning them over to the enemy just because he was personally antagonistic to them. *A common danger from something*—more complicatedly, *a common interest in something*—is a far more potent assurance of future strength and strategic action than is friendship.

Friendship operates between individuals, not between the overgrown corporate fictions which are called nations.

If you were a West German, and if you were absolutely positive that all Americans were lovely people, you would be wise to join the Soviet side. That way, if the Russians win, you will have appeased the enigmatic and implacable Muscovites. On the other hand, if the Americans win and you are sure they are lovely people as well as good friends of yours, they will not *really* mind your having joined the other side as a matter of temporary factual necessity. If a man is your best friend he may jump into the river to rescue you, should you fall in; unfortunately, he might prefer to telephone a rescue squad. But if he is handcuffed to you, you are reasonably sure that if you fall in he will be with you.

Call it propaganda, call it information, call it international communication—under any name the major point remains: *Americans can find trustworthy future allies through commitment to common interest or common danger.* Friendship is pleasant, but not of the essence. In some cases it might be desirable for leaders or key groups in important foreign areas to realize that the United States could be a worse enemy than the Soviet Union, rather than to realize that the U.S. is a friend. If the French were sure of this—that is, that a Soviet-occupied France would get sixty-five hydrogen bombs dropped on it while a U.S.-occupied France would get only three— they might prefer the Americans whether they liked them or not.

Is this kind of communication consistent with American ideals? Perhaps not. Yet *honesty* has always been one of the American ideals and perhaps honesty may take us in the future to a stronger and a wiser position than friendliness has taken us in the past.

NOTES:

[1] Psychological warfare is, of course, neither very psychological nor is it necessarily warfare, indeed, within the context of a rigidly purist and scholastic definition, psychological warfare is not psychological, in that most of its operations are very definitely *not* a part of present-day scientific psychology. Neither is it *warfare* because it can be operated before war, during war, after war, or contemporaneously with and apart from war. As pointed out above, war involves the inescapable content of public lawful *violence*. It is hard to ascribe violence to a short-wave broadcast or to a leaflet. In Korea in 1951 the author heard that a Chinese soldier was found dead—mashed by a leaflet bomb which had failed to explode at the proper altitude. If this story is true, that particular soldier was one of the few genuine *war* victims of military or strategic propaganda both so pretentiously called "psychological warfare" by Americans of the mid-twentieth century.

Anthony Leviero, who summarized American PsyWar in *The New York Times* in a series of articles between 9 December and 14 December 1951, is both an experienced general staff officer and a first-class newspaper man. His comment in 1953 on the new Operations Coordinating Board was encouraging or ominous. He stated in his *Times* dispatch of 4 September 1953 that the William Jackson committee had found that "psychological warfare did not exist as such." If this meant that the new OCB was to sweep aside the limitations of top-secret pedantic definitions and move toward a refreshingly concrete manipulation of the world scene, the news was encouraging indeed. If the new Board was, however, to be dedicated to the manufacture of new, complicated and secret definitions of its own, the news was bad. Given the time-lag on the declassification of Government materials, it may be twenty-five years, or 1978, before the precise definitions of 1953 are available to the public. The tendency of the Board to succeed or to fail will be evident by the time this material is in print; given the personalities involved, the prognosis appeared optimistic.

[2] This kind of issue has not been neglected in our public discussions or our schools. Two sides of one famous case are given in Owen Lattimore, *Ordeal by Slander* (New York, 1951) and the bitterly anti-Lattimore book by John T. Flynn, *The Lattimore Story* (New York, 1953). A serious and intelligent attempt to answer some of the problems posed by PsyWar and the resulting loyalty issues within a democracy are the works of Nathaniel Weyl, *Treason: The Story of Disloyalty and Betrayal in American History* (Washington, 1950), and *The Battle Against Disloyalty* (New York, 1951). A formidable presentation of what the Communists are doing is offered in Ralph de Toledano, *Spies, Dupes, and Diplomats* (New York and Boston, 1952) and in Major General Charles A. Willoughby, *Shanghai Conspiracy* (New York, 1952). The kind of round-table often intellectually conceived and executed within American schools is well portrayed in the special issue of *Columbia Journal of International Affairs* (New York, spring, 1951), in which the entire issue is given to a synthesis of international problems in the propaganda field under the heading "Propaganda and World Politics." Stefan Possony's magistral *A Century of Conflict* (Chicago, 1953) provides an excellent general framework.

[3] Nothing in previous U.S. experience prepared Americans for the invasion of the individual personality which has long been accomplished by the Communists but which was first publicized in adequate fashion after the outbreak of the Korean war in 1950. The pioneer book in this field, and still the best, is Edward Hunter's *Brain-Washing in Red China* (New York, 1951). This author has known Mr. Hunter for twenty-odd years and can vouch for him as a man with a sober respect for fact, though he does have a vivid taste in adjectives; he has seen not only Mr. Hunter but has gone over some of the raw material which Hunter used and can testify to the reality and sympathy with which Hunter portrays this rather gruesome process. On a different scale, Wilbur Schramm has given a description of what happens when *The Reds Take a City* (New Brunswick, 1951), in a book of that name written jointly with John W. Riley.

CHAPTER 17
RESEARCH, DEVELOPMENT, AND THE FUTURE

Psychological warfare is part of civilization. Civilization, no matter how one defines it, is not a static thing. It is an immense fermenting, active, often turbulent composite of the *whys* and *hows* of the way men and women think and behave. The short-run factors in a civilization are often as important as the long-run ones. Though the United States from 1860 to 1960 has been a steady part of the west European, predominantly Christian civilization, the United States has undergone immense changes of fashion, belief, appetite, preference, and behavior. With any changing, developing civilization, "war" may seem like a very static term, so that the Civil War and the war of the Western powers against Germany of 1939-45 may to some degree seem comparable phenomena. They are comparable, but only within sharp limits.

The Meaning of War. Nowhere is the transitoriness and changeability of modern civilization more evident than in the significance which intelligent men and women attach to the term *war*, War was "noble" in 1861-65, but in 1941-45 it was "noble" only for the most perfunctory and most hollow oratory. Push the contrast farther: "psychological warfare" was an unknown element in 1861-65; by 1941-45 it had become fashionable. (One can seriously doubt that President Lincoln ever worried about Northern citizens becoming "un-American" under that rubric, though he had plenty of traitors to worry him.) The years 1945-53 were momentous. A whole string of new ideas, new terms, and new behavior patterns appeared within the USA in a mere eight years. What the next twenty years will bring is deeply uncertain.

War is coming to mean the effectuation or prevention of revolution, not the half-savage, half-courteous armed conflict of sovereign nations. War is getting to be chronic again.[1] War between entirely comparable states such as the United States and Canada, Mexico and Cuba, Indonesia and India, Iraq and Saudi Arabia, or any similar combination, is getting to be more and more unthinkable. War between ideologically dissimilar states, such as North Korea and South Korea, Communist China and Nationalist China, Viet Minh and Viet Nam, USSR and USA, is getting to be virtual normality.

Research into Tension. It is true of all people that they solve particular problems, in many cases, some time after the occasion for solving the problem has passed. What is called "decision" in government, politics, and in personal affairs is very often not the selection of one very real course of action as against another equally real course of action, but the confirmation of a commitment already made. If this is true of every-day life, it is even more true of scholars and experts. One of the disabilities of our time in the field of the social and psychological sciences and the humanities lies in the fact that although government officials recognize problems some months or years after they have arisen and finally attempt to deal with them, scholars frequently get around problems decades after any practical occasion for decision has passed.[2]

Nowhere is this more evident than in the discussion of tensions as a cause of war. Tension certainly contributed very much to the outbreak of war in 1914. It is possible that the tensions and hostilities of Europe in the 1930s which allowed Fascism and Communism to become threatening and powerful also contributed in the end to the outbreak of war in 1939. It is difficult, however, to suppose that the coming of war in September 1939 was itself the result of tension except as a very remote and indirect cause. This author believes that tension leads to a perpetuation of a kind of civilization in which wars are possible, but cannot persuade himself that an additional factor of tension within civilization as we know it can be an immediate cause of war.[3]

Research into tensions has been carried fairly far. It may be that the wartime role of tension can be ascertained by scientific methods, so that the psychological warfare of Power A can cause so much more tension than Power B, either among the elite or among the general population, that Power B cannot further continue the war. Alternatively, it is imaginable that Power A may be able to relax tension so sharply among the elite or broad population of Power B that Power B's potentiality for war, or decision to wage war, can be postponed.

For purposes of research it seems worthwhile to suggest that tension appears to be highly prevalent in the two most powerful military civilizations on earth today: the USSR and its satellites, on the one hand, and the cluster of Western powers, on the other. Tension appears to be caused by the complexity of every-day life, the demands made upon the psychophysiological organization of each individual human being, by the technological facilities available, and through the relief offered within each civilization by the opportunity to discharge hatred against members of the other civilization instead of recognizing self-hatred for the very real problem which it is.

In other terms, it is tough to be modern; the difficulty of being modern makes it easy for individuals to be restless and anxious; restlessness and anxiety lead to fear; fear converts freely into hate; hate very easily takes on political form; political hate assists in the creation of real threats such as the atomic bomb and guided missiles, which are not imaginary threats at all; the reality of the threats seems to confirm the reality of the hate which led to it, thus perpetuating a cycle of insecurity, fear, hate, armament, insecurity, fear, and on around the circle again and again.

Revolutionary Possibilities in Psychology. It is possible, but by no means probable, that the rapid development of psychological and related sciences in the Western world may provide whole new answers to the threats which surround modern Americans, including the supreme answer of peace as an alternative to war or the secondary answer of victory in the event of war. Nothing in the existing academic literature on the subject of psychology of war, the psychiatry of modern mass behavior, the psychology or psychiatry of present-day power politics, justifies the inference that an applicable solution to our "problems" is at all near. The "problems" are almost all aspects of our entire lives and one cannot solve life like a Delphic riddle or a single scientific experiment.

It would be unwise of U.S. military and political leaders to overlook developing strengths within American every-day talk and thinking, whether academic or popular. Too specific a concentration on the problem of winning a war may cause a leader or his expert consultants to concentrate on solutions derived from past experience, therewith leading him to miss new and different solutions which might be offered by his own time. Changes need not always be thought of as weaknesses, which they are if past criteria are retained as absolute standards. Men born in the period 1910-20 may have endowments which are not commonly found among men born in the period 1930-40, yet it is entirely possible that the generation born during 1930-40 may have capacities and resistances which the older generation does not altogether appreciate.

Apply this concept to Communism. Communism loses strength every day that it exists: each day deprives it of novelty, each day makes it a littler more familiar, each day makes its leaders one day older. If Americans can learn how to be flexible and imaginative and to understand themselves as they really are, they might find that the real American appeal to the youth of the world would be much greater than the Communist appeal. It was unfortunately characteristic of the United States in the early 1950s of the Cold War that U.S. propaganda was based on ideals and standards *older* than the ideals and standards competitively presented by the Communists, and that therefore in many parts of the world the struggle between Americans and Communists appeared to be a struggle on our side of the old against the young. Nothing could be farther from the truth. The United States army in Korea in 1950-53 was one of the most revolutionary armies in history, an army dedicated to non-victory, pledging allegiance to a shadowy world government of the United Nations behind the practical reality of the government of the United States. Perhaps never before in many centuries have men fought so matter-of-factly, so calmly, so reasonably. They fought well and did not need to be jazzed up with the hashish of "making the world safe for Democracy" or "establishing the Four Freedoms."

The temper of the U.S. forces in Korea in 1951 was demonstrated by a Reserve sergeant who scarcely knew he was in the Reserves until he was on a boat bound for Pusan. He was a practical man, anxious to get home, but willing to do his share in this war as long as he had to. He was given the assignment of testing the voice plane of U.S. headquarters at Taegu. The loudspeaker was not working quite right, and he was instructed to test the plane at 500, 1,000 and 1,500 feet. The plane flew low over U.S. headquarters. The roar of the engines almost deafened everyone within the building, yet even above the roar of the engines there could be heard the bone-chilling hum of the silent loudspeaker—an immense magnification of the noise one hears from a radio set which is turned on without being tuned to a station. Everyone expected the sergeant to say, "This is the EUSAK voice plane testing; one-ah, two-ah, three-ah!" Instead the immense voice came through clearly, through brick, and plaster, and wood, through air and trees. It must have reached four miles. The gigantic voice of the sergeant seemed to roar over half of South Korea as he said, "Why—don't—you—imperialist—sons o' bitches—go—back—to—Wall—Street—where—you—belong?" It was said that fifty colonels grabbed for their phones simultaneously, but the purely American gimmick to the whole story lay in the fact that the sergeant was not punished. No damage was done. The Americans thought their enemies were funny or silly. We had shown that we were not afraid of Communist ideas. Several South Koreans told the author that they regarded the Americans as inscrutable people indeed.

The development of modern civilization is certain to have developments in war both as to the purpose of war and as to the modes of war. It seems likely that in the face of the supreme danger of atomic and thermonuclear weapons nations will resort more and more to small wars and semi-war operations which will offer the opportunity of strategic advantage without the cataclysmic danger of a world-wide showdown. In a very hush-hush way the U.S. Army is looking into the possibilities of small and irregular kinds of war; security regulations prohibit the author from discussing some of the interesting new developments in this field.

National Research and Development Programs. The United States Government considered as a whole has developed a very adequate scientific research program. Most of this is quite properly keyed to the physical and mechanical sciences, in which the most tangible results are obtained. Substantial strides are being made in the medical and allied fields. Some research is, however, being carried out in fields pertaining to psychological warfare. These are worth describing, but it must be remembered that research on PsyWar may not affect PsyWar itself as much as research in other fields which, by changing the character of war, will change PsyWar too.

Within the general research field, two basic approaches have been recognized by the U.S. Army as being distinct from one another: developmental research and operations research. *Developmental research* consists of that research which creates new weapons, new methods of war, new devices or procedures, doing so by digging through modern science, investigating its applicability to military problems, and then advancing the frontier of science, when necessary, in the military interest. The goals of *operations research* are more modest and, in some respect, more provocative. Operations research takes operations as they exist and reexamines them from beginning to end to discover how much of each operation is scientifically pertinent to its stated goal, what economies, modifications, or changes might be introduced, and how the operation might be improved.

Developmental Research in PsyWar. At the time of the close of the 1950-53 phase of Korean hostilities, the PsyWar being conducted by the United States Army in Korea showed little sign of having been influenced by developmental research into this field of activity. The leaflets were not better than the leaflets of World War II, nor even very different. Because of the peculiar political limitations of the war, the radio program was not as good as the performance of ABSIE under Eisenhower. The tactical use of loudspeakers had shown a very marked improvement over World War II standards, but to a non-engineer such as the present writer neither the Communist loudspeakers nor our own seemed strikingly better or different.

Developmental research had a great deal to offer, but the gap between initial scientific advance and practical military application appeared to be too broad to warrant the assumption that the research had transformed the U.S. PsyWar program.

Operations Research in Korea. Operations research—sometimes slangily called *opsearch*—was applied to the Korean war with highly uneven results.[4]

Among other things, Army officers in the PsyWar field showed, early in the Korean war, that land forces possessed tactical opportunities which combat propaganda could exploit very effectually. Various experiments were tried, none of them so decisive as to affect the outcome of the war, but some of them of real tactical value and others of great importance in obtaining Chinese prisoners.

One of the points examined was surrender as a *process*. Surrendering does not depend upon the disposition of the individual enemy soldier to say *yes* or *no* to the war as a whole. He could say *no* a thousand times and still be on the other side shooting at us.

The actual physical *process* of surrender is an elaborate one consisting of the psychological processes of getting ready to give up on the other side, the physical capacity to surrender when the opportunity for getting captured presents itself, and the alternative, more difficult process of deliberately leaving the other side and getting to our side alive. In 1951 and 1952 there were considerable developments along this line. Americans learned much about how to teach enemy soldiers to surrender. Late in 1952 and

early in 1953 the front had become so static that it took extraordinary heroism for soldiers—outside of a tiny minority engaged in
reconnaissance patrols—to get away from their own side and
surrender to the enemy without being killed by their friends as
deserters or by the enemy as sneak attackers.

The U.S. public did not realize that throughout the Korean war
the Communists—Russian, North Korean, and Chinese—enjoyed a
distinct radio advantage over the UN side both as to funds available for programs and as to number of station-hours on the air.
The language gap between the Americans and Chinese was so extreme that it was hard for Americans to realize that the Chinese
broadcasts covered wider audiences and covered them better than
did our own. American restraint in this field may have been dictated in part by the fact that the war was a limited war consisting
of combat only with those armed Chinese Communists on North
Korean territory, but not with armed Chinese Communists elsewhere in the Far East.

Philosophy and Propaganda Development. In terms of specific
literature of PsyWar it is difficult to find many contributions of
professional philosophers to PsyWar since the end of World War II.
This is curious, in view of the Communist propagation of philosophy,
no matter how perverted its form, as a major weapon. The American
philosopher, Dr. George Morgan, who became a career diplomat,
was simultaneously a Soviet-area expert and a key figure in the
Psychological Strategy Board. There were not many others like him.

Philosophy offers an opportunity for the reexamination of cultural values. The indoctrination of those professors who will teach
the teachers of the generation after next will influence the capacity
of future Americans to have a world-view which will give them the
utmost opportunities for action in the military field while retaining as far as possible the blessings of U.S. civilian civilization. That
U.S. civilization is still civilian and not military is, of course, beyond cavil.

The William Jackson committee was a voice crying in the wil-
derness when it asked for new terms and new ideas against which

to set U.S. propaganda operations in the world of modern strategy. Philosophers may have had the capacity for finding some of the answers, but philosophers, of all people, do not like to be jostled or hurried. The author has never heard of a philosopher employed on a confidential basis by the United States Government to think through the historical and cultural rationale of a U.S. military victory for the future. Writers such as F. S. C. Northrop and Erich Fromm—to name only two sharply contrasting personalities—have written books which possess high significance for the international propaganda field. The connection appears, however, to be tangential.

Literary Contributions. Almost all the best propagandists of almost all modern powers have been, to a greater or less degree, literary personalities. The artistic and cultural aspect of writing is readily converted to propaganda usage. Elmer Davis is a novelist as well as a commentator. Robert Sherwood is one of America's most distinguished playwrights. Benito Mussolini wrote a bad novel. Mao Tse-tung is a poet and philosopher, as well as a Communist party boss. Down among the workers in the field, such American novelists as James Gould Cozzens, Pat Frank, Jerome Weidman, and Murray Dyer, have worked on U.S. psychological warfare.[5]

Though literary men have converted their writing to propaganda purposes, few of them have gone on to define the characteristics of a specific conversionary literature or to compile canons of literary style applicable to the propaganda field. The contributions may lie in the future.

The Social Sciences. The American Association of Public Opinion Research (AAPOR) is the professional league of U.S. propagandists and analysts of public opinion; its quarterly, *Public Opinion*, is the key journal in the field. The members of this association are drawn both from the social sciences and from the psychological sciences, ranging from such practical operatives as Dr. George Gallup and Elmo Roper to austere theorists like Professors Nathan Leites and Hadley Cantril.

A good argument can be presented to the effect that the skills brought from the social-science into the propaganda field are more valuable once they are employed full time in that field than an attempt to apply political science, or sociology, or economics, each as an individual compartment, to the field of propaganda. There is still no book available with the title *The Politics of Knowledge*,[6] even though the reception, control, prohibition, and dissemination of knowledge is a major factor in all modern governmental processes both in and out of the propaganda field.

Psychology and Related Sciences. There has been an immense amount of work done by psychologists, much of it classified, on the held of propaganda. Some of this work is refreshing in the extreme and should provide nasty surprises for the Communists in a major war. Other parts are restatements which if translated into operations might or might not prove feasible with the kind of army we Americans have or are likely to have.

One of the most conspicuous developments since World War II has been the application by psychologists, sociologists, and persons in related field of *quantifying techniques*. The introduction of rigorous scientific requirements of *number* into the attempted reportage of propaganda behavior or propaganda results is having a significant effect. Quantification may not obtain everything which its devotees claim for it. There is a wide area of human behavior which is significant to the ordinary person, or even to the expert in descriptive terms, and which loses much of its significance if the descriptive and allusive terms are replaced by measurements, tables, and graphs. There is, however, no danger that quantification will replace description as the sole tool of research in the propaganda field.

What quantification does do is develop a common area of discussion between propagandists and nonpropagandists. In many instances quantification can demonstrate results where allegations of failure or of success would have nothing more than personal authority to support them. Within our own particular kind of civilization quantification has a special appeal because of the American trust in engineering and in numbers. The conclusions of the Kinsey reports on men and on women seem much more authoritative to the ordinary man because they are presented with an ample garniture of numbers, even though Havelock Ellis's pioneer works in the psychology and behavior patterns of Western sex life may have been much more tangible and much more revolutionary in their time.

Projection and Research. All propaganda involves a certain degree of projection—the propagandist attempts to identify himself with a situation which he does not face in real life and to issue meaningful communications to persons about situations which they themselves do not face *yet*. Much of the psychological research on tactical PsyWar remains yet to be done, although from the quantitative point of view there have been significant U.S. achievements within the past four years.

Another aspect of projection is left unexplored because of its immense difficulty and its dangerously unscientific character. Consider the problem this way: the United States one day before the outbreak of war with a hypothetical enemy, such as the Soviet Union, will possess a certain group of characteristics. Representative individual lives within this country can be determined to possess certain habits concerning mass communication, trust in mass communication, and response to symbols which may come through press, radio, or other mass devices.

One day after the outbreak of war the United States will change *because* the war has broken out.

One month after the outbreak of war the United States will no longer be the USA_1 which existed on war-day. It may well have become USA_{25} because of the rapidity and variety of change. Three Soviet hydrogen bombs and twelve Soviet atomic bombs might change many of our national, economic, political, and psychological characteristics, and no one, not even an American, could predict this change in advance. The best he could do would be to get ready to study the change as it occurred, to understand the rate and direction of the change, and to assess the meaning of the change in light of the conduct of war.

The same would be true of the USSR; that country, like any other major country, would change under the impact of war. Who could have predicted the renascence of Russian patriotism and traditionalism resulting from the Nazi invasion of 1941? Even if we know where the Russians are as of the outbreak of war, we won't know where they will head or how fast they will head there, once war has broken out.

The scientific problem presented by attempted serious study of a U.S.-Soviet war is therefore very difficult indeed. It is really a problem involving three clusters of moving bodies. The first cluster will be the American people, their behavior, and their institutions; the second cluster, the Russians and allied peoples, their behavior and their institutions; the third cluster, the changing methods of communication existing between them.

It can be said even now, simply by referring to the character of the American people and their past history, that if the Communist leaders of the USSR start a general war, the end of that war is sure (under sets of words and ideas which have yet to be developed in the future) to involve the reconciliation of the inhabitants of the USA with the Russian people. In other words, USA_V and $USSR_V$ can and must have certain relationships with each other, preeminent among which are attempts at undoing war damage, at political and cultural reconciliation, and the undertaking of the rebuilding of a world which *both* these great peoples can support with enthusiasm and hope.[7]

USA_V and $USSR_V$ are imaginable. USA_1 and $USSR_1$ for the day preceding the outbreak of war, or, alternatively, the day on which the war occurs, will be known elements. American science in many fields can help U.S. mass communications and therewith help our armed forces if we learn how to ascertain how the Soviet leadership changes, how Soviet elite groups change, and how the Soviet population changes during the course of the war. We must not only be able to guess what is happening to them physically, but must try to appreciate and to understand what is happening to them psychologically and semantically. This is an immense task. It is by no means certain that our research and development facilities can give us an adequate research program to handle the problem.

This much can be said: if the Americans understand the Russians before the war and during the war, it will be the first time that a nation has kept its enemy in wide-awake sight.

The usual process in the past has been the acceptance of a few exaggerated stereotypes of the national characteristics of the potential enemy, the ascription of every possible kind of infamy and inhuman characteristic to the enemy during the war, and the redefinition of the enemy as a friend after the war. It would be strange and wonderful if the U.S. Government and the U.S. propagandists (or conceivably as much as a large minority of the U.S. population) could learn how to fight the USSR in order to *help* the Russians escape from a tyranny which has already hurt them much more than it has hurt us.

The Germans suffered a tragic, overwhelming, and perhaps decisive psychological defeat in the Russian Soviet Federated Socialist Republic and in the Ukraine, when they carried with their field forces such naïve and tragic Nazi misconceptions of Russian and Ukrainian character as to defeat every opportunity they may have had for a serious anti-Communist alliance of Germany with the Russian and Ukrainian peoples. They destroyed themselves not through ignorance, but through what they *thought* they knew. If they had been more calm, less assured, more willing to learn from immediate experience, and less indoctrinated with their own preposterous misconceptions of Russian and Ukrainian character, they might have found Russian and Ukrainian allies who would have joined them in the final extermination of the Soviet system.

The world Communist movement has already suffered very serious setbacks because of its failure to project U.S. behavior successfully from the summer of 1950 onward. If the Russian and Chinese Communists had understood Americans well and had made a correct evaluation of the American response to the invasion of South Korea, they would not have driven the United States from lethargy to alertness, from weakness to military strength, from vulnerability toward Communist and crypto-Communist propaganda to sharp and angry recognition of Communist manipulation of symbols such as "progressives," "people's governments," and "liberation."

Communist Developments. If the U.S. Government agencies know about the scientific development of Soviet propaganda techniques in the last few years, they have certainly not told this author. What is here presented is therefore derived from first-hand interrogation of Communists, from escapers in both Europe and Asia, and unclassified materials.

Sociologically it would seem that the Russian Communists attempted definite improvements of the techniques of Communist revolution and that these improvements have in large part failed in the European satellites. The governments of Rumania, Bulgaria, Hungary, Czechoslovakia, Poland, and East Germany have turned out to be poor governments—despite the fact that from the Soviet point of view it was a sharp innovation to leave them in pseudo-parliamentary form instead of creating outright Soviet facsimiles.

At the Chinese end of the Moscow-Peking axis the sociology of revolutionary propaganda and organization appears to have worked out much more successfully than at the Russian end. The Chinese Communists, perhaps because they were Chinese, perhaps because they were tougher and more experienced Communists than the Russians, got their country under rigid control and then undertook social and political experiments on a very audacious scale. They have managed not to be un-Chinese while creating in China the kind of pervasive dictatorship which Communist control appears to require.

In the manipulation of satellites and in particularization of propaganda, the North Korean Communist army, the Viet Minh army in Indochina, and the Malayan Races Liberation Army on the Malay peninsula, appear to have near-optimum localism and particularism without suffering serious deviation from the main Communist worldwide pattern. In North Korea, of course, Chinese intervention and Soviet support have sharply modified the position of the North Korean People's Army, but the Annamite and Malay Communist forces appear to be fighting with high morale and considerable success, despite the duality of control from Peking and Moscow, and despite the difficulties of reconciling Asian nationalism with Marxian-world doctrine.

Another Communist technique is now known through Edward Hunter's provocative pioneer book[8] by its correct name of "brainwashing." This involves the transformation of a human personality. The author has himself interrogated victims of brain-washing and can attest to the terrifying depth to which this process is carried. The victim of brainwashing is subject to very slight persuasion at the rational level. He is not even given much propaganda as U.S. propagandists of recent years might recognize the product. Instead, the process of brain-washing consists of a frontal attack on all levels of the personality, from the most conscious to the most hidden. The Communists seek through fatigue and sustained interrogation to create a condition similar to what is called "nervous breakdown" in popular parlance. Then they rebuild the personality, healing their victim into Communist normality.

One victim to whom the author talked had been so subject to Communist brain-changing that he thought himself a real Communist even though he had been reared a Catholic. He was completely convinced of the Communist cause and of his own life and place in that cause after the brain-washing had been completed. Unfortunately for Communism, the man got into serious sexual difficulties, difficulties of a kind which any American psychiatrist would recognize as potentially devastating.

As a result of his sexual frustrations he suffered a mild equivalent of the medically recognized phenomenon of the schizophrenic break—that terrible moment of false enlightenment in which the psychotic personality cuts loose with a truth of his own and shuts off most or all communication with normal people—with the consequence that he was walking along Nanking Road in Shanghai, a normal Communist in one instant of time and (as he put it to the author) in a millionth of a second he suddenly realized he was a Catholic, an anti-Communist, the enemy of every man, woman and child in sight—and at war with his entire environment. As this writer understood it, the poor man, though adjusted to the Communist environment after brain-washing, happened to go crazy—crazy enough to come back to our side.

Who can say which is sane, which insane? When two social and cultural systems are completely at odds with one another it may be impossible to be "normal" in both of them.

Scientifically the Chinese process of personality transformation lacked some of the pharmaceutical features apparent in the Western Communist conversions for purposes of confession. It appears to be a combination of audacious practical experimentation with well-known procedures from textbooks of Pavlovian psychology. It is, of course, an interesting scientific question to ask one's self: could Communist psychological researchers do enough psychological research to understand their own difficulties and to de-Communize themselves in the very act of seeking better psychological weapons for Communism? If the people in charge of Communist psychological techniques were scientists, as American psychologists generally are, there might be a real point of discussion. Unfortunately, most of them appear to be artists, believers, and fanatics. The history of the fanatical religions which have inflamed and ripped so much of mankind across the centuries is not such as to suggest that Communism will de-Communize itself by becoming more Communistic or more scientific.

Logically considered, the United States remains the largest extant revolutionary experiment in the world—the first immense human community which survives without profound dogma or profound hatred and which attempts to make short-range, practical, and warm-hearted (though ideologically superficial) concurrence the foundation for a political and industrial civilization. If the United States wins a few more wars it may be that the rest of mankind will be persuaded that our kind of practicality is not only humanly preferable, but scientifically more defensible than the philosophies of competing civilizations. It seems unlikely that Communist research can outstrip us in the propaganda field so far as the race is run in purely scientific terms; artistically and gadget-wise the Communists are just as inventive as we are and often more enthusiastic.

Private PsyWar and Covert Techniques. Another aspect in the development of PsyWar was the inevitable possibility that skills learned in wartime would not be forgotten in time of peace. Many of the background studies made for OWI during World War II have been developed, on the constructive side, into serious scientific contributions to ethnology, anthropology, or psychology. The postwar studies of RAND Corporation have in part been released in unclassified form and add to our knowledge not only of propaganda but of mankind. The RADIR project at Stanford University, the Russian research program at MIT and Harvard, and other governmentally inspired or encouraged undertakings have borne similar fruit for private scholarship and discussion.

On the other side of the coin, it is very hopeful to note that the many and dangerous techniques developed by OSS for covert propaganda, some of which were applied with considerable success in Europe, have not been introduced into domestic U.S. politics, commercial competition, or other forms of private life. After each war there is often a danger that the coarsening of a culture by the war will lead to the application of wartime skills to peacetime situations. This was emphatically not the case in the Presidential campaigns of 1948 and 1952, even though persons of rich PsyWar experience in World War II were on the staffs of both Stevenson and Eisenhower.

It is often forgotten that some of the deadliest and most effective revolutionary enterprises in the nineteenth century were undertaken without the consent or assistance of the existing governments. Karl Marx was certainly not an invention of Lord Palmerston. Bakunin did not operate out of the French Foreign Office.

In the postwar discussion of USA-Communist rivalry, recommendations were often made on the U.S. side that we should counter Soviet covert operations with our own covert operations against the USSR. What has been forgotten in this context is the fact that such operations have been made illegal and dangerous under United States law. Under Federal law as it exists today no Underground Railway could be developed to assist Soviet escapers in the way that Negro slaves were relayed across the Free States

to Canada in the years before Emancipation. One of the chief blocks
to U.S. covert operations is the immense growth in all directions
of the power, authority, and responsibility of the Federal Government; this growth makes it almost impossible to wage revolutionary or conspiratorial operations from U.S. territory without the
prior approval of U.S. authorities—which the authorities, under
traditional international law, cannot give and cannot afford to give.

It would seem desirable, if the Cold War situation persists over
a long period of time, for Americans to reexamine the restraints
which they have placed upon their own citizens and to attempt
a revision of the laws which would permit pro-American secret
activities to be launched without permitting anti-American activities of the same kind to be carried on. One immediately comes to
the conundrum:[9]

How can the Government say *yes* to the one and *no* to the other
without being cognizant of what happens?

The answer would appear to lie in the older body of our law in
that a withdrawal of governmental authority from some fields
would leave the individual responsible and subject to indictment
and trial if his enterprises should prove deleterious to the United
States Government, but not subject to punishment if his enterprises
hurt the known antagonists of the USA.

Phrased in another way, this means that the USA might, in a
long-range Cold War situation, be required to make some domestic recognition of the fact that the Communist states are the antagonists but not the military enemies of the U.S. system of government and that as antagonists of this system of government such
states, their representatives, their property, and their organizations, should not be afforded any more protection under our laws
than is given to the National City Bank of New York in the laws
applicable to the city of Moscow, or the American Telephone &
Telegraph Company in the laws which apply in Budapest. For a
long time the Communist states have treated even the most innocent business enterprise and social club on our side as though they
were attainted with an inherent factor of criminal and subversive
intent. The withdrawal of U.S. legal protection from all things

Communist might allow the American people—or those among them who so chose—to develop proclivities for adventure and troublemaking against the Communists. These proclivities are now sternly repressed by Federal statute.

The Future of Psychological Warfare. PsyWar has become an existing art. Where it had no practitioners at all in the United States between 1919 and 1940, it has had a long and distinguished roster of active and reserve officers, civilian consultants, and demobilized veterans interested in the field ever since 1945. A wide variety of military establishments have had PsyWar responsibilities assigned them. Substantial cadres of officers and skilled enlisted personnel have been recruited and trained. Radio and leaflet facilities are ready to accompany our land, sea, and air forces wherever they may have to go. A U.S. strategic center for global propaganda, instantly convertible to wartime use, exists in the Operations Coordinating Board under the National Security Council.

This is not the end of the story.

One of the paradoxical but deeply true factors in the study and conduct of propaganda is this: the more people know about propaganda, the better they can resist it.

Propaganda was a tremendous bogey in the 1920s. It probably seems very ugly and frightening to most people born before 1920. It does not seem too frightening, so far as the author can judge, to Americans born after 1930. Those born in the period 1920-30 appear to be divided in their emotional reactions to mass persuasion situations.

PsyWar is not magic. It is a valuable auxiliary to modern warfare and a useful concomitant to modern strategy. If a particular strategic policy is sanely and effectively devised as a feasible deterrent to war, the PsyWar procedures supporting that strategy will contribute to the prevention of war. Psychological warfare represents a recognition and acceptance in the military and strategic field of skills which grow about us every day.

In so far as ultra-destructive weapons may have increased the tenseness and bad temper of people who must live under the perpetual but remote threat of atomic bombing, one can say that physicists have upset the nerves of mankind and that it is now up to the propagandists to reassure and to reconcile the peoples.

Whatever PsyWar does, it certainly does not and should not increase the bitterness of war. Fighting itself is the supreme bitterness. Radio broadcasts and leaflets even in wartime only rarely should promote hatred. The situation which the world faces is dangerous because of technological development, not because of psychological knowledge. PsyWar ranks as a weapon, but it is almost certainly the most humane of all weapons.

Apart from PsyWar, what military weapon destroys the enemy soldier's capacity to fight by saving his life? PsyWar tries to bring him over alive and tries to send him home as our friend. No rival weapon can do this.

PsyWar, no matter what it may be called in the future, cannot be omitted from the arsenal of modern war. Neither can it outlast war. Its improvement is a cheap, valuable, and humane way of increasing the military potential of any country whether we think that country to be politically right or politically wrong.

Since 1945 we Americans have written more, studied more, and talked more about PsyWar than have any of the other free peoples. This is a hopeful sign. It can be read as an indication that the American love of the gadget, the American quest for a novelty, can be turned to the arena of the soul. The Communists are better liars, better schemers, better murderers than we shall ever be; they start off by being better fanatics. Is it not in the American spirit that we should out-trick them, out-talk them, and out-maneuver them? We have a very creative and resourceful civilization at our backs. We have no Führer to guide us and no party line to comfort us; we don't even want such things. Hard though it may be, we can live with our own consciences and not seek for keepers.

The Communists have started a fight with us. That fight may go on a long time. If they want to stop fighting we shall certainly try to find peace with them. But if they push the fight to its bitter end—

We shall not fail.

NOTES:

[1] A sharp contrast between the old politics and the new is shown by the unfortunate book prepared in the Department of State and now hastily, even guiltily, allowed to go out of print by the United States Government Printing Office because it showed that some Americans were guilty or naïve enough to try to love and trust the Soviet state within the same system as our own. One does not know whether to laugh or to weep at the spectacle of men lamenting the fact that they were once innocent and hopeful. The book, prepared by the late Harley Notter and others, is Department of State Publication 3580, General Policy Series 15, *Postwar Foreign Policy Preparation* (Washington, 1949) That not all was innocence, even when things so seemed, is amply attested by Freda Utley's controversial but brilliant summary, *The China Story* (Chicago, 1951).

[2] The function of decision-making has been brilliantly though solemnly explored in Richard C. Snyder, H. W. Bruck and Burton Sapin, *Decision-making as an Approach to the Study of International Politics* (Princeton, N.J., 1954.)

[3] For a contrary point of view, see *Tensions That Lead to War*, edited by Hadley Cantril (Princeton, 1950).

[4] The author had the opportunity of observing opsearch in the Korean war on three different occasions: September 1950, March 1951, and November and December 1952 and early January 1953. He visited Korea itself twice and also spent a great deal of time, part of it in a public capacity and part of it as a free-lance author, in the periphery of that war—areas such as Hong Kong, Indochina, Thailand, the Philippines, Malaya, Burma, Indonesia, and India.

[5] Several novels have touched on PsyWar problems. The most hard-hitting of the lot is Jerome Weidman, *Too Early to Tell* (New York, 1946). Covert PsyWar whispering techniques are thinly disguised and much improved,

technically, in Darwin Teilhet, *The Fear Makers* (New York, various dates) The covert side of some of these adventures is portrayed, among others by W. Stanley Moss, *A War of Shadows* (New York, 1952); Ray Franklin Kauffman, *The Coconut Wireless* (New York, 1948); and Chin Kee Onn, *Silent Army* (New York, 1953). As exciting as fiction are Mark Gayn and John Caldwell, *American Agent* (New York.1947), describing the work of an enthusiastic amateur, and L. C. Moyzisch, *Operation Cicero* (New York reprint, 1952), portraying a first-class professional. Alexander Foote, *Handbook for Spies* (London, 1949), and J. V. Davidson-Houston, *Armed Pilgrimage* (London 1949), are interesting distillations of personal experience which touch on espionage and PsyWar.

[6] The author professes he would like to write a preliminary work on this subject himself some day, if no one else essays the task first.

[7] V = Victory day.

[8] Edward Hunter, *Brain-Washing in Red China* (New York, 1951).

[9] If one good book can be mentioned without prejudice to the many other good books in the same field, attention can he drawn to the excellent undergraduate text which explores the present U.S. position on the press, George I. Bird and Frederic E. Merwin, *The Press and Society* (New York, 1951). At the opposite end of the spectrum, see Oleg Anesimov, *The Ultimate Weapon* (New York, 1953). The first book takes the U.S. as it is and does not envisage profound responses coming as the inevitable accompaniment of frightful change; the second book states the outside problem in shocking terms, but asks of Americans things which neither they nor their press are ever apt to approve.

APPENDIX
MILITARY PSYWAR OPERATIONS, 1950-53

On 25 June 1950, when the invasion of the Republic of Korea began, no real military PsyWar organization was tangibly evident. A planning staff headed by Colonel J. Woodall Greene had been re-created in the Far East Command's GHQ in 1947, but it was hardly prepared to direct full-scale propaganda operations on such short notice, especially with a total lack of field operating units. Yet the staff with hasty augmentation did go into action—in effect, became its own operating unit—two days following the invasion, using both leaflets and radio in a strategic campaign that was continued without interruption for over three years.

At the same time that General MacArthur made provision for the PsyWar planning staff in the Far East Command, the Department of the Army's G2 in 1947 directed the inauguration of a long-range program of extension courses to be administered primarily to the specialists of the Military Intelligence Reserve. One such specialty in the military intelligence career program was psychological warfare.[1]

Parallel with the development of training literature based on World War II experience, the Army experimented with the use of PsyWar in field maneuvers. A special unit, called the Tactical Information Detachment,[2] was formed at Fort Riley, Kansas.

Organization of Field Operational Units. Less than a month after the 1950 invasion, the Department of the Army announced the approval of a new organizational concept for PsyWar field

415

operational units. The new concept, profiting by the organizational happenchance in all theaters of operations during World War II, established two functional units: one for *strategic* propaganda support, the other for *tactical* propaganda support.

Radio Broadcasting and Leaflet Group. Although the concept for new unit organization and function was not conceived overnight, FEC's Psychological Warfare Section (PWS) with its dual planning and operating responsibilities pointed up the urgent need for a unit properly manned and equipped to support full-scale strategic operations in any area. So the Radio Broadcasting and Leaflet (RB&L) Group was born. Not only was it designed to conduct strategic propaganda in direct support of military operations, but it likewise was created to support the national world-wide propaganda effort when so directed. It was built on a basic framework of three companies:

Headquarters and Headquarters Company, containing the command, administrative, supervisory and creative personnel necessary for propaganda operations.

Figure 75: UN Propaganda. In some leaflets used in Korea, the United Nations emerged as a major point. Here UN lavishness to South Korea is contrasted with Communist rapacity in the North. The scene does not remind the reader of slums on our side.

Figure 76: Korean Leaflet Bomb, Early Model. An M16A1 cluster adapter being loaded at the FEC printing plant in Yokohama (1 November 1950). The bomb type adapter will contain 22,500 (5" by 8") psychological warfare leaflets.

Reproduction Company, containing intricate equipment and skilled personnel capable of producing leaflets and newspapers of varying sizes and multiple color.

Mobile Radio Broadcasting Company, designed to replace or augment other means of broadcasting radio propaganda.

In 1953 a fourth type company was activated at Fort Bragg, North Carolina—the *Consolidation Company*. This unit was very flexible and had the job of creating and conducting PsyWar in support of consolidation operations in areas under Military Government control.

Loudspeaker and Leaflet Company. The Group's junior partner in the conduct of PsyWar support operations was the Loudspeaker and Leaflet (L&L) Company. This unit specifically supported an army in the field with adequate *tactical* propaganda support. Like the Group, it supported the national propaganda objectives, but it interpreted the directives that came from the theater commander in terms of more immediate objectives. Its targets were smaller, lived under unusual circumstances, and presented highly vulnerable, rapidly changing propaganda opportunities—a real challenge for the L&L Company. Organizationally it was a trimmed-down version of the Group. Its *company headquarters* and *propaganda platoon* were the offspring of Headquarters and Headquarters Company. The *publications platoon* was a smaller, more adaptable version of Reproduction Company. And the *loudspeaker platoon* was the tactical counterpart of the strategic Mobile Radio Broadcasting Company.

The Tactical Information Detachment, moving from Fort Riley to Korea in the fall of 1950, was reorganized as the *1st Loudspeaker and Leaflet Company* and, attached to EUSAK, served as Eighth Army's tactical propaganda unit throughout the campaign. It adjusted its location, equipment and propaganda tone to keep pace with the ups and downs of the Korean war.

Psychological Warfare Center. Paralleling the creation of the Office of the Chief of Psychological Warfare in the Department of the Army PsyWar training was started in the spring of 1951. A faculty was collected at the Army General School to start the world's first formal school of military propaganda.

At the same time, reserve officers whose civilian specialties were in or related to mass communications were recalled to PsyWar assignments. Several RB&L groups and L&L companies were activated and trained at Fort Riley. One of these, the *1st Radio Broadcasting and Leaflet Group*, was deployed to Japan to become the strategic propaganda support unit in FEC, thereby relieving the hard-pressed Psychological Warfare Section of its operational functions. The Group left Fort Riley in July 1951 at the height of the Missouri Valley floods, forcing the unit to take emergency detours by bus and train in order to meet its scheduled port of embarkation call. The 1st was the only group to have been used in active operations. Other groups were employed in training missions. In addition, Reserve groups and companies trained periodically at key

Figure 77: UN Themes. This Korean-language leaflet states: "No soldier would attempt to fight 54 men, yet Communist China is attempting to fight 54 nations. Don't fight for Communist enslavement – Join your comrades who have surrendered into safety."

locations where sufficient specialized personnel were available to keep the units on a ready, stand-by basis.

In April 1952, the PsyWar training activities at Fort Riley were moved to Fort Bragg, North Carolina, where the new Psychological Warfare Center was located. This Center not only provided unit training supervision and facilities, but it fathered a new activity, the Psychological Warfare Board, designed to evaluate and test new PsyWar equipment and techniques. And the Psychological Warfare School, an outgrowth of the classes conducted by the Army General School, was formally recognized and established as one of the Army's specialist schools. More than four hundred officers have received diplomas as PsyWar officers at the time of this writing (1953). Most of the graduates have been Army officers, although successfully completing the course have been students from the Navy, Marine Corps, Air Force, U.S. Information Agency, and from nine Allied nations.

Psychological Warfare Staff, FEC. For nearly two years, the Psychological Warfare Section operated under the general staff

THE UNITED NATIONS

HAS APPEALED TO AMERICAN FORCES IN
JAPAN TO ASSIST YOU PEACE-LOVING
CITIZENS OF THE REPUBLIC OF KOREA
IN YOUR STRUGGLE AGAINST THE UNPRO-
VOKED AGGRESSION FROM THE NORTH.
WE SHALL GIVE YOU EVERY SUPPORT.
BE STEADFAST. BE CALM. BE COURAGEOUS.
RESIST FIRMLY. TOGETHER WE SHALL
DRIVE THE AGGRESSOR FROM YOUR
TERRITORY.

Figure 78: Home-front Morale. When South Korean communications were interrupted, leaflets such as this provided an early boost to Korean civilian morale.

supervision of Intelligence (G2). Since World War I days G2 had been given the responsibility for monitoring PsyWar activity, a practice that was evident throughout World War II. In 1947 the Department of the Army transferred the monitorship and supervision of PsyWar to Plans and Operations (G3). The shift was effected in FEC in 1952.

Early in 1953 PWS was transferred to the staff of the commander, Army Forces Far East (AFFE), a paper transaction to put the staff in a closer position to coordinate the plans and operations of the supporting army PsyWar units.

Throughout the Korean conflict, PWS, like its area commander, wore two hats: PWS was also the PsyWar operations coordinating agency for the United Nations Command.

Broad objectives made possible throughout the war years the development of literally thousands of appropriate themes. One theme so prominent in World War II propaganda, that of *uncon-ditional surrender*, was never used. UN policy denied its use, and PWS enforced the prohibition.

Psychological Warfare Staff, EUSAK. Recognizing the need for PsyWar officers on army and corps staffs, the Department of the Army hastened to make an allocation for these officers to be inte-grated into headquarters structures. The PsyWar officers finally came to rest in the G3 staff section.

Eighth Army's PsyWar division of G3 had the 1st Loudspeaker and Leaflet Company under its operational control. EUSAK's PsyWar officer kept a tight control over the propaganda output of the L&L Company by physically moving the propaganda platoon into his EUSAK staff office.

Each of the corps PsyWar officers had under his operational control one loudspeaker section (with a varying number of teams) from the L&L Company.

Radio Operations. Radio in the Korean conflict was used jointly as a strategic and a consolidation medium. From the beginning of the war, radio was the voice of our military policy. An ambitious network, supervised in 1950-51 directly by PWS and thereafter by the 1st RB&L Group, became known and recognized as the Voice of the United Nations Command. The Korean Broadcasting Sys-tem (KBS) and the Japan Broadcasting System (JBS) transmitted on a cooperative basis, with the U.S. Government buying air time. The 1st RB&L Group's radio unit furnished programming assis-tance through key stations in Seoul (KBS), Taegu (KBS), Pusan (KBS) and Tokyo (JBS). In addition, the Group furnished techni-cal assistance to KBS in order to keep as many as twelve network stations on the air.

Leaflet Operations. As in World War II, leaflets were delivered primarily by two means: aircraft and artillery. B-29s of the Far East Air Force ferried leaflet bombs on night missions deep into strategic areas. Light bombers and liaison craft in support of

Figure 79: The Famous Airplane Surrender Leaflet. This is the controversial Far East Command leaflet that in April 1953 offered "the sum of 50,000 U. S. dollars to any pilot who delivers a modern, operational, combat-type jet aircraft in flyable condition to South Korea. The first pilot who delivers such a jet aircraft to the free world will receive an additional 50,000 U. S. dollars bonus for his bravery." The leaflet was printed in three languages—Russian, Chinese and Korean. In this example of the Russian language leaflet, there are added notations in both Korean and Chinese that "this is a message from the Americans to any jet pilot who can read Russian. If you know such a person, please give it to him. It tells him how to escape to the UN Forces."

EUSAK dropped both leaflet bombs and bundles on tactical targets. The leaflet bundle was a Korean war development. It was wrapped, tied, and fuzed in such a manner that it would open and release its leaflets in mid-air. The 105mm. howitzer remained the principal artillery piece for placing propaganda-loaded shells on pinpoint targets.

Tremendous quantities of leaflets were printed. The 1st RB&L Group on many occasions averaged better than twenty million pieces of printed propaganda every week. To this, the 1st L&L Company in Korea added an average of three and a half million leaflets per week.

Loudspeaker Operations. The airborne loudspeaker was the object of experimentation, but the bulk of loudspeaker broadcasts were made from vehicle mounts, such as tanks, and from emplacements. During the static battle situation of 1951-53, most of the broadcasts were of the latter kind. Range of the voice casts was short, something like two thousand yards under ideal conditions. Personnel and equipment were supplied by the 1st L&L Company, and scripts were prepared by PsyWar Division, G3, EUSAK.

Results of Military PsyWar Operations. When the question was asked, "Just how effective was PsyWar?" the answer was vague. Clear-cut immediate evaluation of the effects of each propaganda campaign was often impossible to ascertain because of the many intangible conditions that were prevalent in the target area—conditions that were constantly changing.

Some critics of the PsyWar operations in the Far East Command charged that there were exaggerated claims of prisoners of war who surrendered as a result of propaganda. They pointed out that a head count of prisoners is an inaccurate measure of *direct* effects of PsyWar used in support of military operations, because rarely is the taking of prisoners the *sole* goal of any major PsyWar campaign.

Other critics expressed the belief that emphasis had been placed on *quantity* rather than *quality* of propaganda. By quantity they meant propaganda measured by bookkeeping statistics. By quality they meant propaganda that, planned with potent intelligence, was capable of exploiting propaganda opportunities with maximum psychological impact.

Did PsyWar achieve its goal?

The effects of planned persuasion in a thousand days of radio broadcasts, in tens of thousands of loudspeaker appeals, in billions of leaflets, may be measured only in retrospect. The question may be answered when reaction in the target area has reached (or fails to reach) favorable proportion, provided that the tangible results of the military operations can be clearly separated from those of concurrent and subsequent strategic international information operations.

NOTES:

[1] The development of this activity was handed to the Chief of Army Field Forces, in whose G2 section Colonel Donald Hall was the PsyWar officer. The first of these courses with its supporting textbook was not ready for release by the Army General School until 1949, just one year before the Korean conflict began. In 1949 likewise appeared the first officially approved Army field manual on the subject of psychological warfare support of military operations.

[2] Teams from this detachment, armed with leaflets end loudspeakers, were sent to and participated in major maneuvers in continental United States, in the Caribbean area, and in Hawaii. These teams were attached to the "enemy" forces, and exposed the maneuver troops to military propaganda in action. The Tactical Information Detachment suddenly suspended its planning of simulated propaganda operations for Exercise PLUTO in 1950. As the only PsyWar operational unit in the Army, the Detachment was bustled off to Korea.

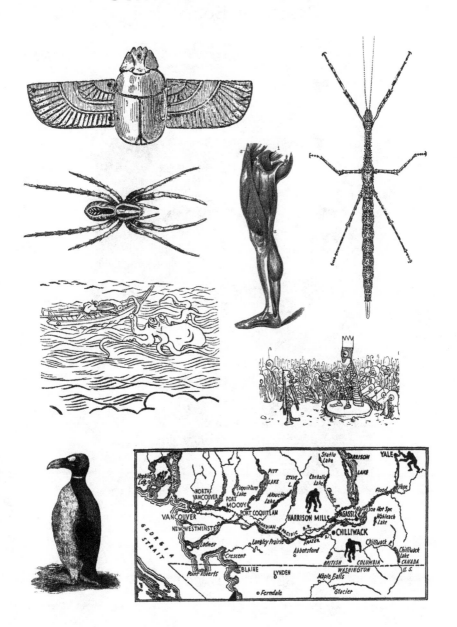

BASTOGNE

The Story of the First Eight Days
In Which the 101st Airborne Division Was
Closed Within the Ring of German Forces

COLONEL S. L. A. MARSHALL

BASTOGNE

ISBN 1-61646-062-8

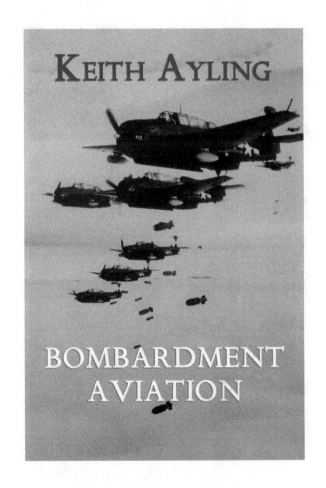

BOMBARDMENT AVIATION

ISBN 1-61646-054-7

TANK-FIGHTER TEAM

LIEUTENANT ROBERT M. GERARD
(FORMERLY OF THE FRENCH ARMORED FORCE)

TANK-FIGHTER TEAM

ISBN 1-61646-023-7

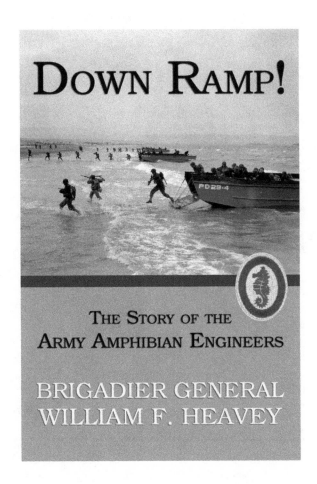

DOWN RAMP!

THE STORY OF THE
ARMY AMPHIBIAN ENGINEERS

BRIGADIER GENERAL
WILLIAM F. HEAVEY

DOWN RAMP!

ISBN 1-61646-057-1

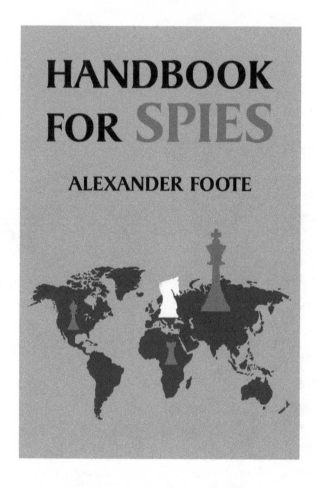

HANDBOOK FOR SPIES

ISBN 1-61646-067-9

TANKS

AND HOW TO DRAW THEM

TERENCE T. CUNEO

TANKS AND HOW TO DRAW THEM

ISBN 1-61646-021-0

CPSIA information can be obtained
at www.ICGtesting.com
Printed in the USA
LVHW040250230723
753116LV00027B/862/J